THE IDEA OF ISRAEL

THE IDEA OF ISRAEL

A History of Power and Knowledge

Ilan Pappe

VERSO

London • New York

First published by Verso 2014
© Ilan Pappe 2014

3 5 7 9 10 8 6 4 2

Verso
UK: 6 Meard Street, London W1F 0EG
US: 20 Jay Street, Suite 1010, Brooklyn, NY 11201
www.versobooks.com

Verso is the imprint of New Left Books

ISBN-13: 978-1-84467-856-3
eISBN: 978-1-78168-247-0 (US)
eISBN: 978-1-78168-545-7 (UK)

British Library Cataloguing in Publication Data
A catalogue record for this book is available from the British Library

Library of Congress Cataloging-in-Publication Data
A catalog record for this book is available from the Library of Congress

Typeset in Adobe Garamond by MJ & N Gavan, Truro, Cornwall
Printed in the US by Maple Press

Contents

Introduction: Debating the Idea of Israel   1

Part I: The Scholarly and Fictional Idea of Israel
  1 The 'Objective' History of the Land and the People   17
  2 The Alien Who Became a Terrorist: The Palestinian in
     Zionist Thought   27
  3 The War of 1948 in Word and Image   48

Part II: Israel's Post-Zionist Moment
  4 The Trailblazers   69
  5 Recognising the Palestinian Catastrophe: The 1948 War
     Revisited   106
  6 The Emergence of Post-Zionist Academia, 1990–2000   126
  7 Touching the Raw Nerves of Society: Holocaust Memory
     in Israel   153
  8 The Idea of Israel and the Arab Jews   179
  9 The Post-Zionist Cultural Moment   197
 10 On the Post-Zionist Stage and Screen   217
 11 The Triumph of Neo-Zionism   247
 12 The Neo-Zionist New Historians   275

Epilogue: Brand Israel 2013   295

Notes   314
Further Reading   336
Index   341

INTRODUCTION

Debating the Idea of Israel

A sober and objective consideration of the facts indicates that Zionism, relative to other ideologies, has succeeded in realising most of its objectives. It has done so perhaps more than any other contemporary movement, particularly in light of its unique initial odds, which caused it to be the weakest political movement of all. For all these reasons, it can serve as an example of the success of modernism.

  – Yosef Gorny, 'Thoughts on Zionism as a Utopian Ideology'[1]

The mutual impact of modern scientific observation and ancient literature as well as archaeology turns the study of the geography of Palestine into the geography of the homeland of the Hebrew people and the study of the culture of the land into the study of Hebrew culture.

  – Yossef Barslevsky, '*Did You Know the Land?*':
  The Galilee and the Northern Valleys[2]

On a hot night in July 1994, hundreds of people packed a university hall in Tel Aviv to listen to a debate about knowledge and power in Israel. The numbers surprised the organisers. They had planned a small, purely intellectual debate and knowingly chose to hold it during the semi-final game of the World Cup, which was being held in the United States. The hope was that attendance would be limited to the few geeks willing to give up a football night for the sake of a scholarly treat. Nonetheless, students crowded into the undersized hall, and so, on short notice, the event had to be moved to a larger venue. According to one account, seven hundred people attended the debate, which featured one 'old' and one 'new' historian of Israel, as well as one 'established' and one 'revisionist' sociologist. I was the new historian.

The debate itself was anything but the dialogue advertised and ended up as four lectures, punctuated by a certain amount of ill-tempered scuffling. But the public seemed to enjoy themselves as much as the fans cheering the semi-finalists on the other side of the planet.[3]

The question posed was significant: Was the Israeli academy an ideological tool in the hands of Zionism or a bastion of free thought and speech? The vast majority of the audience attended because they leaned towards the former conclusion, doubting the independence of Israeli academics. If approval can be judged by applause, the audience sided by and large with my colleague Shlomo Svirsky and myself, representatives of the new history and sociology of Israel, and were less impressed by Anita Shapira and the late Moshe Lissak of the old guard. Most, however, would not walk the extra mile that such a position demanded of them.[4] But some did and, like me, eventually left the country in despair, unable to alter the status quo.[5] And yet that event contributed to the excitement of a historic moment when Israelis doubted the moral validity of the idea of Israel and were allowed, for a short while, to question it, both inside and outside the ivory towers of the universities.

The most memorable remark that evening came from Moshe Lissak, the doyen of traditional Israeli sociology and a winner of the prestigious Israel Prize. Of the story of Israel, he said, 'I accept that there are two narratives, but ours has been proven scientifically to be the right one.' That remark, and my fond memories of that event and of the period as a whole – unique in the history of power and knowledge – inspired me to write this present book. It is a book on Israel as an idea, and it evolved from that short-lived and abortive attempt to challenge it from within.

Every book on Israel attempts to dissect a complex and ambiguous reality. Yet however one chooses to describe, analyse and present Israel, the result will always be both subjective and limited. Nevertheless, the subjectivity and relativity of any representation do not invalidate moral and ethical discussion about that representation. In fact, from the vantage point of the early twenty-first century, the moral and ethical dimensions of such a debate are no less important than questions of substance, facts and evidence. As in the debate in Tel Aviv, versions of reality in Israel are numerous and contradictory, and rarely do they share any consensual ground.

But it must be stressed that they are not just versions of an intellectual debate. They relate directly to issues of life and death, and therefore any attempt to conduct such a conversation in a neutral, objective, purely scientific way is doomed to fail. Israel, or rather the idea of Israel, symbolises for an ever-growing number of people oppression, dispossession, colonisation and ethnic cleansing, while, on the other hand, an ever-diminishing number of people string the same ideas and events into a story of redemption, heroism and historical justice. Along the continuum between these two extremes lie innumerable gradations of strongly held opinion.

In this book, I will argue that these opposing versions are not about Israel as such, but rather about the idea of Israel. Obviously, Israel itself is not merely an idea. It is first and foremost a state – a living organism that has existed for more than sixty years. Denying its existence is impossible and unrealistic. However, evaluating it ethically, morally, and politically is not only possible but also, at present, urgent as never before.

Indeed, Israel is one of a few states considered by many to be at best morally suspect or at worst illegitimate. What is challenged, with varying degrees of conviction and determination, is not the state itself but rather the idea of the state. Some may say they challenge the *ideology* of the state; meanwhile, some Israeli Jews may tell you they fight for the survival of the *ideal* of the state. The optimal term through which to examine the two sides of the argument, however, is 'idea'.

The images and narratives formulated by Zionist leaders and activists in the past, and Israeli Jewish intellectuals and academics in the present, present Israel as the inevitable, successful implementation of the European history of ideas. Ideas are the transformative agents that in any narrative of Western enlightenment lifted Western societies, and in turn the rest of the world, out of medieval darkness and into the Renaissance, and helped restore civilisation following the Second World War. According to Francis Fukuyama, this history of ideas would almost have reached its culmination had not political Islam, national movements in the former Soviet bloc, and Marxist leaders in South America 'sabotaged' the train of progress and modernisation.[6]

Israel was one such transformative idea. To challenge it as such is to challenge the entire narrative of the West as the driving global force of human progress and enlightenment. In the eyes of Yosef Gorny, quoted above, Zionism is one of the few modernisation projects that was successfully implemented, if not the only one, despite the array of counterforces that rejected enlightenment and tried to arrest human progress. This is why he chose to call it not an idea, as would most Zionist scholars, but 'a utopian ideology' that had been translated into a fact. In short, he saw it as an idea successfully fulfilled.[7]

But this is not a book that inquires why the idea of Israel is so negatively perceived by so many people, or why Israeli Jews and their supporters are so adamant about the moral validity of their view and so ready to brand any critique as a display of anti-Semitism. Here I am concerned with those Israelis who share the critical view and harbour doubts about the idea of their state. Doubting the idea of Israel constitutes a serious predicament for an Israeli Jew, as it goes beyond criticism of a given policy of this or that government. It means one is troubled by the very essence of the idea.

Doubting Israeli Jews have displayed their concern mainly through academic work, but also through movies, poems, novels, and the plastic arts. Theirs was an intellectual doubt, which, although expressed by the chattering classes, reflected more hidden and less visible concerns arising from within other walks of life. This intellectual doubt, coupled with increasing international concern, indicates that the idea of Israel is still tentative – a suitable source for moral conversation and political debate.

Ideas can be marketed and commodified. The idea of Israel is no different. The official State of Israel has been doing this since 1948 and has recently produced a booklet to help Israeli tourists abroad sell the mainstream version of the idea. For a time, Israeli travellers were given the booklet on their way out through Ben Gurion Airport; nowadays it can be found on the Internet.[8]

In order to be marketed, the idea must be packaged as a narrative, a story that begins with the birth of the state and its raison d'être. The nation is born as an ideal that becomes a reality that must then be maintained and protected. A successful marketing campaign deepens the idea's validity: while the state can rely on its military, economic and political power, the idea requires scholarly consolidation. Even more for international than for domestic consumption, this validation cannot be won through sheer financial force or moral blackmail; it has to be proven to be just and right. This is the Israeli wish: this is how official Israel, through its intellectual and academic élite, views the issue of the state's legitimisation.

The audience need convincing, even in the case of a state like Israel, which possesses the second most technologised army in the world and enjoys a comfortable $500 billion balance in foreign reserves. The requirement to market and validate stems both from the challenges from without and the potential doubts from within. And the challenges are not merely intellectual or philosophical; they have the power to fuel action against the state and generate solidarity with the state's 'enemies'. The recent Boycott, Divestment and Sanctions campaign (BDS) is an instance of moral doubts being translated into action against the very idea of the state itself.[9]

Since Israel represents itself officially as the 'only democracy in the Middle East' and offers at least the constitutional and formal appearance of being such a regime, the state needs a variety of means to sell the idea as both morally and logically valid. Domestically, it has the power to orientate its educational system towards that goal – although, as we shall see, in the 1990s its grip on that system was temporarily weakened. By contrast, the media and the academia are free agents, at least theoretically, and so cannot be similarly controlled. The former is necessary to the domestic cultivation of the idea, while the latter is useful for international cultivation. With these means in hand, two possible scenarios can develop: either the free agents do not succumb to the state's interpretation of the idea and therefore cannot play the role assigned to them, or they do abide by the state's narrative, either out of true conviction or out of the false conviction that they have reached the same interpretation by way of objective analysis.

When the *idea* of Israel was challenged from within, it meant that the *ideal* of Zionism was deciphered as an ideology, and thus became a far more tangible and feasible target for critical evaluation. This is what happened to a group of Israelis during the 1990s in what I characterise here as Israel's post-Zionist moment.

The challengers focused on the origins of the idea in order to ascertain its present status and interpretation. Political and social processes motivated this search, leading those who embarked on the journey to look beyond current debates about social and economic policies or the fate of the territories occupied in 1967. Their search went deeper into the past.

The journey ended as abruptly as it erupted. After less than a decade, it was branded by the state and by large segments of the Jewish Israeli population as dangerous, indeed suicidal – a trip that would end in Israel losing its international legitimacy and moral backing. Post-Zionism, as the journey was defined by most of its observers and students, became anti-Semitism in the eyes of its enemies. In 2000 it was defeated and nearly disappeared.

This book examines that journey. It charts the departure from the Zionist comfort zone, the arrival at the destination, and the frequent return trip to the comfort zone. Mainly it was an intellectual journey, taken by dozens of academics, a few journalists and numerous artists, who visited the past by delving into national and private archives and by listening empathetically and attentively, for the first time in their lives, to people who regarded themselves as victims of Zionism. They wrote books and articles, made documentary and feature films, composed poems and novels. The common ground was History, a reappraisal of the past so as to understand the present.

Each post-Zionist embarked on the journey for different reasons, yet all were moved by the changing reality around them – a reality that, subsequent to 1967, had been forcing them to consider disturbing questions about their state's conduct present and past. The scholars among them were the last to ask questions, having finally been encouraged to do so by trends in Western academia in the 1990s, where it had become standard practice to pose critical questions about nationalism, state policies and hegemonic cultural positions. Multi-ethnic, multicultural and at times postmodern Western academia showed these local challengers how to deconstruct the impact of power – Zionist ideology – on knowledge embodied in allegedly scientific and objective research. As we shall see, those who delved deep into these questions came to understand their own role, as producers of knowledge, in creating the very reality that disturbed them. Hence they came to challenge the very hegemonic versions of the past that they themselves had researched, learned and taught.

The post-Zionist historians were not mere observers but became part of the process. As a result, their challenge was more noticeable and, for a time, more effective. They participated in global critical practices that encouraged them to adopt a more relativist approach to the history, sociology and national ideology of the State of Israel. Some also found useful the new genre of postcolonial studies as a means of exploring cultural oppression and the attempts to counter it within Israeli Jewish society; others preferred to approach Zionism, Israel and the struggle against them as a purely colonialist situation. Whichever approach they took, they risked incurring the wrath of peers, relatives and eventually the state for being unwilling to accept the prevalent view of Zionism as a just, democratic movement of national liberation. This wrath would lead to their demise.

The historians, sociologists, artists and playwrights who in the 1990s chose to represent victims of the Zionist movement and, later, the State of Israel and to give them a voice did so either because they themselves belonged to a victimised group or because they decided to risk the comfort zone in which they resided and represent the colonised, occupied and oppressed. For them, the idea of Israel had now clearly come to be seen as an omnipotent text that dictated life and death on the ground. The question was, Could it be rewritten? Pondering this question was therefore not an indulgent intellectual pastime; it was an intensely real engagement with an existential situation.

As already mentioned, that challenge is described in this book as post-Zionist. Some would prefer to depict this movement as anti-Zionist; others regard it as a softer version of Zionism. Some post-Zionists were in fact anti-Zionists. But regardless of how far the challengers travelled down that road, they were all searching for an alternative to Zionism. Most of them, not having found one, returned to the ideology's warm embrace; few have become even more anti-Zionist. Some post-Zionists disagreed with their depiction as such, and some who claimed to be post-Zionists were not recognised as such. Clearly the definition is fluid and contentious, but we use it here for lack of a better alternative.

What is uncontended, however, is what was challenged: the consensual Zionist interpretation of the idea of Israel. That consensual interpretation is referred to herein as classical Zionism. Our challengers are the post-Zionists, and the reaction to their challenge is described here as neo-Zionism – the wish to strengthen classical Zionism and provide an unwaveringly patriotic interpretation of the idea of Israel so that it would be immune to such challenges in the future.

Thus did the pendulum swing from Zionism to post-Zionism and thence to neo-Zionism. It can swing again. The political map presents these vacillations very clearly. Classical Zionism was the ideology to which successive governments in Israel, both left and right, subscribed until 1993. Thereafter for a short period, at least until Yitzhak Rabin's assassination in 1995 and possibly until 1999, there was an attempt at a more liberal, possibly even a post-Zionist, approach. Ever since, and until today, a neo-Zionist policy has taken its place.

At the end of day, in other words, the idea was more powerful than its challengers. Its power did not lie in coercion and intimidation; it won legitimacy mainly through acceptance of the idea as being the reality. Its power to regulate everyday life is achieved through invisible means – the very means the challengers sought to expose. Its firm grip ensures widespread support among Israeli Jews – from the worker in the street to the professor in the ivory tower. And this is what makes it such an intriguing case study, not only for assessing the future of Israel but for better understanding the relations between power and knowledge in seemingly democratic societies at the beginning of the twenty-first century.

Methodology and Structure

Methodologically, this book examines the idea of Israel, the challenge and the response, primarily as they appeared in the academic production of knowledge. As I am a historian, this book focuses on the history of the production of and challenge to the idea. That the challenge occurred mainly in academia but also took place elsewhere, most importantly in local cinema and television, enables me to scrutinise the idea of Israel both as a scholarly claim and as a fictional representation. More often than not, the gap between the two is narrow. An almost identical narrative is spun in both these representations of reality, even though allegedly they are diametrically opposed. The uniformity of representation exemplifies the potent grip of the idea; meanwhile, the nation narrates its story and proves its validity through academia, media and the arts and is challenged in these same arenas.

Documentary films occupy a territory between the academic's claim to objectivity and the film-maker's licence to imagine and fictionalise. Documentaries played an important role in the post-Zionist challenge; long after the academic challengers had lost heart, the documentary film-makers continued, as they do to this very day, to criticise openly and courageously the idea of Israel.

When an idea has the power to include or exclude you in the common good of a state, when it can determine your status as enemy or friend, when it is conveyed both as an academic truth and as a compelling movie plot, it is very difficult to escape its influence or dissociate yourself from it. In particular, it is difficult to venture on such an endeavour if you are offered a privileged position in the tale. Risking the privileges, or being unwilling to lose them, is also part of the story recounted in this book.

This book begins with an attempt to chart what was challenged: the Zionist narrative and discourse. The first chapter opens with the representation of the idea of Israel in mainstream Zionist scholarship as the ultimate and most successful project of modernity and enlightenment. Thus a challenge to such a representation does not merely contest a national narrative but also, and perhaps more significantly, a paradigmatic narrative of excellence and uniqueness. To examine this will help us appreciate the distance the challengers had to travel within their own society. Paradoxically, this representation was accompanied by a strong belief in the importance of objective, empirical, scientific research. In confronting the idea, therefore, one either could claim that the facts on the ground did not match the self-congratulatory representation, or could arrive at a better understanding of how the same facts can be manipulated so as to produce differing narratives such as those formulated by the Zionists on the one hand and the Palestinians on the other.

Zionism in this book appears as a discourse. I use 'discourse' in the same way as did Edward Said when discussing the representation of the Orient in the West. In many ways, the Zionist discourse on the Palestinians is both Orientalist and colonialist – at least, this is how the challengers chose to depict it.[10] In order to set the stage for the challenge of the 1990s, I devote the second chapter of the book to the place of the Palestinians in the Zionist discourse. The challengers proposed a total reversal in the common depiction of the Palestinians and Palestine in Israeli Jewish discourse. They suggested transforming the Palestinians from villains into victims and, in some films, even into heroes. In this way, the Zionists became both victimisers and culprits. No wonder some of those who responded angrily to this challenge, whose ideas are covered later in the book, deemed such reversals as evidence of self-hate and mental derangement.

The initial two chapters' general description of the Zionist narrative is followed by a focused analysis of mainstream Zionism's representation of the year 1948, the genesis of the state, in both scholarly and cinematic form. I focus on this year for two reasons. First, the history – and even more so the historiography – of 1948 became a core issue in the post-Zionist challenge. Second, 1948 is the fulcrum for all the debates described in this book: the year represents either the culmination of preceding historical processes or the explanation for everything that happened subsequently. The discussion of what took place in 1948 feeds the historiographical debate about the essence of the Zionist project up to 1948, as well as informing the conversation about the desired solution for the Israel/Palestine question.

The fourth chapter is a tribute to Israel's early Jewish critics of Zionism, who both directly and indirectly influenced the post-Zionist challenge in the 1990s. Although for the most part they were isolated and marginalised in their society, in hindsight one can more fully appreciate their impact on the 1990s, when the challenge matured into a wide-ranging intellectual and cultural phenomenon. The post-Zionist challenge of that decade was the continuation of the brave work and action of certain admirable individuals, some of whom were academics and others journalists of a sort, who in light of their own universalist, humanist approach to life strove single-handedly to critique the truisms of Zionism.

Those early voices were one of three factors that contributed to the emergence of the debate. The second was, as mentioned, the new global, and in particular Western, ideas about power and knowledge. Third, and perhaps most important, were the dramatic socio-economic and political developments on the ground after 1967 and in particular after 1973. A relative calm on Israel's borders exposed the fault lines within the society. Social and economic disparities, ethnic divisions, ideological debates and a deep divide between secular and religious Jews permitted dissent to surface, after its having been silenced for many years.

These developments are described in the fifth chapter, which presents the findings of the Israeli historians – known as the 'new historians' – who set out to challenge the Zionist narrative concerning 1948. They were inspired neither by new theories of historiography nor concepts of knowledge production. Rather, owing to the surrounding social and political upheaval, they read with fresh eyes the newly declassified documents in the archives, even as most of the historians who read the very same documents saw in them no evidence that would force a rewrite of the Zionist version of events.

Global influences were of greater relevance to the developments of the 1990s. Chapter 6 exposes the more profound theoretical discussion that inspired those individuals, consisting mainly of sociologists, who expanded this research chronologically back to the early days of Zionism and forward into the 1950s and thematically to the predicament of Mizrachi Jews, to the Palestinians in Israel, to issues concerning gender, and to the manipulation of Holocaust memory within Israel. Like colleagues of theirs around the world at the end of the twentieth century, these sociologists were interested in the question of how power – be it defined as ideology, political position or identity – affects the production of purportedly scientific and objective knowledge. And, as was the case elsewhere in the world, they answered this query in new and exciting ways.

I then focus more narrowly on this challenge by looking at the role played by the Holocaust in the construction and marketing of the idea of Israel. The book's seventh chapter examines the challenge to the manipulation of the Holocaust memory in the Jewish state – a challenge that touched raw nerves in the society. It exposed not only a Jewish leadership reluctant to do its utmost to save Europe's Jews from impeding genocide but also the alliances upheld by certain Zionist leaders with Nazism until the Nazis' true plan for the extermination of the Jews was revealed. By describing the maltreatment of Holocaust survivors, the challengers demonstrated that in the name of their tragedy, the idea of Israel was sold as the ultimate answer to the catastrophe that befell the European Jews in the Second World War. In addition, they showed that much of what Israel had done since its creation, including its less savoury actions against the Palestinians, was justified by invoking the memory of the Holocaust. Some of the challengers regarded with horror the possibility that the manipulation of the memory had created a society that failed to understand the universal lesson suggested by the horrific event and had instead turned itself into a nationalist, expansionist entity bent on intimidation of the region as a whole.

The most significant challenge to the idea of Israel came from the Mizrachi scholars, many of whom were sociologists, as well as political activists. These Jews had come from Arab and Muslim countries during the 1950s and continually felt discriminated against by the European Jews. This perception of discrimination fuelled their journey into the past and played a role in their rise to power. In their eyes, the idea of Israel was European, Westernised and colonial; absent a transformation into European Jews themselves, it was an Israel in which they could play only a marginal role. Chapter 8 of this book is devoted to the scholarly challenge by and for Mizrachi Jews.

Issues that are mentioned only briefly in the sixth chapter of this book – the scholarly debate on 1948, the Mizrachi Jews, Holocaust memory, among others – did not remain the sole concern of academics. The media became an important venue for such debates, forcing both sides to articulate their respective positions in a more accessible, and at times more simplified and explicit, form. From there the challenge spread to other cultural domains: music, the visual arts, literature. In the ninth chapter, I discuss how this debate contributed to shaping Israeli cultural representations of the idea of Israel. Chapter 10 will revisit these post-Zionist representations on stage and screen.

This book's final section looks at reactions to the post-Zionist challenge and the resultant emergence of a more extreme version of Zionism in the twenty-first century, which has lodged in the heart of the Israeli production of knowledge. I have chosen to name this development the triumph of neo-Zionism. In addition to presenting a general description of it in Chapter 11, I devote Chapter 12 to its manifestations in the new research being conducted on 1948 within Israeli academia. A postscript to this book takes into account the recent upheavals in the Arab world, the stagnation of the peace process, and new developments in the study of Zionism – with particular attention to the emergence of the settler colonialist paradigm – in order to achieve some grasp of future trends in the struggle, inside and outside, over the idea of Israel.

PART I

The Scholarly and
Fictional Idea of Israel

ONE

The 'Objective' History of
the Land and the People

The Objective Zionist Historian

There is a tale that is 66.5 per cent true about Ben-Zion Dinur (né Dinaburg), the doyen of early Zionist historiography in Palestine and one-time minister of education. In 1937, two weeks before the arrival of the Peel Commission, which was charged with finding a solution to the conflict in Palestine, David Ben-Gurion, the leader of the Jewish community, approached Dinur to ask whether the respectable historian could produce some research proving that Jews had occupied the region continuously from 70 CE, the time of the Roman exile, to 1882, the arrival of the first Zionists. I could, said the historian, but this task involves many periods and requires a range of expertise, and will probably take a decade or so to complete. 'You do not understand,' replied Ben-Gurion. 'The Peel Commission is coming in two weeks' time. Reach your conclusion by then, and afterwards you can have a whole decade to prove it!'

From early on, the leaders of the Zionist movement prized scholarly and professional historiography. Whether we choose to define Zionism as a national movement or a colonialist project, it is obvious that establishing its history academically and publicly has always been essential to its survival. Zionism was driven by a wish to rewrite the history of Palestine, and that of the Jewish people, in a way that proved scientifically the Jewish claim to 'the Land of Israel'. As the modern Israeli state came into being, historiography was needed to market the new country as the 'only democracy in the Middle East', to explain the dispossession of the indigenous people who had so recently occupied the land, and to condemn their long struggle to dispossess the Jews of a supposed birthright.

In the pre-1882 Zionist narrative, Palestine was an empty homeland waiting to be redeemed by the exiled Jews. It was a new Germany, Poland or Russia when those places became inhospitable. The early Zionists adapted a patriotic German song about a new Reich to show what 'empty' Palestine became for them:

> There where the cedar kisses the sky,
> And where the Jordan quickly flows by,
> There where the ashes of my father lie,
> In that exalted Reich, on sea and sand,
> Is my beloved, true fatherland.[1]

A youth encyclopaedia on the history of Eretz Israel, written by the best scholars in the land in the 1970s, depicted the pre-1882 territory as 'The Empty Land'. The cover showed a lonely cedar yearning towards the sky on a barren hill, very much as in the poem above.[2] But the land would not be re-appropriated through enthusiastic poetry or inspirational paintings alone – scholarly clout was required, and for that an established academia would have to shape the country's ancient and modern historiography.

Zionist historiography turned professional after Zionism had become a significant social and political force in Palestine; its successor, Israeli historiography, was formulated during the early years of statehood. It was, after all, Ben-Gurion who approached Dinur, not the other way around. As with other national movements that have established nation-states, this professionalisation of history coincided with officialdom's making the political archives accessible to scholarly researchers.

As expected, this generosity was reciprocated by scholarly work that corroborated, rather than challenged, the political élite.[3] Similarly, social scientists in a variety of disciplines determined that developments in the Jewish community during the period of the British Mandate (1918–48) as well as the early years of statehood presented a classic case study in successful modernisation. According to the findings of the academic community, all the preconditions stipulated by the theory of modernisation for a successful transition from tradition to modernity existed in the Zionisation of Palestine. In other words, if you were a Zionist you could confidently participate in the best modernisation project in existence; and if you were a student of modernisation, Zionism was your best case study.

Providing scientific proof for a set of ideological claims was a tricky business. From the outset, most participants in the Zionist movement and later in the State of Israel who did academic work on Zionist and Jewish history have been involved in it, and they were able to do so only by embracing the seemingly impossible combination of a positivist wish to reconstruct reality and an ideological commitment to prove the justness of their cause. The facts, found exclusively in political archives, were treated as the raw material for proving the validity of the Zionist narrative.

Some of these scholarly works were written at a time when theorists globally had begun to challenge the validity of narratives fashioned in the name of nationalism, especially in situations of conflict, and to offer methodologies for exposing the hidden hand of nationalism in such narratives. Nevertheless, the positivist Zionist scholars of the 1970s and the 1980s who were engaged in researching the country's past ignored all methodological and theoretical innovations that might have undercut their confidence in the scientific truth of Zionism. One of the most effective ways to ensure their independence from innovation was their heavy reliance on the deeds of the élite. By taking this biased version of events as an objective, accurate description of fact, ideology and fact were fused and manipulated to produce the same story.

History was recruited to make the ideological and political project look good. Historians who declared themselves Zionists went in search of the roots of Jewish nationalism in the distant past and were satisfied only when they could establish that a national 'Jewish' or 'Hebrew' group existed in Palestine long before the foundation of the Zionist movement in the late nineteenth century. Some were content to seek these early roots in the seventeenth century; others went as far back as biblical times.

The early historians did not see a contradiction between professionalism and ideology. Ben-Zion Dinur explained this abnormality by observing that Zionist historians, by definition, were researchers who fused scientific mastery of the material with a clear and correct understanding of Zionism.[4] The conviction that professionalism demanded strong ideological loyalty became accepted by successive generations of Zionist historians. As the veteran Israeli historian Shmuel Almog remarked, such loyalty was essential for the success of the Jewish national movement: 'Zionism needed history in order to prove to Jews wherever they were that they all constitute one entity and that there is historical continuity from Israel and Judea in ancient times until modern Judaism.'[5]

Almog's colleague Israel Kolatt turned the argument around, claiming that only Zionist historians could provide a quality history of Zionism.[6] These professional historians perceived themselves as taking part in a nation-building project of unique dimensions and proportions under exceptional, indeed extraordinary, circumstances. Even if in every other historical instance ideology and objectivity could not be reconciled, here, they maintained, it could be done.

As a result, fervently committed Zionist historians understood better than anyone else the potency of establishing continuity between ancient Israel and modern Zionism. Already in the 1930s this missionary zeal was embodied in an academic school of thought based at the Hebrew University of Jerusalem and aptly called the Jerusalem School. Among its most famous members were Ben-Zion Dinur, Shmuel Ettinger, S. D. Goitein, and Joseph Klausner.[7] These historians wished to reconstruct the history of the 'People of Israel' with the Land of Israel as its epicentre. They searched for, and believed they found, scholarly proof for a recognition on the part of Jewish exiles that the Land of Israel constituted the focus of Judaism.

Their evidence is at best unconvincing; in fact, it amounts to a claim that Jews in pre-Zionist history possessed an unconscious desire, unknown to the Jews themselves at the time, to return to the land of Palestine. The existence of this recognition was thus claimed in retrospect. In the Jerusalem School's narrative, Jews were connected to the Land whether they were fully aware of it or not. As Benedict Anderson has so pithily commented, it is better for national movements to nationalise the dead than the living because the latter might question their newly imposed identity.

Very little has changed in Israel that might dislodge the primacy of the Zionist historians. Many articles in the two leading journals in Hebrew on Zionist history, *Cathedra* and *Hatzionut* (dominant until the 1990s) managed to tie the Gordian knot between ideology and archival research. In the 1960s and 1970s, the younger writers differed from their predecessors by shunning their proclivity for macrohistory. Rather than setting out to validate grand claims such as a persistent, age-old Jewish urge to settle in Palestine or the emptiness of Palestine prior to the arrival of the Zionists, they sliced up these claims by time frame or topic and provided limited empirical evidence for their validity. Thus they would look at Jewish urges for Palestine during a particular decade or discuss conditions in Palestine during a particular year or season. But whether they reconstructed the historical process as a whole, or focused on a single anecdotal chapter within it, they remained loyal both to Zionism and to scientific truth, as they saw it.

Older and younger Zionist historians alike were interested in political history, but Zionist loyalty restricted the ability of the younger scholars to produce novel ideas or groundbreaking research. Since the aim was to provide scholarly proof for a narrative already told and known, there was little room for revelations of any kind – only confirmations were wanted. Current Israeli historiography of the Mandatory period exemplifies this limitation. Everything one wanted to know, and much of what one did not, about the history of the Jewish community at that time has been covered; there is nothing new to say, because the story has already been told.

Moreover, because the narrative was to be based on sound,

scientific evidence, it could withstand any challenges coming from Palestinian or non-Zionist Jewish narratives. In this respect, the Israeli historians' admiration for the English historian E. H. Carr is quite understandable, especially their fascination with his observation that history is always written by the victors. Thus, ontologically, the historical narrative produced by the victorious is the truth.

This approach, to be sure, is not unique to Zionist historiography. Where it differs from other national historiographies that share this characteristic is that there has been almost no theoretical discussion about the apparent contradictions that such historiography produces. For this reason, until now the many (and there are many) academic historical works in Israel on Zionism and the state have been more descriptive than analytical, or indeed critical, in their overall approach. Analysis has been confined to the deeds of the political and ideological élites – leaving unexamined the nature of the ideology that underlay the behaviour of these élites, as well as the way the historians' commitment to the very same ideology affected their research.

The historical narrative as constructed by the academic system became the principal tool for cultivating and preserving the national collective memory. Historians treated the political archives as shrines of Truth and saw themselves as the attendant priests and protectors. But because the shrine is secular, the truth must be not only protected but also proved. The proof arrives by way of repetition rather than scrutiny; as a result, researchers, teachers, the Israeli educational system, and the officials and administrators responsible for national ceremonies, emblems, and the canonical literature have rarely sought out new material or new angles in the archival material. They simply looked for, and found, the same archival material that had originally provided the 'empirical proof' that justified the Zionist claim to Palestine. How unsettling the 1980s must have been, when these very archives yielded up material that forced difficult questions about Zionism and Israel's moral claims to the Land.

This well-known and efficiently proven narrative reconstructed Zionism as a national movement that brought modernisation and progress to a primitive Palestine. It 'made the desert bloom', rebuilt the Land's ruined cities, and introduced modern agriculture and industry to the benefit of Arabs and Jews alike. The resistance to Zionism resulted from a combination of Islamic fanaticism and pro-Arab British colonialism, along with local traditions of political violence. Against all odds, and despite cruel resistance, Zionism remained loyal to humanist precepts and unrelentingly stretched its hand to its Arab neighbours, who kept rejecting it.

No less extraordinary in this narrative is the story of how the Zionists succeeded in the miraculous establishment of a state in the face of a hostile Arab world. It was a state that, notwithstanding an objective shortage of space and means, absorbed a million Jews who had been expelled from the Arab world and offered them progress and integration into the only democracy in the Middle East. It was a defensive state, which tried to contain the ever-increasing hostility of the Arabs and the apathy of the world. It was a generous state, which ingathered Jews from more than a hundred diasporas and made of them a single new Jewish people. It was a moral and just movement of redemption that, unfortunately, found other people residing in its homeland but nevertheless offered them a share in a better future, which they foolishly rejected. That last bit comes in a second version, in which the country was empty when Zionism arrived so that the reaction of the inhabitants diminishes as a factor.

This second claim was presented in the book *From Time Immemorial*, by Joan Peters, a CBS documentary producer who was initially part of Jimmy Carter's team on the Middle East but then joined the new conservative camp. At first the book was a best seller in the United States and was promoted by the Israeli embassy, but its premise was so absurd that professional historians in Israel disavowed the book, demanding somewhat more sophistication in the construction of the Zionist claim that Palestine belongs to the Jewish people To them, Peters's simplistic denial that there had barely been any Arabs in Palestine before the arrival of the Zionists was little more than a fable.[8] On the other hand, the more sophisticated version – still being argued today, in *Palestine Betrayed*, by Efraim Karsh – is that there were indeed Palestinians residing in Palestine, but their leadership betrayed them by not allowing them to benefit from the numerous advantages brought by the Zionist movement.

The Objective Cartographer

Among the many ways this narrative has been conveyed, domestically and externally, is through maps and atlases. In Israel, the production of elegant atlases, divided into historical periods from biblical times to the present day, is a big industry. Usually maps are associated with the conveyance of strictly geographical information. For some time, however, they have also conveyed biases and agendas above and beyond the graphic, schematic representation of nature. Like the more classical natural atlases, the historical ones are a popular medium for communication, easily understood and appreciated regardless of language or previous knowledge. As D. F. Merriam noted in 1996, a map is a snapshot of an idea – in the present case, the idea of Israel.[9] Already in the late 1980s geographers had begun to doubt the presumption that maps were authentic or scientific representations of natural reality, but were hesitant to say this aloud. But historians have since become increasingly aware of the subjectivity of cartographic representations, as is evident in a statement by the cartographer J. B. Harely:

> [W]e often tend to work from the premise that mappers engage in an unquestionably 'scientific' or 'objective' form of knowledge creation. Of course, cartographers believe they have to say this to remain credible but historians do not have that obligation.[10]

In the case of Israel, this cartographic presentation was also transmitted outside the country. The best known among these is the *Atlas of the Arab–Israeli Conflict*, the most recent editions of which have been prepared by one of Britain's leading modern historians and the renowned biographer of Winston Churchill, Sir Martin Gilbert.[11] This atlas is now in its tenth edition. Not surprisingly, a work that sketches the history of such an eventful process must be revised every now and then. Forty years have passed since the publication of the first edition, and indeed each new edition included new maps of misery and violence. But whichever edition one chooses to consult, it is immediately evident that an atlas conveys not only a reality but also how that reality is perceived.

The *Atlas of the Arab–Israeli Conflict* grants unequivocal scholarly legitimacy to the classical Zionist historiographical version of the conflict, while the Palestinian perspective is reduced to mere propaganda, despite the wish expressed in the preface to present fairly 'the views of those involved'.[12]

A few examples of the annotated maps in this atlas will suffice to show the ideological bent of the ostensibly neutral cartographic representation. The myth of the empty land for the landless people is re-created vividly in the first three maps. The first one shows the presence of the Jews in Palestine prior to the Arab conquest. Fair enough, one may say, as this demonstrates the romantic Zionist claim to Palestine. One would also expect at least one map informing us about the presence of the Arabs in Abbasid, Mameluke, Seljuk, or Ottoman Palestine, but there is nothing of the sort. The second map presents a picture of the Jews in Palestine during those same periods of Islamic history, when they constituted less than 1 per cent of the population. The third map concerns Jewish immigration (or in the words of the atlas, settlement) of 1880–1914.

The maps delineating and describing the clashes of 1920 and 1929 are categorised as showing the violent Arab attacks against the Jews during the first decade of the Mandate. No mention is made of the Zionist contribution to, and in some cases initiation of, these attacks. Thus, one will find neither Ze'ev Jabotinsky's provocation that led to the 1920 riots in Jerusalem nor an indication that the 1929 eruption in Palestine was also directed against Britain's pro-Zionist policy there.

Needless to say, Gilbert does not call the Arab Revolt of 1936–39 by its proper name but rather prefers the term 'Arab campaign' (that is, a campaign against the Jews). The running commentary (presented in small boxes on the margins of each map) tells us of three years of endless killing of Jews and British soldiers. The Palestinian view of this revolt is strikingly absent. The revolt was, after all, the first national Palestinian attempt to overcome clannish and sectarian cleavages in a torn traditional society. It was a rare instance of unity, generated by the belated awakening of Palestinian leaders to the dangers that faced their community from increased Jewish immigration to Palestine. Despite its failure, the Arab Revolt served as a model for the Palestinian uprising of 1987.[13] In Gilbert's atlas, the maps of the revolt form a trail of anti-Jewish bloodshed and nothing more. Yet according to 'conservative' estimates in the Survey of Palestine, prepared soon after the end of the Second World War, about 2,500 Arabs were killed by the British military and police during the rebellion, while the same source puts the numbers of British killed during the conflict (excluding 1937, where breakdowns are not given) at 143 and the number of Jews at 429.[14]

This atlas goes on to reproduce the classical Zionist view of the 1948 war, which is described at length below. The same approach to cartographic representation appears in many American and Israeli atlases. From the 1990s onwards, however, these representations were countered, first by the dedicated research of Salman Abu-Sitta and soon also by the Palestinian Academic Society for the Study of International Affairs (PASSIA), an NGO founded in Jerusalem in 1987. Abu-Sitta produced several huge atlases covering Palestinian history in general and that of 1948 in particular.[15]

In sum, the 'Zionist' atlases clearly show the same position that the historians documented with archives and testimonies – that the land was empty until Zionism arrived. They offer scholarly proof for the first half of the famous Zionist maxim that it was a movement of people without land coming to a land without people. But of course the people were there on the land, and neither the knowledge producers of Israel nor the philosophers who held forth on the idea of Israel could ignore them. And yet they were ignored, and simultaneously depicted in such a way as to justify, a priori and in hindsight, the denial of their existence and their rights as native people of the land.

TWO

The Alien Who Became a Terrorist: The Palestinian in Zionist Thought

> To most people Palestinians are visible principally as fighters, terrorists, and lawless pariahs. Say the word 'terror' and a man wearing a keffiyeh and mask and carrying a *kalashnikov* immediately leaps before one's eyes. To a degree, the image of a helpless, miserable-looking refugee has been replaced by this menacing one as the veritable icon of 'Palestinian'.[1]
>
> – Edward Saïd, *After the Last Sky*, 1998

In January 2012, Israeli television proudly broadcast a co-production titled *The History of Terror* – a joint venture of the Israeli and France 2 TV, and informed by the work of Israeli and French scholars. Tracing the trajectory of modern terrorism in the world, they detected clear roots in Algeria's National Liberation Front (FLN), the Cuban revolution and the Palestine Liberation Organisation (PLO), all of which, in the programme's parlance, displayed 'murderous ideologies' that had since tainted world history. The final segment in this series focused on Hamas and the Arab Spring as a chapter not yet completed.[2]

Much of Israeli media and academia have characterised the Palestinian resistance movement as a key factor in the global history of terrorism. The role of the academics was to validate this depiction with 'scientific' research that both recorded acts of Palestinian violence and proved the applicability of theoretical definitions of terrorism to these acts. Israeli politicians and the media fully accepted this portrayal, although during the period of the brief, failed Oslo Accords it was toned down.

These images of the Palestinians are deeply rooted in Zionist history and go back to the period of the Second Aliyah, at the very beginning of the twentieth century (1904–14). For these settlers, the Palestinians were either not there or, when they were, appeared as aliens who should not have been there. The participants in the Second Aliyah numbered between 20,000 and 40,000 and came mainly from Russia (it should be noted that they constituted only 4 per cent of the Jews who left Russia at the time). It was not a success story. The vast majority of them (some 90 per cent) left quickly, mainly for the United States. At the end of the day, then, this core group was a few thousand strong. But they were achievers: they expelled the Palestinian workforce from the old Jewish colonies – *Kibbush Ha'avoda* (conquest of labour), they called it – and lay the foundations for the future state.

Most of them encountered the Palestinians for the first time under similar circumstances. The encounters began on the Jaffa shore, then while they laboured alongside Palestinians in the more established Zionist colonies or in the towns. Once they realised that indeed the natives were there, they decided, as all settlers do, to build gated communities and strive for an exclusionary labour market and economy. This inevitably required a paramilitary force to guard the enclaves. The British Mandatory authorities quickly recognised this separateness and legalised it within the Mandatory state.[3]

The new arrivals were compulsive diarists and letter writers – they did not miss a single mosquito bite and, in true shtetl style, did not stop complaining. The first anti-Arab entries were written while they were still being hosted by the Palestinians as they made their way to the old colonies or in the towns of Palestine. The complaints stemmed from the settlers' formative experiences, which arose during their search for labour and subsistence – a universal predicament, whether they went to the Zionist colonies or tried their luck in the Palestinian towns. In order to survive, they needed to work shoulder to shoulder with Palestinian farmers or labourers, and through this intimate contact, even the most ignorant and defiant settlers realised that Palestine was in fact an Arab country, with an Arab human landscape. It was a process of recognition of an unpleasant reality, intertwined with early thoughts of how to change it. The subsequent production of knowledge in Israel – and in particular the assigned attributes of the Palestinians in what we are calling here 'the Idea of Israel' – was strongly influenced by these first impressions.

When one leading activist of the Second Aliyah resorted to a medical metaphor by describing the Palestinian workers and farmers as *Beit Mihush* (an infested hotbed of pain), he could then immediately conjure up exclusive Jewish labour as the panacea. In many letters, Hebrew workers appear as the healthy blood that would immunise the nation from rottenness and death.[4] One letter refers to the idiocy of allowing Arabs to work with Jews, and recalls an old Jewish story of a stupid man who resuscitated a dead lion that devoured him.[5]

With regard to the land of Palestine, the settlers talked about it as a *nechar*, a foreign land, or worse, as *yam nechar*, a sea of foreignness and alienation. References to Palestine as barren land were accompanied by descriptions of the Palestinians as savages roaming this wilderness. These references appear in their diaries or in angry letters lamenting that the homeland had become a *shemama*, a desert.[6] Wherever there were Palestinians, there was a sense of barrenness, which caused some of the settlers to rethink the settlement venture and contemplate a return from, as one of them put it, this 'land of nothingness', because the empty land was full of strangers – 'people who were stranger to us than the Russian or Polish peasant', so that 'we have nothing in common with the majority of the people living here'.[7]

True, if you came from Europe, Palestine was objectively foreign. But ideologically it looked foreign because of the foreigners who were living in it, endowing the place with an alien character. And these people were not simply aliens; they were aggressive aliens, and in the terms of this narrative, the aggression was directed at the Jews from the first encounter.

Like all foreigners, the Jewish settlers sailed first to Alexandria, took a ferry to Jaffa, and were taken ashore by small boats. This mundane arrival at the shore appears in the settlers' statements as aggressive and alien treatment: *Aravim Hetikifu Ottanu* – 'the Arabs assaulted us' – is the phrase used to describe the simple act of Palestinian boys helping settlers to small boats on the way to Jaffa;[8] they shouted because the waves were high and asked for baksheesh because this was how they managed to live. But in the settlers' narrative they were assailants. Noise, presumably a normal feature of life in the Jewish townships of Eastern Europe, becomes menacing when produced by Palestinian women wailing in the traditional salute of joy to the sailors returning safely home. For the settlers this was the behaviour of savages, 'with fiery eyes and a strange garrotted language'.[9] Whether the topic is their language, their dress or their animals, reports back to Europe concerning the Palestinians were all about unpleasantness and weirdness.

Alienation and discomfort caused by the presence of Arabs in Palestine was not the only troubling aspect of the Zionists' first encounter with the locals. Another source of aggravation and bewilderment was the demographic fabric of some of the old Jewish colonies. One of the leading figures of this wave of immigration, a man named Yona Hurewitz, wrote in his diary how disgusted he was to find out that some of the houses in Hadera were occupied by Arabs.[10] In the jewel of the Zionist crown, Rishon LeZion, Natan Hofshi (whose family name, meaning 'free person', was invented on arrival) reported back home to Poland how appalled he was to see many Arab men, women and children crossing through the colony. *'Nehradeti'* (I was flabbergasted), he commented, and suggested, 'Maybe it was a terrible mistake and this was a foreign country?' In a later writing he noted that once 'the Arabs were not allowed to pass [through Rishon LeZion] it became home'.[11]

The presence of Palestinians in or near Jewish colonies is often referred to as *Kalon* (shame) which is accentuated by the *laag* (contempt) and *buz* (scorn) shown by the Arabs, who according to this depiction somehow understood how pathetic the situation was. The settlers remembered being called *Masakin* (the poor ones). In their eyes, it was absurd that Palestinians were allowed to guard the property of the early settlers.[12]

The solution for *Kalon* was *kavod* (honour). At the time, the early Zionist Orientalists were explaining how to manipulate the centrality of honour in 'Arab culture' for the sake of the project's success. Again and again, Zionist settlers behaved as a people who had been insulted – either objectively in the form of a physical attack, but more often simply by the very presence of Palestinians in Palestine. One interesting aspect of this quest for honour was the reported continual competition with Palestinian workers on production. In addition, the Zionist settlers instituted retaliation for 'theft', which was how they characterised the rural tradition of cultivating state land, a practice that was legal under Ottoman law. Picking fruit from roadside orchards became an act of robbery only after Zionism took over the land. The words *shoded* (robber) and *rozeach* (murderer) were flung about with ease when Palestinians involved in such acts were described.[13] After 1948 these terms would be replaced with 'terrorist' and 'saboteur'.

But even the most violent encounter and the even more violent discourse about the local inhabitants could not erase the settlers' need to learn from them how to shepherd, farm, and survive. Very soon the 'Arab way of cultivating and dressing and behaving' was presented as a necessary initial evil that had to be abandoned as quickly as possible. This became the principal declared mission of the Second Aliyah.[14]

Although the appropriation of local habits in order to get rid of the locals was regarded as an indispensable but temporary evil, sometimes that evil was prolonged to assist with the Zionist project. Such was the idea conceived by someone named Arthur Ruppin, who proposed that they build a *madafa*, the traditional guest tent or hall, for settling with local notables the final transition of land from absentee landlords to Zionist hands. The notables represented the tenants of the land, and had to be convinced to expel the tenants so as to allow actual Zionist settlement of the land that had been purchased.[15] Cleansing the land of its farmers and tenants was done at first through meeting in the Zionist *madafa* and then by force of eviction in Mandatory times. The 'good' Palestinians were those who came to the *madafa* and allowed themselves to be evicted. Those who refused were branded robbers and murderers. Even Palestinians with whom the settlers sometimes shared ownership of horses or long hours of guard duty were transformed into villains once they refused eviction.[16] Later on, wherever Israelis would control the lives of Palestinians, such a refusal to collaborate would be the ultimate proof for Palestinian choice of the terrorist option as a way of life.

Urban Palestine, especially the town of Jaffa, triggered a different sort of impression. As David Ben-Gurion and others, reported, the town had 'a large number of Christians'.[17] They were educated, they were nationalist, and they more or less grasped what Zionism was all about. They were impertinent and overly assertive.[18] One settler, Israel Kadishman, asserted that 'our wits', and not only power, would be needed to combat the Arabs of Jaffa.[19] Jaffa symbolised everything the members of the Second Aliyah dreaded and detested. In 1967, Jenin; in 1987, Nablus; in 2000, Hebron; in 2008, Gaza; in 2011, Nazareth – all would be similarly depicted as hubs of self-assertive, nationalist Palestinian sentiment and hotbeds of terrorist activity.

The Palestinians, whether rural or urban, disappointed twice – first, by simply being there, and second, by being ungrateful. In a bizarre way, there was very little the Second Aliyah did for the Palestinians, whereas one could at least say that the first wave of immigrants had offered employment, albeit of an exploitative sort. Yet the sense was that the Palestinians were ungrateful.

Faint-hearted humanist views were not permitted. When a Second Aliyah activist, Yossef Rabinowitch found himself indulging in what he called 'a moment of weakness' and was charmed momentarily by the beauty of an Arab village and the sound of a shepherd's flute, he had to remind himself that 'these were foreigners on the homeland'.[20] The need to exclude the Palestinians in order to make Palestine a safe haven for the Jews is the strongest and most frequent message coming from the voices of the Second Aliyah. Yosef Aharonowitz was one of the more zealous fighters against the employment of Palestinians, whom he defined as 'this evil' (*hara hazeh*): 'We are only few and if they uprise against us this is our end.' He also says, however, that here and there he met decent farmers but knew they were potentially '*raa hola*' (malignant evil).[21]

During the years of military rule, the phrase '*raa hola*' was used often in discussions about the future of the Palestinians in Israel. At that time, the possibility of expelling them was seriously considered as an alternative to the emergency regime of British Mandatory regulations, which until 1967 robbed them of most basic human and civil rights.[22]

The metaphor of the Palestinians as a disease that had to be cured continued to feature in the official discourse in the 1970s. 'A cancer in the heart of the nation' was a common reference and was commonly and wrongly associated with the Koenig Report. Yisrael Koenig was the most senior Ministry of the Interior official for Israel's northern regions, where half of the population was Palestinian. He was asked by the first Rabin government (1974–77) to offer a strategy to advance the Judaisation of the region, given its demographic realities. Although Koenig was associated with the cancer reference, he was not the one who coined it. Nonetheless, his report, though less insulting in its language, recommended a series of draconian measures against the Palestinians. As in the diaries of the Second Aliyah, the Koenig Report treated the Palestinians as a disease that threatened to kill a healthy body.[23]

The experience of alienation – both in the sense of feeling alien in the Arab world and depicting the Arabs as hostile aliens – became more institutionalised after 1967 through discriminatory legislation, governmental policies, and official conduct. At the same time, Palestinians were also becoming a subject of academic inquiry. Following the 1967 war, the production of knowledge within Israel about the Palestinians was primarily a project of 'know thy enemy' and of military intelligence gathering. For that reason, both Israeli academics and Israeli media commonly used the term 'terrorism' when referring to any kind of Palestinian political, social and cultural activity. 'Palestinian terrorism' was depicted as having been present from the very beginning of the Zionist project in Palestine and still being there when academic research into it began in earnest. This characterisation was so comprehensive and airtight that it assigned almost every chapter in Palestinian history to the domain of 'terrorism' and absolved hardly any of the organisations and personalities that made up the Palestinian national movement from the accusation of being terrorists. The government, academia, the media, the army, and the NGOs of civil society all took part in constructing the negative image of the Palestinians.

Historicising Palestinian Terrorism, 1882–2009

With its fusion of ideological commitment and empirical research, traditional Zionist historiography assumed that Palestinian resistance to a Zionist presence in Palestine was tantamount to terrorism. Hence, Israeli historians industriously recorded such acts of resistance from very early on and laid them on a timeline of exponential escalation. The Zionist reaction to this evil was poetically captured in the title of a book by one of Israel's leading historians, Anita Shapira – the *Sword of the Dove*[24] – in other words, a reluctant use of force against increasing Palestinian terrorism. Or, as the former Israeli prime minister Golda Meir is quoted as saying, 'We will never forgive the Arabs for what they forced us to do to them'.[25]

The source of this violence and its escalation is never clearly articulated. As we shall see, enigmatic violence, which spread from nowhere and for no good reason, was a major theme in discussing Arab and Palestinian actions in 1948, and is evident in both scholarly historical works and cinematic representations of the war. The recurring assertion was that Palestinian terrorism had no proper motive or explanation and yet it grew in numbers, its cruelty increased, and it arrived in ever-swelling waves. It is extremely difficult to find a discussion that proposes any Zionist action as a possible explanation for Palestinian violence. In the tradition of empiricism without analysis in the service of ideology, Palestinian terrorism came out of the blue – in the land without people against the landless people who returned to redeem it.

When Palestinian violence against Zionism became a scholarly area of inquiry, historians started to search for the very first victims of that violence. As recorded in many sources, the earliest victim was a rabbi who arrived in 1811 for a religious pilgrimage. He was in fact killed in a feud over building materials in Jerusalem in 1851, but was later Zionised by mainstream historiography and is listed as victim number one at a memorial for victims of terror, located in Tel Aviv near the headquarters of the Mossad. As Benedict Anderson remarked (and as mentioned above), national movements can safely nationalise the dead, since the deceased cannot challenge the collective identity imposed on them by the living.

According to this narrative, terror began in earnest after 1917 in the wake of the Balfour Declaration, when Palestinian leaders and activists organised popular protests against the pro-Zionist policy of the new British rulers of the land. In 1920 and 1921, these protests, especially in urban centres such as Jerusalem and Jaffa, turned violent as a result of either Zionist provocation, as in the case of Jerusalem in April 1920, or a Palestinian rage directed towards Jewish areas, as occurred in Jaffa in May 1921. These skirmishes were depicted as the first waves of Palestinian terrorism, a motiveless and unwarranted violence against innocent settlers. This kind of violence turned the Palestinians into terrorists during a period when none of them clearly understood Zionism but when many were nevertheless outraged by the notion that Britain had promised their homeland to foreign settlers.

Al-Hajj Amin al-Husayni was the leader of the Palestinians during the Mandatory period, and under his leadership, when Palestinian protests took a more systematic form in 1929, he too was described as a terrorist. Al-Husayni was pulled between two poles, trying to navigate between on the one hand, a wish to keep a cordial relationship with the Mandatory powers, and on the other, the fierce internal opposition that demanded more active resistance against the pro-Zionist policies of the British Mandatory government. He and other leaders soon realised that the implementation of the Zionist dream of a Jewish state in Palestine would inevitably bring about partial or even total dispossession of the indigenous population. Despite the fact that these leaders represented a decisive majority of the population (almost 70 per cent in 1929), they were ill equipped to confront the twin forces of British imperialism and Zionist colonialism.[26]

The ultimate Palestinian 'terrorist' of the Mandatory period was Izz al-Din al-Qassam, who operated in the early 1930s. A Syrian preacher exiled to Palestine after taking part in the Syrian revolt against the French Mandate for Syria and the Lebanon in 1925, he became an inspiring religious leader who motivated young, mainly unemployed dwellers of shanty towns around Haifa to take up arms against Jewish settlers and British soldiers. His actions and some of his preaching – he did not write much – would later inspire the military wing of Hamas, which is called the Izz al-Din al-Qassam Battalions. Furthermore, these fighters decided to name the main, though primitive, weapon that they used against Israel the Qassam rocket. It is hardly surprising that, early on, Israeli scholarship described al-Qassam as a terrorist.[27]

Israeli and Zionist historiography were no kinder towards the Arab Revolt of 1936–39, a popular uprising that took the British authorities in Palestine three years to quell and for which Britain called in the Royal Air Force and resorted to a repertoire of collective punishments as brutal as those the Israeli army would use years later in the West Bank and the Gaza Strip during its nearly fifty years of occupation. This was a complex resistance that included strikes, petitions, and guerrilla warfare, as well as attacks on some of the Jewish colonies and neighbourhoods in the mixed towns of Palestine.

In Israel, this revolt usually appeared as a chapter in the history of Palestinian terrorism.[28] In both Palestinian and less biased historiography, it appeared as the first, and in many ways, one of the few, successful popular revolts of the Palestinians that achieved some significant political gains, notably the British White Paper of 1939, which limited Jewish immigration and land purchase. This new British policy, together with the emergence of Nazism in Europe, led to a Jewish Zionist revolt against the British Empire. It was a heroic deed against all odds in Israeli historiography, amounting to terrorism in the eyes of not only the Mandatory government of the day but subsequently, leaders of the Irgun and the Stern Gang, such as Menachem Begin and Yitzhak Shamir, were regarded as personae non gratae in the United Kingdom because of their terrorist past in Palestine.

An episode in the life of al-Hajj Amin al-Husayni, in which he cooperated with the Nazi regime in Germany, succeeded in further demonising the Palestinians and facilitating a depiction of him as not merely a terrorist but also a Nazi. Al-Husayni had been expelled by the British for his role in the Arab Revolt in 1937, which forced him to seek new allies, and pushed him into the hands of both the Nazis and the Fascists. He resided in Berlin during the Second World War and served the Nazi propaganda machine. To this day, this episode has made it easy for Israeli historiography to add Nazism and terrorism to its characterisation of the Palestinian resistance to Zionism, and to avoid a more serious and complex deconstruction of al-Husayni's activities.[29]

The Palestinian rejection of the United Nations partition resolution of 29 November 1947 was regarded as an act of terrorism as well – more significant than previous acts, and genocidal besides, since it intended to destroy the Jewish community in Palestine altogether. This viewpoint is reiterated in the introduction to Benny Morris's recent mainstream historiography *1948: A History of the First Arab–Israeli War*.[30] Morris, a neo-Zionist historian, looks at 1948 within the 'clash of civilizations' paradigm: as a war between Islam and the West. In order to prove this, he quotes from public statements by Arab leaders such as the Saudi king, Ibn Saud; representatives of the religious establishment; and spokesmen for popular Islamic movements, the Muslim Brotherhood foremost among them. In Morris's eyes the war was, for the Muslims, a jihad.

Morris's earlier work, *Israel's Border Wars*, did more justice to the Palestinian resistance, questioning the depiction of Palestinian infiltrators in the 1950s as terrorists.[31] In fact, these were Palestinian refugees who attempted to enter the Jewish state to retrieve lost herds, uncollected crops, and abandoned properties. Very few came for revenge. In the mid-1950s, this energy was channelled into the fedayeen movement, which was at first encouraged and organised by Muslim Brotherhood branches in the Gaza Strip and the West Bank but later turned into an independent national movement committed to recovery from the trauma of the 1948 Nakba. From these beginnings, Fatah emerged in the late 1950s. As the principal independent national movement, it eventually took over the Palestine Liberation Organisation, the PLO – the less genuine and more cynical organisation created by the Arab world in 1964 to redeem Palestine. The takeover occurred in 1968 following the failure of the pan-Arab effort to defeat Israel in the war of June 1967.

Under the rubric of 'terrorism', Israeli historiography lumped together the sporadic and desperate acts of expelled Palestinians with the guerrilla warfare of Fatah. This was presented as a direct continuation of the Palestinian terror in the pre-state period. A summary of this point of view can be found in English in, for instance, a book by the pro-Zionist novelist and essayist Jillian Becker, who relied heavily on Israeli sources and perspectives.[32] It is certainly true that some Palestinian actions were directed against innocent citizens in Israel; the worst instance of this was an attack on an ordinary passenger bus on 17 March 1954, in which eleven passengers were murdered. A serious historiographer would no doubt regard such an act as terrorism, but would not characterise an entire national movement as a 'terrorist organisation' because of individual acts such as these.

By 1954, Israeli retaliation policy against the more innocent infiltrations was well known: to shoot on sight any Palestinian attempting to enter or return to Palestine. Around five thousand people lost their lives in these infiltrations, and yet it was they who were depicted as terrorists. State policies of any kind, even as brutal as shooting on sight, are not mentioned in Israel apart from the aforementioned work by Benny Morris.[33] The idea that Palestinian resistance on Israel's borders was pure terrorism was used by the Israeli government in 1956 to justify the collusion with Britain and France on the confrontation over the Suez Canal. Updated historiography, especially that provided by Avi Shlaim, has revealed that the principal objective of this operation was a wish to topple Gamal Abdul Nasser, who was a thorn in the side of Britain (because of his nationalisation of the Suez Canal), of France (because of his support of the FLN), and of Israel (because of his attempts to radicalise Arab states that were somewhat favourable to Israel, including Lebanon and the Hashemite regimes of Jordan and Iraq).[34]

The occupation of the West Bank and the Gaza Strip in June 1967 by Israel and the defeat of the pan-Arab military forces sharpened the focus of the Palestinian national movement. Between 1967 and 1974, under the influence of Third World revolutionary theories, armed struggle came to be deemed the exclusive means of ending the Israeli occupation and even of achieving the liberation of Palestine as a whole. In practice, the movement was engaged in an abortive attempt to organise a popular revolt against the Israeli occupation of the West Bank and the Gaza Strip and a more successful effort to attract world opinion to the plight of the Palestinians.

During those years, the armed struggle resorted to every possible tactic: terrorism, guerrilla warfare, and direct military confrontation with the superior army of Israel. Terrorism was manifested mainly in the hijacking of airplanes, a speciality of the Democratic Front for the Liberation of Palestine (the DFLP, led by Naif Hawatmeh) and the Popular Front for the Liberation of Palestine (the PFLP, led by George Habash). Here, for the first time, several Palestinian groups linked up directly with what the professional literature would define unhesitatingly as pure terrorist groups, including the Baader-Meinhof Gang and the Japanese Red Army, but also with other liberation movements, such as ETA and the IRA. These were, however, short-term associations. The 1972 murder by three members of the Red Army of twenty-six (some say twenty-four) passengers at Ben Gurion Airport (then still known as Lod Airport) was the most notorious operation of that kind – unquestionably an act of pure terrorism. There were also growing tensions between the PLO and the Hashemite Kingdom of Jordan, on whose territory the units had trained and operated, and as a result of that deterioration, ending with the massacre of several thousand Palestinians by the Jordanians in September 1970, the PLO moved to Lebanon. These developments marked the end of that revolutionary moment.

The guerrilla operations included attempts to infiltrate the occupied West Bank in order to organise popular resistance there. After 1970, there were similar operations based in Lebanon, which targeted civilians in Israel for purposes of kidnap and negotiation. Quite often these ended in disaster, including the murder of civilians, either because of an aggressive Israeli salvage action despite prudence having dictated further negotiations, or because of the callousness of the kidnappers. One infamous operation took place at the 1972 Olympic Games in Munich, where eleven Israeli athletes were killed. Another took place in Ma'alot, where a school was taken; during the salvage operation, twenty-two students were killed. It must be said that today Israeli scholars do refer to Ma'alot as a failed salvage operation but nonetheless present it as a classic case study of Palestinian barbarity and terrorism.

Another chapter of the guerrilla efforts was a war of attrition that went on until September 1970, in which the PLO bombarded Israeli settlements in the Jordan valley. After the Munich operation, the Mossad initiated its own campaign of terror, with names such as Operation Wrath of God (killing PLO personnel in Europe) and Operation Spring of Youth (the assassination of PLO leaders in Beirut in 1973). The most famous of the Israeli retaliation operations took place at Karameh in 1968, a confrontation that the Israelis called *Mivtza Tofet* (Operation Hell), which triggered unexpectedly fierce Palestinian and Jordanian resistance.

Judging by the balance sheet, Palestinian actions were a failure – not one square inch was liberated. But some change was achieved: the PLO became the sole and authentic liberation movement, even though losing the battle of liberation while winning the struggle for legitimacy did transform its strategy. In the mid-1970s, the organisation developed what its commanders called the stages plan: a realistic political strategy that accepted the failure of a pure military solution and opted for a diplomatic effort and resolution of the conflict with Israel.

Israel, however, did not reciprocate this pragmatism. On the ground, the occupied territories became a mega-prison under strict military rule – which in many ways continues to this day. The Israeli discourse of peace was soon exposed as an attempt to conceal the vast Judaisation of the Palestinian territories while confining the Palestinian population to the rest of the territories. With time, the Palestinians would be offered to turn these circumscribed areas into a state and to declare the conflict at an end, which they would refuse to do.

Nor was pragmatism manifested in the continued depiction of the PLO as a mammoth terrorist organisation, at least prior to the signing of the Oslo Accords in September 1993. The PLO and Israel were employing all kinds of means, including actions that would be defined by scholars as terrorism whether executed by states or by non-state actors. (See, for instance, the scholarly description of the PLO, terrorism, and Oslo in the entry 'PLO' on the popular Israeli website Ynet, an offshoot of the widely read daily paper *Yedioth Ahronoth*.)

Since the beginning of the occupation, Palestinian paramilitary activity included attacks on three different kinds of targets: the military, the settlers, and civilian targets inside Israel. The latter began in earnest only after the failure of the first uprising, the First Intifada, which erupted in 1987. There are few academic analyses of the First Intifada in Israel, but there are journalistic assessments that have appeared as books and that represent mainstream perception. Although the uprising consisted mainly of stone throwing and mass demonstrations, and occasionally even successful short-term takeovers of villages and neighbourhoods, the more popular books still summed it up as another chapter of terrorism.[35]

In the mid-1970s, the Israeli Orientalist Yehoshua Porath published two volumes, which later appeared in English, about the emergence and history of the Palestinian national movement between 1918 and 1939.[36] He was the first to refer to the people who lived in Palestine before 1948 as Palestinians. This was a novelty. Despite the famous remark by Golda Meir that there was no such a thing as the Palestinian people, they have been referred to ever since as Palestinians, including in discussions of the period before 1948.

Palestinians appear in Porath's book as petty politicians of a clannish society, concerned only about their own interests and united solely by their negation of Zionism. Porath's books make an ideal case study for Edward Said's model of Western Orientalism. Although they do recognise the existence of the Palestinians as a people before 1948, the local population is described in one-dimensional terms as primitive, moved only by tradition, religious fanaticism, and a shifty urban élite. Nowhere in these works is the proposition that the Palestinians were, at least in their eyes, struggling against a colonialist movement mentioned or explored.

Yehoshafat Harkabi, a head of military intelligence during the 1950s, who moved to academia in the 1970s, wrote a more contemporary history of the PLO and came to the conclusion that it was purely a terror organisation determined to destroy the State of Israel: 'The objective which has been proclaimed day and night by the Arab leaders is the liquidation of the state of Israel', he wrote in 1974. This position left no space for Arab leaders' various debates about Zionism ever since 1882.[37] A decade later, however, some of his students – and in the 1990s, towards the end of his life, he himself – developed a new approach that differentiated between the different PLO positions towards Israel. One student of Harkabi's, Matti Steinberg, who also came to academia from the security and intelligence world, employed theoretical tools to show that pragmatism was an inevitable development in organisations like the PLO, and he advocated dialogue with the movement.[38] Other of Harkabi's students, such as Moshe Shemesh, Avraham Sela and Shaul Mishal, to mention but a few, adopted similar views.[39] Their analysis was less demonising and more informative, at least about the history of the PLO since its inception and until their own time.

The Palestinians in Israel: Between Orientalism and Terrorism

The Palestinian minority in Israel was first researched by non-professional writers who wished to present either the official Israeli line or the individual grievances of members of the community. This genre continued to be pursued, mainly by Israelis involved in one way or another in shaping policy towards the Palestinian minority. But even the more academic works that appeared in the late 1970s were not devoid of ideological leanings and biases, even though their methodology was professional and their reliance on factual infrastructure more solid. Broadly defined, their research lay on a spectrum between Zionist and anti-Zionist positions.

Among those scholars who wrote within the framework of Zionism, the paradigm of modernisation was their favourite theoretical point of departure. If we apply for a moment Noam Chomsky's analysis of how academics in the West in general and in the United States in particular relate to hegemonic ideology, we have here a rare example not merely of academic bowing to an interpretation of past and present realities in such a way as to satisfy the powers that be but also of basing the interpretation on a solid theoretical infrastructure for the validity of the ideology. As social scientists, they were not only loyal to Zionism for emotional and utilitarian reasons but also convinced that the theory of modernisation validated the ideology – in this case, reinforcing the attitude towards the Palestinian minority in Israel.[40]

The Palestinian minority was regarded as a potentially subversive element and hence was put under severe military rule. In the euphoric mood that sprang up after the 1948 war, politicians and generals, who regarded the minority community as a 'fifth column' and a grave security risk, were willing to let military rule continue and even contemplated the Palestinians' forceful removal from the state.[41] But change came with the end of the Ben-Gurion era. Ben-Gurion was supremely paranoid in regard to the future of the minority; following his disappearance from the political scene, the politicians abolished the straightforward military rule that had been imposed on the Palestinian minority and substituted it for a more complex matrix of discrimination, dispossession and colonisation.

Meanwhile, academics were developing hopeful scenarios for the future. In both its self- and its external image, Israel had become a new regional superpower, ruling over vast areas of Egypt, Palestine and Syria. Academically, this translated into a sense of mission.

But the 'mission' was not easy. One of the most progressive of those who chose the Palestinians in Israel as his subject matter, Sammy Smooha, wrote at that time:

The cultural differences between Jews and Arabs in Israel are due to stark differences in fundamental values ... there are significant differences in ways of thinking, personal traits, impulses for achievements, patterns of leisure, etc.[42]

In short, the Jewish community was a progressive, modern society, whereas the Palestinian minority was a primitive one. Modernisation was slow and could lead either to a clash of civilisations that, owing to the imbalance of power, would end in the demise of the Palestinian minority in Israel or to its integration within a modern society. Smooha predicted that the latter scenario was the more likely. To his credit, in later works he moved away from this essentialist, Orientalist depiction of Palestinian society and cast as much blame on Israel's discriminatory policies as on the intrinsic problems of Arab society and culture – before joining everyone else after 2000 and returning to his earlier point of departure in his 1978 book *Israel: Pluralism and Conflict*, which, after trials and tribulations and attempts to think out of the box, the prediction that the Palestinian minority would be Israelised, but with great difficulties, became his main mantra about the Palestinian minority in Israel. In brief, it was a non-modern group that recognised the superiority of modern Jewish society and wished to integrate into it but was hindered by, on the one hand, the Arab nationalism around it and, on the other, Jewish racism in Israeli society.[43]

Smooha's articles from that period indicate that, both inside and outside Israeli academia, the Palestinian minority was considered not only to be primitive and non-modern but, as shown through surveys among Jewish citizens at that time, also one that would never become modern unless it was de-Palestinised and de-Arabised.[44] The dominance of the modernisation theory as the principal prism through which the reality of the Palestinian minority should be viewed was facilitated by the august presence within Israeli academia of one of the world's renowned theorists on modernisation, Shmuel Noah Eisenstadt, a favourite target of the new sociology. His students at the Hebrew University presented the Palestinians in Israel as a classic case study of a successfully modernised and Westernised community in transition and added scholarly weight to the more ideological aspirations of the political élite towards this sizeable minority.[45] Their basic assumption was that the community at large was a traditional society that was modernised through its incorporation within the State of Israel. More specifically, it was seen as a society in 'transition' between traditional and modern phases. These academic observers were looking for quantifiable evidence of the transformation of an Arab society and its adoption of a Western way of life.

This methodology was also applied to the *Mizrachim*. Both were conceived as ideal subjects for the study of modernisation and Westernisation and as proof of one of the more successful implementations of these enterprises. Thus, for instance, Israeli sociologists attributed the lower fertility rates of the *Mizrachim* after their arrival in Israel as 'adopting modern Western patterns of fertility', which rescued them from the fate of remaining primitive and poor. The subsequent increase in fertility rates was seen as a sad failure of modernisation among some segments of the Mizrachi Jews.[46]

This school of thought would have a large number of successors, who followed the search for modernisation with a more focused examination of the minority community's chances for 'Israelisation' versus 'Palestinisation'. Successful Westernisation was equated with a collective acceptance of being part of the Jewish state; whereas adherence to a Palestinian national identity was considered a failure. The problem with this approach was that it was not clear that the political élite in Israel in fact wished to Israelise the Palestinians in the state: a great number of them harboured a vision of a pure, ethnically Jewish state, and, more important, there was a risk that successful modernisation could, perhaps paradoxically, have led to further Palestinisation of the Arabs in Israel. As the theorists among these researchers knew only too well, if you modernise a society, you also increase its politicisation and nationalisation. Thus arose a bizarre model of modernisation, which saw Palestinian acceptance of Israel as a Jewish state as a positive outcome of the process and yet regarded modernisation as questionable if it produced an impulse among the Palestinians in Israel to continue their struggle in the name of Palestinian nationalism and against the Zionisation of the country.

A more cautious approach was developed in the 1970s by Israeli anthropologists, who, like their peers in the overall field of Middle Eastern studies, condemned the accelerated modernisation that undermined the rural areas while not providing adequate infrastructure elsewhere. Nevertheless, mainstream anthropological efforts came under severe criticism from non-Zionist scholars – criticism that in some instances seems valid. These anthropologists developed intimate relationships with the Palestinians themselves, spoke quite good Arabic, and sometimes became truly close to the culture and the region. They, too, became ostracised – condemned as traitors during the neo-Zionist epoch that commenced in 2000 and still exists today.

It should be noted that the modernisation approach continues to be used, albeit more marginally, in research on the Palestinians in Israel, although it has been challenged, initially, in the early 1970s, by Palestinians doing research abroad as well as interested scholars who began to appreciate the value in a closer examination of this case study.[47] What was entirely absent from even the most advanced social-science research on the Palestinian minority in Israel was their history: how did the indigenous population of the land, once an almost absolute majority, become a minority? As the official Palestinian and Zionist narratives both associated the refugees only with the events of 1948, this community – about 10 per cent of the Palestinian population in Mandatory Palestine – was forgotten, its connection to the events of 1948 disregarded.

But it was not only the role of Israel's Palestinians in the events of 1948 that was hidden; in their entirety, the historical events were depicted and narrated in a very particular way. The mainstream Zionist depiction of 1948 and the denial of Palestinian suffering during it remained the locus of the idea of Israel before it was challenged in the 1990s. And when that challenge was successfully defeated, the society and the state reverted to the mainstream affirmation of the Zionist narrative of 1948 and the denial of that of the Palestinians.

The 1948 chapter is the core of the story of Israel, both as the culmination of two thousand years of exile, abnormality and the danger of extinction, all of which ended in 1948, and also as the redemption, the renaissance and the success story of the modern, liberated Jews in their own homeland. To tackle this as a fable, or worse, as an intentional fabrication, would trigger the most significant challenge to date of the moral basis and validity of the idea of Israel.

THREE

The War of 1948 in Word and Image

Israel's victory in the war was a miracle performed by divine authority, by a God who has not deserted his people in their hour of need. In a generation that saw the destruction of the magnificent Jewish civilisation in Europe, God has comforted his people ... [T]his is a new period for the sons of Israel to celebrate their liberty in their own homeland.

In front of our eyes the huge miracle of Israel's redemption is recurring. We are witnessing the huge victories of Israel's army which are engaging in one campaign after the other against their many enemies. The spirit of the *Hashmonaim* [the Maccabees who fought the Greeks in ancient times] is reawakening. We have occupied every piece of the Holy Land.[1]

– Netanel Lorch, historian

The preceding paragraphs are found in the history book on 1948 that was used as the main professional text in Israel for many years – *The Edge of the Sword*. As we see, this account, although secular, nonetheless allows for the possibility that the outcome of the war was a matter of divine authority. It summarises well the way the war was researched and presented by the university departments charged with the teaching of Zionist history. For these

departments, the events of 1948 were the culmination of the tele-
ological process of redemption and renaissance of the Jewish people.
Thus, the role of the historian was limited to the reconstruction of
this miracle that had begun with the awakening of the national movement in the 1880s and had ended with the 1948 'war of liberation'
against the British. The Israeli terminology employed to characterise the war was carefully constructed so as to confer upon Zionism
the status of a Third World liberation movement rather than a war
against the Palestinians. Indeed, the two terms used above to refer to
the 1948 war do not indicate any direct conflict with the Palestinians
or with the neighbouring Arab states; rather, the narrative is of 'independence' from the British (*azma'ut*) and 'liberation' from the yoke
of the diaspora (*shihrur*).

   This did not mean, of course, that the Arabs did not appear in
Zionist historiography of the war. When the story of 1948 or the preceding years of the Mandate was told, researched, or taught, the Arab
side was mentioned as yet another hardship that the Jews had to bear.
The message throughout the story was clear: the Jews in Palestine
won against all odds, and this imbalance was supremely evident
in 1948, when the community, consisting of Holocaust survivors
who could barely fight, was faced with a hostile British government
and a united Arab world preparing for a war of annihilation. Since
the victory was a miracle and was won thanks to the ingenuity of
David Ben-Gurion and the heroism of the soldiers on the ground,
all that was left for historians to do was to re-create this battlefield
heroism while analysing the tactical decisions that made the miracle
come true.[2]

   The task of exploring and describing the Arab side of the story was
entrusted to Israel's established, Orientalist historians. On the whole,
these scholars were more neutral in their research than their colleagues in the Jewish studies departments, but most of them seemed
interested neither in the Palestinians nor in the 1948 war. Even the
most prominent among them, Yehoshua Porath, who, as mentioned
in the previous chapter, provided the first balanced Israeli view on
the Palestinians, never wrote about 1948. He was content to recount
Palestinian history up to 1939; beyond that date he lost interest and

sympathy.[3] The few Israeli Orientalists who did write about the 1948 war avoided dealing with the Nakba as a human or national tragedy, and showed no understanding of its impact for the Palestinian side. Instead, they focused on political and military manoeuvring in the Arab world outside Palestine before and after the war. Similarly, when more recent generations of Orientalists dealt with the Palestine Liberation Organisation, they did not (with the notable exception of Moshe Shemesh[4]) take 1948 as a starting point. The Palestinians of 1948 were erased from Israeli academic discourse.

The absence of the Palestinian tragedy from the Israeli historical account was indicative of a more general Israeli Orientalist view. The historiographical view of the Palestinians up to the 1980s was monolithic and based on stereotyping. The local population in late Ottoman times was mentioned only in passing as a marginal component in the geographical panorama of the promised and empty land waiting to be redeemed. From 1948 until 1967, the Palestinians were mostly ignored as academic subject matter, except for being mentioned here and there as refugees. Post-1967, they were depicted as threatening terrorists, as was shown in the previous chapter. But even in this portrayal, the Palestinians were not granted an independent role; instead they were presented as pawns within an all-Arab conspiracy to annihilate the Jewish state.

There was a reason for this. Recognition that there existed an independent Palestinian (even if small and weak) national group fighting for its rights contradicted the Zionist self-image of underdog, as well as the Zionist myth of the few who had miraculously beaten the many. The heroic Zionist story of 1948 has an internal paradox (probably more than one) that troubled, at least for a while, those loyal Zionists who tried to reconstruct the events of 1948 without challenging the foundational mythologies. If the Palestinians fled without fighting, then what was so heroic about 1948? And even if the story told is not one of Palestinian heroism, it would still be one of Palestinian tragedy. The best way to deal with this predicament, academically, was simply not to deal with the Palestinian side of the story at all and, if possible, not to deal, beyond reverence and obedience to the ideology, with the history of 1948 altogether.

Those who did deal with the Palestinians and the Arab states in the context of the 1948 war focused on motives, or rather the absence of any 'logical' motives for Arab behaviour during that year. The Arabs appear to have been animated by an emotionalism that defeats any logical explanation. As a result, it remains unclear why the Arabs launched a war against Israel in 1948. Such books as *The History of the Resurrection* (1959), prepared by the History Branch of the IDF; *The History of the War of Independence* (1963), by Netanel Lorch; the popular version of Jon and David Kimche's *On Both Sides of the Hill* (1973); and the prefaces and annotated material accompanying the publication of David Ben-Gurion's *1948 War Diaries* (1984) offered the same explanation, or rather the lack thereof.[5] As Ben-Gurion noted in the diaries, 'immediately after the decision in Lake Success [the venue where the UN partition resolution was adopted] the troubles began in the country'.[6] Here is the portrayal, then: troubles seemingly erupt out of the blue and Arabs assault Jews, just like that. Thereafter, this is the essence of the 'troubles' – attacks driven by incomprehensible and unintelligible hate, against which the Jewish forces defend themselves with valour and determination.

Evil that is not decipherable is especially cruel. Every Arab operation, in the official historiography until 1982 and from 2000 onwards, was murderous – a boundless spree of bloodthirsty and heartless barbarian acts. This unexplained violence was identified academically as an essential feature of Arab culture and life. It is shocking but true that this portrayal recurs, without amendment, in Volume 6 of the *Encyclopaedia Hebraica* (the Israeli equivalent of the *Encyclopaedia Britannica*), in the relevant entries that deal with 1948 and the earlier clashes between Arabs and Jews during the Mandatory period.[7] This sixth volume is devoted entirely to Eretz Israel and has been only slightly revised in recent years). All through these encyclopaedic descriptions of the period, the Palestinian resistance to Zionism at notable historical junctures such as 1920, 1929, 1936, and 1948 is portrayed as the end product of the incitement of a mob that lacked any will or intention of its own.[8] The incited mob recurs as the weapon used by anti-Zionist British officials or fanatic Muslim notables for the purpose of destroying the future Jewish state. Never are the Palestinians considered to be endowed with a desire to defend their homeland or to be part of a national movement struggling for independence.

As for the Israeli violence, there was a clear distinction in the classical version between mainstream Jewish forces and splinter groups. On the eve of the 1948 war, three main paramilitary groups stood at the disposal of the Jewish community. The main one was the Hagana, founded in 1920; this group was ideologically close to the Labour movement, which dominated political life in the Jewish community before 1948 and for the next thirty years within Israel. The second, the Irgun, was founded in 1931, by officers of the Hagana, who left the mother organisation because of what they deemed its focus on defensive rather than offensive operations. This group was associated with the Revisionist movement, which later became the Herut Party in the newly founded state, headed by Menachem Begin; already in the 1930s it had targeted British forces as well as the Palestinian population. The third group, the Stern Gang, was founded in 1940 by people who had left the Irgun, feeling that even that organisation was not assertive enough in its struggle against the enemies of the community.

In 1945 an umbrella organisation for the Jewish Underground movements was established to coordinate strategy for all three paramilitary outfits. However, when the Israel Defence Forces (IDF) was officially created on 26 May 1948, it included only the Hagana. Several days later, Menachem Begin's organisation joined, as did the Stern Gang, and for most of the war these two groups continued to act independently in the area around Jerusalem. Thus, during the crucial stages of the war, when the urban space of Palestine as well as sizeable areas of the countryside were being depopulated by the Zionist forces, the splinter groups remained independent.

The vast majority of historians who have written on the 1948 war, both before and after the appearance of the more revisionist history, belonged to the Labour movement, which was responsible for the 1948 ethnic cleansing of Palestine. When doubts were first raised about the moral validity of the policy, they made a clear distinction, according to which the Hagana never engaged in violence for the sake of violence, and that if atrocities were committed, they were the doing of the other two splinter groups. This is best illustrated by the work of a leading Zionist historian, Anita Shapira. In her book *Walking Along the Horizon* (1988) she writes,

> In the attitude to the Arabs of Eretz Israel, and even to the British, the readiness to use force was not taken for granted. It was accompanied by severe internal dissent and moral agonising. But its demonic magic attracted quite a few, and in time of trouble a justification for its use was offered, while using socialist argumentation.[9]

Shapira could reach this conclusion because her history of the Zionist use of violence does not reach as far as 1948. She could thus avoid the need for a thorough discussion of the moral dimensions of the Zionist project and of Israel's early history. Earlier historiographical treatment of Jewish behaviour on the battlefield ignored such insights as well. Instead the narratives of the battles of 1948 chronicled heroes fighting Arab villains, and this heroism was presented as a salient feature of Jewish history from time immemorial.

In his famous and well-read introduction to the voluminous history of the Hagana, Ben-Zion Dinur reproduced the myth of heroism and redemption that had been invented by earlier Zionist historians. Like them, he lumped together the heroic days of King David, the anti-Roman Bar Kokhba revolt, and the Warsaw Ghetto partisans with the heroes of the 1948 Jewish community.[10] This representation was reinforced at the time by commemorative academic institutes such as Yad Tabenkin and Yad Ben Zvi, as well as by commemorative museums such as the Hagana Museum. At Yad Vashem, Jerusalem's Holocaust History Museum, invited and captive (often VIP) visitors are taken on a guided tour from extermination camps through the Warsaw Uprising to the heroic 1948 story of revenge – namely, that Arabs paid for what the Nazis did to the Jews. Only with the advent of the 'new historians' of the 1990s was the 1948 war treated as anything other than a show of heroism, with no reference to the origins of the violence or its potential victims.

For example, in 1976 the scholarly journal *Cathedra* devoted its first issue to a discussion of the military moves of the 1948 war. Although conducted almost thirty years after the event, the discussion did not raise any new questions of historiographical research, and the agenda was exactly the same as that of the official history books published by the Ministry of Defence soon after the war.[11] Yet the discussion was presented as being historiographical, and revolving around the following questions: Who was the first Israeli officer that called to his soldiers, 'Follow me'? How long did the war last (a question that would at least not be considered historiographical in regard to the Six-Day War of 1967)? What were the different stages in the war? Was the war a single campaign in a wider conflict or a separate and exceptional historical event? Should the war be discussed within the context of operative or tactical military history? And finally, how was the war financed?

That first question is of a particular interest: Who issued the call of battle? It was an exploration of heroism that blurred the boundaries between telling fables and spinning mythologies on the one hand, and conducting an ostensibly neutral, professional inquiry on the other. The call 'Follow me' is more like a slogan. It is not part of what happens on the ground, and one doubts that anyone really used it on the battlefield.

The boundaries were further blurred in 1985 when in another Israeli journal, *Hatzionut*, a messianic tone replaced the scholarly language. In an article titled 'The Prophecy of a Jewish State and its Realisation', it was claimed that the success of the Zionist movement to establish a state in Palestine defeated any logical analysis or rational explanation. The project should have been a failure, and yet it miraculously succeeded. This assertion is quite similar to the depiction of the war in the present chapter's opening quotation by Netanel Lorch. It does not necessarily mean, however, that the author thinks divine intervention lay behind the success, as religious scholars would contend, but that only a unique group of people could have defied history and fate against all odds in pursuit of a manifest destiny.[12]

It is thus evident that the classical scholarly representation of the

1948 war consisted of several foundational mythologies. The most important one was that the Jewish community faced the danger of total annihilation in 1948 – a danger that predicated everything that happened afterwards and that justified in hindsight the future extreme use of force. The second, better-known tale is that of an Israeli David facing an Arab Goliath – a mythology portrayed mainly through cartographic images in which thick arrows of Arab armies pour into Palestine, where they are met by almost invisible trickles and flecks of Jewish forces. From the viewpoint of professional and populist historians, that this clash ended in a total Zionist victory was miraculous.

According to this version, the odds were very bad. British policy was especially hostile and worsened further when Ernest Bevin was appointed foreign secretary. Bevin is often portrayed as an anti-Semite; I myself still remember burning Bevin effigies in bonfires, along with those of Gamal Abdul Nasser and Hitler. Indeed, when Bevin's biographer, Allan Bullock, visited Israel for a series of lectures in the 1980s, he was bewildered by the depth of hate still expressed towards his subject. Yet even before the appearance of the 'new history', this image changed. Research in British archives done during the 1970s by sensible Zionist historians such as Gavriel Cohen and Michael J. Cohen revealed a far more pragmatic and sensible Bevin than was depicted in the myth.[13]

Nevertheless, the narrative became an intricate sequence of interdependent elements. Thus, while the *Yishuv* (the Jewish community in Mandatory Palestine) faced annihilation from a barbaric Arab world, as a hostile British Empire and an indifferent international community looked on, it had no time to bother with the indigenous population. According to this narrative, these native people became refugees because their own leaders, and those of the Arab League, told them to leave, paving the way for an all-Arab invasion. Only then could they return to the liberated Palestine. Into this collective remembrance were interwoven the individual recollections of Jewish leaders and city dwellers who urged their fellow inhabitants – their Arab neighbours – not to leave and who, alas, failed in convincing them not to do so.[14]

The story culminates in the image of a moral war, one that produced the most famous Israeli oxymoron: the 'purity of arms'. This was a war against all odds, fought against the worst of enemies, and won while the army adhered to the highest precepts of moral conduct on and off the battlefield. The 'pure arms' can only be Jewish, are fired only in defence, and do not permanently scar the warrior; on the contrary, they make the warrior a far better human being. Films, such as those produced in Israel until the 1980s, are adept at conveying these sensations in a highly explicit way.

A Children's Horror Film: 1948 in the Cinema

The Cinema Album, edited by David Greenberg in the late 1960s, was an early attempt to summarise the history of Israeli cinema. Greenberg declared that until 1967, all the feature films on the 1948 war were produced by foreigners who failed

> to comprehend the full meaning of this glorious period, but nonetheless helped to publicise it globally. This topic still awaits an Israeli director who will illuminate it from a novel vantage point; one which caters to the aspirations of the Israeli filmgoer.[15]

Although, according to Greenberg, the average Israeli filmgoer sought more realistic films and was not content with the beautification of the war, it is hard to find evidence for this. The local film industry continued to depict the war, whether in feature or documentary films, in heroic, idealistic terms, much the same way as did the foreign producers.

More to the point is the work of Nurith Gertz on this period. In various articles and in the only book of hers that appeared in English, *Hirbet Hiza'a and the Morning After,* she proposed that in the 1960s, the Israeli cinema was still a nationalist, Zionist and heroic medium, which located the troops and their adventures at the centre of cinematic production.[16] Cinema was treated as a means for national propaganda; in fact, the officials appointed by the state to supervise and encourage local cinematic production stipulated that their offices would assist 'educational and constructive films which would reflect the Israeli mentality'.[17]

Films of that period, as Ella Shohat has commented, focused on mythical Israeli heroes, all of them Sabras (Jews born in Palestine), kibbutzniks and soldiers. Many of these films used the Arab–Israeli conflict as the background for a story of one Israeli, or a group of Israelis, fighting a large number of Arabs, epitomising the struggle of Israel against the Arab world. Among such films were *Hill 24 Doesn't Answer* (1955), *What a Gang* (1963), and *Five Days in Sinai* (1969), all of which related a personal story of heroism in the face of Arab barbarism and aggression. Quite often the Zionist warriors in these films ended up dead, and quite a few of the films end with a famous Israeli mantra from 1948 that was integrated into every speech given ever since by politicians on Yom HaZikaron, the Day of Remembrance for fallen soldiers: 'In their death they gave us our life'.

Until the 1980s, nearly every film conformed to Zionist ideological guidance. The cinema reconstructed and maintained the mythology of the war and in particular left untouched the stereotypically negative image of the Arab. Because of the visual dimension of cinema, on the one hand, and the commercial demands of the industry on the other, the engagement with the Arab was more pointed and extensive than in any other medium (perhaps apart from children's literature).

Actual Arabs rarely appear in these films; when they do, we know nothing about them – they are anonymous. Thus, although the hit film *He Walked Through the Fields* (1967) deals with the 1948 war, not one battle scene appears in it. In *Hill 24 Doesn't Answer*, the Arabs are unseen but continually appear in the film's narrative as the hidden threat. The Druze, Israel's allies in that war, are fully visible (played by Jewish actors), as are the Jews themselves.

One of the leading myths was that the Jewish community faced an existential danger on the eve of the 1948 war. This is the theme of *Hill 24 Doesn't Answer*. The film's opening scene shows a strategic map of Israel, accompanied by a narration explaining the movement of the forces during the conflict. The arrows charted on the map present an alarming picture of an all-Arab assault on the Jewish community, and depict the entire country as a besieged bastion.[18] The film was a pseudo-documentary, fully staged – a docudrama. This same depiction would later appear in the popular Israeli Carta atlases and in the current edition of Martin Gilbert's *Atlas of the Arab–Israeli Conflict*.[19]

Cinema added its own dimension to the myth of annihilation and associated the Nazi ideology of human extermination with Arab intentions in 1948, as can be seen in films such as *Hill 24*, *They Were Ten* (1960), and of course *Exodus* (1960). An especially blunt version is to be found in the feature film *Amud Ha'Esh* (Pillar of Fire, 1959); not to be confused with a television series discussed later on with a similar name. It is the story of a small southern kibbutz locked in a desperate fight against Egyptian tanks.[20] The American Jewish director Larry Frisch staged the film as a classical western, where the cowboys have to fight the savage Indians, who do not appear in the film but are implicitly present as targets whenever the brave Zionist soldiers shoot someone in the dark. In one scene, there are obscure images in the distance that seem to be dangerous Arabs.[21]

Some of the films directly associated the Palestinian or Arab threat with that of the Nazis. In a joint Italian–Israeli co-production, *Judith* (1966), Sophia Loren plays the wife of an ex-SS officer who was smuggled to Israel by the Hagana so that she could identify her husband, who was now helping the Arabs in the 1948 war. The same association appears in the film *Exodus*, adapted from Leon Uris's famous novel, in which a sadistic Nazi expert orchestrates murderous Arab assaults on the Jewish community. Finally, in *Hill 24*, a humane Israeli soldier helps a badly wounded Egyptian soldier who turns out to be a German-speaking Nazi who tries to kill him at the first opportunity – although the Israeli soldier does not then kill the Nazi but merely defends himself.

Amud Ha'Esh, a TV documentary series directed by Yigal Lusin for the first, and that time the only, Israeli TV channel in 1981, gives the viewer a good sense of why the Israelis call the 1948 war the War of Independence. That year is described as the culmination of an anti-colonialist struggle against the evil British Empire. The British were defeated and so, according to this narration, left

Palestine because they could not withstand the Jewish resistance against them. Meanwhile, the professional historiography indicated that the British decision to withdraw from Palestine arose from the overall and inevitable global collapse of the British Empire. This wider context informed the financial and regional strategic decisions that led to the end of British rule in Palestine.[22]

The lengthiest feature film on 1948 during those years was *He Walked Through the Fields*, based on a novel by Moshe Shamir. It presents the 1948 war almost exclusively as a war against the British; the Arabs are hardly there.[23] The film tells the story of Uri (played by Moshe Dayan's son, Asaf Dayan) – a fighter in the Palmach, the storm-troopers of the Hagana – and his love for an immigrant girl. He is a kibbutznik, the first child born in Palestine in the fictional kibbutz. Uri deserts his girlfriend in order to receive training under the nose of, and for the purpose of attacking, the British troops in Palestine. During training, Uri dies. This film is a good example of cinema being able to convey marginalisation and exclusion in a far more powerful way than is offered by the cool heads of historiography; primarily because of cinema's potent visuality.

Dan and Sa'adia: The Ultimate Mythology

Intertwined with the myth of annihilation was the myth of the 'few against many', which the popular film *Dan and Sa'adia* illustrates better than any other. The full name of the film was *Dan Quihote V'Sa'adia Pansa* the obvious inferences of which have been aptly analysed by Ella Shohat. Here I am concerned with treating it as a cinematic representation of the classical historical version of the 1948 war.[24]

The film engages with all the foundational mythologies of the war and represents them through a fictional tale of individual Jewish heroism on the day of Israel's independence. The film was produced in 1956 and was directed by Nathan Axelrod, one of Israel's leading cinematic figures in the early years of statehood. His later documentary films were highly regarded, the best known of which was

Etz o Palestine (*The True Story of Palestine*, 1962), named after the images found on the two sides of a Mandatory Palestine coin. Before the invention of modern cinematic appetisers, that film, which was the basis for the newsreel *The Carmel Dairies*, preceded every feature film.[25]

Israeli academics generally refer to *Dan and Sa'adia*, Axelrod's first feature film, as a pioneering movie that broke away from Zionist pathos, and they characterise it as a fairly realistic and even cynical film about the ideology and mythology of the state. But viewed from a critical perspective, it seems deeply entrenched within the Zionist historical narrative.

The same can be said of the feature film *Waltz with Bashir* (2008) and the documentary *The Gatekeepers* (2012, nominated for an Oscar in 2013). Israeli Zionist critics would hail both as bold and courageous cinematic revisitings of the 1982 war on Lebanon, in the case of the former, and the evil of the occupation of Palestinian areas in the latter. In fact, it is possible to see these works as attempts to have one's cake (support and participate in the Israeli invasion of Lebanon or the occupation) and eat it too (display public remorse and regret until the next invasion or while the occupation continues).[26]

Dan and Sa'adia tells the story of Dan, an Ashkenazi boy who is an avid reader of detective stories and lives in an imagined world of adventure and excitement, and Sa'adia, a Yemeni boy who shines shoes and is Dan's friend and partner in his detective games. Dan is considered a troublemaker and is therefore sent to boarding school, where most of the film's scenes take place. Sa'adia sneaks into the car that takes Dan away, and stays with him. All this happens just a few days after the State of Israel was declared on 15 May 1948 and war broke out. The head boys in the boarding school are busy collecting weapons, hiding them from watchful British eyes, and training for the real fighting. Dan and Sa'adia continue their detective games, steal a crate full of hand grenades (not knowing the its contents), and hide the crate as pirates' treasure.

Fear of an Arab attack leads to the children being evicted from the boarding school, leaving behind the two young companions, the teachers, and the military troops. The teachers worry that the ammunition they have accumulated before the war will not be enough to repel the attack. To their rescue come Dan and Saadia, who avoided the eviction and now understand that the treasure they hid could save the *Yishuv*. When they go to the orchard where they hid the crate, they happen to eavesdrop on a meeting among Arabs who are contemplating a night attack on the Jews (they are able to follow the conversation, because Sa'adia the Yemeni knows Arabic). Using the hand grenades, the children prepare a deadly trap that saves their boarding school from destruction.

Fear of annihilation and the almost miraculous acts that avoid it are recurring motifs in this film. Fear and pride are conveyed through a microhistorical focus on the conflict as a reflection of the macrohistorical picture. The boarding school is 'surrounded by Arabs' and is saved by the valour of the two boys – one Ashkenazi and the other Mizrachi – signifying another foundational myth, the unity of Jewish exiles from all over the world.

These two new Jewish heroes face Arab danger without for a moment losing their humanity. Although the peril of extinction would normally raise suspicions against anybody who is an Arab, the two schoolboys, unlike all other teenagers in the world, resist this tendency. The viewers see this when, in Dan's imagination, an innocent Arab woman momentarily turns into an Arab wearing a keffiyeh and holding a gun. Arab violence is responsible for the demonisation in young Dan's mind, which in turn can explain the collateral damage sometimes meted out to the Arabs by the Zionists. But the woman soon transforms back into the innocent person she is. Apart from this scene, however, the Arabs are shown as an incited mob, complete with keffiyehs and guns – in other words, the potential terrorists portrayed in scholarly works up to the 1980s.

As a rule the Arab characters in *Dan and Sa'adia* are anonymous and part of a crowd, while the Jewish forces are humane, courageous individuals. The Arabs are always seen as a massive throng, emphasising the myth of the many against the few, but their numbers are also testimony to their inferiority. The inferior, incited Arab mob used to be as common a theme in Israeli movies about 1948 as it is in British films about the British Empire. Even after it became clear that 1948 was not a war between few and many, Arabs still appeared for a while as a dangerous mob. Later, during the First and Second Intifadas, and despite the many transformations in the interim in the image of the Arab, mob scenes similar to those in *Dan and Sa'adia* reappeared in the visual and written descriptions of Palestinian resistance of 1987 and 2000.

The incited Arab mob, like the 'Arab villain' archetype in Israeli cinema then and now, is motivated by sheer callousness, embedded in 'Arab nature'. For scholars, the force of these archetypes meant that Arab violence need not be explained, merely described. Thus one does not have to wonder why the Arabs in the orchard wished to destroy a boarding school. In the film, as in mainstream Zionist historiography, it is also unclear why the Arab states launched a war in 1948. In the opening scene, news headlines tell the story of the Arab invasion of Israel, the sirens in Tel Aviv. One headline reads, 'A Boarding School Is Surrounded by Arabs'. Factual and fictional events mingle in the representation of a reality in which Israel was under siege and in danger of being annihilated. This siege mentality would not subside even as it became increasingly difficult to furnish support for its existence.

The absence of a logical explanation for the Arab attack on Israel in general and on the boarding school in particular signals the worst kind of violence: meaningless and cruel assault. Film is good at conveying unexplainable evil and special cruelty. This same theme appeared even more forcefully in an older film, *Ha-Fuga* (Intermission), made by Amram Amar in 1950, which tells the story of Miriam, a female Jewish soldier caught in the fighting by two Arabs and saved by Gideon, a typically omnipotent Zionist who is the new Jewish male and who is in love with both Miriam and another woman.

The romance is the main theme of the film but its depictions of Arabs are quite striking. In the main, they represent the absolute opposite of the new Jew, Gideon. They are potential rapists and worse. They have no respect for guns or friends. One of the captive Arabs is invited to play cards with the soldiers and shows himself willing to gamble away his rifle and that of his friend – the ultimate sin and crime in the eyes of a militarised society such as Israel.

Dan and Sa'adia, too, engage directly with Arab characters. Although the Arabs are the enemy that defines the reality, their basic function is to provide the setting and background for a closer examination of the internal tensions in Jewish society between men and women, Ashkenazi and Mizrachi Jews, the individual and the collective. The Arabs in *Dan and Sa'adia* do not seem to enjoy the ordinary things in life, whereas the staff at the boarding school – the principal, the teacher Aviva, the poet Uri, the shepherd Yoram (who is in love with Aviva, who is in love with the principal) – are three-dimensional, humane characters. These people get hurt and wounded; they love and ache. They are real human beings with emotions and personalities, and thus the viewer forms a bond with them. Not so the Arabs who meet in the orchard – we know nothing about them, not even their names.

Another dismal, pathetic character who crops up in this and similar films on the war is the new Jewish immigrant, who is easily identified by his heavy accent in Hebrew and is often overweight and cowardly. This anti-hero is also an anti-Sabra. The immigrant appears as stereotypical as the Arab, but there is a difference between the two. The immigrant will eventually be modernised and national-ised, mainly through military service. But the violence of the Arabs is explained by their savagery, which directly as well as indirectly leads to thoughts, not of how to modernise them, but rather how to get rid of them.

Cinematic representation of the early chapters in the Zionist nar-rative relies in part on the visual apparatus of marginalisation and exclusion. Thus, for instance, Axelrod's *Tree or Palestine* focuses on the history of the Jewish community during the closing ten years of the British Mandate. It is a collage of documentary footage, edited in both an amusing and a nostalgic way. It begins with a scene in which one can see Arabs and camels resting beneath trees. In the back-ground plays the Zionist song 'Anu Banu Artza' ('We Came to Our Homeland'). The Arabs in this scene appear as a pagan, primitive tribe. The narrator explains that they know nothing about mecha-nised agriculture. 'Is this our coveted homeland?' asks the narrator in a lamenting voice. The answer is no, not as long as 'they' are there.

This is no different from the representation of the Arabs in *Dan and Sa'adia*: essentialist, simplistic, reduced. It is typically Orientalist, but with one important variant: above and beyond the familiar Western condescension are additional thick layers of animosity, suspicion and racism. More blunt than dry academic discourse, cinema carries these emotions straight to the viewer.

More important, film presents the Arab as a danger to be removed, although it was not until the emergence of post-Zionist cinema in the 1990s that their actual removal was addressed in any Israeli feature or documentary about 1948. Nevertheless, the fate of the Arabs is an issue that arises in such films. They expose the typical colonialist dilemma concerning the evil enemy of the benevolent empire who foolishly decides to resist the takeover and occupation of his home-land. He is both harmless because of his primitive essence and yet dangerous because of his savagery, and therefore needs to be countered by a combination of sophistication and exceptional heroism.

This dual colonialist view of the indigene appears repeatedly in adventures such as the tales of Jules Verne and Rudyard Kipling. But in *Dan and Sa'adia*, there is a different formula: the savage enemy is defeated by children. One must then ask, How dangerous could the enemy be if children can outsmart and crush him? And indeed, *Dan and Sa'adia* directly and clearly exposes the problematic messages of the annihilation myth – how to reconcile the pathetic Arabs that appear on-screen as stupid grown-ups who can easily be overpowered by two children, with the belief that Arabs are as bad and dangerous as the Nazis? The film presents the Jewish community in Palestine as facing destruction, and yet the threat comes from a handful of pitiable Arabs. As a result, the contradictory messaging about the nature of the menacing Arabs undermines the myth of annihilation, even though this contradiction is softened somewhat by the contention that the unsophisticated Arabs are dangerous because of their numbers rather than their capabilities. In Hollywood, it requires physically and mentally superhuman heroes, such as those played by Arnold Schwarzenegger or Bruce Willis, to defeat Arab and Islamic evil. Not so in Zionist cinema. There, the contradiction between a pathetic enemy and the myth of Zionist heroism is not so easily resolved.

Another example of the heroism of the young is the popular children's story *Shemona B'Ekevot Ahat* (Eight Trail One), which was also made into a 1964 film, tells the story of eight children in a kibbutz who succeeded in a capturing a dangerous Arab spy whom the army had failed to catch. Throughout the film, the children sing, 'We are united and fearless / Forward going and courageous / We will defeat the enemy.'[27]

All told, the Israeli sense of pre-eminence, as manifested in cinema, is a combination of a racist superiority complex intertwined with pathological hate. Just as the Israeli is the eternal villain in the Palestinian national ethos, so too is the Arab the eternal villain in the Zionist ethos. Often, one does not even know whether the villain is Palestinian, Syrian or Egyptian, since the Israelis did not recognise the Palestinians as a separate nation.

Court Film-makers and the Documentary

Documentary films that deal with 1948 are not easily liberated from the foundational mythology and negative image of the 'other'. A prime example is a series of documentary films titled *The Palmach Tents*, which follows the war through the history of the Hagana's storm-troopers, the Palmach. Some instalments in the series appeared as late as 1988.[28] These films can be found in every secondary-school film library and show how little had changed in Israeli documentaries until the late 1980s. The first film in the series proudly surveys the story of the *Mista'arvim* (literally, 'those who became Arabs'), the spy unit of the Hagana. It relates their adventures during their infiltration of the throngs of refugees expelled from Israel in 1948. Prior to this episode, the refugees had almost never appeared in documentary films; here they appear, visually speaking, but are not referred to as refugees. Rather, they are simply shown, unnamed apart from being identified as Arabs who left. It would take a long while for film-makers and historians to refer to the Palestinians as refugees, and even longer to ponder in hindsight the immorality of such espionage.

The ideology and culture of documentary films depend greatly on the historiographical consultants who work on these projects. In the case of *The Palmach Tents*, parts of the series, including the story of the *Mista'arvim*, were produced with the help of the official historians of the IDF. The second episode in the series was about the Negev Brigade; for that episode, the consultant was Meir Pa'il, whose challenge to the classical Zionist narrative on 1948 went as far as possible without exiting the Zionist parameters. Pa'il was the first to debunk the myth that the 1948 war was fought between a Jewish David and an Arab Goliath. Basing his analysis on a sober assessment of the number of troops involved, and their level of preparation and quality, he contended that the Jewish side had military superiority on every level in the 1948 war. This was the first-ever documentary to admit that Plan Dalet, which was prepared by the Hagana in March 1948, was in essence a blueprint for the takeover of rural and urban spaces in Palestine. In the film, Pa'il even goes so far as to declare that some villages were uprooted by force, although he maintains that they were the exception, and that most of the villagers simply fled.[29] The third film in the series conformed more closely to the work of the official historians and returned to a one-sided presentation of the history and stereotypical images of the Arabs.

At the same time, during the first couple of decades after the 1967 war, when documentary films were still loyal to the mainstream Zionist version of the idea of Israel, a small group of brave and unusual individuals began to question the validity of this version in general and the 1948 chapters in particular. They paved the way for a substantial challenge that in turn fostered more open, and less Zionist, documentaries as well as fictional representations of the 1948 war. The following chapter tells their story.

PART TWO

Israel's Post-Zionist Moment

FOUR

The Trailblazers

Towards the end of his life, one of the early anti-Zionists in Israel, Maxim Ghilan, became my friend. When I met him, he was living in dire conditions, barely making ends meet in the harsh reality of Tel Aviv. And yet with the last penny in his pocket, along with my own small occasional financial contribution, he produced a fascinating monthly called *Mitan*, which literally means in Hebrew both a load and an IED, an improvised explosive device. The journal was produced on the best quality of paper I have ever seen, which of course tripled the expenditure and reduced Maxim's living conditions even more. 'Why do you insist on using such an elegant and costly format?' I asked him. After all, as with all anti-Zionist publications in Hebrew that appeared both before and afterwards, we had more contributors than readers. 'This is obvious', he answered. 'After the catastrophe hits Israel – and it will – only the best-quality paper will survive in the ruins, and people would then adopt our progressive ideas.'

Ghilan's life story is not very different from the other individuals of the first generation of anti-Zionist thinkers in Jewish Israel. They were individualistic, marginalised, and in many ways quixotic. Their nonconformist and lonely existence should be juxtaposed with what we call in this book the post-Zionist moment, when their views were briefly held by a large number of people. This chapter tells their story and tries to follow its trajectory up to the appearance of the post-Zionist moment in the mid-1990s.

There are two ways of becoming a Jewish anti-Zionist in the State of Israel. You either leave the tribe of Zionism because you witnessed an event conducted in the name of Zionism that was so abhorrent it made you rethink the validity of the ideology that licensed such brutality, or you are a thinker by profession or inclination who does not cease to ponder and revisit the concepts and precepts of Zionism, and the internal paradoxes and absurdities cause you to drift gradually towards a more universal, and far more anti-Zionist, position in life.

This combination of disgust at the way Arabs were treated in the state and the intellectual rejection of the very logic of the dogma motivated the early anti-Zionists. The academy was the last to be affected by such doubts and critiques, but when it was, its output was prodigious, reaching a volume never seen before or since. While future Jewish critics in Israel would rely on high-profile international gurus or well-known theories to explain their criticisms of Zionism, pioneers such as Ghilan attributed their views to a transformative personal moment.

The political home for these early Jewish doubters of Zionism in Israel was the Communist Party, but soon most of them left the party, continuing on their path either individually or within new, smaller groups that eventually sought alliances with the PLO, and in particular with its left-wing factions, such as the Democratic Front for the Liberation of Palestine. Others were closer to the Chinese version of communism, and, as is typical of radical left groups, their internal arguments caused splits and divisions, followed by attempts to reunite. Their debates addressed the issue of how far nationalism, even Palestinian nationalism, deserved support from international-ist communists, Maoists and Marxists. Later in this chapter I will describe these debates; here it suffices to note that there were two logical conclusions for the participants. Those who saw the Palestinian national movement as the principal vehicle for implementing a social-ist, Marxist or Maoist agenda eventually joined the movement in one way or another. The other way was to remain an internationalist, a path that usually led to self-exile or to joining groups that were more internationalist. Either path was treated in Israel as high treason, and most of these activists paid a very high personal price. Most of these pioneers have been forgotten, and the price they paid has not been properly recorded. For that reason, it is important to tell some of those stories here.

Maxim Ghilan was born in Lille but spent most of his childhood in Spain during the Spanish Civil War; his father, a leading figure in the Republican camp, was murdered by the Fascists and the family escaped in 1944 to Palestine. Like so many others who challenged Zionism in the early years of statehood, Ghilan went through a nationalist phase and also fought with the Stern Gang during the last days of the British Mandate. In 1950 he was arrested as a right-wing activist, still loyal to the Stern Gang, which sought to overthrow the progressive Mapai regime that dominated Israeli politics for many years. Once in jail, Ghilan was changed by what he saw.

Witnessing the torture of Palestinian prisoners made him question Zionism during his first stint in jail. As a poet and a journalist, he had no qualms about using soft pornography to attract readers to anti-Zionist texts. He became famous as an investigative journalist when he exposed Israeli involvement in the assassination of Mehdi Ben Barka, leader of the Moroccan opposition in 1966, for which he was sent to jail for quite a long time. Ghilan's entanglement in this affair was typical of him. Apart from his being comfortable with the use of eroticism as a means of attracting readers to challenging views in *Bool* (meaning 'hit on' in Hebrew), the journal of which he was an editor, he would sometimes plant stories of Israel's involvement in the Arab world, some based on documents he received and some arising from his imagination. When Ben Barka was murdered, Ghilan wrote that Mossad agents were involved in the operation. Later, when the Secret Service came to arrest him, he claimed he did not know it was true. He was jailed for four and a half months for disclosing secret information to the enemy. But in fact he did not possess any such documentation. He was merely a keen observer of subversive Israeli activity in the Arab world, and it seemed likely to him that a pro-Palestinian Moroccan leader – someone who annoyed a royal house that was not hostile to Israel – could be a target of Mossad.[1]

Like so many of these lone warriors of peace and justice, in 1967 Ghilan became a voluntary exile to Paris and, again like so many of them, returned after the signing of the Oslo Accords in 1993. Before leaving Paris, he asked close friends to find out whether the Secret Service would arrest him upon arrival. The agency later claimed that such a conversation never took place, but in any case, Ghilan was no longer a thorn in the side of the Israeli security apparatus. Nor was Israel a changed place, as far as Ghilan could determine, and when he died in 2005 he was as disillusioned with Zionism as he had been in 1948.[2]

Being an eyewitness to a different kind of brutality changed the life of another pioneer of anti-Zionist thought, Israel Shahak. One day in 1950, he watched, to his horror, a religious Jew's refusal to help a wounded Palestinian citizen because it was the Sabbath and because Jewish law, the Halachah, prohibits such an act. This traumatic event turned him, according to his own narrative, into an anti-Zionist – a strong reaction triggered by his difficult biography. During the Second World War he had escaped the Warsaw Ghetto in his occupied home city before being recaptured and sent to the extermination camp of Poniatowa. Once again he escaped, this time with his mother; he temporarily survived the Nazi horror but was eventually arrested for a second time and spent the last days of the war in Bergen-Belsen.

The twelve-year-old survivor and his mother reached Palestine in 1945, where Holocaust survivors were not welcomed by those who made the decision to leave Europe before the Holocaust. Born Israel Himmelstaub, Shahak, like so many other Jews, Hebraicised his name once he landed in Palestine. But his full initiation into Israeli society was completed only when he served in an élite unit of the IDF and was then appointed to the Israeli Atomic Energy Commission.[3]

In the newly founded State of Israel, Shahak encountered the daily interpretations of Jewish rabbinical law and was distressed by the way it was applied towards non-Jews, namely, the Palestinian citizens. He asserted that what he saw was a literal implementation of certain Jewish theological texts according to a tradition that stretched back to the early days of the religion. After researching these texts and global Jewish history, he concluded that the Palestinians were not only the victims of colonialist and oppressive military policies, but had also fallen prey to an overarching racist/theological ideology.

Writing later about his life, Shahak added another transformative event: the Israeli attack on Egypt in 1956. In the wake of this event, he felt, as he put it later, betrayed by Zionism and in particular by its leader, David Ben-Gurion. It was not simply the Anglo–French–Israeli collusion in itself that reshaped the ideological and moral world for Israel Shahak; more significant for him was the narrative that accompanied it. This appeared most strikingly in the rhetoric of Ben-Gurion, who continually referred to the Sinai operation as the dawn of a new era which heralded the re-establishment of the biblical Jewish empire. This new messianism alarmed Israel Shahak and reaffirmed his worst fears about the new Jewish state. In his words, the State of Israel appeared to be a sinister and destructive war machine that would stop at nothing in its battle against the entire Arab world and specifically the Palestinian people. To his horror, this machine was fuelled by Jewish theology and modern nationalism.

The fusion of nationalism and religion was a lethal combination that reminded Shahak of the policies that ran roughshod over his life in Poland as a child. This association must have been extremely painful for a survivor of a Nazi concentration camp who had only recently begun, after settling safely in Israel, a retrospective journey into his past. From that time on, his writings and activities were directed against the abuses and injustices perpetrated by his new state, as though such a commitment was the best way of confronting the horror he had undergone in Bergen-Belsen and elsewhere during the Holocaust.

One object of Shahak's study was an especially sacred claim by Zionism: that Jews were persecuted all over Europe and hence needed a refuge, which should naturally be their ancient homeland in Palestine. Within Israel, the life of Jews in Eastern Europe had been, and still is, portrayed as a perpetual and relentless tale of

Christian and European persecution that ceased only with the emergence of Zionism and the creation of the State of Israel. To Shahak,
this hegemonic Israeli narrative of modern Jewish life was manipulative and misleading, and he challenged it head-on.[4]

In the Zionist narrative, the modern history of anti-Semitism, as
distinct from that of the medieval period, began in 1648, when the
Cossacks of Ukraine, led by Bohdan Khmelnytsky, rebelled against
the Polish-Lithuanian Union of those days. It was a popular revolt
in the sense that vassals and other marginalised groups, such as the
Tatars, joined forces against an oppressive feudal system. 'Khmel the
Evil' was the name by which contemporary Jews knew him, since he
oversaw a wave of pogroms against Jewish communities in the area of
the rebellion. Quite a few Jews died because of a plague that raged at
the time; others were captured and forced to convert to Christianity
or were sold into serfdom. A desperate letter written by a local rabbi
to Oliver Cromwell, then the Lord Protector of the British Isles,
states that 180,000 Jews were killed. In the Zionist narrative, it was
pure anti-Semitism that imposed this fate on Jewish communities in
Eastern Europe in the second half of the seventeenth century.[5]

Shahak was not the first to point out the fact that, in the eyes
of the rebels, the Jewish communities sided with the oppressors, as
tax collectors and moneylenders. Most of the time, the landowners
were not present; Jewish agents acted as their managers, although of
course most of the Jews slaughtered were not part of this arrangement. Shahak wanted the narrative to reflect some degree of Jewish
responsibility, to assign a role to the Jews' lack of empathy or identification with the oppressed peasants. He attributed this lack to
Judaism's separatism and sense of superiority. For Shahak, Jewish
participation in the exploitation of others played a part in the chain
of events in 1948 and the formative events that gave birth to modern
Zionism.

To any Israeli who experienced the official educational system,
this truly was heresy. In Israel's history books, curricula, and popular
programmes, the Jews were the helpless victims of a Christian anti-
Semitism that targeted Jews because of who they were and not because
of anything they did. The same explanation applied to the hatred and

aggression of Arabs or Palestinians against Israelis: Jews had done nothing that warranted such an attitude. The only reason for it was that Muslims held the same anti-Semitic views as Christians.

The memory of the Khmelnytsky pogroms was the cornerstone on which indoctrination in Israel was erected. The massacres appear prominently in official educational publications. I myself recall how it was hammered into us that the only way to stop this never-ending calamity was to create a Jewish state in Israel. Moreover, we also learned that Arabs, mainly Palestinians, were the modern-day Khmelnytskys, but that they would be unable to implement their evil schemes because the Jewish state had an army that would use every means in its possession against this last bastion of anti-Semitism.

Shahak did not pretend to be a theologian and did not demand that the holy Jewish texts be revised, but rather suggested they be superseded for the sake of more universal philosophies of human-ity and liberty. His was a call for the universalisation of Holocaust memory, underscored by the recognition that the poison of racist supremacy lies dormant in the blood of every nation, including the Jewish one. He warned that continued adherence to anti-Gentile religious texts would retain this venom in the Jewish people.

Moreover, Shahak was the first historian, albeit not a professional one (he was a professor of chemistry), to revise the dominant Israeli tale of how Zionism emerged and operated. In his alternative nar-rative, Jewish life in the era of the Jewish state is informed by an exclusionist, chauvinist ideology. It was a seemingly outrageous con-clusion, broadcast by a Holocaust survivor who did not hesitate to include both Nazism and Zionism in his historical case studies of dangerous exclusionist ideologies. He does not compare them per se; instead, he warns of the magnetic attraction that ideologies of racial superiority and supremacy can have for people and the horrific dangers they pose. So powerful are these ideologies that they can appeal to people – such as the Jews, the recent victims of horrid man-ifestations of these very ideologies – who should know better. With a moralising voice heard loud and clear, Shahak cautioned his fellow Israelis that those who did not learn from history were condemned to repeat it. More specifically, he admonished Jews who refused to come to terms with the Jewish past, that they had become its slaves, repeating its immoral message through their adherence to Zionist ideology and their unwillingness to challenge Israeli policies.

The focus in Shahak's work was on Jewish life, but his message was universal: a cry against any and all fanatical religious or nationalist ideologies. It was also a call for the replacement of ethnocentrism by what he called normalisation, the adoption of a humanist approach to human beings. The final words of one of his most famous books, *Jewish History, Jewish Religion: The Weight of Three Thousand Years*, elegantly summarise his point of view:

> Therefore, the real test facing both Israeli and diaspora Jews is the test of their self-criticism which must include the critique of the Jewish past. The most important part of such a critique must be a detailed and honest confrontation of the Jewish attitude to non-Jews. This is what many Jews justly demand from non-Jews: to confront their own past and so become aware of the discrimination and persecutions inflicted on the Jews ... Although the struggle against anti-Semitism (and of all other forms of racism) should never cease, the struggle against Jewish chauvinism and exclusivism, which must include a critique of classical Judaism, is now of equal or greater importance.[6]

In 1978 Boaz Evron, a leading journalist and pundit, listened to a monologue from an Israeli soldier serving in the occupation that transformed his intellectual views in such a way, as to turn him, like Shahak, into one of the pillars of anti-Zionist thought.

Evron was born in Jerusalem, a second-generation Sabra, and hence belonged to a kind of local Zionist aristocracy. His life in Mandatory Palestine was very similar to that of Ghilan. Like him, he fought for the Stern Gang in the 1948 war and tended towards what was then called the Canaanite ideology.[7]

The Canaanite movement was founded in the 1930s by a Ukrainian Jew by the name of Adolph Gurewitz, who soon found his first name a bit troublesome. As a student of classical and ancient history, he went in search of a biblical name (he chose 'Adiya') and a new identity. At first he was close to Ze'ev Jabotinsky's Revisionist movement, but he wanted that movement to divorce itself totally from Judaism and to reinvent the Jewish community in Palestine as the new Hebrews or, in his words, the new Canaanites, so that the Palestinians, too, could identify with both the 'return' of the exiled Hebrews and the new-old identity offered to them. When Gurewitz arrived in Palestine in the 1930s, he worked with others in the Revisionist movement who shared his views. Most famous among them was the poet Uriel Halperin, who, like everyone else in this movement, soon changed his name to a Hebrew one, Yonatan Ratosh. The Canaanite platform proposed a joint Semitic state that would belong to both people on the land – an idea that has never succeeded in winning even one Palestinian to its ranks and was not very popular with the Jews in Israel either.

In his youth, Boaz Evron was drawn to the Canaanites, which officially became a group in 1939, and it was from the Canaanite perspective that he developed his critical views on Zionism. But he also became a leading journalist and essayist for *Haaretz* and *Yedioth Ahronoth*, and from that key base he produced an impressive tract that would include most of the elements of the later internal Israeli critique of Zionism.

According to Evron's account of the soldier's monologue, which sowed the seeds that grew into this tract, the soldier told of how he and his friends had entered a Palestinian school, locked about twenty eight-year-old boys in a classroom, threw gas grenades into the room, and held the doors closed, causing such panic that at least half the children jumped out of the windows, breaking their legs in the fall.[8] The soldier characterised this action as a punishment for stone throwing by students from a nearby college, who were not caught.

What attracted Evron's attention was not so much the horrific story itself, which later appeared in a Kibbutz Movement publication under the title 'A Tear-Gas Monologue', but the fact that the soldier seemed to believe that telling the story absolved him and his friends from the deed. Similarly, soon after the June 1967 war a group of soldiers agreed to a series of interviews that were published as a book titled *Conversations with Soldiers*.[9] Evron's uneasiness turned into a review of liberal Zionism and its role in beautifying and hiding the horrors of Zionist colonisation and occupation since 1882.

The participants in this book were, among others, Amos Oz, Avishai Grossman (a leading intellectual of the Kibbutz Movement), and one of Ehud Barak's brothers. In the conversations included in the book, soldiers speak with one another, and the main theme is the necessity to kill in order to defend the homeland and to maintain one's humanity and morality. Recently, it came to light that certain references to atrocities committed during the 1967 war were deleted by the military censor. The omitted pieces have not yet been published; the researcher who discovered them is awaiting permission but has stated that they describe war crimes committed by the soldiers who participated in the conversations.

Listening to the soldiers strengthened Evron's critique. In his 1988 book *A National Reckoning*, he questions whether the Zionist claim that the Jews were a territorial nation wishing to return to its homeland has any basis in fact or reality.[10] He proposes instead that the Jewish state was a European project meant to solve the problems of the religious minority, the Jews, living within an anti-Jewish Europe. For most Europeans, emancipation of the Jews did not mean their integration on the Continent but permission for them to colonise Palestine and build their own Europe there.

Like Shahak, Evron saw anti-Semitism both as the Christian refusal to accept the Jews as equal but also a response to the Jewish religious insistence on exclusivity and uniqueness. What the Zionists called the forced exile from Palestine by the Romans, ending in the 'return to Zion' in the late 1880s, was deemed by Evron to be a conscious Jewish wish not to be part of the society around them. Zionism, in his eyes, benefited from two developments in the first half of the twentieth century in Eastern and Central Europe. One was the continued wish of a large number of Jews to remain in their own separate communities and to insist on the uniqueness of the Jewish existence – a position that leftist and liberal forces in Europe did not accept because of their search for universalism and secularism. Plekhanov, for instance, construed the desire of the Bund, the non-Zionist Jewish socialist movement, to retain a Jewish identity within the global workers movement as unacceptable and called them 'seasick Zionists' – that is, Jews who remained in Europe only because they dreaded the trip across the Mediterranean to Palestine.[11] The other development was the unwillingness of the Rightist and conservative forces in Europe to accept even the most secular and patriotic Jews as equal or legitimate members of society.

Evron was the first Israeli to question the narrative of return. He did so not only because he saw no connection between the early Zionist settlers and the Jews who lived in Roman Palestine, but also, and mainly, because he felt that the myth of return was invented only after secular Jews had realised they would not be able to assimilate as equals into European society.[12] Furthermore, he contended, because immigration as such was, from a modernised Jewish perspective, not a good enough solution, they looked for a more sublime reason to explain their failure and their need to leave Europe. Hence Palestine was invented as the ancient homeland, and the immigration described as return. Evron concluded this 'heretical' explanation by adding another, more mundane reason why the invention included the colonisation of Palestine: colonisation became possible because it meshed well with British imperial designs towards the Middle East.

At the time of publication, Evron's book and views were ignored. But while he was articulating this comprehensive challenge to Zionism's most basic truism, another voice – far more powerful in its effect – began to be heard in the public arena.

The voice of Yeshayahu Leibowitz was not so easily silenced as were the voices of previous doubters of Zionism in Israel. Leibowitz was a religious Jew who, although possessed of a physique that was the antithesis of the almost Aryan images of the Sabras and the new Jews of Israel, gained respect among many as if he were the bravest general returning triumphantly from the battlefield. Born in Riga, then part of the Russian Empire, he showed signs of being a chess prodigy but was prevented by his religious parents from choosing that as his career. Following the First World War, his family went to Berlin, away from the Russian revolution. In Berlin his career flourished, and by the time he emigrated to Palestine in 1935, he already held a PhD in chemistry and had engaged in considerable study of medicine. Leibowitz participated in the Zionist religious and political movements and served in the 1948 war in the Jerusalem area. He was a Renaissance man of vast knowledge, a man of major achievements and positions in disciplines ranging from the biological sciences to Jewish theology.[13]

Leibowitz's first doubts about the hegemony of Zionism were, as was true of other critics, aroused by a formative event. In his case, it was the Israeli operation in Qibya in 1953. This was an offensive retaliation for the killing of a mother and her two children by Palestinian infiltrators from Jordan. Despite Jordanian readiness to punish the culprits, the Israeli army attacked the village from which they believed the perpetrators came and, in the process, massacred sixty villagers, most of them women and children. Leibowitz wrote:

We have to ask ourselves where this youth of ours emerged from – young people who had no mental inhibitions about committing this atrocity? What inner motivation for such acts could have been at work here? This youth is not a mob but the product of Zionist, humanist and social education.[14]

His answer was that the state and Zionism had become more sacred than Jewish and humanist values: 'If the security of the people and the homeland are sacrosanct, and if the sword is *Zur Israel* [one of God's names in Judaism], then Qibya is possible and feasible.'[15]

Leibowitz's most famous references to Israeli conduct in the occupied territories were to call the settlers 'Judeo-Nazis' and the state the 'Shabak State'.[16] On many occasions in the 1970s and on into the 1980s, he argued that Israel could easily become a fascist, or even a Nazi state, and called on society to initiate civil war against such a scenario. Such remarks, along with his similarly uncompromising critique of Israel's policies, lost him the maximally prestigious Israel Prize, which is regarded as the country's equivalent of the Nobel Prize and is awarded, in a regal ceremony on Independence Day, to scholars and artists for a lifetime of achievement. When the committee of experts announced in 1993 that Leibowitz would be offered the

Israel Prize, his opponents rushed to attack the decision on the basis of his past comments. In response, Leibowitz declined the award.

Yitzhak Laor, a poet, writer and essayist for *Haaretz* – and one of the few Israeli intellectuals who has remained, since the beginning of his career, a firm critic of Zionism and of Israel's treatment of the Palestinians – has analysed well the relationship between the Zionist left and Leibowitz. While defining him as the 'spiritual authoritative voice of the Israeli left', Laor nonetheless wondered how a secular group of people, who usually detested any religious authority, were willing to accept his moral guidance. Perhaps this was due to his high national and international standing as a scientist that turned Leibowitz into a secular guru, or perhaps it was his directness and his journey from analysis to prognosis. From the time of the 1982 war in Lebanon, he had continually called for soldiers to refuse to serve in the occupied territories. According to Laor, what differentiated Leibowitz from the Zionist left was that his call for refusal was not merely a tactic in the struggle against occupation. Rather, it was a principled, pacifist point of view, which the Zionist left in fact condemned. 'War belongs to the filthiest layer of human existence', said Leibowitz. As Laor said, with such a view, Leibowitz challenged not only the occupation but also the sacred militarism of Israeli society.[17]

He was, however, not an anti-Zionist, and his post-Zionist followers of the 1990s went much further than he did. Leibowitz refused to criticise pre-1967 Israel. In his eyes, it was the occupation of the West Bank and the Gaza Strip that corrupted a legitimate ideological movement. His mantra remained the same with regard to the Arab–Israeli conflict: 'What is important is that we do not rule over Gentiles and that Gentiles do not rule over us'.[18] He predicted that 'people like me would be put in concentration camp by the new political powers'.[19] In this he was wrong. After his death, his fundamental acceptance of Zionism rehabilitated him, and a street in Jerusalem was named after him. None of the other thinkers mentioned in the present chapter have been honoured in this way. And yet he was so versatile and so powerful in his articulation of injustice that he was undoubtedly one of the major influences on the post-Zionist critique of the 1990s.

Also within the Zionist frame, but nearly breaking out of it, is Uri Avnery. Born Helmut Ostermann in Germany in 1923, he was taken by his parents in 1933 to Palestine when the Nazis came to power. As a young man, he wandered ideologically between the Canaanite movement and the Revisionist movement until he found his way, during the 1948 war, into one of the Hagana's élite units, Samson's Foxes, which took an active part in the war's ethnic cleansing of southern Palestine. A book he wrote while fighting, *In the Fields of the Philistines – 1948*, summarised his experience of the war and immediately became a best seller. Although meant as an anti-war document, it was not received as such.[20] Avnery therefore wrote another, more explicit critique, *The Other Side of the Coin*, which was less successful but better reflected his disillusionment with the State of Israel's policies towards the Arab world and the Palestinians.[21]

Avnery was badly wounded in the war, and with the money he received for rehabilitation, he purchased a failed journal called *HaOlam HaZeh* (This World) and turned it into a subversive political publication. It was a yellowish paper in many ways – a lot of gossip and soft pornography decorated its pages – but it was also an important investigative publication that exposed corruption inside Israel and Israeli aggression outside its borders. Avnery was elected to the Knesset in 1965, and several times later on.

Following the Six-Day War of 1967, his public profile rose – fame that in 1975 nearly got him assassinated. Soon after the war, he became one of the leaders of the anti-occupation movement and of a group of intellectuals and activists who sought direct dialogue with the PLO (he went to Beirut in 1982 to meet Yasser Arafat while that city was under Israeli siege). In 1975 he co-founded the Israeli Council for Israeli–Palestinian Peace, which was in many ways the first significant mechanism that enabled mainstream Israeli politicians to meet clandestinely with the PLO in an attempt to find a solution. Since 1992, Avnery has been active in the peace group Gush Shalom, which he founded; the group has attempted, unsuccessfully so far, to create a similar dialogue with Hamas and has been urging a worldwide boycott of products exported from Jewish settlements in the West Bank.[22]

Like Leibowitz, Avnery did not represent an anti-Zionist point of view, and saw the 1967 war as the source of evil in Israel. But his exposures of pre-1967 oppressive policies towards the Palestinians in Israel and the aggression towards the Arab world were an important source in the 1990s for academics who were prepared to embark on a more fundamental challenge of the Zionist narrative or the idea of Israel.

Other activists, such as Akiva Orr, Michel Warschawski, Ilan Halevi, and Uri Davis, stood outside, and clashed directly with, Zionism. Each of them had an epiphany, so to speak, triggered by an event that changed their perspective on the Zionist reality in Israel. In fact, there are so many others of whom the same can be said that I cannot mention them all in this chapter. Most seemed to follow a similar trajectory, in which a formative, sobering event exposed Zionism as colonialism, Israel as an apartheid state, and the United States as an imperialist nation.[23] For the benefit of future historians, there is now a 'dissident archive', thanks to the psychotherapist Avigail Abarbanel, who recently induced a large number of Jews and Israelis to describe their experiences.[24]

The late Akiva Orr was born in Berlin in 1931 and emigrated with his family to Palestine as a toddler. As did many teenagers at the time, he joined the Hagana in 1945 and served in the Israeli navy in 1948 (as a youth, he was a local champion in competitive swimming). Later he served in the commercial national fleet, where he witnessed a sailors' strike being brutally broken by the police, with the tacit support of the Labour-led trade union, the Histadrut. While completing his studies in the sciences, he became active in several political groups on the anti-Zionist left.[25] In 1964 he left Israel and moved to London, where he became an important member of the Palestine solidarity movement and also participated in British socialist groups. He published extensively in the *Black Dwarf*, a newspaper edited in the 1960s by Tariq Ali, and joined the London-based organisation Solidarity, founded by the Greek philosopher Cornelius Castoriadis. In the 1990s he returned to Israel, where he stayed until his death in early 2013.

Although Orr published extensively on democracy, socialism and politics, one of his early publications – *Peace, Peace and There Is No*

Peace, written with his colleague Moshe Machover and published in 1961 – reads as though it were written in the 1990s by a post-Zionist. Machover was born in Tel Aviv in 1936 and was a lecturer in mathematics when Akiva Orr arrived at the Hebrew University as a student. *Peace, Peace* is five hundred pages long and includes chapters on the ethnic cleansing of the Palestinians in 1948 as well on the atrocities committed by Israel against the Palestinian citizens of Israel. It was the first structured analysis in Hebrew of Zionism as a colonialist movement, and the first to suggest that the struggle for peace in Israel and Palestine must be anti-colonialist.

Michel Warschawski, known as Mikado, was born in central Europe, as were so many of the other challengers mentioned so far (I discuss in a separate chapter the Arab Jews who challenged Zionism later in the state's history). He was born in Strasbourg to an Orthodox Jewish family; his father was the chief rabbi of Strasbourg and a partisan in the Second World War. In 1961 Warschawski's family sent him to a yeshiva in Jerusalem that was also attended by future leaders of Gush Emunim, the settlers' movement in the occupied territories. Warschawski went in the opposite ideological direction, pushed there by his own formative event – the expulsion of the residents of three Palestinian villages near the monastery at Latrun (between Tel Aviv and Jerusalem) in 1967. The Israeli army had tried in vain to occupy these villages in 1948, losing many soldiers in the attempt, but the Arab Legion bravely defended them. Finally the Israeli army succeeded in capturing the villages in June 1967, expelling the residents with vengeance.

Mikado was an eyewitness to this expulsion. When he began to study at the Hebrew University in the late 1960s, he joined with like-minded students to organise a solidarity movement with the Palestinian struggle on both sides of the Green Line. For a while he also dreamed of importing the 1968 Prague Spring. In 1984 he put his energies into something far more permanent, the Alternative Information Center, which has continued ever since to track the abuses of the Israeli occupation in the West Bank and the Gaza Strip and the oppression of Palestinians inside Israel. Deep analyses, wide reportage and strategic discussion made its publications an important source for activists inside and outside Israel before the Internet revolution provided even more accessible and immediate tools for apprehending and reacting to the reality on the ground. Again, like so many other activists, Warschawski paid a high price for his views and activity: sitting in jail for months while he was a young father of two.[26]

Two other trailblazers were willing to do even more than pay the high price of being jailed or being condemned as traitors by their own society. These two – Ilan Halevi and Uri Davis – actually went over to the 'other' side.

Halevi was born in Vichy France to an extraordinary family. His father had been born in Jerusalem and, after travelling the world, joined the International Brigades during the Spanish Civil War; his mother was a Resistance fighter in Paris. As a teenager, he was sent to the United States after the separation of his parents, and there joined the Black Panthers. He also came to know Malcolm X quite well. Years later, he would say that his darker complexion made him feel like, and be accepted as, an African American. Like his father, Halevi chose a cause and finally landed in the newly liberated Algeria as a guest of the FLN. In 1965 he arrived in Israel and joined a kibbutz, Gan Shmuel, near Hadera, but was eventually thrown out of the kibbutz because of his radical views.[27]

Halevi's political career took a turn in 1976 when he left Israel for France and from there began frequent visits to Beirut and the PLO headquarters until he received an official appointment to the organisation in 1982. He represented the PLO in the Socialist International and in the 1991 Madrid peace conference. His highest position in the PLO was as deputy to the PLO's foreign minister, Nabil Shaath. He was more of an activist and politician than a writer. But the interviews he left behind give us a glimpse of his worldview: he uncompromisingly rejected Zionism and declared himself to be '100 per cent Jew and 100 per cent Arab'.

Uri Davis followed suit and joined the PLO in 1984. He was born in 1943 in Jerusalem and grew in Kfar Shmaryahu, a well-to-do suburb of Tel Aviv. He was already thinking out of the Zionist box when he succeeded in avoiding military service by substituting civil service for it instead (a very rare move for a young Jewish man in the early 1960s). After completing his national service, he was drawn into the Palestinians' struggle in northern Israel against the expropriation of their land. His focus was on the land taken from several villages for the construction of the new, Jewish-only town of Karmiel on the road between Acre and Safed. In 1964 he began demonstrating there, sometimes all by himself; at the height of his struggle, he undertook a hunger strike and moved to one of the villages as a resident. The expropriated areas were declared closed military zones, but he violated these orders and was arrested for doing so; all told, he was incarcerated for half a year, during which he again began a hunger strike. After several forays into local and municipal politics, he adopted a different mode of action and joined Fatah, of which he remains a member of the Revolutionary Council.[28]

Davis was one of the first to fuse his professional qualifications – a doctorate in anthropology – with his political commitments. As an anthropologist, he exposed the apartheid nature of the State of Israel.[29] In many ways he set an example for the following generation of how to confront Zionism within Israeli academia and within one's own discipline – the inevitable price for which was the loss of his job.[30] It was possible in Israel to teach the sciences and hold anti-Zionist views, but it was not permissible for a dissident social scientist or humanities professor to teach Zionism in an Israeli university. Until Davis's daring scholarly work, critiques of Zionism were dismissed as purely political and ideological tracts.

But even lone fighters need a home, and most of these activists – most of the time, in one way and another – were connected to Matzpen, the longest-standing anti-Zionist Jewish movement in Israel (apart from the Communist Party), or to one of its many offshoots.

The Anti-Zionist Movements: Matzpen and Its Offshoots

In 1962 Moshe Machover, Akiva Orr, Oded Pilavsky and Yirmiyahu Kaplan were expelled from the Israeli Communist Party. They were among the younger cadres of the party, and their sin was their continued critique of party policies, specifically its blind obedience to the Soviet Union. On various occasions, they argued that the party had, since 1948, failed to advance the conditions and realities of its natural constituencies: the Palestinian minority of Israel and the socio-economically deprived classes of the Jewish state.[31]

Feeling that what was needed was a clearer discourse about a socialist revolution in Israel and the Middle East as a whole, they decided to found a new political organisation that would better reflect their views. They also proposed that the workers in Israel create councils that would make major decisions on the policies to be pursued and actions to be taken, rather than follow the practice of the Communist Party, in which the Politburo made all the decisions. Their early publications declare clearly their rejection of Zionism (for the Communist Party, this was never a clear issue) and fully endorse the demands of the Palestinian national movement (in 1962 these were not yet clear, since the Palestinian National Charter, which defined these demands, was not produced until 1964).

These ideas came out in the public manifesto of the new group, which called itself Matzpen (Compass). At their first meeting in 1962, the participants defined themselves as a voluntary organisation of Israelis committed to a social revolution within the territory of Israel and Palestine. In the next few years the group succeeded in recruiting dozens of Palestinian and Jewish Israelis. Consisting mostly of students, it had more Jewish members than Arabs; most of the Jews came from the kibbutz movement, while the Palestinians came from the cities. In 1965, Matzpen joined Uri Avnery in the founding of a parliamentary party that would compete in national elections, although none of the Matzpen members were willing to be in the actual list – they only lent their support.

Having started with twelve members, the movement grew significantly after the June 1967 war. On June 8 it burst into the international arena when it published a joint ad in the *Times* of London, together with the Palestinian guerilla organisation the Democratic Front for the Liberation of Palestine, calling for the abolition of the Zionist character of Israel and the creation of an 'a-national' federal-socialist state. The ad further stated that in the desired new state, everyone would enjoy equal cultural and civil rights and that the state would be committed to the economic and political union of the Middle East. Soon after, leading members of Matzpen, such as Akiva Orr and Moshe Machover, joined exiled Palestinians in Europe to create a pro-Palestinian solidarity movement. Inside Israel, it became the most vociferous lobby against the occupation – an approach that frequently led to the arrest and detention of its members.

In the 1970s Matzpen underwent an ideological crisis, when some members found it to be too passive and departed to create a number of splinter groups. The first was the Workers' Union (called also Avangard). This group criticised Matzpen for being insufficiently active within workers communities in Israel and for preferring the international stage. From this group sprang another one, the Revolutionary Communist Alliance – the RCA, whose publication was named *Ma'avak*, 'Struggle' – which proposed that the political strategy had to focus on the creation of a binational state over the entirety of historical Palestine. Some RCA members were still active in the 1990s, in a new organisation called Derech Ha-nizoz (Through a Spark) and were arrested for their connections to left-wing organisations within the PLO.[32] Nowadays some of them are part of the parliamentary list, the Da'am Workers Party, which focuses on the rights of workers and has thus far not succeeded in entering the Knesset.

From those two basic groups emerged a third, the Red Front, which chose, among other things, to be associated directly with the armed Palestinian struggle. The best-known, outside of Israel, of their members was Udi Adiv, a young member of Kibbutz Gan Shmuel (Ilan Halevi's kibbutz) who, after serving as a paratrooper in the Israeli army, joined others in creating an underground web of connections with the PLO. The members of the Red Front were arrested in December 1972 and charged with the creation of an Arab–Jewish sabotage and espionage network in Israel. It seems they had never gotten, nor did they intend to go, that far. In any case, they were sentenced and jailed for long periods but were released in 1985, when three Israeli soldiers captured in Lebanon were traded by the Palestinian organisation Ahmad Jibril for more than a thousand Palestinian prisoners, including the arrested members of the Red Front.[33] Finally, I should mention a fourth group, the Revolutionary Communist League (also called Matzpen Marxist). All of these groups, as well as their own splinters, shared a stronger affiliation with Maoist or Trotskyite variants of communism and were willing to participate in actual military struggle against the state.

For the Israeli public, these dissident Jews should have symbolised everything Zionism was proud of. Many were young, handsome members of kibbutzim who had served in the élite units of the army. Although there were only a handful of them, the society as a whole was bewildered that such members could subscribe to such revolutionary and counter-Zionist ideas.

Aside from the specifics of these splinter groups, it is Matzpen that is most important within the context of the history of ideas that I wish to chart here. Matzpen's positions were very much the same as those put forward by the challengers of the future. I myself can attest that while I had not read any Matzpen publications prior to writing my books challenging the Israeli version of the 1948 war and depicting Zionism as a colonialist movement, I was amazed to discover – when, in 1997, Akiva Orr handed me the book *Peace, Peace and There Is No Peace*, along with several issues of Matzpen's official publication – the degree to which we shared the same analysis and prognosis.

This holds true for other works that appeared in the 1990s as well. They, too, would reflect Matzpen's views of Zionism as colonialism and of 1948 as a catastrophe, and would share the movement's critique of Israeli policies towards Arab Jews, the Palestinian minority, and the occupied territories. The later critics had neither access to the archives nor an interest in scholarly academic work, and yet the end result would be the same. More than anything else, the courage displayed by the members of Matzpen was inspiring. These young men and women could be seen in small groups, carrying provocative banners and not being deterred by the prospect of verbal or even physical assault by bystanders or the police. Through that commitment and determination, they showed the way for the few who, still today, do not give up regardless of the opposition.

Few members of the academy belonged to this group. But in the 1970s there emerged academics who found themselves developing similar doubts about Zionism. They differed from the earlier activists in that their trigger for questioning the idea of Israel was not some specific formative event or a personal epiphany. Their beliefs began to be shaken when their professional research exposed the false assumptions and historical fabrications on which the idea of Israel was based.

The Pioneering Academics

In the wake of the groundbreaking work by these pioneering activists, there appeared the first voices from within the Israeli academy expressing profound doubts about the nature of the state, its ideology and policies. Until the war of October 1973 – sometimes called the Yom Kippur War – academia was obedient, highly patriotic and overwhelmingly Zionist. Dissenting teachers paid less of a price than did activists in terms of imprisonment or public condemnation, but being a lonely voice in the wilderness made such academics feel quite marginalised and out of place in the Israeli universities.

One such voice was Uriel Tal. A professor of modern Jewish history at Tel Aviv University, Tal wrote extensively on Jewish secularisation in modern times but also voiced consternation about the way Israeli academia was being pressed into the service of the nation and of Zionism.[34] In a series of lectures delivered to colleagues in the Department of Jewish History at Tel Aviv University in the 1980s, Tal posed some poignant questions about the newly formed discipline in Israeli academia known as Jewish studies. Since the 1970s every university had a department of Jewish history; some had gone further and opened Eretz Israel history or studies departments, which taught and researched according to a specific disciplinary logic and methodology. Tal objected to any insistence that the study of Zionism, Judaism, and the history of the Land of Israel required both ideological loyalty and particular methodological tools. He sought instead a universal approach towards all these topics. To his mind, there was no such discipline as 'Jewish history' – there was only history – and whatever history's methodologies, theories and tools were, they should apply equally to the study of an African, European or Jewish past and present.

Tal failed in this quixotic quest. Universities continued the zealous cultivation of the 'disciplines' of Jewish and Eretz Israel studies. The politicised academic structure, displaying continued indifference to what was going on in the rest of the world, remained impenetrable to any genuine interdisciplinary influence, let alone any comparative studies. Zionism and the Zionist version of Judaism continued to be taught and researched as unique case studies that lay outside the framework of general historiography.

Nevertheless, what Tal had noticed in mid-1980s Israel soon became obvious. Formerly acclaimed Israeli scholars working on Israel and Zionism started to lose their prestige abroad and became regarded as propagandists for the national narrative. A short while later, international criticism began to have an impact within Israeli academia itself. Tal's critique had been shaped by his interaction with the academic world outside Israel, but most of the early academic challengers were less engaged than he was in philosophical or theoretical criticisms of Israeli academia. Their problem with the national academy was that it was indifferent to the predicaments of the society around it; predicaments that began to surface forcefully after the 1973 war.

That war is a turning-point in its own right. The Syrian–Egyptian surprise attack that month on the occupied Golan Heights and the Sinai Peninsula, which had been under Israeli control since 1967, shook the earth beneath the feet of many Israelis. The aftershocks reached the academy before they affected Israeli culture as a whole. The war ended a period of euphoria and consensus in Israeli society and exposed cracks in Israel's moral smugness. In many ways, it served to prod academics and others to embark on an introspective search for answers to a number of troubling questions about the moral validity of the state, including both past and present policies, and eventually to revisit the essence and implications of the idea of Israel itself.

Until the third day of the war, the sense among generals, politicians and indeed the general public was that Israel was lost. There was even serious discussion of the possibility of using nuclear weapons as a last resort in case the United States would not come to Israel's aid. By this time, Syrian forces were deep inside the Golan Heights, while Egyptian forces had advanced into the Sinai Peninsula; dozens of Israeli soldiers had been captured, and the famously invincible Israeli Air Force found it difficult to operate against the enemy's anti-aircraft system. An American airlift and a successful strategy in the north tipped the balance later on, but these did not lessen the sense of insecurity and suspicion about the leadership's ability to sustain the Jewish state. In the early days of the debacle, the Labour government, headed by Golda Meir, was handed the blame. Although a committee of inquiry absolved politicians such as Meir and her minister of defence, Moshe Dayan, from responsibility for the failure and cast the blame on the army and the intelligence chiefs, the electorate thought differently. In order to save the Labour Party from defeat in the elections of 1974, the 1967 war hero Yitzhak Rabin was brought back from Washington, where he had been serving as ambassador, and he indeed won the election for Labour. But in 1977 Labour ran his rival, Shimon Peres, who was easily defeated by Menachem Begin and his Likud Party.

But this was more than just a changing of the guard. The war traumatised the society, and many Israelis lost, albeit for a short moment, their sense of perpetual invincibility – not only because of the army's poor performance on the battlefield, but also because of the raising of doubts about Israeli policy among traditional supporters of the state in the world at large. By itself, the 1973 war was not enough to cause loyal adherents of the idea of Israel to doubt the whole plot. Earlier developments had already planted these doubts in a few corners of the public mind even before the war. In the aftermath of the 1967 war, the state's highest officials and ministers had become entangled in highly publicised cases of personal corruption. Most of those suspected and later indicted were members of the ruling Labour Party. As a result, the founding movement of the State began to lose its prestige and its hegemony – politically, socially and culturally – for the Jews of Israel.

But the war did stand at the gateway to two decades, the 1970s and 1980s, that exposed some basic Zionist truisms as doubtful at best and as fallacies at worst. In the relative calm after 1973, these tensions brought to the fore certain demons that had been safely hidden away, the most important of which was the claim that the state was a successful melting pot in which a new Jewish identity had been forged. What became apparent was that the society was ridden with tensions between various cultural and ethnic groups, and was only precariously cemented together by the lack of peace and the continual sense of crisis.

It was at this time that social and cultural undercurrents of dissatisfaction and antagonism in Israeli society began to erupt. These were transformed into social protests against the evils inflicted by the state on deprived Jewish communities, mostly North African in origin. Young and vociferous activists tried to emulate the dissent voiced by African Americans and so, in the early 1970s, established their own Black Panther movement, led by a group of extraordinary young men.

Reuven Abargel, who was born in Morocco, arrived in Israel in 1950 at the age of three. His family settled in Musrara, a Palestinian neighbourhood in Jerusalem from which the residents had been evicted in 1948; in those days, it served as a buffer zone between Jordanian East Jerusalem and Israeli West Jerusalem. It was a slum, one of the poorest neighbourhoods in the city. Occasionally the respective armies exchanged fire.

Abargel spent some time outside the neighbourhood and was educated in a kibbutz in the Negev. When he came back, he, like so many other youngsters, lived on the margins of the law and normative society. Seeing his family's poverty and lack of hope, in 1971 he decided jointly with friends from the neighbourhood to found a protest movement that would demand government investment in the educational, transportation, and housing infrastructure in the poor neighbourhoods.[35] Abargel's friend Charlie Biton, who also arrived in Israel in 1950, came from Casablanca at the age of two; his family, too, had been thrown into the slum of Musrara. Other friends from the neighbourhood included Saadia Marciano and Kochavi

Shemesh. Together with another ten friends, and with the help of social workers who operated a community centre in the neighbourhood, they founded the Israeli Black Panthers.

The movement demanded a new and fairer distribution of the economic resources of the state and a share in the definition of its cultural identity. The protesters failed to move the Israeli left but attracted the attention of the right, which skilfully manipulated their protest into a mass movement that brought Menachem Begin to power in 1977. In this shifting landscape, the Israeli left lost the working classes, the natural constituency for such movements in the West. In addition, some of its adherents in academia began to drift away from Socialist Zionism and began to view critically their former political home. In particular, they saw the Labour Party's defeat at the polls in May 1977 as an indication of the potential failure of the Zionist project as a whole.

Meanwhile, protests and discontent continued against the ongoing discrimination against Israeli Jews of North African origin, whose second generation expressed grievances against the Ashkenazi-dominated national memory. They pointed to the exclusion of the North African experience from the collective story of early statehood. The protests exposed the deep-rooted racism played out in practice within the ideal of Israel as a 'melting pot' society. They highlighted the continual institutional discrimination against the Mizrachi Jews.[36] When academics joined this protest movement in the footsteps of activists on the ground, they not only investigated the discrimination in their own time but also sought its roots in the early years of statehood.

The first group of academics to respond to Mizrachi grievances operated at the University of Haifa. The university itself had been established in 1963 as a branch of the Hebrew University in Jerusalem but gained its independence in 1972. This was an ideal place for novel thinking, located along a ridge of Mount Carmel – where it became a familiar feature of the northern scenery, with its eerie thirty-floor tower designed by the communist Brazilian architect Oscar Niemeyer during the tenure of the legendary megalomaniac mayor Abba Hushi. The university boasted a fresh and innovative department of sociology, and until they were tamed, these sociologists challenged the orthodox methodology and Zionist commitment of the leading Israeli sociologists of the day.

One of their main targets, and the best known among their former Hebrew University professors, was Shmuel Noah Eisenstadt. A Polish Jew who emigrated to Palestine at an early age, he was groomed to be the doyen of Israeli sociology under Martin Buber. He introduced the theory of modernisation as both an academic pastime and a guidebook for future Israeli government policies towards anyone who was neither Western nor modern. The theory was that anyone who encounters a Western society is, at the end of the day, bound to be Westernised, which is to say to be modernised and introduced to the world of economic progress, social stability and liberal democracy. Nevertheless, such an integration cannot be expected to happen voluntarily or autonomously – the new recruits must be coached into becoming modern.[37]

When that theory became policy in the 1950s, it signified that the state had the power first to define who was and who was not modern, and then to choose the means by which to modernise them. These means included de-Arabising Mizrachi Jews, secularising Orthodox Jews, and breaking traditional practices of rural or immigrant societies while at the same time compensating or rewarding these people by locating them at the social and geographical margins of the society until the process of modernisation was successfully completed.

In the era of nationalism, the idealisation of one group often requires the demonisation of another. The idea that Israel epitomised modernity meant that Palestine signified the precise opposite: primitiveness. Similarly, if modern Judaism epitomised enlightenment, then Arab nationalism was the heart of darkness, and as Ashkenazi Jews were progressive, Mizrachi Jews were regressive. These antitheses wounded and scarred society in such a way that only a constant state of emergency and near-war could suppress the pain and anger. On the other hand, as this view was the fruit of theoretical research, the Zionist narrative and highly positive self-image was accepted as scientifically valid.

In response, the University of Haifa challengers approached their research on Israeli history and society with critical distance, paving the way for post-Zionist scholarship. Common to their multifaceted works and interests was the underlying assumption that collective memory was constructed officially through the educational system, the media, and the academy. Directly and indirectly, they accused Israel's mainstream sociologists of employing methodologies that suited Zionist claims on the land and the Jewish people, and that excluded marginalised groups and narratives that did not fit the self-image of Israel as a Western, Jewish society.

With the help of historical and sociological research, this group of social scientists hoped to represent as valid and worthy the agendas of deprived groups in Israeli society. They unearthed the hidden voices of the past in Israel – those of North African Jews, Palestinian citizens, women, all those who had been submerged by the Zionist narrative. These scholars made their way into history from departure points suggested by the political organisations that represented these groups.

Universalism was the key factor that separated these researchers from the traditional historiography and linked them with the critical voices of the future. Politically, they also broke traditional barriers by grouping Palestinians and Mizrachi Jews into a single subject, as was especially evident in the work of Sammy Smooha and Shlomo Swirski. They used a typology that ran contrary to everything that Zionism and Zionist academia had stood for.

Swirski, an Argentinian Jew, would become the main non-academic expert on social and economic problems in Israel, consulted and listened to by the media as well as politicians. During his early days in Haifa, he was involved in the establishment of a high school based on Mizrachi values and perceptions; later he opened the Adva Centre, which is today the only reliable information source about poverty and inequality in Israel. Smooha came from Iraq with his family in 1941 and experienced personally the discrimination against Mizrachi Jews. Although an excellent pupil in his elementary school, he was refused entry into a prestigious high school in Tel Aviv and had to work hard as a boy to finance his studies.

Swirski and Smooha, each in his own way, became severe critics of established sociology in Israel. Swirksi focused on, among other things, the major works of the mainstream sociologists in Israel (S. N. Eisenstadt, Dan Giladi, Dan Horowitz and Moshe Lissak) and the way they depicted the history of Zionism in Palestine. He described how the major actions taken by Zionist settlers were always ascribed to an ideology, but without any discussion of what that ideology entailed or how it acted as a motivation (he sought, for instance, to engage with Karl Marx's hypothesis that reality informs cognition and not vice versa). He and others suggested that economic interests might be the reason behind the colonisation of Palestine, the oppression of the Mizrachi Jews, and other policies invoked under the rubric of ideology. But more than anything else, Swirski opened the door for the next generation of critical sociologists not to look at ideology, and in particular Zionist ideology, as an object of inquiry which exists outside the reality on the ground. It was part of the reality, he insisted – sometimes a manipulation of that reality and at other times a justification in hindsight for actions taken by individuals and collectives.

It was a question of responsibility and accountability. Mainstream sociology explained settlement as an ideology and everything that happened afterwards as normalisation – namely, a process in which ideology no longer played, nor did it have to play, an important role. According to later, critical sociologists, Zionism as a colonialist project developed an ideology that justified the continued and thus far never-ending dispossession of the indigenous population. Swirski was more interested in the failure of these works to explain why the settlers' utopian socialist ideas had in fact created a capitalist society:

The main problem of these works is that due to their approaches and assumptions, they do not engage in a serious discussion about Zionism as a social project. Whereas in history, the Zionist movement – and in particular the socialist Zionist part of it – was infested with internal debates and hesitations, it is depicted by these authors as a process of selection that produced the best alternative possible. While today still a lot of people ask what should be the future orientation of Zionism, the impression these works leave is that there is no debate anymore, since the natural development that ensued after the right selection has turned Israeli society into a mature and healthy one.[38]

Sammy Smooha tackled the works of the mainstream sociologists from a different angle. He painted a picture of social scientists in Israel in the early 1980s as a White Ashkenazi establishment that displayed patronising, and at times racist, attitudes towards Arab culture.[39] Smooha called this school of thought in Israeli academia 'the cultural approach', and he highlighted sociologists who assumed that an 'inferior' culture could absorb a 'superior' one as happened in 1977. He explained that mainstream Israeli sociologists depicted this political change as the end of the era of universalist, liberal democracy in Israel and the beginning of an 'ethnocentric, fanatic, pre-modern and irrational' era in the state's history. He took issue with this depiction on two grounds: first, the cultural hegemony of the Ashkenazi Jews did not end with Likud's rise to power and said it was incorrect 'to characterise the political Mizrachi culture as nationalist, extreme and anti-Arab'.[40] Instead, he contended, the vast majority of the Mizrachi Jews supported the peace with Egypt in 1977 because it was brought about by the Likud and not by the hated Labour Party.

The Haifa sociologists published their findings in the Hebrew journal *Notes on Critique and Theory*, still a valuable source for an alternative view of the history and sociology of the idea of Israel. Not long afterwards appeared the work of two Israeli sociologists who were similarly engaged but, like Uriel Tal before them, were lonely voices within established departments of sociology. Baruch Kimmerling worked in the department at the Hebrew University of Jerusalem, and Yonathan Shapira in the department at Tel Aviv University. Their input was invaluable for the future deconstruction of the mainstream Zionist historiographical enterprise. They employed conventional sociological theories to explain the domination of the Labour movement in Zionist life and how marginal groups were both co-opted and coerced into full collaboration with a small élite that had held all the power and resources since 1882.[41]

These two scholars were the first to suspect that the forefathers of Zionism and modern Israel were not altruistic, committed politicians but rather were motivated by more cynical reasons, such as the wish to remain in power at all costs. This determination rested less on the basis of new evidence and more on their theoretical choice to appraise Zionism as a normal rather than an abnormal chapter in history. They were also the first to explain the malaise of 1970s Israeli society by way of historical research on the Mandatory period. In their new retelling, the Jewish Mandatory political system was far less democratic and egalitarian than it appeared to be in work done by their peers from the Eretz Israel departments.

Kimmerling and Shapira painted a picture of a far more dictatorial, and at times even sinister, political and social system whose practices and conduct afflicted the politics of Israel for years to come. The most notable of these was its nurturing of mediocre successors who would not endanger the leadership. The researchers showed how party affiliation and ethnic origin, namely, Labour membership and Ashkenazi origin, were the main criteria for being admitted to the better jobs and positions in society and government. Yonathan Shapira characterised Israeli democracy during its first thirty years as a system that gave no room to any kind of opposition, whether ethnic or ideological:

> Israel was not a liberal democracy; it did not nourish individual and minority rights against the power of the majority rule, and therefore did not have an effective opposition party, which is the basic guarantee for a liberal democracy … the public was exposed to a limitless and uncurbed indoctrination and intervention of the hegemonic ideology in its life. This condition of dominance by the ruler, manifested both in institutional and cultural dominance … was what characterised the rule of Mapai in the Israeli political system.[42]

These two researchers were also the first to describe the Israeli policy of land purchase as a regime orientated entirely for the sake of creating more space for the Jews at the expense of the Arab minority in Israel. As Kimmerling put it,

> The state made sure that the Palestinians in Israel would be confined geographically, socially and politically through the apparatus of the military rule [imposed on the Palestinians in Israel until 1966] and the general trade unions, the Histadrut, discriminated against the Palestinian citizens, favouring the Jewish workers in terms of salaries and place in the labour market.[43]

Yonathan Shapira was born before the creation of the State of Israel and finished his graduate studies at Columbia in 1964, before returning to help found the Faculty of Social Sciences at the University of Tel Aviv. Although part of the university management and leadership, he engaged with Zionism and Israel in a way that was liberated from the reverence and awe his predecessors had showed to the state's founding fathers. Shapira re-examined the historical origins of the leading Zionist Labour party, Mapai, and found there a propensity for domineering and brutal politics and little trace of pure socialist ideology or a Zionist vision devoid of narrow-mindedness and egotism. He then attributed some of the contemporary problems of Israeli society to the tyrannical nature of the ruling groups within Mapai, which had prevented the emergence of a competent élite during the early years of statehood.[44] Shapira was a charismatic lecturer and in many ways ensured that what Mapai's founding fathers had done – allowing only mediocre successors to grow beside them, so as to leave their authority intact – would not happen in the university. He left behind him a cohort of impressive scholars who continued his work in the same vein of boldness.

Baruch Kimmerling had a powerful impact of a different kind. Born in 1939 in Romania, he was afflicted with cerebral palsy that would confine him to a wheelchair for the rest of his life. His family arrived in Israel in 1952 after narrowly escaping death in the Holocaust. Kimmerling's physical disability did not prevent him from pursuing a successful academic career at the Hebrew University in Jerusalem, where he taught until his death. He spent most of his adult life in Mevaseret Zion, a suburb of Jerusalem built on the ruins of the Palestinian village Qalunya, which had been destroyed in 1948 and its inhabitants expelled. Kimmerling would digest this fact only in the late 1990s, but when he did so, it further radicalised his critical position towards Israel and Zionism. An obituary in the London *Times* described him as 'the first academic to use scholarship to re-examine the founding tenets of Zionism and the Israeli State'. He may not have been the first, but he was indeed among the first.

This fragile, crippled man wrote and spoke, with the help of others, in a loud, clear voice until disease defeated him. There was an intriguing disjunction between his definitive criticism of Zionism as an ideology, as well as his pioneering analyses of Zionist intentions in the 1948 war, and his low public profile and lack of political involvement. Nevertheless, his writings have had an enduring effect on Israel's understanding of itself.[45]

Kimmerling's most important input to the new debate was his application of the settler colonialist paradigm to the historical study of Zionism. Through this approach, he and the colleagues who followed him brought critical Israeli sociology as close as possible to the Palestinian narrative. This theoretical perspective was first offered by Jewish activists within Israel, such as those of Matzpen, and was adopted earlier by leading scholars of the European and in particular the French left.[46] The French Marxist scholar Maxime Rodinson was one of the first after 1967 to identify the Zionist project as colonialist in his famous article '*Israel, fait colonial*', published in Jean-Paul Sartre's journal *Les Temps Modernes*.[47]

Kimmerling constructed the bridge between Rodinson's ideas and a more systematic and paradigmatic method of research. He defined Zionism as an 'immigrant-settler' movement, created for the purpose of a new subcategory of colonialism. He placed the Zionist phenomenon within the wider context of global colonisation and decolonisation processes, viewing it as an intriguing case study of a human project carried out against difficult odds – and at the expense of other human beings. He explained its success as the result of a fruitful combination of British colonialism and Jewish settlement activity, on the one hand, and Jewish nationalism and revivalism on the other. In addition, he pointed to the importance of the protection provided by the British Empire to the Zionist project, which had enabled the Jewish community in Palestine to attain its principal goal of reaching significant demographic growth despite the Arab majority in the land. Kimmerling was, so to speak, more ideologically secure from the wrath of the establishment because his theoretical perspective allowed him to look at Zionism as a colonialist movement without his being accused of a wholesale adoption of the Palestinian discourse. However, in the neo-Zionist atmosphere described later in this book, it did not completely immunise him from the vicious attempt to brand any such criticism, including his, as treason.

In the footsteps of Shapira and Kimmerling came Gershon Shafir. He, too, was a precursor of the later and more comprehensive attempt to challenge Zionism in Israel. Shafir began his career at the University of Tel Aviv before emigrating to the United States; his work there, in many ways, was a continuation of that done by the Haifa critical group of the 1970s, complementing Kimmerling's voyages into the questions of colonialism and Zionism. Shafir was more blunt than his predecessors. He reconstructed Zionism as an orthodox colonialist movement in a colonialist era despite its atypical characteristics, such as the absence of a proper mother country, the marginal role played by capitalist profit-and-loss considerations in the Zionist project, and the evident nationalist discourse and motivation. These exceptional historical circumstances led the leading Zionist scholars to reject strongly, indeed to condemn, any reference to Zionism as a colonialist movement.

Shafir's explanation of Zionism's distinctive features stands in stark contradiction to that of Zionist historians such as Anita Shapira, a leading figure in the historiographical establishment. She has insisted on the uniqueness of the Zionist case study, which therefore excludes it from being treated as a colonialist project like any other – an exclusion authorised by the movement's highly exceptional moral standards.[48] Zionist historiography likes to characterise the project in Palestine as colonisation without colonialism, and has even invented a Hebraicised term with a Latin connotation when responding to the charge that Zionism was a colonialist movement: Zionism was a *Colonisatoring* movement, meaning that it colonised but was not a colonialist movement. Think of it as decaf or diet colonialism.[49]

Shafir did not ignore the uniqueness of Israel but preferred to stress particular geographical and economic conditions as the unique features of the Zionist movement. For him, Zionism was an intriguing example of colonialism, since the movement succeeded in establishing a state notwithstanding its lack of vast military or financial means. Thus, for Shafir, the jewels in the Zionist crown – the kibbutz and the *moshav* – were types of settlers' colonies that could be found in the plantations of whites in South America, the Caribbean, Australia and elsewhere.[50]

In addition, Shafir debunked another self-proclaimed Zionist achievement: that of building an independent national market under the British Mandate. In the Zionist parlance it was called *Kibbush Ha'avoda* (conquest of labour), and it epitomised the Zionist dream of creating a 'new Jew' by delivering the Eastern European Jews from their dismal location at the margins of the Continent's labour market prior to the rise of Zionism. The early ideologues of the movement condemned the pre-Zionist occupational map of European Jews as based entirely on what they called in Yiddish *luftgescheften* (hot air business) – non-productive and parasitic jobs forced upon the Jewish communities at times of persecution and anti-Semitism.

For the purpose of *Kibbush Ha'avoda*, there was a need to move out those in Palestine who were employed as more productive labourers, i.e., the Palestinians. In Shafir's dictionary these strategies were typical colonialist means of excluding the native from the labour and land markets and replacing him with the settler. Two other Israeli historians of labour, Deborah S. Bernstein and David De Vries, would soon closely examine this policy in similar terms and expand our knowledge of the period.[51]

Although Shafir certainly broke new ground, it must be said that for many scholars outside Israel, his analysis of Zionist policy in its early stages was accepted as the most natural way to describe what happened there. Ernest Gellner, who was a friend of the state and the

movement, while discussing examples to show how national movements nationalise past events so as to fit them to a new narrative,
chose the kibbutz as one such example. Like Shafir, he asserted that
this form of collective settlement was the cheapest and most effective
way of colonising Palestine at the time, and that only in hindsight
did historians attribute a socialist or communist agenda as being the
principal motivation behind the kibbutz and the *moshav*.

This pathway recurs often in history and has even a theoretical
reification: symbolic realism. A certain action is taken by people – in
the case at hand, leaving a country for another, alien country – for
a variety of discrete and individual reasons. Then they choose the
most functional way of surviving during the early stages of their settlement in an alien landscape. When the project becomes successful,
these individual stories and practical solutions are narrated in such
a way as to fit the objectives of the newborn state. In our case, the
narrative becomes that the Jews did not come to Palestine because of
their personal troubles nor did they live in kibbutzim because it was
cheaper. No, they did both things because they were Zionists in the
first instance and socialists in the second. And the articulators of this
new narrative were those who became leaders of the group, either by
choice or by force.

Shafir viewed the tale of a socialist dream as a retrospective justification for the brutal takeover of Palestine. A few years later, in 1999,
Zeev Sternhell would articulate the same idea in an elegant book
titled *The Founding Myths of Israel: Nationalism, Socialism, and the
Making of the Jewish State*.

Each of these three pioneering sociologists – Shapira, Kimmerling
and Shafir – had a profound influence on the next wave of historical
revisionism in Israel. Whereas Shapira and Kimmerling normalised
the historiographical picture and opened the way to self-criticism,
Shafir was the first scholar to investigate the principal chapters in the
Palestinian narrative that related to the genesis of the Zionist project
in Palestine.

Nevertheless, an identification with the Palestinian vantage point
should not be mistaken for a wholesale adoption of Palestinian collective memory and history. At the time books by these sociologists

were published, Palestinian historiography was less nuanced in its treatment of Zionism. It would become more so, as a result of dialectical and mutual influences, only after the emergence of more comprehensive post- and even anti-Zionist scholarship in Israel. In fact, only when some hope for introspective Zionist criticism arose did Palestinian historiography respond in kind. In many ways, the appearance of the Israeli 'new history' of the 1948 war held the potential for such an introspective view and a favourable Palestinian response.

FIVE

Recognising the Palestinian Catastrophe: The 1948 War Revisited

S oon after his victory in the 1960 election, President John F. Kennedy became deeply involved in US global policies. Among other issues that attracted his attention were the Middle East and in particular the question of Palestine. He decided to continue the policies of his predecessor, Dwight D. Eisenhower, who was convinced that only the repatriation of a significant number of Palestinian refugees to their homes in what became Israel would help resolve the Arab–Israeli conflict, which was disrupting US efforts to create a solid base against the Soviet Union in that region. That is why Kennedy ordered his ambassador at the UN to support the efforts by Arab countries in the General Assembly to force Israel to repatriate a large number of refugees from the UN camps in which they had lived ever since being ethnically cleansed in 1948.[1]

The astonished Israeli government, which had already successfully fended off an attempt by Eisenhower's secretary of state, John Foster Dulles, to impose such a policy on Israel, had to come up with new ways of responding to the new pressure. (One of the major decisions taken by the government at that time was to create a pro-Israel lobby to ensure that future American administrations would not stray down that same path.) The Israeli prime minister, David Ben-Gurion, convened an emergency meeting in his office to discuss the matter. 'We need to tell the facts. [These people] fled voluntarily … As far as I know, only the Arabs of Lydda and Ramla were forced to leave', he said.[2] As I and others have shown, his diary from 1948 showed that he was aware, if not responsible, for the forced expulsion of Palestinians from almost every corner of the land. What he meant by 'we need to tell the facts' was that he wanted to tell the facts in a way that would ease American and international pressure on Israel.[3]

Ben-Gurion explained that he was going to provide Israeli academia with the necessary archival material to show the world that the Arabs voluntarily left their homes in 1948. He chose the Shiloah Institute at the Hebrew University of Jerusalem (in 1965 this institute moved to Tel Aviv University). Reuven Shiloah was the first head of the Mossad until 1952 and then remained a senior adviser to the government on Mideast affairs. The Israel Oriental Society decided to commemorate his activity by naming after him the first ever university centre for research on the Middle East. The centre (which in 1983 became the Moshe Dayan Center for Middle Eastern and African Studies at Tel Aviv University and still operates there today) has close ties with the Israeli security apparatus and in many ways was part of their research infrastructure. At the same time, it was recognised across the world as an important academic entity.[4]

The task at hand was entrusted to the institute's deputy director, Rony Gabbay, an Arabic-speaking Iraqi Jew who emigrated to Israel in 1950 and later wrote a PhD on the origins of the Palestinian refugee problem. In his 1959 thesis, Gabbay contended that the Palestinians became refugees mainly due to a policy of destruction and dispossession that was executed by local Israeli commanders in many places during the war, although at the time he found no evidence for a systematic policy of expulsion.[5] This was hardly the conclusion Ben-Gurion wished the Shiloah Institute to draw, with or without the examination of documents and archives.

Now the plot thickens. Under Gabbay's name, the Shiloah Institute provided a report, which provided Ben-Gurion's desired narrative. The main reason for the creation of the Palestinian refugee problem, it said, was that Palestinian leaders as well as leaders in neighbouring Arab countries encouraged them to leave. Even better, as Gabbay wrote in a letter in 1961, 'The last chapter of the report shows that the local Jewish leadership tried to stop the exodus of the Palestinians but to no avail'.[6]

Gabbay moved to Perth, Australia, decades ago because he found the Israeli academia to be racist towards Iraqi Jews like himself. He says he does not recall writing these conclusions. Recently he told a PhD student from New York named Shay Hazkani that he drew no conclusions; he only collected and summarised the documents, which showed that there was no encouragement from any Arab or Palestinian leaders and that there were plenty of cases of expulsion. Hazkani published a long piece in *Haaretz* on the subject in May 2013.

Ben-Gurion took a personal interest in the affair; he read Gabbay's report and was disappointed, so he asked one of his advisers on Arab affairs, Uri Lubrani, to write a new report. Lubrani in turn gave the mission to Moshe Ma'oz, who would later become one of Israel's leading Orientalists and was about to go to Oxford to complete a PhD. Ma'oz explained in a letter to another member of the institute that 'we aim to show that the exodus was caused by the encouragement by the local Arab leaders and Arab governments and was facilitated by the British government'.[7] Indeed, this conclusion – reached before the documents were even inspected – was the very same one reached afterwards.

Ma'oz told Shay Hazkani that today, in retrospect, he regrets playing such a role in the fabrication of history (indeed he later became a champion of Palestinian rights). In the meantime, this report's conclusions were the main Israeli argument used to fend off further American and international pressure. As it happens, the pressure ended when Kennedy was assassinated in November 1963. The new administration, under Lyndon B. Johnson, ceased any attempt to force Israel to repatriate the refugees, and any continued UN insistence on it was regarded by both Washington and Jerusalem as insignificant and irrelevant.[8]

Those involved in this episode recall that the documents were shredded and their reports shelved. Hazkani discovered some of it in Israeli archives decades later, but at the time, in the early 1960s and until the late 1980s, the professional as well as the popular historiography subscribed to the narrative presented above, in the third chapter.

By now, readers of this book should be familiar with the term 'new historians' of Israel. We are a group of professional Israeli historians, myself included, who have challenged the official version of the 1948 war and about whom more will be said later. In many ways, the 'new history' was nearly born in 1961, fathered by none other than David Ben-Gurion! Shelving the Gabbay report precluded that outcome.

A more familiar chapter in the local challenge to the official Israeli version of events surrounding the 1948 war began with the journalist Simha Flapan. He was an unlikely candidate to challenge the official version of the war. If anything, in the public mind after 1967 he was remembered as someone who brilliantly demolished Jean-Paul Sartre's call, upon his visit to Israel, for the unconditional return of the refugees Israel had expelled in 1948. Flapan refuted the allegation and rejected out of hand the philosopher's demand. Years later, however, he would embrace both the allegation and Sartre's solution.[9]

Born in Poland in 1911, Flapan joined the Zionist left group Mapam after arriving in Palestine in 1930. He joined Kibbutz Gan Shmuel – which appeared in our fourth chapter as the residence of several early anti-Zionist pioneers in the State of Israel – and became interested in Arab culture and language. As with many others who showed such inclinations, his knowledge was used to defeat Arab culture rather than cultivate good relations with it. In the 1930s he was already a member of the Hagana and took part in the war.

Mapam was the second largest party in the Knesset. It defined itself as a Zionist socialist party and had very strong ties to the Soviet Union until Stalin's death. In the late 1950s Flapan became the head of the party's Arab section, which succeeded in creating a constituency of a sort inside Israel's Palestinian community. He worked in the party's daily *Al HaMishmar* until he joined Martin Buber in founding the English-language journal *New Outlook* in 1957. While the journal rejected many of the oppressive policies against the

Palestinian minority inside Israel, nothing in it challenged the official
Israeli version of the 1948 war.[10]

All this changed when in retirement, in the early 1980s, Flapan
went to Harvard and met Walid Khalidi, the doyen of Palestinian
historiography at the time and someone who had devoted his life to
the chronicling of the 1948 Palestinian catastrophe. It was Khalidi
who convinced Flapan that the official Israeli version, the one Ben-
Gurion invented, was a fabrication. As Flapan wrote, 'Like most
Israelis, I had always been under the influence of certain myths that
had become accepted as historical truth.'[11] It was not until he was
seventy-three that he decided to investigate the foundational mythologies of the State of Israel. The book which summarises his findings
came out in 1987 under the title *The Birth of Israel: Myths and Realities*
(which, sadly, was published posthumously). In the book he debunks
each of these myths in an effective and convincing way.[12] The work of
those who followed him was in many ways an attempt to sustain his
research through the use of newly available material.

The first myth was that Israel accepted the UN partition resolution of 1947 and therefore agreed to the creation of a Palestinian
state next to the Jewish one over more than half of Palestine. Flapan
explained that this acceptance was 'tactical' and 'a springboard for
expansion when circumstances proved more judicious'.[13] He proved
quite convincingly that Ben-Gurion ignored the territorial dimension
of the partition resolution, which divided Palestine into two states,
and continually referred to the resolution only as granting international legitimacy for the idea of the Jewish state whose borders the
Zionist movement, and no one else, would determine.

The second myth was that all the Palestinians followed al-Hajj
Amin al-Husayni, the Grand Mufti of Jerusalem, in his resistance
to any UN peace plan. Flapan showed that al-Husayni was not very
popular and did not succeed in organising any significant resistance
to the resolution or to its implementation. In his book, Flapan introduces assessments written by Ben-Gurion's chief advisers on Arab
affairs that reaffirm his own analysis: the advisers reported to the
Zionist leader that the vast majority of Palestinians accepted partition. He further claimed that in most cases, the Palestinians resorted

to violence only for self-defence. Flapan's unconventional description of how the Palestinians reacted to the UN policy was based in part on his own memories from that period, during which he was close with top political and military leaders of the Jewish community in Palestine.[14]

The third myth was that the Arab world was determined to destroy the Jewish state in 1948. First of all, explained Flapan, the Arab world was fragmented and did not have a unified policy on the question of Palestine. Iraq and Transjordan, important powers in the Arab world and both of them Hashemite kingdoms, were seeking an understanding with the new Jewish state. As a result, Ben-Gurion concluded a secret treaty with Jordan, under which the two sides agreed to divide Palestine between them after the British withdrawal from the country. In fact, that agreement had already been reported in two sources. One was the memoirs of Abdullah al-Tall, the Jordanian commander of the Jerusalem front, who had decided to disclose these secret details because he fell afoul of his masters in the early 1950s and had to flee to Egypt.[15] The other source was Israel Baer, who was a strategic adviser to Ben-Gurion in 1948; his reason for betraying this secret was his arrest in 1961 on the charge of spying for the Soviet Union. While in jail he wrote a book titled *Israel's Security: Yesterday, Today and Tomorrow,* in which he disclosed the existence of this treaty.[16]

The fourth myth was that the Palestinians left their homes because they were told to do so by their leaders and the leaders of neighbouring Arab countries. There is 'no evidence' for such an allegation, declared Flapan. Furthermore, it made no strategic sense for the Arab side to demand such a flight, which would only have made the battlefield more complicated for them.[17] The reason the Palestinians became refugees was that the Zionist leadership was determined to reduce their numbers by all possible means.[18] Although Flapan had no access to official documentation and was only postulating that there were no direct orders of expulsion, he was convinced that there was no need for such orders, since the atmosphere was such that military commanders knew exactly what to do: namely, expel the Palestinians from their villages and towns.[19]

Yet a fifth myth was that Israel was a David that miraculously defeated an Arab Goliath. Flapan was convinced that at any given stage in the confrontation of 1948 'the superiority of the Jew[ish forces] ... was never in dispute'. In addition, the 'Goliath' was disunited and weakened by internal strife and animosity.[20]

Flapan's sixth and final myth was that Israel extended its hand for peace after the war and was rejected by the Arab states and the Palestinians. He refutes this assertion by pointing to the Lausanne Protocol, signed on 12 May 1949 by Egypt, Jordan, Lebanon, Syria, and Israel in an international peace conference on Palestine convened by the United Nations. That protocol set three principal guidelines for peace in Palestine: recognition of the earlier partition plan and therefore, the existence of Israel, the internationalisation of Jerusalem, and the repatriation of Palestinian refugees. Flapan further showed that there were serious initiatives for peace on the part of Syria and Jordan that were rejected by the Israeli government.[21]

One year later, in 1988, in the liberal, American Jewish journal *Tikkun*, the historian Benny Morris discussed Flapan's work along with his, mine, and that of Avi Shlaim as constituting a new wave in Israeli historiography concerning 1948, and he coined the term 'the new history of Israel'.[22] The term caught on and has been used ever since. The following year, in an article in *Haaretz*, the prominent Israeli historian Shabtai Teveth adopted the term 'new history' for the books we have written; he also rejected our findings and accused us of treason.[23] This was the start of a long discussion on our findings, which led to a more general debate on the scholarly challenge of the idea of Israel and which is discussed in subsequent chapters. But in Israel at least, 'new history' until today refers to that group of historians who challenge the accepted version of the 1948 war.

And yet this term, borrowed from the 'new history' in Europe, is misleading. The European 'new history' was an interdisciplinary effort to place diplomatic and élite history in a wider social and non-élite context. The Israeli 'new historians', in contrast, questioned only the élite analysis of politics. For this reason, they/we would more aptly be described as revisionists, in a sense similar to the revisionist school in American historiography on the Cold War. One difficulty with this term, however, is that it creates confusion with the Revisionist historians – namely, historians who belong to the Revisionist Zionist movement of the right.[24] An additional problem with the term is that in Germany, France and Italy, 'revisionist' is also associated with those who tend to minimise the horror of the Holocaust or the Nazi-Fascist experience.

In any case, what all our works had in common was that they jointly debunked the fundamental Israeli mythologies of the 1948 war. Let me now recap who we were and what were our motives, as well as our main contributions and how they related to the mainstream narratives on both sides.

The 'New Historians'

Let us first look at the period during which we produced our challenge. The Israeli assault on Lebanon in June 1982 appeared to be a retaliation for the abortive assassination attempt on the Israeli ambassador in London but was really an operation meant to destroy the PLO's base in Lebanon. The assault failed to win public support in Israel itself, and thus became the first non-consensual war in Israel's history.

The oppositional public opinion concerning the war set a precedent. It branded the war in Lebanon as unnecessary and a war of choice. Questioning the logic or justification for a war had hitherto been taboo. For professional historians, the assault on Lebanon was a watershed, as it opened up the inquiry into Israel's previous wars. Further doubts arose, especially among the intellectual and cultural élite, when the First Intifada – an unarmed uprising in the occupied territories – was brutally crushed by the Israeli army in 1987.

The Palestinians now appeared, not as the enemy, but as the victim: the weaker party in the balance of power. The First Intifada was a clash between an army and a civilian population, and consequently it reminded at least some of us of the clashes of 1948. Many confrontations during the 1987 uprising took place in the refugee camps of 1948 and were seen by the Palestinians themselves as part of the same struggle they had been involved in ever since their dis-possession forty years earlier. Thus the 1980s brought back, for both sides, memories of the 1948 war. And for some of us it also triggered new thinking about the past.

The work on 1948 was executed while an inevitable comparison was consciously or unconsciously affecting our reconstruction of the past. The attitudes and policies of 1987 looked relevant to the 1948 war. That even the mainstream Israeli press called the situation in 1987 a war with the Palestinians and explored the similarities to 1948 only accentuated the fact that what was done and condemned in 1987 had already been done in 1948. As for the atrocities Israel had committed in Lebanon, we felt unable to identify with the war's goals and plans, even though we were all Zionists in one way or another. Additional doubts, for myself, and I think as well for the other two 'new historians', appeared when we found ourselves unable to iden-tify with the brutal Israeli response to the uprising in the occupied territories that broke out in December 1987.

Benny Morris was born in Israel in 1948 to an Anglo-Jewish family. His father was an Israeli diplomat serving in various Western posts, including the United Nations in New York, where Morris spent much of his youth. He graduated from the Hebrew University of Jerusalem and finished his PhD studies in Cambridge with a thesis on modern European history. His interest in the history of the con-flict was aroused by his journalistic work, which he started at the *Jerusalem Post* in the late 1970s, and in particular through his cover-age of the 1982 Israeli invasion of Lebanon. In 1988, as a reserve soldier, he refused to be posted in occupied Nablus. For his refusal, he spent three weeks in jail.

That same year, Morris published *The Birth of the Palestinian Refugee Problem, 1947–1949*, in which he confirmed Flapan's refu-tations of the fourth foundational myth: that the Palestinians left their homes because they were ordered to do so by their leaders in and outside the country. Like Flapan – and before Flapan, the Irish journalist Erskine Childers – he found no evidence for such a state-ment. As for Flapan's claim that the refugee problem was caused by multiple instances of expulsion and dispossession, Morris was able to verify this by mining the Israeli archives of both the IDF and the paramilitary organisations.

Israel followed British law and so declassified political documents after thirty years and security documents after fifty years. Thus, by 1978, both the British and the Israeli documents on 1948 were open to the public. Morris worked mainly in the archives of the Hagana and the IDF, looking at reports from the battlefield and discussions among the politicians of the day. He concluded that the archival material did not indicate a systematic plan to expel Palestinians but that the residents' inevitable fear and the consequences of the fighting were the major causes that led people to leave their homes. But in a very detailed manner, he did adduce quite a few cases in which local commanders in fact decided to expel the population. In addition, he pointed out that there was a deliberate policy not to allow them to return. When this book was published in Hebrew in 1991, it was for many Israeli readers their first encounter with the possibility that their army had expelled people by force. The fact that Palestinians were not allowed to return seemed to all of Morris's reviewers and readers the only possible policy that a Jewish democracy could have adopted.

Avi Shlaim made similar use of the declassified material, in his case to reaffirm Flapan's refutation of the third foundational myth: that the Arab world was united in its determination to destroy the future Jewish state. Shlaim was born in Baghdad in 1945 and emigrated to Israel in 1951.[25] As a sixteen-year-old, he was sent to England to complete his high school studies. He went back to Israel, served in the army, and then returned to England, completing his BA in history at Cambridge and then a PhD at the University of Reading in the early 1970s, where he was a lecturer until moving to St Antony's College at Oxford in the 1980s. As with Morris, Shlaim's doctoral dissertation dealt with European history, and it was the 1982 Israeli invasion of Lebanon that orientated him towards the history of the Arab–Israel conflict in general and that of the 1948 war in particular.

Shlaim focused on the secret negotiations between the Hashemite Kingdom of Jordan (Transjordan until 1949) and the Zionist leadership. His book *Collusion Across the Jordan: King Abdullah, the Zionist Movement, and the Partition of Palestine* followed these negotiations from the moment they began in the 1930s until their culmination in a tacit understanding that allocated to Jordan parts of Palestine that the UN defined as the future Arab state in its partition resolution of November 1947.[26] This pre-1948 war agreement neutralised the Jordanian army and confined its activity to the Jerusalem area. In many ways, Shlaim showed that this tacit understanding explained the Jewish success on the battlefield. The Jordanians had the only modern army in the Arab world; it had battle experience and included a strong contingent of British officers. The Arab Legion was thus the ablest Arab army, and so its neutralisation and limitation to one front, the Jerusalem front, removed a serious threat to the existence of the young state. The claim of a prior agreement also forms an important chapter in the Palestinian narrative.

In my own career as a historian, the 1982 war loomed large. It was an assault that ended in the loss of tens of thousands of Palestinians and Lebanese, and culminated in the brutal Israeli occupation of Beirut. The massacre of Palestinians in Sabra and Shatila by Christian Phalangists, with the full knowledge of the occupying Israeli army, caused hundreds of thousands of Israeli Jews to demonstrate, for the first time in the state's history, against an ongoing army operation.

I was born in Israel in 1954 and graduated from the Hebrew University in 1979. During the research phase of my doctorate studies at St Antony's College, Oxford, the 1982 war broke out. I had been working on British policy during the 1948 war. In the resulting book, *Britain and the Arab–Israeli Conflict, 1948–1951*, I relied mainly on British documents released in the 1980s.[27] In so doing, I completed the picture of collusion drawn by Avi Shlaim by highlighting Britain's part in it.

In classical Zionist historiography, Britain was mainly pro-Hashemite and played a highly negative role. But it turned out that even the 'villain' Ernest Bevin opposed the idea of an independent Palestinian state and supported, as did the rest of his staff, the partitioning of post-Mandatory Palestine between the Jews and the Hashemites, which he viewed as the best means of safeguarding British interests in the area. Shlaim and I thus corrected the demonised image of Britain in Israeli collective memory; we showed Britain's behaviour to have been neutral in the conflict and even, on various occasions, pro-Israeli.[28]

But in *Britain and the Arab–Israeli Conflict* I accuse British forces of indifference towards the dispossession of the Palestinians. The British troops watched the expulsion of the Palestinians and at times, such as in Haifa and Jaffa, played a dubious role by exerting pressure of their own on the resident population to leave or be exposed to the Zionist occupation, undefended by the British. As a result, they facilitated the transfer of the Palestinians from both these cities.

I have also shown that the British intelligence documents reaffirm Flapan's refutation of the story that the war of 1948 was fought between an Arab Goliath and a Zionist David. The British chiefs of staff wrote a highly detailed assessment of the balance of power on the eve of the war, which was to be sent to the cabinet in London. It was based mainly on reports submitted by the various British advisers to the heads of the Arab armies at the time. Each in turn, the Arab armies were assessed as being unable to endure for more than a brief period on the battlefield.[29]

For a book I wrote shortly afterwards, *The Making of the Arab–Israeli Conflict, 1947–1951*, I also excavated available Arab documentation of the war.[30] I looked at the reports of the military commanders to their political masters, in which they drew a dismal picture of their armies' level of preparation, commitment, and ability to perform on the battlefield. As I have shown, this led the Arab League, and most of the Arab leaders to request the international community to prolong the Mandate over Palestine and to seek a new peace plan. But the massacre at Deir Yassin, in which 250 innocent civilians were slaughtered on the north-western slopes of the Jerusalem mountains, together with the forced depopulation of most of the Palestinian towns, pushed public opinion towards a demand for action in Palestine. In any case, the international community disregarded these desperate calls and insisted that only the UN partition plan was the way forward. And yet, as I showed, one day before the actual war broke out, most Arab leaders were still trying to avoid a military operation that they knew only too well would end in a fiasco. The final decision to enter Palestine was taken on May 14, 1948.

In addition, I confronted one of the main arguments raised against Flapan: that his depiction of the balance of power as favouring the Zionist side could not be right because of the high number of Jewish casualties in the war (one per cent of the community). In fact, considerable numbers of casualties were caused by local and civil clashes during the period preceding the war itself; regular Arab troops were not involved in these confrontations, and therefore the losses could not have been attributed to their firepower or superiority. I also stressed that Ben-Gurion's policy of trying to defend isolated settlements led to some unnecessary and desperate battles that did not necessarily reflect the overall balance of power. Finally, I argued that the great number of casualties in the battle for Jerusalem and its vicinity could have been avoided, since the parties involved (the Jordanians and the Israelis) had already reached non-aggression arrangements regarding other fronts in Palestine.[31]

The balance of power was further enhanced in Israel's favour due to a successful diplomatic campaign. The achievements on that front were attributable to a rare cooperation between the two warring superpowers in 1947, with each for its own reasons supporting the Zionist cause against the Palestinians.

The Truman administration was probably the first ever to succumb to the power of a Jewish lobby (although in those days there was no AIPAC or a structured effort). In February 1948 the administration was still giving serious consideration to replacing the partition plan with a new scheme that would extend the Mandate over Palestine for an additional five years and would seek a new solution. But this approach was abandoned after prominent Jewish leaders visited the president in the White House to exert pressure on him. Although his secretary of state, George Marshall, was not enthusiastic about the creation of a Jewish state, his military strategists hoped it would become an asset in the ensuing Cold War. I have also shown that Truman was moved by his visit to the Holocaust sites and that he accepted the Zionist contention that the best response to the atrocity was the creation of a Jewish state in Palestine.

As for the Soviet Union, it hoped that the Jewish state would be on its side in the Cold War because of the prominent role played by socialist parties in the Jewish community – Israel's second-largest party, Mapam, respected Stalin and his policies, and Stalin's death became an official day of mourning for the Kibbutz Movement. The Communist Party was also very loyal to Moscow, and some of its members helped the Hagana purchase weapons in the Eastern bloc (Britain and France had imposed an embargo on arms sales to both sides).

This dual backing also ensured victory in the United Nations. 'The world' was not 'against us', as the Israeli myth declared. In fact, the world opposed the basic Palestinian demand to recognise their demographic majority as a basis for the creation of an independent state in Palestine. Generally speaking, the Zionists succeeded in persuading large segments of world opinion to accept the idea of Israel as the best response to the horrors of the Holocaust. Against such a claim, even able Palestinian diplomats – and there were not many in those days – could hardly win the diplomatic game, as was faithfully reflected in the UN Special Committee on Palestine, UNSCOP.[32]

Taken together, these points showed that the success of the Jewish side was explained by the overall parity of forces on the ground, the understanding with the Transjordanians, and international support and pressure. Clearly, victory had not been delivered by some kind of miraculous good fortune, as the official historiography would have it.

In my book I also took some issue with Benny Morris's analysis of the making of the refugee problem. It was a scholarly debate that turned bitter in the next century. For purposes of the future marketing of the idea of Israel, the myth of the Palestinians' voluntary flight was the most important myth challenged by the 'new historians'. This is why many of the documents on the expulsions and atrocities committed by Israeli soldiers have been reclosed to the public.

Morris, as was pointed out, debunked this myth in his book. Nevertheless, he did not accept the Palestinian historiographical claim, first made by Walid Khalidi in 1961, that the expulsion was part of a master plan.[33] This difference of opinion showed that there was still a gap between the Palestinian national narrative and the 'new history'. It did not seem crucial at the time, but this distinction would later become perilous and would reveal Morris to be more loyal to the Zionist narrative than he had seemed to be at first. The casting of blame and responsibility on Israel was not simply an argument about historical accuracy; it was also a debate about the solution to the refugee problem.[34]

For example, the intentional expulsion, which I have elsewhere called 'ethnic cleansing', located the Israeli actions in 1948 within the history of war crimes, and even crimes against humanity, with wider implications for a future solution of the problem.[35] Later, Israel's responsibility for the Palestinian refugee problem would become an important issue in the diplomatic war with the Arab world. World opinion – however elusive that term may be – while supporting Israel's right to exist, nonetheless sympathised with the plight of the refugees. Moreover, even pro-Zionists could not ignore Israel's responsibility for the problem, a problem that has been persistently shunned by Israeli governments to this day.

Lastly, my second book tackled the final myth that Flapan refuted: Israel's relentless and unreciprocated search for peace. This chapter in the 'new history' was missing from the Palestinian narrative. I claimed that there was a genuine willingness on the part of most of the Arab governments, along with what was left of the Palestinian leadership, to negotiate a settlement over Palestine after the war. This agreement was based on the Arab acceptance of the 1947 partition recommendation and the repatriation of the refugees. Avi Shlaim, in another, later book, *The Iron Wall: Israel and the Arab World* (2000), further undermined Israel's self-image as the relentless peace seeker and claimed that it had failed to exhaust opportunities for peace with its Arab neighbours from 1948 until our own time.[36] Both of us showed that Israel did not extend its hand in peace, and in fact rejected such gestures on the part of a considerable number of Arab leaders. It was the intransigence of Ben-Gurion (his foreign minister, Moshe Sharett, had been more forthcoming) that had blocked the chances for peace in that era.

Two additional books should be mentioned. The first was Tom Segev's *1949: The First Israelis*, which exposed documents that strengthened the major points made by the above-mentioned 'new historians' in our work. Segev was born in 1945 in Jerusalem to

German Jewish parents who arrived in Palestine in 1935; his father died in the 1948 war. After graduating from the Hebrew University in Jerusalem, he completed his academic studies at Boston University with a PhD on the commanders of the Nazi death camps. Since 1979 he has written for *Haaretz*; periodically he publishes books on the modern history of Israel. In his book *1949*, Segev collated documents that exposed the attitudes of the Jewish political and cultural élite to whoever was different from them, beginning with the way Palestinians in the occupied villages and towns were treated from the first moment of their surrender or occupation.[37]

The second book was published in 2002 but belongs to this slightly earlier group of works: Meron Benvenisti's *Sacred Landscape: The Buried History of the Holy Land Since 1948*.[38] This work helped complete the historiographical picture of the dispossession of the Palestinians in 1948. Having been born in Jerusalem in 1934, Benvenisti was half a generation older than Morris, Shlaim, and I were. After a short initial academic career, he became involved in local politics in Jerusalem and served, from 1971 to 1978, as the deputy to the city's legendary mayor, Teddy Kollek. He became internationally renowned for a project he conducted on Jewish settlement in the West Bank and the Gaza Strip, concluding that the settlements had become such a fait accompli that it would be impossible ever to dismantle them. As a result, he called for a binational state as the only feasible solution.[39]

In between writing, as he still does today on that particular issue, he wrote one book on the 1948 events. In it he explored the enthusiasm with which Israel erased the Palestinians' abandoned villages and transformed them into cultivated land or new Jewish settlements. Archaeologists and architects also took part in the festivities by demonstrating that Arab villages were located on ancient biblical places and suggesting that the Jewish settlements built over them might carry a Hebrew name that sounded like the Arab name of the village, thereby creating a narrative that claims that a given site was first a Jewish place, in biblical times, before becoming Arabised for a time, and was now being properly redeemed. Thus, Lubya became Lavi, Saffuriya became Tzipori, and Maan remained Maan.

All the works discussed above have reaffirmed through archival documents what Flapan found between the lines of the published material available to him at the time. But their significance also lies in the ways they challenged mainstream interpretation of the idea of Israel. The situation was changing. There was now an atmosphere in which it was easier to write a historical version that was as alive to the Palestinian narrative as to the Zionist one. The peace activity on both sides allowed for a more open dialogue between Israeli and Palestinian scholars, and finally one could begin to hear on Israeli university campuses academic versions of the Palestinian narrative of 1948. In some cases, the recognition of the other side of the story, even to the point of adopting it as the rightful interpretation, was the result of a newfound ideological stance; in others, it was the consequence of adopting a more relativist and multi-narrative approach to history; in still others, it was both.

The Significance of the 1948 Historiography

The 'new history' signified a new chapter in the production of knowledge in Israel because it was the work of professional Israeli historians whose specialised area of inquiry was the Arab–Israeli conflict. But their impact was limited, because of the scores of Israeli historians who entered the Public Record Office in Kew Gardens and the Israeli State Archives in the basement of the prime minister's offices in Jerusalem (nowadays it moved to a new place in the south of the city), only a few emerged as 'new historians' – that is to say, historians convinced that the evidence they had seen challenged a formative chapter in the consolidation of the idea of Israel. Indeed, documents are not the only bricks with which a historiographical picture is built. The prism through which one interprets the evidence differs from one historian to another, and that prism is suffused with his or her ideological background and political outlook. The documents we have been discussing became an explosive and even sensational discovery only when scrutinised though a highly critical prism on Zionism in general and Israeli contemporary policies in particular.

The 'new history' of the 1948 war had a twofold effect on Israeli historiography: it legitimatised the historical narrative of the Palestinians, and it offered a potential for normalising the national collective memory. It did not adopt – and this is worth reiterating – the Palestinian narrative in its entirety. In the case of the 1948 war there are specific chapters in the new Israeli narrative, such as the claim that the British were neutral, that are still rejected by Palestinian historiographers. Nor does the reference to an Arab willingness to compromise with Israel after the 1948 war – even though it portrays Israel as the intransigent party – appeal to what may be called either the collective Palestinian memory of the period or the pan-Arabist memory, inasmuch as it shows a lack of serious Arab commitment to the cause of Palestine. But those caveats do not undermine the overall contribution. With regard to the history of knowledge production on Palestine, and the challenge to the Zionist marketing of the idea of Israel, the 'new history' of the 1948 war is the most profound legitimisation given by Israeli scholarship to any chapter in the Palestinian narrative.

The 'new historians' thus presented, in a purely positivist way, what they believed was the true nature of Israeli behaviour – or rather, misbehaviour – towards the Arab world and the Palestinians in 1948. They drew a picture of which most Israelis were unaware, and it provoked angry reactions from public figures and press commentators. As mentioned, Shabtai Teveth, the respected biographer of David Ben-Gurion and a senior journalist for *Haaretz*, branded the 'new historians' as traitors. Others followed suit, although more soberly, and were willing to engage in some degree of public debate about the findings but a far greater degree of debate about our motives. Name-calling characterised the initial response to the publication of the work of the 'new historians'. I recall a conference at the University of Haifa, an early conference devoted to the 'new history', at which the head of the history department suggested that the research being pursued by the new group was tantamount to treason during a time of war. Later, in an article in *Haaretz*, he called me Israel's Lord Haw-Haw.[40]

Nevertheless, when Morris and Shlaim began to study the

aftermath of 1948 and on into the 1950s, the early years of state-hood, they took the same critical approach to the Zionist narrative. Before 1967, Israeli policy had never been depicted as aggressive, to say nothing of occasionally brutal and inhuman and quite often morally unjustifiable. While there was little in the work of the 'new historians' that dealt with historiography, and specifically Zionist historiography, their/our works did serve to highlight mainstream academia's repression of the truth and its participation in the fabrica-tion of the national narrative about 1948.

Revisiting the First Decade of Statehood

The research on 1948 that was carried out during the 1980s paved the way for a more fundamental criticism of Zionism and its role in Israeli academia. In addition, the media coverage of this issue en-couraged scholars to go beyond the topic of 1948, both in themat-ics and in chronology. The same socio-economic and political back-ground that produced what I have called the academic pioneers and the new history also contributed to the shaping of a new research agenda about the first decade of statehood. This period, 1948–58, seemed to attract not only professional academics but also novelists, film-makers, playwrights, musicians, poets, artists, and journalists, who represented their version of events in a way that did not tally with the collective memory nurtured and maintained by the state through all its agencies and apparatuses.

What differentiated this new energy, apart from the choice of topics and methodology, from anything that preceded it was its almost matter-of-fact acceptance of Zionism as an ideology and not as an ideal reality. As such, scholars could not be neutral about it; they must be either for or against it. This aspect of the debate was absent from the 'new history'. Our new history of 1948 was based on a new ideological approach, even though Morris and Shlaim denied that this was the case and thus upheld the claim to academic objec-tivity with the same vigour and conviction as had their predecessors. As for myself, I was inclined to engage with the impact of power on knowledge as an overall part of our work. The present book is in many ways the result of this engagement.

The next wave of new historiography in Israel, however, was motivated by just such an impulse. This new approach emerged among a group of young Israeli social scientists who added a historical perspective to their attempt to understand contemporary Israeli society. Their challenge was not based on new evidence; rather, they read the documents differently. More important, they searched for a different kind of evidence that could not necessarily be found in the political archives. As a result, they were as critical of the past as they were of the present social situation in Israel. In fact, they attributed the contemporary unease of, and cleavages within, the society to government policies in the early years of statehood and, in particular, to the inherent contradiction between Zionism and values such as democracy and liberalism.

This new wave of challengers, to which I devote the following chapter, started a conversation at the heart of which lay several questions never before asked in Israel: How is academic knowledge produced? How does it serve or abuse the interests of the society, and how can it be made more equitable and democratic? The answers were drawn both from far away, from the United States, and from very close to home, from the social reality around them.

SIX

The Emergence of Post-Zionist
Academia, 1990–2000

In the autumn of 1994, a group of mainstream Israeli scholars met their young challengers for an open discussion at the secular mausoleum of Zionism, the burial place of David Ben-Gurion, on the desert plateau that the Israelis call the Negev and the Palestinians al-Naqab. Today the grave is still a ceremonial space for commemorating past glories and spelling out bold visions for the future.[1]

It was a bit ironic that the defamers and violators of the shrine, myself included, were asked to come and share the sacred space. The introduction to the volume that came out of this meeting shows that there was a hope of converting us back to Zionism even while embracing the principle of free exchange of thought and ideas. Nevertheless, since a discussion at Sunday Mass on the existence of God is by itself a refreshing moment in the history of any religion, this discussion on the existence of Zionism was no exception. It was there that I heard the term 'post-Zionism' for the first time as a description of the renegades who dared question the truisms of Zionism.

The year 1994 was a good one for apostates like us. It was the year after the Oslo Accords were signed between Israel and the PLO. There was a hopeful public atmosphere, and it made possible a meeting such as the one that took place at the very heart of the Zionist establishment. Nor was it a unique event. Anyone who visited Israeli academia in the 1990s would have sensed a changed place, one that had nothing in common with what preceded (or, as it turned out, succeeded) it. From every poster-crammed wall you would be invited to conferences and seminars to discuss topics that had hitherto been taboo in the Jewish state: Zionism as colonialism, the Nakba, discrimination against the Arab Jews, the manipulation of Holocaust memory. Even more daring were the articles you could have read during that period, both in academic journals and in the popular press, about these and similar topics that before (and after) the 1990s were deemed subversive and unprofessional.

These winds of openness and adventure blew not only in the corridors of academia but also across the public domain. New conversations about the past, as well as the present, seeped into chat shows on radio and television. There was a sense that these discussions could perhaps serve as a new source of inspiration for textbooks and high school curricula. Soldiers and officers were invited to attend debates and discussions on 'the new history of 1948' or Israel's policies in the 1950s.

As a whole, the 1990s were a decade in which the entire idea of Israel was questioned. The evidence for this enterprise is readily available: dozens of books in English and Hebrew, hundreds of articles and conference papers, similar numbers of op-eds, numerous appearances on television and radio talk shows. All show academics pointing a guilty finger at their own milieu for providing the scholarly scaffolding for acts of repression, oppression and discrimination. This deconstructive effort affected virtually every discipline in the Israeli human sciences: arts, history, philosophy, political science, literary criticism, and many other fields in the social sciences and humanities. The local press labelled this new energy 'post-Zionist', but was ambivalent about whether it was a positive development or a dangerous deterioration. The term 'post-Zionism' became generic for describing any academic critique on Zionism from within Jewish Israel. It was used equally by those who complimented themselves and gladly identified as post-Zionists because they challenged Zionism head-on, and by those who condemned the challengers as traitors to the idea of Israel. There is no easy Wikipedia definition for 'post-Zionism' and, like so many other such phenomena, it is preferable to describe it in full rather than attempt to define it.

What Is Post-Zionism?

Nearly twenty years after I first heard the term near the burial place of the state's founder, I think 'post-Zionism' warrants some elaboration. In the course of those twenty years, no one has been able to come up with a definition shorter than four pages, dotted with endless recurrences of 'but' and 'nonetheless', in an attempt to clarify this elusive phenomenon. Clearly there is no simple definition for this working term, whose claim to fame is that it enabled interested parties to lump together a disparate group of a few hundred academics and cultural challengers to Zionism in the 1990s. However, it is worth trying to provide at least a moderately focused and detailed reflection of the motivations of these academics, their areas of inquiry, and their impact on media and society.

But first allow me to chart some common characteristics of these challengers, in so far as that is possible. The easiest way forward is to detect their internal debates so that the scope of their critique may be appreciated. The most important debate among them concerned ideology. This group included anti-Zionists as well as Zionists. The former despised the adjective 'post-Zionist' when it was applied to them and insisted that it better suited those who, despite their critique, remained Zionists, whereas the latter gladly adopted an adjective that they hoped would not brand them as traitors to their own society.[2]

Another discussion concerned the importance ascribed to the debate about Zionism in the 1990s. Among the challengers one could find those who regarded it as a local conversation about the production of knowledge in Israel and academia's role in it in particular. Others, by contrast, took it far more seriously and believed they were deliberating the very essence and soul of Zionism, in hopes of impacting the identity and nature of the state in years to come.

The different ambitions were also manifested in the personal projects undertaken by these challengers of Zionism. Some were truffle hunters, if I may use the favourable term employed by the French historian Emmanuel Le Roy Ladurie and adopted by the British historian Lawrence Stone when describing microhistorians, who knew everything at the level of historical anecdote about the life of Zionism and Israel but did not contextualise their particular research in a more general challenge to Zionism. Others were parachutists, to use Stone's image of macrohistorians, who offered a comprehensive overview of Zionist and Israeli past and present realities but without providing concrete evidence for their challenge.[3] The best works were, of course, those that were able to integrate both approaches to history.

Another debate was between positivist and relativist historians. The former regarded the Zionist narrative as a fabrication of historical fact and saw their work as offering the truthful version of Israel's history. The latter sought only to legitimatise additional narratives and versions of the past and the present, with the goal of undermining the hegemonic role of the Zionist narrative.

Finally, there was uncertainty whether this endeavour was a Western or an anti-Western project. Because the challenge that inspired them was directed at Western civilisation, some of those who exposed the injustices and wrongdoing in Israeli society analysed them as the inevitable illusions and fallacies created by 'the Enlightenment', 'modernity', and 'Westernisation'. Others critically reviewed Zionism and Israel as a failed case study of those very same processes, which they viewed as highly positive.

So can Zionists and anti-Zionists – whether light-hearted or serious, modest or ambitious, relativist or positivist, academic or artistic – be regarded as part of the same phenomenon? As I cannot offer a sound-bite definition of post-Zionism, let me instead propose a generational identity card.

We were a Jewish group, ably representing Israel's Jewish ethnic mix. While most members were secular, it was possible to find religious Jews among us as well. As has already been mentioned, the group included academics, film-makers, playwrights, journalists, artists, educators, writers and poets; the academics came from a variety of disciplines but were mainly historians and sociologists. All of us, in one way or another, in our professional work, challenged basic truisms of Zionism. The more sacred the cow we slaughtered, the more anti-Zionist we were deemed, by ourselves or by the public.

But this raises a legitimate question I have often been asked: why not call the individuals anti-Zionist, and the entire phenomenon anti-Zionism? Indeed, a reasonable case can be made for the adjective 'anti-Zionist'. After all, the hundreds of academics described here as post-Zionist were the successors of the anti-Zionist critics who had emerged when Zionism itself arose. In more than one respect, this challenge from within is a link in a longer chain that goes back to the late nineteenth century. Like those I have named the trailblazers, these early disputants, too, left behind them the comfort zone of consensual Zionism because its actions and ambitions clashed with the universal values they believed in as Jews and as human beings.

So why not call them anti-Zionists? First and foremost, most of them refused to be identified as such and marketed themselves as post-Zionists, a choice that should be respected. According to an explanation frequently offered by some of them, they chose this term because it fitted the 'post-' era in which they lived, with its postcolonialism, post-nationalism, post-structuralism and postmodernism. All these 'posts' were ways of asserting a certain degree of break from a thesis – the -ism – but not a total negation of it. Whether this can be done or not is another question, and in fact, quite a few self-defined post-Zionists would later call themselves anti-Zionists.

Watching this phenomenon both from the inside, as I was one of these people, and from the outside, as a historian of the movement, I think the prefix 'post-' signalled a measure of caution and a sense of insecurity about the project the dissenters had undertaken. Their doubts were articulated in a far more guarded way than that chosen by the trailblazers of Chapter 3 above, and their commitment to scholarly discourse tamed and even at times watered down their criticism. They felt themselves to be part of Zionism and wished to retain some of its ambitions and aspirations while negating especially the negative mainstream ideological perceptions of the Other, whether a Palestinian, a Mizrachi Jew or a Holocaust survivor. As Hannan

Hever, a scholar of Hebrew literature who recently joined the faculty of Yale University, commented, by calling himself a post-Zionist he felt he took responsibility for the evils as well as the achievements, of Zionism.[4]

On questions of definition, it is always helpful to listen to those who have watched a phenomenon from the outside and are less pre-occupied with the issue of an accurate definition, but nonetheless have a grasp of what they see. Sometime in the early 1990s, soci-ologists of knowledge in Israel and abroad noticed that the critique voiced in the past by individuals was now being articulated in a sys-tematic, scholarly way and acknowledged by a relatively large number of academics, who offered reflexive and intuitive descriptions, two of which I have found particularly helpful.

Edward Said in 1998 and Perry Anderson in 2001 described post-Zionism as a welcome movement of self-critique on what was wrong and dangerous about Zionism and Israel in the past and the present, although both lamented that it did not go far enough; in addition, both visited Israel during the hyperactive phase of post-Zionism and were thus able to convey the tenor of the post-Zionist atmosphere to their readers.

After a 1998 meeting in Paris, organised by *Le Monde Diplomatique*, between Palestinian historians and a handful of Israel's new histori-ans, Said said he was impressed that 'home truths can be heard which are blasphemy in the diaspora',[5] but he was also disappointed that the Israelis he met still wished to determine the research agenda and were blind to the Palestinian side of the story:

> Only Ilan Pappe, an avowed socialist and anti-Zionist historian at Haifa University, was open in his espousal of the Palestinian point of view, and, in my opinion, provided the most iconoclastic and brilliant of the Israeli interventions. For the others in varying degree, Zionism was seen as a necessity for Jews. I was surprised, for instance, when Sternhell during the final session admitted that a grave injustice was committed against the Palestinians, and that the essence of Zionism was that it was a movement for conquest, then went on to say that it was a 'necessary' conquest.[6]

He was equally disappointed with Benny Morris:

> One of the most remarkable things about the Israelis, again except
> for Pappe, is the profound contradiction, bordering on schizo-
> phrenia, that informs their work. Benny Morris, for example, ten
> years ago wrote the most important Israeli work on the birth of the
> Palestinian refugee problem ... Morris' meticulous work showed
> that in district after district commanders had been ordered to
> drive out Palestinians, burn villages, systematically take over their
> homes and property. Yet strangely enough, by the end of the book
> Morris seems reluctant to draw the inevitable conclusions from
> his own evidence. Instead of saying outright that the Palestinians
> were, in fact, driven out he says that they were partially driven out
> by Zionist forces, and partially 'left' as a result of war. It is as if he
> was still enough of a Zionist to believe the ideological version –
> that Palestinians left on their own without Israeli eviction – rather
> than completely to accept his own evidence, which is that Zionist
> policy dictated Palestinian exodus.[7]

And this is what Perry Anderson had to say: 'The emergence of a
"post-Zionist" scholarship and – as yet small – sector of opinion is
one of the most welcome developments in recent years. The context
in which it has appeared, however, is a warning against any exaggerated optimism.'[8]

Said and Anderson made two valid points. The first is that post-
Zionism is a convenient term for measuring the distance that these
scholars travelled out of the Zionist camp. And it seems that many of
them did not go far enough, as Said and Anderson lamented. (As a
result, one might add, under the pressure of events and public wrath
after 2000 they were still close enough to the tribal space to return
to its warm embrace.) The second is that, more than anything else,
post-Zionism was a mood, and that when it changed, as moods do,
it could easily be declared dead, which is what one Israeli journalist declared in *Haaretz* in September 2001. Alas, at least from the
perspective of this writer, it was. This book is in many ways post-
Zionism's post-mortem.

Why 1994?

I have artificially located the emergence of post-Zionism in 1994 and have connected it to the Oslo process. Of course, developments such as a new discourse or a new academic orientation are not born in a specific moment, and yet that year symbolised the coming-together of the processes I already described as the background for the 'new history of the 1948 war' a decade earlier. In many ways, post-Zionism was a delayed reaction to the same socio-political and socio-economic processes that had produced the earlier critique at the University of Haifa and among the activists of Matzpen and similar groups in the 1970s.

It took a few years for perceptive academics to digest the wider implications of the First Intifada and the peace treaty with the PLO. Ironically, the short-lived emergence of a post-Zionist point of view seems to have been the only positive result of these two monumental events, which otherwise failed to change even modestly the daily reality of the Palestinian people, whether they were under direct occupation in the West Bank and the Gaza Strip, second-class citizens within Israel, or refugees. It would be, as we shall see, another monumental event – the Second Intifada – that would bury this positive reaction for the time being.

Ironically, when the 'new historians' published their first works, around 1988, the full impact and meaning of the first uprising in the occupied territories had not yet been fully taken on board. This unarmed Palestinian protest movement, the First Intifada, dramatically tilted world opinion in the West against Israel. This shift impressed Israel's cultural élite, although it was totally ignored by the political sector. The academics, journalists and artists of Israel were and are an organic part of the Western cultural and academic scene. Hence, a shift in their global milieu was bound to impact the way these Israelis were viewing the present and, by extension, also the past. Moreover, the corpus already published by the 'new historians' made it easier for others to follow suit, each in his or her field.

The 'new historians' began as three or four people; the earlier anti-Zionist scholars numbered only a handful as well. Nevertheless, the

1990s saw the endorsement of their views by scores of academics, inspired by twin developments. The first was the transformation of Israeli society from being relatively homogenous to being multicultural. In this new environment, two groups in particular attracted the attention of academics: the Mizrachi Jews and the Palestinians inside Israel and under occupation. To a lesser extent, this was also the time when feminism made inroads into Israeli politics and universities.

The academics' decision about what to revisit was influenced mainly by the agenda of social activists who had been engaged in protest movements since the early 1970s. Academics quite often lag behind social activists when it comes to challenging realities that are taken for granted. But when they do, they themselves become social activists (a role many of them do not like, which may be another factor in the demise of the movement). The decision about how to revisit these uncomfortable chapters of the past was imported from the West, in particular from the United States.

The focus of the new research was history, of which one particular period attracted these challengers: the first decade of statehood, the 1950s. It appeared in their work as a formative period in which most of the ills of Israeli society emerged for the first time, formulated either as policies from above or as attitudes from below. Established academics viewed the first decade of statehood, or rather the first nineteen years of statehood, up to 1967, as exactly the opposite. To them it was the golden age – if mistakes were made, they could be forgiven and absolved because this was a pioneering era. To some extent, that benevolent view had to do with admiration for the great men of the past, who inevitably erred from time to time, but mostly it came from the attitude that the problems faced by the society were not the outcome of bad policies or immoral ideology, and that the policies pursued were the only options at the time. As Israel was still a poor country during the early years of statehood, the only way it could receive immigrants from the Arab world was by pushing them into poor 'development towns' and allowing them only unskilled work and technical careers.

Similarly, the Arab–Israeli conflict justified the imposition of military rule over the Palestinian minority in Israel, as well as brutal retaliation against Palestinian infiltration from the Gaza Strip, Lebanon, the West Bank and Syria. In this vein, mainstream historians justified Israel's decision to join Britain and France in the attempt to topple Gamal Abdul Nasser in the autumn of 1956. They also saw no harm in the way individuals and children were mistreated or abused under the collective education of the kibbutz or the way women were ordered back into the kitchen for this Zionist experiment in socialism. Finally, they applauded the diplomats of the young country for securing Israel's international legitimacy by persuading the world to accept the Jewish state as the only moral and just response to the horrors of the Holocaust.

The critical post-Zionist scholars of the 1990s, however, rejected these explanations. Marginalisation and oppression were seen as the outcome of an ideological bias, both economical and financial, against *Mizrachim* and Arabs alike, yielding a cheap labour force made of *Mizrachim*, women and Palestinians. What for classical Zionist scholars was an inspiring ideal of nation-building was for the dissenters an oppressive ideology that was ruthlessly used to crush any opposition to the dominant, domineering Eastern European culture.

Initially, the treatment of the Palestinian minority in Israel was a topic of research dominated mainly by Palestinian scholars, although several post-Zionist Jewish scholars soon joined them to expose the nature of the oppression imposed on the Palestinians during the years of military rule, 1948–67. The mainstream justified these policies as responding to the 'objective' problems of security and scarcity of resources in the young state. The challengers attributed them to a racist and segregationist ideology. For example, Oren Yiftachel, a geographer from Ben-Gurion University, wrote:

> The territorial restructuring of the land has centered around an all-encompassing and expansionist *Judaisation* (de-Arabisation) program adopted by the nascent Israeli state, following the 1947–49 flight and expulsion of close to 800,000 Palestinians. This created big 'gaps' in the geography of the land, which the authorities were quick to fill with Jewish settlements inhabited by

migrants and refugees who entered the country en masse during the late 1940s and early 1950s.[9]

There are many other examples. Sarah Ozacky-Lazar, who was working at the leftist Zionist institute of Givat Haviva as a historian of the state of Israel, wrote that 'the military regime imposed on the Arabs in Israel became a tool for political, economic and cultural control of the state in the lives of the Arab minority'.[10] Dan Rabinowitz, an anthropologist from Tel Aviv University, wrote extensively on the need to adopt the term 'the Palestinians in Israel' as a replacement for the Israeli establishment's term 'Arabs in Israel', which was meant to rob the minority of its Palestinian roots and identity. He also took a critical stance on the flourishing of workshops and NGOs in the 1980s and 1990s, which 'at close examination, however, reveals the key aspects … were designed primarily for Israeli consumption. Palestinian participants and moderators thus tend to become objectified, mere illustrations in an all-Israeli debate which takes place, as it were, above the Palestinian's head.'[11] Hillel Cohen, a historian from the Hebrew University, was one of the first to write about the internal Palestinian refugees inside Israel – those who lost their homes and became refugees in their own country. Yoav Peled, a political scientist from Tel Aviv University, wrote on the need to recognise the just side of the Palestinian demands in the negotiations, including that of the right of return.[12]

The study of gender and feminism was also part of this new post-Zionist energy. In many ways it was the most impressive import from America, a culture that more often than not had a negative impact on Israeli society. In the case of post-Zionism, however, it opened up constructive and crucial vistas of research and commitment for local scholars. As a result, during the late 1970s, under the strong influence of gender studies, feminist activism, and politics, a feminist movement emerged in Israel as well.

The feminist movement grew in parallel to the American feminist movement and was greatly influenced by it. One of the main propellants was an American Jewish activist, Marcia Freedman. She was born in the United States in 1938, emigrated to Israel in 1967, and immediately became involved in left Zionist politics. A new party called Ratz, dedicated to peace and civil rights and founded by the female politician Shulamit Aloni, invited Freedman to become a candidate. Both women did well in the 1973 elections, and Freedman became a member of the Knesset. With other women, she founded the first refuge for battered women in Israel; she and other women members of the Knesset were also responsible for progressive legislation on gender equality and women's issues. Freedman came out of the closet as a lesbian at around that time – one of the first women to do so in Israel. In recent years she has divided her time between Israel and the United States.[13]

Preceding the establishment in the 1980s of the first women's studies programme in an Israeli university, Israeli NGOs were intensely active, united in the wish to push forward a progressive feminist agenda but divided on the strategy for doing so. The resulting feminist research addressed a variety of topics and included the rewriting of women's history in the Zionist movement and in Israel, highlighting the misogynist attitude of the society and state in the 1950s, and the discovery of unknown stories of feminists in the pre-state period and the early years of the state.

Another import from America was queer theory. Scholarship on gay and lesbian politics now began to develop in Israeli academia and to become fused into the post-Zionist agenda. The academics who were involved in introducing these issues to the scholarly community, such as the sociologist Yuval Yonay from the University of Haifa, also wrote extensively on the occupation and oppression of the Palestinians. But in many cases the focus on gay and lesbian rights inside Israel was not associated with the oppression of other groups within the state. Nevertheless, the raising of gay issues was a revolutionary development, given the hostile attitude of Judaism to homosexuality.[14] The first public activist on this issue was a German Jew named Theo Meinz, who came out openly as a gay man in 1956.[15] For many years, gays had to be content with being active within the Association for Civil Rights in Israel, founded in 1972, as any other reference was forbidden in Israel. But the 1980s saw a flourishing of NGOs and university study modules that investigated gay issues, thus adding to the sense of pluralism in the local academy and society.

Unfortunately this new openness was later used by mainstream academia to deflect any attempt to criticise it for complicity in the occupation or the oppression of the Palestinians. The Israeli academic establishment attempted to fend off calls for an academic boycott of Israel earlier in the 2000s by turning to gay and lesbian lobbying groups around the world – a move that was later dubbed 'pinkwashing'. Broadcasting Tel Aviv as the most gay-friendly city in the West (a title it wins frequently) was one of the main campaigns supported by the government in order to undercut the boycott. Quite a few groups, including some powerful ones in the United States, refused to partake in the 'Brand Israel' campaign and were fully aware that while life may go on happily for gays in Tel Aviv, a few kilometres away millions of people are incarcerated in the huge megaprison of the West Bank and the ghetto of Gaza.

More familiar areas of inquiry developed impressively in the 1990s, such as political economy. Scholars such as Michael Shalev and Shimshon Bichler, joined the critical sociologists in pointing to the economic interests and materialist realities that lay behind the ideological project – not only in the 1948 war, but also thereafter. They were followed by others, such as Dalit Baum, who described the economic realities and benefits behind the continued occupation of the West Bank and the Gaza Strip.[16]

As the group of challengers grew, the chronological and thematic scope of the research expanded enormously. Earlier, even ancient, periods were now revisited, as bold, new, and previously taboo themes were tackled. The ancient past was revisited under the influence of critical theories on nationalism as an invented, engineered story that told us more about the nature of modern Zionism than about what really happened in those distant years. Baruch Kimmerling opened the way through his exposure of the invented tale of two thousand years of exile, and how it was used to justify the colonisation of Palestine.[17]

Yael Zerubavel, an Israeli historian who taught in the United States, added to this the intriguing insight that the ancient stories of heroism, such as Masada, that were the fulcrum of the Zionist meta-narrative, were actually tales of defeat and total failure, as were many later acts of heroism.[18] Similar but probably even more outrageous from a Zionist point of view was the anger voiced by the sociologist Nachman Ben-Yehuda about Zionism's chosen and revered ancestors: the Jewish rebels against Rome.[19] As Zerubavel rightly commented, their rebellion ended in total failure. Ben-Yehuda went further: he called them a bunch of thieves and murderers, and cast a blaming finger at the Zionist archaeologists for providing what he saw as false scholarly scaffolding for that narrative. Shlomo Sand and Gabriel Piterberg, each in his own way, would later shed more light on how the past, even the biblical one, served to create a society suffused with romantic nationalism in the eyes of Sand and a settler colonialist society in the eyes of Piterberg.[20]

The more recent past, such as the centuries preceding the emergence of Zionism in the late nineteenth century, has not been extensively revisited, but in this respect the work of Amnon Raz-Karkozkin should be mentioned. (In fact, Raz-Karkozkin, who regarded himself as an anti-Zionist, was quite unhappy about the term 'post-Zionism' but nonetheless took part in many of the workshops, conferences and publications that pushed the academic critique of Zionism.) In a two-part article published in the main venue for post-Zionist critique during the 1990s, *Theory and Criticism* (founded in 1991 at the Van Leer Jerusalem Institute), he explored what he called 'the Zionist denial of Exile'.[21] The first part shows how the depiction of Jewish life in Europe as exilic since the end of Roman times was used in order to deny the Palestinians' right to their homeland; the second part examines the distortions created by this depiction, as Jewish life in Europe did not centre on or relate to Palestine. Raz-Karkozkin also examines in this article how this idea of Jewish life in history as a life of exile determined the negative attitude of Zionism towards the Arab Jews, who, from the Zionist-narrated perspective, unnecessarily extended the exile longer than anyone else. Some years later, a professor from the University of Haifa, Gur Elroi, would demonstrate the mundanity of the motives of most of the settlers who came to Palestine – their emigration had nothing to do with the establishment's narration of their journey as a wish to return home from their exilic life in Europe.[22]

The Mandatory period was a topic frequently revisited. Historians and sociologists, such as Zeev Sternhell, belittled the role of socialism in the Zionist project in Palestine and depicted it as romantic nationalism.[23] A more positive approach was taken by historians who showed that the natural instinct of Palestinians and settlers was to coexist and collaborate on the basis of class association in industrial struggles – an instinct crushed by the Zionist trade unions. Lev Greenberg examined the joint industrial action of drivers; David De Vries examined the industrial action of junior clerks; Deborah S. Bernstein described in detail the policies of the Zionist trade unions.[24]

In addition to all of this, militarism – never before deemed relevant in Israeli academia – emerged as a new field of study. It began with a close look, provided by a couple who began their work in the Haifa group mentioned earlier. Shulamit Carmi and Henry Rosenfeld worked as a team to expose the mammoth growth of the military industry in Israel, claiming that it had arrested overall economic growth over the years.[25] They were followed by a young sociologist, Uri Ben-Eliezer, then a member of the department of sociology in Tel Aviv, who depicted the militarisation of Israel not only as an inevitable product of the state's precarious existence in the midst of a hostile world but also as a means of obtaining the wholehearted commitment of every citizen to the state, which is why women are still recruited and men are called for reserve duty until the age of fifty-five.[26]

The work on militarism later focused on two aspects. The first was the state and pre-state history, which showed how from very early on, the use of military force was more than tactical – that it was part of the ideology. The formative years were the 1950s, when 'special forces' units were created to punish and challenge Palestinian refugees who were trying to return clandestinely to their homeland, and who later organised themselves into guerrilla units, leading to the official founding of Fatah in the mid-1960s). The aura of these special forces – the most important of which was Unit 101, whose commander was Ariel Sharon – transformed them into the main core group from which Israel's most famous leaders, such as Ehud Barak and Benjamin Netanyahu, were recruited. Their world view would turn Israel into an extremely active and aggressive agent on the regional scene, espousing the belief that the language of military power was the best means of ensuring the state's existence and success.

Yagil Levy, a sociologist now at the Open University of Israel, associated militarism with the treatment of new Jewish immigrants from Arab countries.[27] His work showed that the decisions of where to settle new arrivals and how to integrate them into Israeli society were made not only by politicians but also by generals. Locating them on the borders of the Arab world served more than one purpose: confronting them with Arab hostility would help to de-Arabise them; they would serve as a human presence on the long borders that Israel shared with its 'enemies', and recruiting them into the army was regarded as the best means of 'Israelising' them.

Indeed, identifying the nexus between education and the militarisation of the society was part of the new post-Zionist agenda. Hagit Gur-Ziv, Rela Mazali, Nurit Peled-Elhanan, Diana Dolev and many others examined the impact of militarism on the educational system and reached some dismal conclusions about the possibility for change from within Israeli society in regard to issues of peace, democracy and equality.[28] Their works exposed the highly militarised space that Israeli Jews inhabited from cradle to grave.

Not only was the army examined at close range – academia, too, became a new object of inquiry. The analysis of its role was provided mainly by Israeli graduates of the New School, a university in New York's Greenwich Village that became the alma mater of progressive social scientists around the world. One such graduate, Uri Ram, was particularly influential in the new post-Zionist approach to methodology. He was one of the first to introduce post-structuralism and postmodernism to the local academic scene. For more than a decade, he has taught at Ben-Gurion University of the Negev.[29]

Ram showed how, in their analysis of Israeli society, Zionist sociologists elaborated theories to fit notions such as the 'ingathering of the exiles' and the 'melting pot'. They described a modernised society in which the white, Western component – the Jewish immigrants from Europe – coached the rest, be they Jews from Arab countries or Palestinians who remained in Israel, on how to emulate them and become better citizens in a Jewish democracy. The modernisation theories embraced by the Israeli sociological establishment disregarded the heterogeneous, multi-ethnic and multicultural society that had developed since 1948.[30] To these sociologists, Israel was a paragon of successful modernisation process and progress. Ram not only challenged the validity of this claim but argued that the sociologists provided academic justifications for the discriminatory and oppressive policies that resulted from such an interpretation of the idea of Israel.

The scholars who worked on the history of the State of Israel were in tune not only with the realities around them but also to the contemporary global debates about power and knowledge. An important component of the new research, in addition to aspects of history and society, was a lively inquiry into theoretical questions. As a result, there arose a vibrant local conversation about knowledge and power that yielded important texts relevant not only for local consumption but for more general use elsewhere.

Because of this interest in theory, tremendous effort was directed towards the translation into Hebrew of major works, foremost among them those of Michel Foucault, as well as the revisiting of archaic translations of Marx and Marxist literature. These books were published by a Tel Aviv publisher, Resling, and the articles in *Theory and Criticism*. This effort also required expertise and familiarity with new methodologies, so that academics, within their professional remit, would be able to expose the production of hegemonic knowledge and, even more important, offer ways to intervene in the process.

Post-Zionist Methodology

Post-Zionist scholars continued to accumulate new evidence about the past and new data about the present, within the restrictions imposed by the thirty-year delay in declassification of materials in the Israeli archives. The new archival evidence exposed previously unknown domestic and foreign policies, some of them quite horrific. One example was the forced kidnapping of Yemeni Jewish babies in the 1950s from their mothers, on the grounds that they were unfit parents, so that the babies could be given over for adoption by Ashkenazi parents. The babies were taken while the mothers were still in hospital; they were told that the babies were dead. These revelations caused a Yemeni Jewish rabbi, Uzi Meshulam, to barricade himself and family members in a house in the centre of Israel in 1994, demanding truth and justice.[31] Also found in the archives were nasty and unpleasant statements about anyone who was not an Ashkenazi Jew – quotes from top ministers and journalists in all the major newspapers. The archives shed new light as well on the activities of the Israeli intelligence services in Arab countries, including both active interference in Arab politics and ways of triggering the emigration of Arab Jews to Israel.

But the vast majority of academics were not focused simply on the collection of new evidence. They were more interested in the deconstruction of existing evidence and knowledge for the purpose of exposing the realities that lay behind the accepted vision of Israel. So they reread newspaper articles, speeches, and novels; they looked again at art and movies. This second look enabled them to pose a more fundamental challenge to the idea of Israel.

Thus, Zvi Efrat revisited the iconic photography of the 1950s, which in fact recorded the destruction of Palestine even though the photographs were commissioned to commemorate the forestation of the country; the Jewish National Fund had planted European pine trees all over the villages destroyed and depopulated by the IDF during the 1948 war.[32] Galia Zlamansov Levi examined how the Bible was taught in Israeli schools as a text that justified military occupation and dispossession, minus any exploration of moral issues or questions of justice. Alexander Kedar looked at the Israeli land law regime and presented it as a colonialist structure in its intent, praxis and objectives.[33] Haim Bereshit deconstructed the history of urban planning in Jaffa as a microcosm of the Zionist policy of de-Arabisation of the country.[34] Ilan Gur-Ze'ev discussed the physical

structure of the University of Haifa, built on Mount Carmel, as
a project aimed at 'erasing the existence of the other cultures on
the mountain … its phallic towers eradicating the memory of the
destroyed Palestinian villages as well as the natural flora of the area'.[35]

Every medium through which the historical narrative of Zionism
and the essence of the idea of Israel were conveyed was examined,
deconstructed and exposed as a text that hid, distorted, rejected and
oppressed the Other, whoever that might be. Like their colleagues in
the West who ventured in a similarly critical way to question their
own national ethos and idealism, the post-Zionists sought to salvage
hidden or repressed voices of Israeli society.

Critical theories on nationalism, relativist historiosophies,
postmodernist hermeneutical techniques, and deconstructive methodologies were all employed in the service of understanding how
the Zionist interpretation of reality affected the life of everyone who
lived, or used to live, in Israel and Palestine. Jonathan and Daniel
Boyarin, for instance, developed a subfield of postcolonial Jewish
studies that, among its other issues, examines how Zionism transformed Judaism and turned the Jewish victim into a victimiser,
while Hannan Hever reread the literary Israeli canon through the
lens of the most up-to-date postcolonial theoretical analyses.[36] One
of the most intriguing samples of such work was a reaction to the
UNESCO declaration that an area of old Tel Aviv that was built in
the 1930s–50s be labelled a World Heritage site. Sharon Rotbard, an
Israeli architect, used a postcolonial prism to show how the so-called
White City could not exist without the Black City, the depopulated
and now gentrified town of Jaffa.[37]

As I am rereading these sources, it seems that whether these and
other scholars were using the term 'postcolonial' or 'colonial' as the
preferred adjective in their studies, for ordinary Israeli readers the
overall message was the same. Even when a scholar applied updated
theoretical prisms to the case study of Zionism, the project could
not but be described as a nineteenth-century colonialist enterprise that continues to this day to focus on erasing the Palestinians
from the land in any way possible. The only drawback was that
the theories, especially when translated into Hebrew, brought with

them a highly specialised language which was not accessible to a wider public.

Two tools attracted this new scholarship in particular: deconstruction, as offered by literary criticism and hermeneutics, and positionality as defined by cultural anthropology. In simple terms, and as it was understood in Israel, positionality is the right of scholars to position themselves vis-à-vis their research in accordance with whatever identity they choose. As a result, whatever your identity, or your politics of identity, it plays a crucial role in why, what, and how you research a given topic. The more representative academia becomes of the full range of positions, the better its work will be – and if significant positions are not represented, then the research will be biased against the very groups whose representatives are absent. The best way to fully appreciate the nature of positionality is to juxtapose it with the older idea that it does not matter who the researcher is, since all research is scientific, even that done by humans on humanity, and is therefore accurate and truthful.

Deconstruction enabled scholars in Israel to treat the Zionist interpretation of the idea of Israel as a text that could destroy, or elevate, real people's lives and fortunes. The gist of the approach was that the power of Zionism, either as a national movement in the eyes of some or as a settler colonialist movement in the eyes of others, is the omnipotent narrator; and that in many ways is lived according to, or in defiance of, this narrator's script or plot. Consequently, every human cognition, action and emotion can be examined as a literary text in which one can identify the plot, the heroes, the villains, and the genre.

From the deconstructionist perspective, Zionism figures as a powerful story, and one's place in it determines in real life one's fate under the Jewish state. If you are a Palestinian, you are the villain in the story; if you are the Mizrachi Jew, you are the primitive relative. Comparing these depictions as they appeared in everything from scholarship to cinema was the first step in implementing this methodology. The second was an attempt to correlate actual policies and strategies from above with the images in both the popular and the high culture of the society. Thus, if you were depicted as marginal or hostile, this was reflected in the authorities' attitude towards you in mundane as well as existential matters. What this meant was that the power of the interpretation could be detected in every aspect of life, in such disparate areas as radio commercials, the characters of sitcoms and soap operas, children's literature and textbooks, the government's policy papers, politicians' speeches, and so on.

In addition, one could refer not only to what was present in the written or visual form to find how you, the Other, or anyone else was represented or misrepresented; you could also research what was absent from the text. As Edward Said pointed out, the attitude of Jane Austen and her contemporaries to colonialism was evident from the sheer fact that the colonies are hardly there in the novels. Similar absences of Arabs, Palestinians, *Mizrachim* and women were noted in scholarly Zionist work, films, museums, novels, national ceremonies and emblems – and that is not an imaginary list, as it objectively represents what was deconstructed in the 1990s. In fact, almost everything in sight was deconstructed, so much so that one sometimes had the impression that the process went too far in its depiction of every piece in the puzzle of one's reality as a legitimate area of inquiry. All in all, though, deconstruction was an impressive salvage operation of hidden or silenced voices, unheard in the texts written by the oppressors or the rulers. It introduced oral history as a legitimate academic genre, and so even those who, because of illiteracy or destruction, left no written evidence could now tell their stories through the work of these scholars.

Nevertheless, the measure of a scholar's academic relevance had more to do with that other tool, positionality, which was also imported from abroad in the 1990s. This method demanded from scholars that they go beyond the indulgence and pleasure of slaughtering sacred cows or deconstructing to death the presentation of reality by the powerful. Now they were expected also to show commitment to the real people who were being victimised by that presentation. The process was far more difficult and much less enjoyable.

Positionality meant that you had to locate yourself not in the national, Zionist narrative, but against it. When you defied the national claims for a collective past, identity, and future, you entered the arena of the politics of identity and multiculturalism. The most vibrant academic embodiment of this arose in 1970s America. In those years, quite a few US academics were involved in what became known as the 'culture wars' or the 'campus wars': heated debates about identity and its politics as legitimate criteria for assessing such matters as admission to the universities (whether as students or staff), promotion, the shaping of curricula, and the quality of one's academic work.[38] Even Hollywood succeeded in conveying that atmosphere in the memorable 1970 film *Getting Straight*, directed by Richard Rush, in which Vietnam veteran Harry Bailey (played by Elliott Gould) appears as a graduate student facing the pressures of the anti-war movement on campus on the one hand, and the conservatism of his examiners on the other.

The striking feature of American identity politics in those years was that they were tangibly manifested on campuses: in the composition of departments, their teaching agenda and research orientation. Thus a department of history was asked to give voice to multiple historical narratives that had been ignored or misrepresented in the past by the hegemonic white American narrative. Hispanic, gender, African American, and gay histories were now offered, along with similar perspectives on culture, literature and other fields of inquiry. At times the debate was regarded as a war, because in some circles it was held that for these points of view to be fairly represented in academia, members of those very groups were the best candidates to put them across. Affirmative action and positive discrimination were sometimes the solution. Lawsuits, the disintegration of departments, and the sacking of staff members were the more extreme manifestations of this discussion. But, as in any academic war, nobody died or was even wounded.

Israeli academics tried to follow suit. They wished to represent the Palestinian, the Mizrachi, and the feminist sides of the story, to demand their introduction into the national narrative, and even to claim a place for them in the cultural canon. They had the strong conviction that by representing these groups within Israeli academia, one was not only exposing their mistreatment in the past and present but also offering redemption for these evils in the future. The former goal – presenting the trials and tribulations of repressed, oppressed and marginalised groups – was achieved to a certain extent; the second, not at all. Indeed, the only group in Israel that is better represented today than in the 1990s is women. Palestinians, Mizrachi Jews, and in particular Palestinian and Mizrachi women, constitute a mere fraction of the ten thousand or so members of staff in Israeli academia (less than one per cent for Palestinians, 9 per cent for Mizrachi Jews, and one per cent for Mizrachi women).[39]

For the Israel academic to be able even to experiment with what is called affirmative action – and I say 'experiment' because I am aware of the drawbacks of this technique – these scholars had to become activists against Zionism. For most of them, however, political activism did not go beyond writing articles or books. The price would have been too high.

Demanding representation of other groups was thus a complex and risky endeavour. One could hide for a while behind politically correct jargon borrowed from the United States. This oversensitive, and at times exaggerated, language was about as useful as the postmodernist discourse that had earlier been adopted from Europe. In fact, to challenge the idea of Israel through the elusive idiom of postmodernism – which in Hebrew is even more undecipherable than it is in English and is understood only by like-minded people – meant that one would be, in effect, protected from swift repercussions.

There were exceptions, to be sure, as can be seen in the work of, for instance, Tanya Reinhart, who followed the example of her mentor, Noam Chomsky, in the use of clear and unambiguous prose. Chomsky showed the submissiveness of the American academy when faced with hegemonic ideologies; Reinhart demonstrated the obedience of the local academia to its political masters. In addition, Chomsky's double engagement – his expertise as a linguist, combined with his commitment as a conscientious, knowledgeable commentator on world affairs – served as a model for Reinhart and some of her colleagues in the department of linguistics at Tel Aviv University, such as Rachel Giora and Mira Ariel.[40] They were joined by members of the philosophy department such as Anat Biletzky and Anat Matar, who, as professional moral philosophers, questioned and condemned

Israeli academia's apathy at best, or collaboration at worst, with the occupation and discrimination against the Palestinians. As Biletzky wrote:

> We must, as academics, never forget our political agenda: the eradication of evil. And the Israeli occupation of Palestine is the epitome of evil. We must constantly, as academics, identify with Palestinian teachers and students in conditions of severe repression. We must constantly, as academics, criticise the acquiescence of others in Israel to the occupation. And we must constantly, as academics, call for condemnation of the occupation.[41]

However, Biletzky did not support the idea of an academic boycott, whereas her Tel Aviv colleagues Anat Matar in the department of philosophy, who equally demanded that academics become more active against the occupation, endorsed Palestinian civil society's call for an academic and cultural boycott when it was declared:

> When the flag of academic freedom is raised, the oppressor and not the oppressed is usually the one who flies it. What is that academic freedom that so interests the academic community in Israel? When, for example, has it shown concern for the state of academic freedom in the occupied territories?
>
> On the other hand, members of the Israeli academia staunchly guard their right to research what the regime expects them to research and appoint former army officers to university positions. Tel Aviv University alone prides itself over the fact that the Defense Ministry is funding 55 percent of its research projects and that DARPA, the Defense Advanced Research Projects Agency in the U.S. Defense Department, is funding nine more. All the universities offer special study programs for the defense establishment.[42]

The Tel Aviv University philosophers and a handful of others offered – either because they were influenced by similar conscientious voices, or because of their own integrity, or both – a different interpretation of what being an academic meant, beyond the professional career. What was wanted was a new breed of activist scholar, which alas, in the case of Israel (and, one should add, elsewhere in the West), more often than not turned out to be an oxymoron. But before the decline in the 2000s, at least in the 1990s it was attempted.

Even becoming an activist against male chauvinism proved difficult. Activism and scholarly feminism did not always see eye to eye: the activists far more clearly connected gender issues to Zionism and nationalism, while those who remained in academia took a more cautious approach to linkages and associations. Eventually there arose much dissent and discord between the Mizrachi and Palestinian feminist agenda and what was regarded as a Western variety of feminism masquerading as a universal one. A crucial moment in the development of gender studies was the creation of feminist organisations that wished to be more closely associated with the politics of identity. In 1991, Al-Fanar, the Palestinian feminist organisation in Israel, was established; shortly afterwards, Achoti (Sister) for Women in Israel left the overall feminist movement to represent more faithfully the particular agenda of Mizrachi women.

This was a local conversation that reflected a more general one, in the Middle East as a whole, between Islamic or Muslim feminism and Western feminism. In addition, the unwillingness of Israel, the state and the society alike, to be integrated into the region – its insistence of being an integral part of the West – affected issues of gender as well.

Thus, a feminism that could have been regional, could have built bridges with feminist movements in the Arab world, failed to connect with a feminism that strove to grant equal rights to young women in the army, so that they could serve as fighter pilots or commando troops, and as a result, become unacceptable to the Arab world. Israeli fighter pilots and commando troops are prepared for one mission: to brutally police the occupied West Bank and the Gaza Strip, or to punish southern Lebanon. Despite these rifts, feminist activism and cooperation flourished through organisations such as Isha L'Isha (Woman to Woman), Achoti, and Al-Fanar.

This does not mean that the feminist movement in Israel, whether we speak of its academic wing or its political/activist wing, did not have an impressive list of achievements. It is mainly in the sphere of legislation and changes in attitudes that these achievements are visible. However, as with so many other aspects of life in Israel, the formal and official façade covers up a far more depressing reality: a high rate of women being murdered (both in Arab and Jewish societies), occupational inequality, the growing influence of ultra-religious forces. These factors combine to create a renewed marginalisation and, in certain cases, exclusion of women in the already socio-economically deprived sectors of Jewish society.

But the feminist challenge, especially in academia and subsequently in civil society, was influential in two areas. One was in importing into academia the theoretical and methodological frameworks that have helped feminists around the world to salvage women's voices and experiences from the past and to empower them in the present – a toolkit that has also been used successfully by other oppressed and marginalised groups. Second, it was the progressive feminist research on the Israeli educational system that pushed forward a new agenda of anti-militarism and even pacifism as possible goals for a protest movement inside Israel. This worked better in the sphere of civil society than in academia, but in both places it was a fresh, bold move to deconstruct the Israeli educational system as a militaristic and manipulative tool that ensured youthful obedience to and admiration of the army, as well as the securitisation of the society.

Mothers were invited to reconsider the wisdom of sending their children to die in the name of the idea of Israel. Towards the end of the prolonged Israeli presence in Lebanon (1982–2000), such reflections were translated into a short-lived political movement called Four Mothers (a reference to the four famous mothers of the Bible), which served as an effective lobby to pressure the Israeli government to withdraw its forces from southern Lebanon. The attempt to recruit motherhood in a similar way to end the occupation of the West Bank and the Gaza strip failed dismally, however. Several years ago, mothers of sons who were physically able to serve in élite Israeli units but were commissioned for non-combat and logistics service demonstrated in anger at the main recruitment centre near the Tel Hashomer Hospital in Tel Aviv.

Towards the end of the 1990s, what took place in the arena of gender – when the real action moved from campuses to civil society – affected post-Zionist scholarship as a whole. When the academic impulse petered out or was curbed, the same agenda would be taken up on a smaller but more committed scale by civil society and its NGOs, the most notable of which was New Profile. This group was established in 1998 by a group of feminists in Israel dedicated to persuading young people not to serve in the army. In Israel, a 'profile' is the overall assessment of eligibility for the army, especially for men. A 97, which is the highest profile, means that the young recruit can join the combat units; a 24 means he is mentally unfit to serve (which in many cases means that the candidate exhibited pacifist tendencies), a profile that can impact his chances of getting a studentship and a job. Hence, the idea of a 'new profile'.

One topic was not even engaged with openly by these courageous NGOs, and that was Holocaust exploitation. Only a handful of scholars addressed this matter, and they deserve to be recorded in the next chapter as the people who probably went further than anyone else in examining the validity of the idea of Israel.

SEVEN

Touching the Raw Nerves of Society: Holocaust Memory in Israel

In August 2005, the Israeli government evicted from the Gaza Strip eight thousand settlers who had occupied the region since 1967. In a desperate attempt to thwart the government's action, the settlers' crusade adopted insignias meant to link the evacuation with the Holocaust: sewing yellow stars of David onto their clothing while tattooing numbers onto their arms. During the actual removal, many of the settlers, crying and shouting on their way to the luxury buses that whisked them off to Israel, re-enacted scenes they had seen in Holocaust films or museums. They cursed soldiers and police as Nazis, and likened senior army officers to Hitler.

This was a supremely ugly manipulation of the memory of the Holocaust, witnessed in a state that had perfected such manipulation as a diplomatic tool in its struggle against the Palestinians. But even when the manipulation has been excessive or indeed pathetic, Israeli academics have nonetheless been very careful about criticising such occurrences.

The protection of the Holocaust memory in Israel from any critique is consensual and widespread. For that very reason, recording those who in the 1990s did dare to ask some pertinent questions about it within academia must be an important part of this book. Their effort was as unique as those who challenged the 1948 foundational mythology, and so perhaps it is not surprising that, in both cases, the persons most associated with the academic research on the topic later retracted, becoming neo-Zionist defenders of Zionism as well as the chief critics of their former colleagues. These persons are Benny Morris, in the case of 1948, and Ilan Gur-Ze'ev, in the case of Holocaust memory.

As is often true, there were in fact earlier attempts, most of them not by scholars, to understand the impact and significance of Holocaust memory in the constructing and marketing of the idea of Israel. The search for truth was driven by moral and ethical concerns, and paved the way for the initiation of scholarly inquiry when a more amiable atmosphere developed in Israeli academia in the 1990s. A more open approach to Holocaust memory in Israel showed the connection between the state's narration of the Holocaust – its causes and impact – and its justification of harsh policies towards the Palestinians. This connection became a major theme in the post-Zionist critique of Holocaust memorialisation in Israel.

One of the first persons to voice a genuine concern about the way Holocaust memory was brought to bear in Israel was none other than Nahum Goldmann, founder and president of the World Jewish Congress through the late 1970s. Despite his senior position, he condemned as sacrilegious the way Israel manipulated Holocaust memory in order to justify its oppression of the Palestinians.[1] Many years later, in our own century, Avraham Burg, a speaker of the Knesset and subsequently chair of the Jewish Agency, would voice similar concerns. He summarised his thoughts on this issue in a book whose title says it all, *The Holocaust Is Over: We Must Rise From Its Ashes*, in which he states: 'In fact, the only hope we have to make peace with the Arabs is if we free ourselves of our Shoah mentality, and stop acting like a small Eastern European shtetl'.[2]

The strongest voice came from Holocaust survivors. The first was Israel Shahak, in whose writing one can often encounter the phrase 'the falsification of the Holocaust':

I disagree ... that the Israeli education system has managed to instil a 'Holocaust awareness' in its pupils. It is not an awareness of the Holocaust but rather the myth of the Holocaust or even a falsification of the Holocaust (in the sense that 'a half-truth' is worse than a lie) which has been instilled here.[3]

In another passage, Shahak refers to the fear felt in Israel about explaining how crucial Jewish collaborators were in helping the Nazis carry out their extermination of the Jews, and he justifies the killing of these collaborators by the Resistance at the time, just as he indicates an understanding of why the Palestinians killed collaborators during the First Intifada:

> If we knew a little of the truth about the Holocaust, we would at least understand (with or without agreeing) why the Palestinians are now eliminating their collaborators. That is the only means they have if they wish to continue to struggle against our limb-breaking regime [referring here to Yitzhak Rabin's famous call, during the First Intifada, for the Israeli soldiers to break the limbs of the Palestinians].[4]

Shahak was also the first to bring up the enthusiasm felt by certain leading Zionists for the Nazis in the early 1930s, an enthusiasm which, he acknowledged, ceased in the late 1930s. About one of the most revered liberal Zionist philosophers, Martin Buber, he wrote: 'Buber glorified a movement holding and actually teaching doctrines about non-Jews not unlike the Nazi doctrines about Jews'. And, he wrote, Joachim Prinz, later a leading figure in the post-war American Zionist establishment,

> congratulated Hitler on his triumph over the common enemy – the forces of liberalism. Dr Joachim Prinz, a Zionist rabbi who subsequently emigrated to the USA, where he rose to be vice-chairman of the World Jewish Congress and a leading light in the World Zionist Organization (as well as a great friend of Golda Meir), published in 1934 a special book, *Wir Juden* (We, Jews), to celebrate Hitler's so-called German Revolution and the defeat of liberalism.[5]

Obviously Shahak did not mince his words. He characterised an attempt by religious Jews during the Litani Operation in 1978 (in which Israel occupied southern Lebanon as retaliation for a PLO attack on a bus on the outskirts of Tel Aviv) as an effort 'to induce military doctors and nurses to withhold medical help from wounded "Gentiles" ', calling this 'Nazi-like advice'.[6] He referred to the Jewish settlers in a similar vein. Following the 1980 assassination attempts by Jewish terrorists in which Mayor Bassam Shak'a of Nablus lost both his legs and Mayor Karim Khalaf of Ramallah lost a foot, Shahak reported to his readers: 'A group of Jewish Nazis gathered in the campus of Tel Aviv University, roasted a few cats and offered their meat to passers-by as shish-kebab from the legs of the Arab mayors'.[7]

Boaz Evron echoed similar concerns in his 1980 article 'The Holocaust – A Danger to the Nation'.[8] He questioned the uniqueness of the Jewish experience within the overall Nazi programme, saying that the extermination of the gypsies 'disproves the false assumption that the Nazi extermination policy was exclusively directed against the Jews'.[9] He further argued that Holocaust memorialisation in Israel was responsible for creating a 'paranoid reaction' among Israelis and even a 'moral blindness', which posed a real 'danger to the nation' and could lead to an occurrence of 'racist Nazi attitudes' within Israel itself.[10]

Eight years later Yehuda Elkana, who, like Shahak, was a young child in Nazi Europe, repeated these very ideas in an article in *Haaretz*.[11] Elkana was ten when he was imprisoned in Auschwitz and fourteen when he arrived in Israel in 1948. He became an international star in the philosophy of science – receiving his PhD from Brandeis University in Massachusetts, teaching at Harvard for a while, having a long and distinguished career at the Van Leer Jerusalem Institute, and finally becoming the president and rector of the Central European University in Budapest.

In 1988 Elkana witnessed with growing unease two simultaneous displays of Israeli power and force. One was the brutality of the Israelis during the early months of the First Intifada; the second was the trial of John Demjanjuk in Jerusalem. Demjanjuk was allegedly a notorious guard, 'Ivan the Terrible', in the Treblinka extermination camp. He was sentenced to death in 1988, after having been extradited from the United States, but was exonerated in 1993 by the Israeli Supreme Court on grounds of lack of decisive evidence for his true identity.

On 2 March 1988, Elkana published an article in *Haaretz* titled 'The Need to Forget'. Israeli society, he recommended, should ease its excessive and obsessive preoccupation with the Holocaust. He argued that Israeli Jews suffered from a surplus of memory and would do well to unburden themselves of the symbols, ceremonies, and purported lessons of their traumatic past. While it may be 'important for the world at large to remember', wrote Elkana, '[f]or our part, we must learn to *forget*!' He warned that there was no greater danger to the future of Israel than to be preoccupied from morning to night, with symbols, ceremonies, and lessons of the Holocaust, and he exhorted his country's leaders to uproot the rule of historical remembrance from their lives.[12]

Elkana saw the trial of Demjanjuk as an example of excessive preoccupation with the Holocaust, but he also connected this obsession with the supposedly 'anomalous' behaviour of Israeli soldiers towards Palestinians in the First Intifada. Searching for ways to understand this behaviour, he attributed the soldiers' actions to the negative effects that the manipulation of Holocaust memory had on the younger generation, contending that it perverted their moral judgement and values.

In his view, Israelis harboured an exaggerated sense of themselves as victims, and this self-image, itself the result of wrong lessons learned from the Holocaust, prevented them from seeing the Palestinians in a more realistic light and impeded a reasonable political solution to the Arab–Israeli conflict. Elkana worried that a Holocaust-induced image of the Jews as eternal victims might encourage Israelis to justify the crudest behaviour toward the Palestinians. Drawing parallels between the excesses committed by soldiers in the territories and what took place in Germany, Elkana voiced his concern that Israeli Jews could end up mimicking the behaviour of the worst of their enemies and thereby grant Hitler a 'tragic and paradoxical victory'.[13] Amos Elon, the famous Israeli journalist and essayist, agreed with

Elkana and in response to the latter's article wrote 'a little forgetfulness might finally be in order'.[14]

These early public ponderings about the manipulation, overusage and potential harm of Holocaust memory set the stage for the more scholarly post-Zionist academic challenges of the 1990s. The academics' readiness to go that far was also influenced by a surprisingly rich literature from the American Jewish community. Conscientious Jews in the United States – such as Peter Novick, Lenni Brenner and Norman Finkelstein – had begun to rebuke their own community's manipulation of Holocaust memory in the service of Israel.[15] It is through the work of these scholars that one can appreciate the crucial role played by the Zionist representation of Holocaust memory in marketing the idea of Israel in the United States. Novick summarised his criticism by claiming that American Jewry turned 'inward and rightward' in recent decades, mostly because of the 'centring of the Holocaust in the minds of American Jews'.[16] He also drew more general conclusions from what he termed 'Holocaust consciousness', which encouraged Jewish self-aggrandisement and prevented other victimised peoples from receiving a proper share of public attention and sympathy.

The most vociferous American critic, however, has been Norman Finkelstein. Born in 1953 in New York to parents who were Holocaust survivors, he chose an academic career as a political scientist very early on, and his postgraduate studies took him to Paris and then to Princeton University, where he completed his doctorate. He has taught at several American universities, encountering real hardship in gaining tenure because of his forthright criticism on Israel, which he has voiced in numerous articles and several books. Most of his work has focused on Zionism and Palestine.

In 2000 he published *The Holocaust Industry: Reflections on the Exploitation of Jewish Suffering*. The book sought to indict 'the Holocaust' as an ideological representation of history that was fraudulently devised and marketed to the American public in order to revive a faltering Jewish identity and to 'justify criminal policies of the Israeli state and US support for these policies'. Finkelstein decries the fact that Israel, 'one of the world's most formidable military powers, with a horrendous human rights record, has cast itself as a "victim" state' and looks for ways of garnering 'immunity to criticism'. The industry is not only about images; it is in fact more about money. People who have made money out of the misery of the Holocaust: are 'a repellent gang of well-heeled hoodlums and hucksters' seeking enormous legal damages and financial settlements from Germany and Switzerland – money which then goes to the lawyers and institutional actors involved in procuring it, rather than to the actual Holocaust survivors.[17]

Very much as in the case of the sensitive issue of 1948, scholars demanded more than just strong conviction and could only be satisfied when presented with hardcore evidence that shook their confidence in the hegemonic narrative. Nor did the archives and the newspapers of the past disappoint on that score either. Reappraisal of declassified documents exposed several issues, of which three were especially important: the Zionist leadership's past stance towards fascism, Nazism and the Holocaust; the attitude towards the survivors of the catastrophe who arrived as immigrants to Palestine during and after the catastrophe; and the nature and significance of the uprisings in the ghettos.

'What Italy Can Achieve, So Can Yehuda!'

The first topic the new scholars dared to tackle in the new and relatively open atmosphere were the sympathies shown in the early 1930s towards fascism and Nazism by some participants in the Zionist movement. Even when leaders of the movement were unenthusiastic about the ideologies themselves, the very fact that Italy and Germany were Britain's enemies, as many Zionist activists saw it, was enough to allow for contact with both powers during the years leading up to the Second World War. In addition, before they became aware that the Nazis planned to exterminate the Jews, pragmatic Zionist leaders wanted to exploit the Nazi wish to expel them, because these leaders saw expulsion as benefiting the Jewish community in Palestine.[18]

The picture that emerged when all three themes were fused into one challenging new narrative was, to say the least, embarrassing. Leading intellectuals of the Jewish community, such as Itamar Ben-Avi (the son of Eliezer Ben-Yehuda, reviver of the Hebrew language) and Aba Ahimeir, sang the praises of fascism loud and clear. Ben-Avi even suggested that the Italian Fascist model was suitable for the *Yishuv*, the Jewish community in Palestine. As he wrote, 'what Italy can achieve, so can Judah!'[19]

In 1928, Aba Ahimeir, who became a leading member of the far-right wing of the Revisionist movement, wrote a regular column in the Hebrew daily *Doar Hayom*, edited by Ben-Avi. The title of the column was '*Mipinkaso shel Fashistan*' (From a Fascist's Notebook). In 1931 he played a central role in the founding of Brit Habiryonim (Union of Thugs), an underground group modelled on European fascist groups and devoted to opposing British policy in Palestine. At the trial of members of this organisation who were accused of disrupting a left-wing event at the Hebrew University in early 1932, their lawyer declared, 'Yes, we Revisionists have a great admiration for Hitler. Hitler has saved Germany ... And if he had given up his anti-Semitism we would go with him.'[20]

In the summer of 1932, Ben-Avi commented in the pages of *Doar Hayom* that one should accept the inevitability of Hitler's rise to power. What he meant was spelled out in another newspaper, *Hazit Ha'am*, edited by Aba Ahimeir and Yehoshua Heschel Yevin, which declared that unlike the socialists and democrats who were convinced that Hitler's movement was an empty shell, 'we believe that there is both a shell and a kernel. The anti-Semitic shell is to be discarded, but not the anti-Marxist kernel'.[21]

The mainstream leadership did not exhibit such sympathy, but refused to adopt an aggressive stance against the Nazi regime. The archives revealed a Zionist leadership so focused on the project in Palestine that the boycott declared by Jews around the world against the Nazis in the 1930s seemed to these Zionists the wrong policy. At the time, the leader of the Jewish community in Palestine, David Ben-Gurion, said: 'Zionism bears the obligations of a state; it therefore cannot initiate an irresponsible battle against Hitler as long as he remains a head of state'. The 'irresponsible battle' was the boycott.[22]

In order to convince his listeners, Ben-Gurion further pointed out that other countries hostile to Germany, even the Soviet Union, had not severed their ties with the Third Reich. Instead of joining in with the other Jewish communities in a worldwide boycott of German goods, the Zionist leadership adopted a different stance – the only Jewish community to do so. It struck an agreement with the Gestapo that in return for the Zionist movement agreement not to support such a boycott, the Jews of Germany would be allowed to liquidate their holdings and possessions and bring them along when they moved to Palestine.[23]

The contacts with the Nazis were less an issue of sympathy and more a matter of practicality, and yet exposing these contacts required a self-assertive, confident academic. Moshe Zimmermann was such a person.[24] He was a well-known expert on German history at the Hebrew University and was used to public notoriety and abuse. He attracted the nation's attention with a very blunt condemnation of the settlers and their youth movement.[25] So perhaps it is not surprising that he was willing to excavate this uncomfortable topic. Greatly assisted by the US historian Lenni Brenner, Zimmermann discovered that Zionist contact with the Nazis had begun in earnest in 1933. The main supporter in Germany of this contact was the German journalist Leopold von Mildenstein, who was close to the Zionist ideologue and leader Arthur Ruppin, a German Jew. Early on, Zionist leaders offered an alliance with Germany, since, at the time, they saw Germany primarily as Britain's enemy.[26]

When, a bit later, the anti-Jewish nature of the Nazis' policies was revealed, the Zionists' agenda turned to the promotion of an agreement that would enable the immigration of German Jews exclusively to Palestine. In late 1936, a joint delegation of the Jewish Agency and the German immigrant association in Palestine approached the German consul general in Jerusalem with a proposal that Germany send a representative to the Palestine Royal Commission, the famous Peel Commission, and support the Zionist stance (the plan was rejected).[27]

Zimmermann probably went further on the issue than many other scholars would have. Without hesitation, he identified the common goal shared by the Zionist movement and Nazism: the exodus of European Jews from the Continent. Of course, when it came to light that the Nazi plan called for the extermination of the Jews, the joint vision evaporated and the Zionist–Nazi collaboration ended. When the Palestinian scholar Joseph Massad recently implied such an interdependence on Al Jazeera's website, the network briefly bowed to pressure and removed the article, but then republished it.[28]

The most elaborate research into the attitudes towards and contacts with the Nazis was carried out by the Israeli journalist and historian Tom Segev, whose area of expertise was German history, specifically Nazi history. Segev's doctoral dissertation dealt with the commanders of the extermination camps, and his other work focused on the Mandatory period and early statehood. In his research on Holocaust memory, he showed that the contact continued well into 1937; not only did he describe the contact but, like Zimmerman, condemned it. Segev exposed meetings between the Hagana, the main Jewish military group, and senior Nazi personalities, the most important being Adolf Eichmann. Most of the meetings involved the heads of the Sicherheitsdienst, or SD (the security service of the SS), in the winter of 1937.[29] According to the later claims of Zionist organisations, the Hagana wanted to direct the exiting German Jews to Palestine, not to anywhere else. The German foreign ministry did not encourage these meetings, however, as it did not see the formation of a Zionist state to be in the German interest; the Hagana emissary countered by asserting that a Jewish majority in Palestine would in fact serve Germany's purposes, because it would rid the country of its Jews and would serve as an anti-British base. Segev is unsure about this emissary's degree of authority, but as Zimmerman has shown, the line he took was not contrary to the one taken by the Zionist leadership.[30]

It is obvious that once the true nature of Nazism and its extermination policies was recognised, this attitude changed and contact ceased (until an attempt was made to save the Jews of Hungary in 1944 by offering the German army money for ammunition). But then a different issue emerged: How much was the Zionist leadership willing to invest in the rescue operations once it came to recognise the fate of the Jews in Europe?

On that question, Segev proved to be Zionist policy's severest critic. In his book *The Seventh Million: Israelis and the Holocaust*, he describes a Zionist leadership interested only in saving Jews who were willing to emigrate to Palestine or who were physically and mentally capable of contributing to the success of the community. Segev begins this thesis in the pre-war years, when saving the Jews of Europe was important to the Zionist leadership only in so far as it contributed to the building of a Jewish state. 'If I knew', said David Ben-Gurion,

> that it was possible to save all the children in Germany by transporting them to England, but only half of them by transporting them to Palestine, I would choose the second – because we face not only the reckoning of those children, but the historical reckoning of the Jewish people.[31]

The practical manifestation of this attitude, Segev found, was that rescue operations not connected directly with the Jewish community in Palestine were not undertaken. He describes in his book a community that went about its mundane affairs while its leaders revealed themselves to be people of limited imagination whose rarefied self-image as national leaders stymied their willingness to engage in the duplicity and stratagems necessary for underground activity. Not wishing to invest heavily in rescue operations was not only a matter of prioritisation; it was also a condemnation of those Jews who were unwise enough to ignore Zionist warnings. Or, to put it differently, the priorities regarding the allocation of monetary and human resources for salvage operations reflected a more deeply embedded stance. This dismissive attitude towards the diaspora Jews, even at their hour of need, was part of a wider distaste for the diaspora itself.

This situation was among the most daring components of the post-Zionist challenge to the idea of Israel. Segev claimed, for example, that the negation of the diaspora remained the ideological cornerstone of Zionist doctrine. Negation was expressed, he writes, in the

Yishuv's 'deep contempt, and even disgust, for Jewish life in the diaspora' and their feeling of 'alienation [towards] those who suffered'
in the Holocaust.[32] Elsewhere in his book, Segev ventures a more
conspiratorial explanation for the *Yishuv's* policies. He detects a tacit
alliance between the Jewish community in Palestine and the British
Empire. The Zionist movement was promised a favoured status after
the war if it kept quiet about rescue operations and let the Allies
pursue their war efforts without interference.

It all adds up to quite an uneasy read. *The Seventh Million*
appeared first in Hebrew and was then made into a documentary
film, screened in prime time in the happy days of post-Zionist media
openness.[33] It showed the more questionable side of the 'new Jew'
born in Palestine, hero of the idea of Israel. Segev pointed out that
in many ways the commemoration of the Holocaust became the new
religion for the secular Jews of Palestine – or, as he put it, since religion had no importance for the identity of many secular Israelis, in
its place came homage to Holocaust memory, a tribute that often
transmogrified into a bizarre obsession with death.

Segev was a post-Zionist researcher par excellence. He not only
told us what he found in the archives, he also condemned the previous generation of scholars, especially historians, for ignoring these
unpleasant facts because of their loyalty to the Zionist interpretation
of the idea of Israel. In that interpretation, those who died in the
Holocaust went 'like sheep to the slaughter' instead of rebelling, as
did the few among them, who were immediately recognised not only
as the brave ones but also as the Zionist ones, who belonged to us,
even if they made the mistake of not emigrating sooner to Palestine.

'The Ancestor of the Warsaw Uprising Is the State of Israel'

Mainstream Israeli historiography, the underpinning of the political
élite, characterised the revolts in the various ghettos and camps as
a chapter in the long Zionist history of struggle against those who
wished to destroy the Jewish people. This was one narrative. The very
idea that there might be another narrative was a bold suggestion,

made by post-Zionist scholars in the 1990s. To them, these upris-ings had been Zionised in Israeli collective memory and mainstream academia. They saw this process of Zionisation as a typical instance of how national movements tend to define people's past identity in accordance with the needs of the present national movement.

In early 1942, the Nazi regime in Poland began to despatch Jews to death camps. This triggered the unusual attempt by the Warsaw Ghetto's inhabitants to resist by force this transfer to death. Two groups of Jews in the ghetto decided to rebel – one closer to Jewish Socialist movements, such as the anti-Zionist General Jewish Labour Bund, and one closer to the Zionist Revisionist movement. Both were aided by the Polish underground. Among the leaders of the former was Marek Edelman; born in 1919, he had joined the Bund as a youth. The actual revolt broke out in January 1943, when a second wave of transports began, and held on until the beginning of May until they succumbed to the superior military might of the Nazi forces.

After the war, Edelman studied medicine in Poland and became a cardiologist. In 1976 he joined the famous Solidarity movement led by Lech Walesa and became one of Poland's revered intellectuals. In his writing he often addressed issues of human and civil rights around the world and often criticised Zionism and Israel for their discriminatory policies towards the Palestinians. In the late 1980s he became a member of the Polish parliament. In 1993 the Israeli prime minister, Yitzhak Rabin, led an Israeli delegation for the jubilee com-memoration of the Warsaw Ghetto Uprising. Polish president Lech Walesa asked Edelman to be among the chief speakers; heavy pres-sure from the Israeli delegation removed him from the list at the very last moment.[34]

In keeping with the observation by critics of nationalism, such as Benedict Anderson and Eric Hobsbawm, that it is best to nationalise dead people since they cannot claim an identity different from the one ascribed to them, one can imagine how troublesome was Marek Edelman, this major figure in the Warsaw uprising.[35] At the time he was a member of a non-Zionist organisation; after the Holocaust he remained a Polish socialist; and still he was alive and kicking. It was bad enough that Edelman did not fit the image that the official cultural producers in Israel wished the leaders of the rebellion to have; worse, he actively contested it. In 1945 he wrote a book on the uprising called *The Ghetto Fights*, which appeared in Hebrew only in 2001.[36] He disliked the way he and his friends were portrayed visually and textually in Israeli scholarship – 'none of them had ever looked like this … they didn't have rifles, cartridge pouches or maps; besides, they were dark and dirty', hardly the ideal type of handsome, Aryan-like young Jews seen in the Israeli museums of the Holocaust and in the pictures decorating official texts.[37]

Edelman explained that for him the uprising was a human choice about how to die (as Primo Levi, too, claimed). But death was not a simple issue for the political élite in Israel, which is always busy shaping the collective memory of a society of immigrants, while at the same time colonising a population and an area that resisted, at times violently. The leaders felt in the past, as they do today, a need to rank death in a hierarchy – to idealise one type and condemn another. Death in rebellion against the Holocaust was commendable; death in the Holocaust without resistance was questionable. Death for the sake of the nation was to be the sublime act of humanity.[38]

Edelman was ignored in official Israeli texts and representations of the Holocaust. He is known now thanks to Idith Zertal, who, in the relative openness of the public debate during the 1990s, introduced his story to the world.[39] Zertal was the editor of *Haaretz*'s prestigious weekend supplement and edited *Zmanim: A Historical Quarterly*, the main publication of Tel Aviv University's School of History; today she teaches in Switzerland. In her book *The Nation and the Death* (in English it was titled *Israel's Holocaust and the Politics of Nationhood*), she discussed the Warsaw uprising. As Zertal came from the heart of the establishment, she was able to get a mainstream publishing house to publish her highly subversive book. In it, one encounters Israel as a necrophilic nation, obsessed and possessed by death, and particularly the death camps of the Holocaust – unable to comprehend the atrocity, and yet quite able to use and abuse its memory for the sake of its political aims.

Through Zertal's book, we become able to see how deep the

institutionalisation of Holocaust memory went in the young Jewish state. She describes the construction of a selective narrative that adapted the history of the Holocaust to Israel's strategic and ideological demands. Two themes were important in this respect. The first was planting in the public mind a clear contrast between the new 'brave' Jews of Israel and those who went 'willingly' to the slaughter in Europe's extermination camps; the second, nationalising, or Zionising, the rebellions, particularly the Warsaw Ghetto Uprising, as precursors of the resurrection of the Jews as a new nation in their 'redeemed' homeland. To use a phrase from Benedict Anderson, who served as an inspiration for Zertal's work: 'The ancestor of the Warsaw uprising is the state of Israel'.[40] When the two themes are taken together, it is clear that the Jews who participated in the uprising were constructed by the young Jewish state as 'proto-Zionists' and not, as Primo Levi and others saw them, as people who wished to choose their own kind of death in the face of massive extermination.[41]

In the official version of the collective memory, the uprisings were part of the narrative of Palestine, in which, whether in the Warsaw of the Second World War or north of the Galilee in Roman times, brave Jews stood firm in the face of their enemies. 'The flame of the rebellion has been ignited in the ghettos in the name of Eretz Israel', declared Zalman Shazar, who later became Israel's third president.[42] According to this account, the rebels drew courage from the Jews who had withstood the Arab attacks of the 1920s. This reductionist approach, explained Zertal, was not just a cynical construction of a tale; it also served a psychological yearning to comprehend the Holocaust: 'By [the rebels'] acts, the impossible and inconceivable became both possible and conceivable'.[43]

Zertal relied heavily on Hannah Arendt's work. In the wake of the Adolf Eichmann trial in Israel in 1961–62, Arendt challenged Israel's crude distortions of the Holocaust.[44] She was even more fiercely rebuked than Edelman and to a degree demonised. Arendt not only philosophised about the historical narrative but, far more important, contemplated the moral implications of nationalism, Judaism, and evil. She offered an alternative humanist and universalist view of the Holocaust and contemporary Judaism.

In the 1990s, the educator Yair Auron went as far as to propose a radical change in the way the Holocaust was taught in Israel, suggesting that it be taught as part of the history of modern genocide.[45] He was supported at the time by a University of Haifa philosopher of education, Ilan Gur-Ze'ev, who in the 1990s was a strong voice in favour of a universalist approach. Gur-Ze'ev decried what he called 'the Israeli educational industry's desire to dominate the memory of the Holocaust' and to exclude any universalisation of the event. The Shoah, he wrote, 'became the Totem of Zionism'.[46] The educational system in Israel acts as a conservative, non-reflective, manipulative tool and labels as taboo any other approach to the event and its implications.

After the Second Intifada, Gur-Ze'ev would come to regret his own post-Zionism and embrace afresh the old Zionist narrative and interpretation of the Holocaust. The philosopher Adi Ofir, editor of *Theory and Criticism*, on the other hand, remained steadfast in his criticism. Already in 1986, he depicted the Israeli preoccupation with the Holocaust as religious practice. He claimed that anyone who would dare 'to offer a different representation' or 'even claim he or she knows what really happened there' would be branded as a heathen and traitor.[47]

The Embarrassing Jews: Demonisation of Holocaust Survivors

Part of this more humanist and universalist approach to the history of the Holocaust was de-Zionising the revolts and also providing space for the different narratives of those who had survived the camps and the atrocities. This new angle also enabled a revisiting of the way the survivors themselves were treated once they reached Palestine and, later, Israel.

Until the 1990s, Holocaust studies in Israel was a widespread discipline; almost every university and college had a special department or centre devoted to extensive research on it. Their brand of inquiry, however, was quite limited and focused mainly on the Nazis themselves and the uprisings against them. The vast majority of scholars seemed to ignore Yeshayahu Leibowitz's famous comment when he was asked by the film-maker Eyal Sivan, in the documentary *Yizkor: Slaves of Memory*, about Holocaust memorialisation in Israel (more on this film in Chapter 9): 'Why should the Holocaust interest us? We are the victims. It is the Germans who should be concerned with what they have done'.[48]

In the 1990s post-Zionist scholarship, in the course of extending the scope of research, juxtaposed for the first time the Jewish state and its political élite with individuals who survived the inferno and chose to become citizens of Israel (or were forced to do so). These survivors did not fit the image of the Sabra – the new Jew – a disparity reflected in the documentary films of the 1940s and 1950s. This pattern was discovered by Nurith Gertz, a literary scholar at the Open University who contributed significantly to post-Zionist work on cinema. She showed that the survivors appeared in those films as obstinate, strange Jews who were unwilling to integrate into their new society. She called this representation the silencing of memory, as the films gave no room for either the personal or collective narrative of these survivors. Their narrative, wrote Gertz, was 'stifled by the collective narrative of Holocaust and heroism'.[49] Their memories, she continued,

> erupt in the present and disrupt the Zionist narrative that leads from the obliteration of the Diaspora past to the formation of the Israeli present and future. This is the narrative of people who remained foreign and 'other' in Israeli society, who did not exchange their identities as Zionism expected of them. The films attempt to integrate these people into the Israeli collective.[50]

And nothing could mitigate this negative image. As Tom Segev noted, even the fact that a third of the soldiers who fought in Israel's war of independence were survivors of Hitler, or that some of them had indeed rebelled, was of no help to them. The young State of Israel was still, in Segev's words, 'embarrassed by the Holocaust'. The Jewish state was founded on the concept of the 'new' Jew: tough, proudly speaking Hebrew, working the land, self-reliant. The Holocaust victims, it was said, had gone like sheep to the slaughter. They were the 'old' Jews: Yiddish-speaking exiles, urban and mercantile.[51]

The State of Israel, so it seems, coped much better with dead Holocaust Jews than with Holocaust survivors. As a Ben-Gurion University historian, Hanna Yablonka, put it, in general the Zionist sense was that those who survived were guilty by the sheer fact that they were alive, and thus represented a past that the Israelis wished to forget.[52] Idith Zertal, too, in her earlier book *From Catastrophe to Power: The Holocaust Survivors and the Emergence of Israel*, focused on the lofty and dismissive attitude of the Sabras towards the survivors and their plight, and she noted that this attitude left deep scars in the souls of those who survived the Holocaust and reached Palestine.[53]

But the survivors were not simply despised; when necessary they were recruited, quite often against their will, to the Zionist cause in Palestine. It began on their day of liberation from the death chambers in Europe. This much we now know because of the work of Yosef Grodzinsky, a neurolinguist from Tel Aviv University. His father was a survivor and a member of the Bund, an organisation that even after the Holocaust continued to maintain that there was an international socialist alternative to Zionism.[54] This personal history motivated Grodzinksy to step out of his field of inquiry and take the unusual step of writing a historical study of how people like his father were treated by the Zionist movement after the Holocaust, when, having survived the war, they were put in 'displaced persons' (DP) camps all over Germany.

The DP camps played an important part in the Zionist diplomatic battle over the fate of post-Mandatory Palestine. In those days, the Palestinian counter-argument against the idea of the Jewish state was based on the idea that, among other things, the Arabs in Palestine, constituting an absolute two-thirds majority, had the democratic right to determine what kind of state they wanted at the end of the Mandate. Zionist propaganda worked hard to associate, initially only in vague terms, the Jews all over the world and the fate of the Jewish community in Palestine. In this way, the demographic balance on the ground became immaterial – it had to include all Jews, wherever they were, and therefore the Jews were a potential majority in Palestine.

But this approach was deemed too academic, for instance by the Anglo-American Committee of Inquiry charged in 1946 with proposing a solution to the conflict in Palestine. It was clear that a more concrete association had to be established between the fate of the European Jews and those in Palestine. To prove that point, the people in the DP camps would have to wish, en masse, to emigrate to Palestine. One member of the Anglo-American Committee, Richard Crossman, was unimpressed by the general argument at the time he was appointed, but changed his mind once he visited the camps and was told that most of the people there wanted to come to Palestine. If he had actually consulted the American and British commanders of those camps, they would have told him that the vast majority in fact wanted to emigrate to Britain or the United States.[55]

Grodzinsky found out why the Anglo-American Committee and its successor, the UN Special Committee on Palestine (UNSCOP), heard only one voice in the camps. In his book *Good Human Material,* he describes a reign of Zionist terror against anyone else trying to help the DPs emigrate to places other than Palestine (the American Jewish Joint Distribution Committee, for instance, was very active in trying to help Jews go to the United States). In the camps were recruitment offices for the Hagana where the DPs were sworn in as soldiers; for such soldiers to change their mind was tantamount to desertion. Grodzinsky described other unsavoury means for Zionising survivors who were fit for military action and for barring other organisations from establishing a presence in the camps.[56]

Moreover, the Zionist leadership continued to utilise the survivors after they left the camps and were on their way to Palestine. This has become evident in post-Zionist scholarship through a reappraisal of the case of the SS *Exodus,* or *Exodus 1947,* the ship that sailed from Europe with more than four thousand Holocaust survivors on board and was refused entry to Palestine by the Mandatory government, its passengers ultimately forced to return to Germany.

On 11 July 1947, SS *Exodus* left France in the middle of the night with its cargo of Jewish Holocaust survivors from Europe's DP camps. None of them had a certificate to enter Mandatory Palestine. The British Royal Navy trailed the ship and finally intercepted it.

This was the intended outcome of the incident, as the Jewish Agency wanted to attract world opinion to the blockade Britain had imposed on large immigrant ships attempting to reach Palestine. A mainstream Israeli historian, Aviva Halamish, showed that the refugees were told to prepare for the interception and were instructed how to resist the British forces when they boarded the ship.[57]

The passengers were returned via three smaller ships to France, where they refused to disembark. The British government decided not to attempt forced disembarkation and made the ships sail to the place from which most of the DP had departed: Germany. Returning Holocaust survivors to Germany in 1947 was a shocking move, and the Jewish Agency made all the PR capital it could out of it.

The incident became part of what Novick, and later Finkelstein, called the Holocaust industry in the United States. A well-known American writer, Leon Uris, wrote a novel on it that was published in 1958. Uris was a freelance war correspondent for several American newspapers in the 1956 Israeli–British–French attack on Egypt. He was, as would be said today, embedded with the Israeli forces, and it was during those years that he used the *Exodus* affair as a basis for a tale that faithfully reflected the Zionist narrative. The book's protagonist, Ari Ben Canaan, is a fearless kibbutznik who commands the *Exodus 1947*. Other characters, by their very life story, represent chapters from the Zionist narrative. Ari Ben Canaan came vividly to life when Paul Newman played the part in Otto Preminger's adaptation of the novel into a Hollywood film in 1960.[58] For the mainstream, this was the modern story of Masada; indeed, it was the redemption of Masada. It was such a powerful narration that as a heroic tale, through Leon Uris's book and the subsequent film, it became one of the main media sources through which American public opinion was galvanised in favour of the Zionist story.

The post-Zionist reading of this event was diametrically opposed to the way it was narrated by mainstream historiography. In the alternative narrative that emerged in the 1990s, *Exodus* is a tale of cynicism and manipulation. In it, the immigrants appear as pawns in the struggle for the international recognition of a future Jewish state. The wretched survivors demanded, or so the world was told, to be allowed to settle in Palestine; if refused, they would end up being sent back to the displaced-person camps in Germany. This message was directed specifically at the UN Special Commission on Palestine, which in mid-1947 visited Palestine in an effort to find a solution after Britain's declaration several weeks earlier that it intended to end its Mandate over the torn country. But Britain still held responsibility for law and order and was adamant about preventing massive Jewish immigration or, alternatively, Arab military intervention before the last British soldier left the land.[59]

The *Exodus* affair was meant to prove to UNSCOP that only the Judaisation of Palestine was the correct solution for these and all the other Jews who had survived the horrors of the Holocaust. If they would not come to Palestine, they would have to be sent to the killing fields of Germany. The gambit proved partly successful: the ship was not allowed to disembark in Palestine and was indeed sent back. But public opinion, and especially the UN committee, now clearly associated the fate of the Jews in Europe with the future of the Zionist project in Palestine. Consequently (and also because of the overall strategic decision by the United States and the Soviet Union to support the Zionist project), the UN decided in favour of the Jewish community and recommended the creation of a Jewish state in Palestine. Once that was achieved, however, hardly anyone in the Zionist leadership took any more interest in the fate of the *Exodus* refugees, who were shipped back to Germany to face horrible conditions.

Even after the post-Zionist critics had salvaged the survivors' point of view, few survivors actively challenged the tale told by the state about them and their fate. Their silence did not arise from fear; it was a much deeper response to the horrors they had witnessed, as has already been articulated by Arendt, Levi, and many others. Arendt highlighted silence as a defence mechanism against an inconceivable horror that overpowered 'reality and [broke] down all strands we know'.[60] Levi pointed to the link between survival and achieving a relatively privileged position in the death camps. This uncomfortable conclusion meant, in Levi's words, that 'we, the survivors, are not the true witnesses' to the Holocaust.[61]

But beyond their traumatic experiences, possibly beyond the reach of any description or analysis, the survivors who managed to make it to Israel could not obstruct, but rather had to collaborate with, the construction and manipulation of official memory. Ex post facto, they became Zionists during the Holocaust, whether they wanted to be or not, and those of the survivors who had not played an actual role in the resistance became second-rate Zionists. Worse, unless they belonged to the leadership of the communities (the *Judenräte*) which were incorporated into Israel's ruling élite, the survivors were at risk of being judged for their activities in the camps. Some were brought to trial for being ex-capos (which is perhaps understandable) or for collaborating under coercion (in order to survive) in any of the hideous ways made available to inmates by the Nazis.

This insane persecution of survivors was the result of the wish to bring the Holocaust itself to trial – with very limited success. Only in 1960 did the Israelis succeed in capturing an arch-Nazi, Adolf Eichmann, and in staging a show trial the following year, which was more of a didactic move than a search for justice. But most of the architects of the Holocaust were dead, gone, or tried at Nuremberg, and in the absence of other arch-Nazis, alleged collaborators were targeted.

Such was the case of Elsa Trank, a Jewish survivor who for a while was a forced supervisor of a block in Auschwitz and, as such, did indeed contribute to the misery of her fellow prisoners. She was appointed by the Nazis to keep order in one of the camp's shacks. Trank was identified in Israel by a survivor and brought to trial on the charge of beating her fellow prisoners. In court, it was established that she hit them with her hands, not with any weapon; she was found guilty.[62]

The Zionisation of the struggle omitted, or deleted, the daily heroic struggles of those who 'just' survived. The main stage for conveying this message was the Eichmann trial. The impact of this trial on the institutionalisation of Holocaust memory, when viewed from the post-Zionist perspective, added an angle of which Hannah Arendt was unaware, and which emerges forcefully in the work of Idith Zertal. She connects the trial to the impact of the manipulation and instrumentalisation of Holocaust memory on attitudes towards, and perceptions of, the Palestinians within Israeli Jewish society. The most important theme in this connection is the Nazification of the Palestinian struggle. Hence, they too became victims of this manipulation.

The Nazification of the Palestinians

Zertal exposed how the case against the Palestinians evolved out of the story of al-Hajj Amin al-Husayni, the exiled leader of the Palestinians who foolishly flirted with Hitler and Mussolini in hopes of forming an alliance against Britain and its pro-Zionist policies. Palestinians, however, were not the only target of this case-building, which was orchestrated and directed by the Israeli prime minister, David Ben-Gurion, during the Eichmann trial and coincided with crucial elections for his party. Also under fire was Egyptian president Gamal Abdul Nasser. Already in 1956, Ben-Gurion had equated Nasser with Hitler: 'The danger of the Egyptian tyrant is like that which afflicted the European Jews', he said in the Knesset to help prepare the ground for an aggressive war against Egypt.[63]

Nasser was similarly vilified before the June 1967 war. Israeli propaganda repeatedly likened him to Hitler and raised the threat of a second Holocaust. But the focus on Nazification shifted shortly afterwards to the Palestinians in general and the PLO in particular. The most notorious incident in this respect occurred during the First Lebanon War in 1982, when Israeli troops occupied Beirut, laying siege to Yasser Arafat's bunker. Beirut became Berlin in the last days of Nazism, Arafat was Hitler awaiting his fate in the bunker, and the PLO charter became *Mein Kampf*. It was the Israeli prime minister at the time, Menachem Begin, who continually used these references. On the day the invasion of Lebanon began, Begin declared, 'The alternative to fighting is Treblinka, and we have decided there will be no more Treblinkas'.[64] Even some Zionists at the time found that too much: the novelist Amos Oz wrote of Begin, 'Again and again ... you reveal to the public eye a strange urge to resuscitate Hitler in order to kill him every day anew in the guise of terrorists'.[65]

Another of the many illuminating examples of Nazification was provided by Peter Novick, which is that the al-Husayni entry in the Israeli–American *Encyclopaedia of the Holocaust* is longer than that of any other person apart from Hitler! Apparently Himmler and Goering paled in comparison to the crucial role played in the destruction of the European Jews by a pathetic Palestinian leader whose sin was to serve as a wartime broadcaster to the Arab world from Berlin.[66]

A less obvious objective was to manipulate Holocaust memory in such a way as to help the political and military élites in Israel to move public opinion behind them when they needed support for taking a crucial decision during the struggle against the Arab world or fending off a real or imagined threat. From vindication of the brutal killing of Palestinians in 1948 and subsequently, in the war against Palestinian infiltrations, through the instigation of public panic on the eve of the 1967 war, to the justification of intransigent official positions on peace following the war, to the present oppressive policies against the Palestinians in the occupied territories – Holocaust memory has been a supremely useful and accessible means of silencing criticism and pushing a policy of belligerence.

And so we now arrive back in 2005, where we began this chapter. How easy, how familiar it was for the fanatical settler movement in the territories occupied by Israel in 1967 to exploit Holocaust memory in order to justify its expansionist, theocratic, and racist version of Zionism, which eventually turned against the state itself.

Maintaining a Nation in Trauma

Compelling a nation to be constantly at arms was not just a matter of Nazifying the enemy – there was a need for continual angst, which could easily be conjured via Holocaust memory. Even this kind of manipulation became a subject for post-Zionist academic research. Notable among those who did such research was the philosopher Ilan

Gur-Ze'ev, who asserted that a universalist commemoration of the Holocaust would liberate society from such manipulation.[67]

Even more important in this respect, however, was the work of Moshe Zukerman, a Tel Aviv University sociologist who showed how the powers that be seek to re-traumatize the newly formed Jewish society and keep alive its constant angst about a second Holocaust. Zukerman introduces as a prime example the Israeli government's attitude during the Persian Gulf War of 1991. His book *Holocaust in the Sealed Room* describes in minute detail how Israeli society was unnecessarily exposed to a trauma that was meant to bring them back to the Holocaust and learn the lesson that only the Jewish state could save them from a similar fate.[68]

The sealed room, *Haheder Hatum* in Hebrew, refers to the safest room in the house, in which, during that 1991 war, you sought refuge from a possible chemical or biological attack. Once the siren was sounded, you ran to the room, put a gas mask on your face, and sealed the room. For many, like my late mother, the combination of gas, siren and a sealed room, was an enactment of the extermination chambers of the Holocaust; reinforced by depictions of the man who might launch such attacks, Saddam Hussein, as a new Hitler. In fact, Saddam's army launched primitive missiles that could kill you only if they hit you directly in the head, and the only Israeli casualty of the war was an old Jew who panicked because he got entangled in his gas mask.

One important segment of Israeli Jewish society was not easily manipulated this way was the Jews from Arab and Muslim countries. When post-Zionist Mizrachi Jews engaged with the subject of the manipulation of Holocaust memory, they discovered that all the Arab Jews were victims of this official and collective manipulation. As a result, certain leading activists decided in the 1990s to commemorate the Holocaust in a new way, different from that favoured by the state.

Two of these activists, Shlomo Svirsky and Sami Shalom Chetrit, founded an academic high school that was meant to salvage the culture and value system of Jews in Arab countries while enabling its graduates to become fully matriculated. That school was named Kedma

(Towards the East, in biblical Hebrew). There on Yom Hashoah, the official day of Holocaust remembrance in Israel, students commemorate not only the Holocaust but also other genocides that have taken place in the world, thus giving a more universal meaning to the event. In the official ceremony at the Yad Vashem museum, dignitaries light six candles, one for every million Jewish victims of the Holocaust – a ceremony repeated in every Israeli school. At Kedma, a seventh candle is lit for the Armenian genocide that took place during and immediately after the First World War. The additional candle also represents other persecuted minorities, such as Native Americans and African Americans.[69]

Identification with other minorities, and in particular African Americans and Native Americans, is one of the main features of the post-Zionist scholarship that has focused on Mizrachi Jews, or as they prefer to call themselves, the Arab Jews. The next chapter tells their story.

EIGHT

The Idea of Israel and the Arab Jews

In January 1952, two agents operating clandestinely for the Zionist movement were hanged in Baghdad. They were accused of planting bombs against Jewish targets in the Iraqi capital so as to prompt the local Jews to feel unsafe in their homeland and then emigrate to Israel. Acts like these rattled a veteran community that was probably the oldest in Iraq, an organic part of the society and its history. The successful Zionist actions were not the only reason for the exodus of Iraqi Jews. The nationalist government, headed at the time by Nuri al-Said, wrongly suspected that the vast majority of Iraq's Jews had become Zionist and hostile to the state. Al-Said also coveted their assets and belongings, and thus ordered them to leave.

In the days following the executions, the Israeli government orchestrated mass protests and ceremonies of mourning and commemoration all over the country; however, they had to work hard to persuade the hundreds of thousands of Iraqi Jews who already resided in Israel to partake in these events. Most of them had arrived only a few months earlier from a country where they and their ancestors had lived for hundreds of years and where they would probably have stayed had not the State of Israel come into being. Declassified documentation, released in the late 1980s, revealed that an astonished Israeli political élite learned that quite a few of these immigrants, who were crammed into refugee camps upon arrival, reacted by exclaiming, 'This is God's revenge on the [Zionist] movement that got us where we are [namely, in the hated camps]'.[1]

The Tel Aviv University sociologist Yehouda Shenhav who found this document and similar evidence in the Israeli archives became one of the first scholars to expand the work of the 'new historians' beyond the trials and tribulations of the native Palestinians. Shenhav, like the new historians, found that with a certain frame of mind a visit to the local archives can end in a direct challenge to the state's foundational mythologies and truisms. The particular chapter he challenged was depicted in the official state historiography as a prime example for the humanity and validity of Zionism: Operation Ezra and Nehemya. This was allegedly an operation to save the Iraqi Jewish community by 'repatriating' them to the lost homeland. Ezra and Nehemya were biblical prophets who instigated the return of the exiled Hebrew tribes from Babylon in the sixth century BCE and were said to be the builders of the Second Temple in Jerusalem.[2]

In the Zionist narrative, the repatriation of the Iraqi Jews occupied the same heroic pedestal as the attempt to save the Jews of Europe from the horrors of the Holocaust. But Shenhav and other post-Zionist scholars doubted whether it was indeed a salvage operation, because they found little evidence for an Iraqi Jewish desire to come to Palestine. It is true that in one particular nasty incident during the Second World War – the Farhoud, in April 1941 – Jews were attacked and killed after a long history of peace and excellent relations with the other Iraqi communities. This exceptional eruption unsettled the community and caused some members of its élite to emigrate, mainly to the United Kingdom. But this did not produce either massive panic or a wish to leave; the Jews of Iraq by and large shared in the excitement of witnessing and participating in Iraq's struggle for independence, which was a quiet affair compared with many other anti-colonial wars and campaigns.

For Shenhav, Operation Ezra and Nehemya was not a rescue mission. In his eyes, it was a manipulative move by the Israeli government intended to counter mounting international pressure to allow the repatriation of the Palestinian refugees. What the Israeli government had in mind was to convince the international community that a kind of population transfer had occurred in the Middle East and that it was better for everyone: the Palestinians left for the Arab countries and the Jews of Iraq returned 'home'. Later this official argument was used in a more negative way, with the late 1940s and early 1950s depicted as an extension of the post–Second World War period of mass transfer, displacement, and the reshaping of borders. The international community has never accepted either depiction. Annually, the United Nations reaffirms its commitment, dating back to December 1948, to facilitate the repatriation of the Palestinian refugees. This reaffirmation, however, is not supported by the United States and its allies and therefore has not amounted to much – so far.[3]

The new documents Shenhav unearthed also showed that the government was fighting hard against a tendency of many Iraqi Jews to emigrate to Europe and the United States instead of Israel. He had the impression that the official narrative on why and how the largest Arab Jewish community had arrived in Israel distorted the truth, and this impression was reinforced by a series of interviews he conducted with immigrants from that period. As he explained in 1999,

> The motive for conducting this research is the wide gap between the official version, the one taught in schools, and the life stories of the immigrants from Iraq with whom I have talked. Many among them refute the official version and talked about the brutality and the coercion of the Zionist agents, in their efforts to recruit these Iraqi Jews for the national [Zionist] struggle … [T]heir life stories are the alternative to the Zionist narrative; an alternative that was repressed. My commitment to this silenced position of a large community among the Iraqi immigrants informs my attempt to expose new evidence in this historiography.[4]

This challenge by Shenhav was more than just a question of historical accuracy or fabrication. He doubted the mainstream Zionist narrative in Israel about Mizrachi Jews: that they were Zionists who were eager to come to Israel and that the state saved their lives by

bringing them 'home'. Shenhav questioned the assumption that
Zionism played any important role in the life of Jews in the Arab
world in general, and in Iraq in particular. While acknowledging that
they did have a religious affinity to Eretz Israel, he suggested that
they never perceived it as a place of residence or displayed any wish to
colonise it. Shenhav also stressed the patriotism Jews felt for Iraq and
other Arab countries – another reason they did not feel compelled
to leave. And he goes further still, claiming that they were brought
in as a cheap labour force to replace the expelled Palestinians and
to help redress the demographic imbalance in the new state. In the
early years of statehood, Israeli leaders realised that despite the 1948
ethnic cleansing, a Palestinian minority remained within the Jewish
state and that not enough Jews had come from the West to settle in
Israel. Not mincing his words, Shenhav cast doubt about the pretence of the Zionist movement to be a liberation movement: it may
have liberated the European Jews, he asserted, but it enslaved the
Mizrachi Jews.

Shenhav was too young to recall the events himself. But Ella
Shohat remembered all too well what it meant to be an Iraqi Jew in
the young State of Israel. Today she teaches at New York University
and is a leading figure in cultural studies, a topic she tried unsuccessfully to promote in Israeli academia. As a young girl in 1960s
Israel, Shohat tried to lose her Arabic accent and refused to take as
her school lunch the kinds of food that would identify her as an
Arab. She further noticed that most of her neighbours Hebraicised
their family names, and therefore she, too, tried to adapt (later she
returned to her Arabic names as part of her personal struggle for
recognition and equality).[5]

Out of this experience came a long career of activism and scholarship that acquainted her with the world of textual and cinematic
analysis, and a close association with the works of Edward Said and
his deconstruction of Orientalism. She was the first to coin the term
'Arab Jews' and in many ways pioneered the 1990s post- and anti-
Zionist Mizrachi challenge to the idea of Israel.

Only Slightly Better Than Arabs

Hiding their origin was common to many Jews who came from Arab countries. Ariella Azoulay – another cultural studies scholar, and a curator of several important post-Zionist exhibitions in Israel during the 1990s – tells the story of her father, born in Oran in Algeria. Upon his arrival in Israel, he took the first step on the way to Israelisation by declaring proudly, when the immigration official asked him for his place of birth, that he was from Oran, France. Nobody, she wrote, wanted to admit to being of Algerian origin.[6]

What Ella Shohat and Ariella Azoulay's father went through was individually and collectively experienced by many Arab Jews upon arrival to Israel. They were patronised and resented by the host community, and this disdainful attitude was felt from top to bottom. Prime Minister Ben-Gurion led the way by describing the Arab Jews as being without 'the most elementary knowledge' and having not even 'a trace of Jewish or human education'. Ben-Gurion was worried that the arrival of Arab Jews would turn Israel into an Arab state. 'We do not want the Israelis to become Arabs', he said. 'We are bound by duty to fight against the spirit of the Levant that corrupts individuals and society'.[7]

Other Israeli politicians shared similar views. Abba Eban was worried about the 'prominence of immigrants of oriental origin'.[8] Nahum Goldmann, at that time the chairman of the Jewish Agency, asserted that 'a Jew from Eastern Europe is worth twice as much as a Jew from Kurdistan' and suggested repatriating only a small number of them.[9] And Golda Meir wondered aloud, 'Will we ever be able to elevate these immigrants [to Western civilization]?'[10]

The politicians' views were echoed by Israel's leading journalists. Already in 1948 one of them wrote:

> We are dealing with people whose primitivism is at a peak, whose level of knowledge is one of virtually absolute ignorance and, worse, who have little talent for understanding anything intellectual. Generally, they are only slightly better than the general level of the Arabs, Negroes, and Berbers in the same regions. In

any case, they are at an even lower level than what we know with regard to the former Arabs of Israel. These Jews also lack roots in Judaism, as they are totally subordinated to savage and primitive instincts. As with Africans you will find among them gambling, drunkenness, and prostitution … chronic laziness and hatred for work; there is nothing safe about this asocial element. [Even] the kibbutzim will not hear of their absorption.[11]

By the early 1970s, Mizrachi activists had had enough. They went on a campaign to convince the establishment that they were not Arabs.

Are We Arabs?

From very early on, Mizrachi activists and politicians rebelled against these negative images. Much of the wrath was directed at the Labour Party establishment, which ruled Israel from 1948 to 1977, and so it was not surprising that the natural home for such frustration was the right-wing opposition parties, led by the Likud. Menachem Begin, Likud's Polish leader, captured the anger and channelled it into his electoral campaign in 1977, a campaign that brought him and his party to power. The Likud is still there today, helped by a new group of frustrated immigrants. Now it is those who were brought from the former Soviet Union and the Eastern Bloc.

Likud's main answer to these negative images was that the Mizrachi Jews were modern and Jewish, not Arab – that they were in fact as European as the other Jews. Scholarly proof of this assertion was provided by mostly left Zionist scholars whose expertise lay in Jewish communities in the Arab world; their approach was to show that these communities had their own identity, culture and life – 'untainted' by the surrounding Arab culture.

Alas, the European Jews still perceived the Arab Jews more as Arabs than Jews. This explains the desire felt by many Arab Jews to become integrated as quickly as possible as Jews and Westerners in 'the only democracy in the Middle East'. The fact that many of them had an Arab appearance complicated the integration; quite often, their appearance led to arrest or maltreatment by the security forces. Thus they were forced to work hard at de-Arabising themselves in the eyes of the Ashkenazi community around them. Wearing a huge Star of David medallion on the chest and a conspicuous yarmulke reduced the instances of mistaken identity by the powers that be.

That desire was very different from the one that motivated the post-Zionist Mizrachi scholars and activists of the 1990s. What they claimed was that their Zionist and Jewish credentials were being overlooked, denied or ridiculed by the Ashkenazi Jewish establishment. On the other hand, the new generation also wanted to be recognised as Arabs, both ethnically and culturally, if not necessarily nationally. This, as we will see towards the end of this chapter, opened an unbridgeable gulf between the 1990s challengers and their natural constituencies.

However, there was also a common thread. The scholars' revelations about the scope and depth of past discrimination were welcomed by the community of Mizrachi Jews, who also accepted the allegations that the *Mizrachim* were still being discriminated against in modern-day Israel. Yet they detested the comparison with the Palestinians and rejected any non-Zionist visions of the future, such as cultural integration of the Jewish community within the Arab world.

In this challenge too, there were trailblazers. Certain members of the most influential Mizrachi movement of the 1970s, the Black Panthers, not only took issue with the Labour establishment, they did not support Likud in its stead; moreover they also had doubts about Zionism as a whole. This is why some leading members of this movement developed close ties with the Israeli Communist Party, whose leadership saw the plight of the Mizrachi Jews and the Palestinians as a class issue. A well-known leader of the movement, Charlie Biton, served as a member of the Knesset on the Communist Party's parliamentary list. There were also strong links between this movement and the Marxist sociologists at the University of Haifa in the 1970s.

As a result, Marxist analysis remained a possible basis for Mizrachi action, provided that the former dimmed its critique of Zionism. But the post-Zionist scholars of the 1990s who were Mizrachi Jews themselves or were Ashkenazi Jews concerned about the plight of this community were far more interested in the politics of identity than in issues of class. The most important impact on their work came from postcolonial studies, especially the work of Edward Said.

The Orientalist Jewish State and Its Jewish Orientals

The impact of Said as a Palestinian and as someone who confronted Western Orientalism head-on was quite significant during Israel's post-Zionist moment. Said himself did not always move easily between his general critique of Orientalism and his commitment to the Palestine issue, and this open-ended twin interest explains also the nature of the post-Zionist engagement with his work and thoughts. It was possible to engage with him as a universalist when convenient but not as a Palestinian nationalist if that posed a problem.

There is a tendency to separate Edward Said's theoretical work on literature and culture from his writings on Palestine. It is true that he dealt with the two themes in separate books and essays, in which not only the content but also the style differed. However, it is possible to trace a dialectical relationship between them. This is particularly true with regard to his writings on Palestine, in which he directs the reader to theoretical contexts when discussing certain issues specifically connected to Palestine, but it is also present in his theoretical writings even where he does not explicitly mention Palestine.

This interconnection between the general situation and the Palestine case study, however, created a permanent tension within Said's work. The former entailed a sharp critique of nationalism, while the latter had to be more tolerant, if not reverent, towards it. This may explain why so few other authors on Palestine employed Said's paradigms. It may also account for the paucity of Palestinian historians who followed his lead. The reasons for this are complex and understandable, but it was not until the Oslo Accords of 1993 and the unattractive manifestation of statehood under the Palestinian Authority in the occupied West Bank and Gaza Strip that pioneering works began to denationalise Palestinian history in the same way Said did.

The universalised approach towards the study of Palestine, and his use of a deductive prism, did not at first win Said many followers within Israel. As we have shown, until the arrival of post-Zionism, academic work in Israel was primarily Zionist. But when Zionism was eventually challenged, Said became a natural source of inspiration. It seemed that quite a few critical Israeli academics, media pundits, and literati could not resist Said's desire, and ability, to engage with humanity.

Said's impact can be detected in several major areas: the analysis of Israel as an 'Orientalist' state, the examination of the dialectical relationship between power and academic knowledge within the local context, the introduction of the postcolonial prism into the study of the society, and the critique of the current peace process and the search for an alternative way forward. But more than anything else, it was Said's methodology of exposing images of the Orient and his assertions of what those images signified that had the most notable effect on how Mizrachi scholars and intellectuals viewed the past and present conditions of the Arab Jews within the State of Israel.[12]

Among the early work in this vein was that of Eli Avraham, who investigated the media portrayal of the *Mizrachim* in the 1980s and 1990s. He found a number of recurring themes, including violence, crime, social unrest, unseemliness and neglect, and other unsavoury attributions such as having a primitive, herd mentality that disabled them from ever being 'like us (the *Ashkenazim*)'.[13] The most notable Saidian work in this respect, as mentioned, was the research of Ella Shohat. Inspired by Edward Said's essay 'Zionism from the Standpoint of Its Victims', Shohat wrote about Zionism from the standpoint of its Jewish victims.[14] In her view, the Arab Jews were part of the Orient, disparaged by the West and, in particular, the European Jewish settlers. By taking that approach, Shohat drew different lines of conflict on the land of Palestine: not between Israelis and Palestinians, but between ethnic Arabs (belonging to all three monotheistic religions) and European Jews. In her eyes, it was primarily a clash between East and West.

Indeed, Said's main impact was to allow these scholars to understand the delicacy of identity politics in a Jewish state that had brought in more than a million Jews from Arab countries in the 1950s. This re-examination began by looking at how Zionism affected the question of Jewish identity in modern times, arguing that the transformation of Zionism from a national movement in Europe, where a Jew was defined as a non-Gentile, into a colonialist project in Palestine produced a new definition of a Jew: a non-Arab person.

The issue of identity appears prominently in the writings of the Mizrachi challengers. This new, Orientalist definition of a Jew in the context of Palestine owed much to Said's claims in *Orientalism* – that the notion of the Orient helped to define Europe, and the West, as its ultimate opposite in perception, in ideas, in personality and in experience. Thus, from this Saidian angle, Zionism destroyed the Arab Jewish sense of community and culture and superimposed on it the Zionist and Israeli identity, which was an Orientalist construction, a collective identity that idealised European features by demonising Arab characteristics.

In many ways, however, these Mizrachi scholars went beyond Said. They not only deconstructed Orientalist Israeli attitudes toward the Jews who came from Arab countries; they also tried to offer a different narrative on how the Arab Jews lived before they arrived in Israel. They negated the depiction of life in the Arab and Islamic countries as supposedly primitive and pointed out that the cities where these Jews lived and were active were far more culturally developed than the small shtetls of Eastern Europe.

The assertion that the prior identity of the Arab Jews was not merely different but also contributed to peace played an important role in the new Mizrachi challenge. Moshe Behar, an important activist of the 1990s who now teaches at the University of Manchester, saw the superimposition of a Western identity, which was in Middle Eastern terms a colonialist one, as a crucial factor in making any reconciliation in Israel and Palestine a failure. Thus, he introduces a narrative that is accepted all over the world but denied by mainstream Israelis: life as a Jew in Arab and Islamic societies was a life of integration and coexistence.[15]

As Behar insisted, only once in ancient history were Jews forced to choose between Arabism and Judaism, and suffered from 'communal schizophrenia' as a consequence. This was during the days of the Caliph Harun al-Rashid (763–809), who forced Jews to wear yellow patches. Zionism, it seems, reintroduced this schism in modern times. On the other hand, for the Mizrachi scholars, this history of organic cohabitation made the Arab Jews the ideal facilitators of peace and reconciliation between Israeli Jews and the Palestinians, including the refugee communities. Sadly, this view remained a matter of wishful thinking, and the role of facilitator has not yet been fulfilled.[16]

The Saidian prism explained why the attitude of the nascent Jewish state was so hostile and indeed racist. From a Zionist perspective, the new state promoted the arrival of a million Arabs after expelling exactly that number in order to ensure Jewish supremacy and exclusivity in Palestine. As the works of Chetrit,[17] Shenhav, and others clearly show, the Zionist leadership would have preferred to leave the Arab Jews where they were had it not been for the Holocaust and the lack of any significant immigration from the West after 1948. The dilemma was solved, however, by de-Arabising those Jews upon arrival. Once de-Arabised, the new immigrants contributed to the demographic balance and minimised the number of 'real Arabs' inside Israel.

It is because of this paradigm shift that questions such as those posed by Shenhav were asked about the motives behind the immigration of Jews from Arab and Muslim countries to Israel. The Zionist narrative asserted that the main reason for such immigration was the Arab Jews' devotion to Zionism. It was a groundless replication of the story of the rise of Zionism in Europe. The critical scholars, however, showed two reasons for the immigration: aggressive Zionist lobbying and the emergence of local, anti-Jewish Arab nationalism.

Similar revision of the official narrative was offered with regard to the motives behind the government's discriminatory and abusive treatment of the immigrants. Mainstream historiography argued that there were objective problems, such as scarcity of resources or security concerns; the new Mizrachi researchers exposed a racist attitude towards these Jews as Arabs and a wish to modernise and

Westernise them, with little consideration for their traditions and roots.

Under Said's influence, Mizrachi scholars exposed the sociological, anthropological and historiographical discourses used in research on 'Arabs', whether they were Palestinians in Israel, the inhabitants of neighbouring Arab states, or Mizrachi Jews. Therefore, when the early critics at Haifa made Arabs, Palestinians, and oriental Jews a single subject for scholarly research in Israel, they revolutionized the field. This tendency was strengthened in the post-Zionist discourse of the 1990s, and it made even more sense if one adopted the critical paradigm of Orientalism offered by Said. In fact, for years, such a grouping or reification was taboo, as Ella Shohat learned when she was faced with the condemnation that forced her to leave the country.

On this score, a highly unusual development in Israeli knowledge production occurred as a result of the deep engagement with Said's work. *Orientalism* differentiates between the colonialist Orientalism of the nineteenth century, which had its own reasoning and features, and the one that continued to be exercised after colonialism ended in the second half of the twentieth century, often defined as the postcolonial period. In every corner of the world where the attitudes of the colonial past were still held and implemented by Western states, institutions, or people towards whatever or whoever was non-Western, this was discussed as a postcolonial phenomenon – because in practice there was supposedly no more colonialism. Palestine, however, was not yet decolonised, even at the end of the twentieth century. So the question was which aspect of Said's work applies better: his approach to historical colonial case studies, or his approach to societies that were formerly colonialist.

This question was seriously debated in the spring of 2002 in the leading post-Zionist journal, *Theory and Criticism*, which devoted a special issue to postcolonialism as it was understood and applied by Israeli scholars.[18] This was a difficult title for scholarship within a state that many believed was still colonialist. The reality that was described appeared to be much closer to colonialist-era reality, while the discussion relied on tools which assumed that real colonialism was already over. This was never mere intellectual babbling. Until today, the Palestinian national movement and its supporters have failed to provide a clear analysis of what Zionism is all about: was it a colonialist movement and thus the Palestinian struggle is anti-colonialist, or is Israel a state with a colonialist past but the struggle with it today is between two national movements? This conundrum was eventually solved a few years ago when scholars such as Patrick Wolfe, Edward Cavanagh and Lorenzo Veracini offered a new paradigm for situations such as the one prevailing in Palestine. They proposed that settler colonialism is 'as much a thing of the past as a thing of the present'.[19] They would not accept 'neocolonialism' or even 'postcolonialism' as terms that describe the reality that prevails in Palestine, where colonialism still rages on, albeit through twenty-first-century means.

This is an intellectual quandary with political implications that have only recently been grasped. Earlier, the Mizrachi scholars had more urgent issues to resolve. The main problem for those who adopted the Saidian prism was that it led to a direct clash with their immediate constituency in the State of Israel. On two major aspects of the analysis, the scholars and the politicians of identity differed: how to deal with Zionism, and what sorts of alternatives to offer the Mizrachi Jews?

The politicians endorsed what they saw as a popular wish among the *Mizrachim* to be admitted as 'good Zionists' and saw this as the key to integration and success. Such a route, however, was deemed disastrous by the challengers. Said had offered an answer as to why that approach became so popular. Inspired by Frantz Fanon's ideas of how native populations react to their negative image in the eyes of the colonisers, Said invoked the process of internalisation. Victims of racist colonialism begin to absorb and accept the negative images the colonialists have of them. They try to solve the problem by becoming the colonisers, and their failure puts them in an even more vulnerable position than they had occupied before.

Ella Shohat explained that this political behaviour was the result of years of Ashkenazi oppression. In her view, the Mizrachi Jews internalised the condescending Ashkenazi attitude towards them to such an extent that they turned into self-hating *Mizrachim*. In other words, the East came to view itself through the West's distorting mirror. Shohat quoted Malcolm X, who said that the white man's worst crime was to make the black man hate himself. She maintained that Mizrachi hatred towards the Arabs was no more than self-hatred caused by long exposure to Ashkenazi oppression.[20]

The second bone of contention was that many of the post-Zionist Mizrachi scholars regarded the *Mizrachim* as Arabs, who therefore suffered the same way as the Palestinians did. This approach seemed alien, and still does, to the community's leaders and pundits. And indeed, while many of these scholars were inspired by Edward Said's work on Orientalism, to mainstream Israeli scholars Said was an enemy – a Palestinian.

We Are Proud Arabs!

By associating themselves with the kind of critique offered by Said, post-Zionist scholars broadcast that they were content to be counted among the Arabs. Scholars such as Shohat and Shenhav, along with many others, were seeking their roots as Arabs, not necessarily as Jews. In many cases, that meant relearning Arabic – which their parents had asked them to forget – as part of an attempt to widen their identity as Arab Jews and diminish their identity as *Mizrachim* in Israel.

The most passionate articulator of this sentiment was the sociologist Sami Shalom Chetrit. He was part of the Moroccan Jewish community, the largest group of North African Jews in Israel. He taught at several Israeli universities before having to pursue his academic career elsewhere. Like Shohat, he went to the United States. Born in Morocco, he grew up in Ashdod, a development town built near the evicted Palestinian town of al-Majdal. In his fascinating work, he fuses personal memories with scholarly research on the Arab Jews in Israel. Like his colleagues, he made substantial forays into activism. [21]

Together with Shlomo Svirsky, Chetrit opened Kedma, the school mentioned in the previous chapter. He was also instrumental in founding an organisation named the Mizrachi Democratic Rainbow Coalition, a group (and think tank) that articulates demands such as increased social and cultural rights for their fellow *Mizrachim* and redistribution of the state's wealth and resources, such as housing, among the ethnic Jewish groups within Israel. Their greatest achievement was to allow *moshavim* – generally poor Mizrachi Jewish settlements, collective in their nature – to enjoy the same rights and access to privatised public land as granted many years earlier to the predominantly Ashkenazi kibbutzim. (That land, of course, had been confiscated from the Palestinians in 1948, a point the Rainbow was not always willing to acknowledge fully.) In fact, fearful of the anti-Arab tendencies in its potential constituency, the Rainbow refused to include the Palestinians in Israel as a group whose lack of any share in public land and housing should be addressed by the Rainbow itself. Universalism was not really one of its tenets.[22]

The Second Intifada fractured the Rainbow. The wish to be part of a newfound consensus in Israel in the wake of the demise of the Oslo Accords – the effects of which are discussed in the final chapter of this book – pulled most of the Rainbow members back into the Zionist fold. A minority became even more critical than before towards Zionism and the idea of Israel as a Jewish state. Chetrit was among the latter group. He remained both a universalist and, more than anything else, an Arab Jew. He is also a poet, and sometimes his and his fellow *Mizrachim's,* angst and frustration come through best in his poems:

> When I hear Fayruz singing, 'I shall never forget thee, Palestine',
> I swear to you with my right hand
> that at once I am a Palestinian.
> All of a sudden I know:
> I am an Arab refugee
> and, if not,
> let my tongue cleave to the roof of my mouth.[23]

In the 1990s, these scholars had to confront not only the right-wing orientation of most Mizrachi Jews in Israel but in addition a new tendency to adopt a far more religious, and at times fundamentalist, approach in their politics of identity. The new orientation was a mixture of ultra-Zionism with ultra-Orthodoxy, which stressed the superiority of the Mizrachi religious tradition in Judaism over all other trends and attitudes. This tendency was institutionalised when a charismatic North African rabbi, Ovadia Yosef, with the help of a leading ultra-Orthodox rabbi of Ashkenazi origin, Eliezer Shach, founded a new party, Shas, which became increasingly popular among the Arab Jews who were still stuck on the lower rungs of the social, economic and geographical ladder of the modern State of Israel.

The slogan of Shas, *Le'hahzir atara l'yoshna* (to return the crown to its place – in other words, to redeem our greatness) was by itself not something the critical Mizrachi intellectuals were opposed to. They shared the wish to salvage a forgotten, repressed and marginalised religious and cultural tradition. But the wish to reinvent this tradition as a Zionist one, and at the same time as a pointedly anti-Arab and anti-Palestinian one, separated the politics of identity of the scholars from that of the Mizrachi politicians.

And yet what is really impressive about the post-Zionist Mizrachi scholars of the 1990s is that they were quite a large group, and that they persisted in their defiant outlook into the next century, at a time when their immediate constituency rejected their agenda even more categorically than before. They remained relevant, despite the ideological gap between them and other societal forces championing Mizrachi rights, because the discrimination remained intact. The combination of Shas and a relatively open door for Mizrachi politicians within Likud (and later, even in the Labour Party) did reform the status of this community in the political and cultural realm in the late 1990s. *Mizrachim* held key positions in government and in the army. But there was still good reason for a scholar or any other kind of knowledge producer to continue the search for the roots and realities of discrimination against Mizrachi Jews, since the socioeconomic gap did not narrow and in many ways worsened. One of the main reasons for this was the mass immigration of Russian Jews in the 1990s. This led to a prominent voice in the anti-Zionist group of Mizrachi challengers, Smadar Lavie, who attacked the Israeli government for its attempt to 'whiten the Jewish people' by bringing in large numbers of Russian Jews, many of whom were in fact Christians.[24]

By the end of the twentieth century, still nearly 90 per cent of upper-income Israelis were Ashkenazi Jews, while 60 per cent of the lower-income families were *Mizrachim*. Yoav Peled, a political scientist at Tel Aviv University, noted in the 1990s that there was in Israel 'a cultural division of labour' – that is to say, there was a correlation between ethnicity and income.[25] Thus, the vast majority of the low-income and impoverished families were of Mizrachi origin, while the lower-middle class consisted of both Ashkenazi and Mizrachi families, with a small Ashkenazi majority, and the upper-middle and upper classes were almost exclusively Ashkenazi.

Even though the *Mizrachim* account for almost half of Israel's population, even as late as 2000 there was still only one college-educated Mizrachi for every four college-educated *Ashkenazim*.[26] Indeed, education is one of the areas that Mizrachi activists, whether Zionist or not, cannot ignore. Sami Shalom Chetrit argues that the gap in the educational realm is the outcome of state policies that have not changed significantly since the 1950s. In areas more densely populated by Ashkenazi Jews, high schools have focused on preparation for higher education and careers in academia or more prestigious professions. By contrast, in areas that are primarily Mizrachi, the state has built special high schools (called *Makif* and *Amal*) that offer mostly vocational training. Differences in levels of education have led to differences in occupation and income.[27]

Another scholar, Yaakov Nahon, noted that despite intermarriages and the process of Mizrachi socialisation into Ashkenazi society, the gaps between the two groups not only did not close but even grew at the end of the twentieth century. Although he observed certain 'objective differences', such as the larger Mizrachi families, the gap was still, in his eyes, the result of early and present state policies of discrimination and prejudicial social attitudes.

The post-Zionist Mizrachi challengers were pointing to the reality of discrimination, a reality that also informed the actions of Mizrachi politicians. In this respect, whoever represented the *Mizrachim* in Israeli politics shared parts of the analysis of the post- and anti-Zionist Mizrachi scholars. What the politicians refused to accept was the scholars' explanation for why discrimination had occurred and would continue to occur as long as the state remained Zionist.

Around 2000, the post- and anti-Zionist Mizrachi scholarly challenge reached its peak. It was an important challenge, but not, as we have shown so far in this book, the only challenge to the way the idea of Israel was marketed inside and outside the state. To a certain degree, the other challenges petered out after 2000. Yet the critical Mizrachi viewpoint persisted into the twenty-first century, since both mainstream Zionist politicians and scholars of Mizrachi origin shared major elements in its critique. The claims of discrimination were not denied. If scholars continued to observe its existence in the twenty-first century, and if poets, film-makers, and artists continued to protest it, this was all perfectly legitimate. As a result, the analysis continued while the debate about the prognosis was pushed aside.

In the present century, Mizrachi scholars have tried a softer approach, requesting recognition of their cultural rights. They have demanded that the state's educational and cultural policies be based on a more multicultural perspective; today, in the midst of the second decade of this century, this demand is still regarded as quite reasonable, provided it is wrapped in a Zionist discourse and frame of mind. Unlike the scholars, some artists, poets and writers, each in his or her own way, have continued the agenda of Arab Judaism that was first set forth by the scholars of the 1990s. To this day, the Mizrachi contingent of culture producers continue to pose some sort of challenge and alternative to the idea of Israel as presented by the establishment and as understood by the vast majority of Jews within the state.

NINE

The Post-Zionist Cultural Moment

In a little town in the south of Iraq, Basra, there were thirty million palm trees, but there was not even one sunflower by Van Gogh … George Shemesh was among those who left the rivers of Babylon and arrived in Jerusalem. There he found out that Zarisky [a well-known Israeli Ashkenazi painter] was the king of painters. And this truth was also revealed to Benny Efrat from Lebanon, Ben Haim and Doctori from Iraq and many young 'Franks' [derogatory term used by Ashkenazi Jews to refer to *Mizrachim*] who arrived in the land. But from these 'Franks', Zariskies did not emerge; nor did they engage with 'Jewish' or 'Zionist' art … However, when they arrived in America they learned from Matisse the Frenchman and Sol Lewitt the American that everyone [in the West] was talking about Islamic art and for a short moment this reignited their memories.

– George Shemesh, text accompanying the exhibition
Six Israeli Artists from Arab Countries, Tel Aviv, 1978[1]

In the spring of 2002, the Mother Tongue Festival was launched with exhibitions, a film festival and an academic conference. In more ways than one, it summed up the 1990s attempt to produce, or at least point to, the existence of a distinct Mizrachi discourse. The gist of the films, the visual arts exhibits and the talks delivered at the conference had to do with connectivity – the strong, almost undeniable ties that had been exposed between Arabism and Mizrachi Judaism. Yet this theme captured the paradox of the event: could Mizrachi culture return to its roots without re-adopting at least the mother tongue of that civilization, Arabic?

Most of the films and discussion at the events were in Hebrew, reinforcing the fact that the Arabic language was not part of the new culture. The participants in the event were, in their own eyes, Arab Jews, but culturally they wished to be defined as *Mizrachim*, the Orientals. Loyalty to Hebrew was probably pragmatic, not ideological. Or perhaps the use of Hebrew involved deeper layers, for as one acute Mizrachi observer noted, this attitude to the Arabic language in the new post-Zionist Mizrachi culture, including music, was also an attempt to run away from the role played by Mizrachi Jews in the oppression of the Palestinians:

> We did all kinds of things there; we were governors in the occupied areas of 1948, agents in the Mossad, agents in the Secret Service, officers in the military rule inside Israel until 1967 and then in the occupied territories [the West Bank and the Gaza Strip].[2]

The documentary films produced by the *Mizrachim* tried to revive the contribution of Jews to Arab culture in general, especially Egyptian and Iraqi culture. An example of this is the fiim *Desperado Square* by Benny Toraty, a feature film about one of Tel Aviv's poorest neighbourhoods, Shechunat Hatikva, which ironically means 'neighbourhood of hope'. Hatikva, located on the southern outskirts of the city, was populated by North African Jews in the 1950s; lately the government has dumped tens of thousands of Eritrean refugees there, a move that is the source of constant friction between two disadvantaged communities locked in a slum separated from the rest of Tel Aviv by a highway.

The film tells the story of the neighbourhood through the chronicles of one family. The father used to own a cinema and, after it closed, beseeched his children never to operate it again. There are two sons, who, after their father's death, decide to defy his request, as one of them claims he was granted permission to do so by his dead father in a dream. To celebrate the reopening of the cinema, the brothers look for a copy of the Raj Kapoor film *Sangam*. The search for the rare copy reveals the neighbourhood's subculture, in which dreams are fulfilled only on the screen.

Many Mizrachi film-makers and visual artists regarded themselves in the 1990s as Arab Jews. But the Arabic language appeared only as it does in the testimony of a prominent Arab Jewish author, Shimon Ballas – in a dream, or rather a nightmare.

In addition to including Arab Jews, the Mother Tongue Festival featured North African Jewish writers who asserted that it was not only the relearning or re-respecting of Arabic that could pose a linguistic challenge to the idea of Israel. Some of them regarded French similarly. Before emigrating to Israel and becoming Zionised, North African Jews conversed mainly in French. The Mizrachi author Dror Mishani even suggested that a return to French as the strategy for cultural definition might be less alienating to the general Israeli Jewish public. After all, it was not the language of the enemy. Or, as Mishani put it, it would create a linguistic space 'where the Mizrachi Jew is not disturbing the cultural scene'.[3]

In fact, the Mizrachi Jews had not only lost their Arabic or French; they also lost their ability to speak Hebrew in an accent that could capture the similarities among the Semitic languages, especially the closeness of Arabic to Hebrew. This loss is beautifully expressed in a poem by Sami Shalom Chetrit:

> On the way to 'Ayn Harod [a veteran Zionist settlement]
> l lost my trilled *resh* [the letter 'r' in Hebrew].
> Afterwards I didn't feel the loss of my guttural *'ayn*
> And the breathy *het* [the letter 'h' in Hebrew)
> I inherited from my father
> Who himself picked it up
> On his way to the Land.[4]

Post-Zionist Music

If there was a clear point of dialogue between the Mizrachi constituency that emerged in the 1990s and the post-Zionist challengers, it was a longing for the music they had left behind but could still listen to on the radio and television and more recently via the Internet. There has been a concerted attempt to market Israel as a Western, modern state in the midst of a sea of Arab primitivism and barbarism. But music is part of the local culture and, like Arabic food, it may have the potential to play a more significant role some day in integrating a new kind of Israel into the Arab world. At present, however, it serves no such purpose.

This was the motivation behind the West-Eastern Divan Orchestra, the Arab–Israeli philharmonic orchestra founded by Edward Said and Daniel Barenboim. If the fortunes of Arabic music in Israel are any indicator, one cannot be too sanguine about the prospects. The popularity of Arabic music demonstrates a process of appropriation by local Mizrachi musicians of Arabic music as exclusively Mizrachi music. Yet the music had no political or substantial cultural implications for the identity or behaviour of the society or state, and indeed, on occasion, right-wing parties have played it at the very rallies at which they have vented anti-Arab rhetoric. Even the West Bank settlers' Gush Emunim radio station, *Arutz 7* (Channel 7), energetically broadcasts a somewhat Hebraicised version of Arabic music. Despite all these caveats, in the 1990s, music was one of the many means by which Ashkenazi cultural hegemony was challenged.

Mizrachi music, minus any Arabic language, became a salient feature of the post-Zionist musical revolution that took place in the 1990s. It became a genre by itself – Hebrew lyrics set to Arabic-style music. Today, Israel's national airline, El Al, offers an audio channel designated 'Mizrachi music', a category that also appears in music shops and on radio and TV channels. Back in the 1990s, even Arabic music itself – that is, the music emanating from the Arab world – became popular, whether classics such as Umm Kulthum or the new genre of North African *Ra'i*.

The optimistic mood of the 1990s meant that Mizrachi scholars regarded the growing popularity of such music as an indication that Israel was slowly integrating into the Arab world around it. They saw the musicians – especially the early ones who, since they did not have the money or connections to employ established studios, had to produce music on illegal audio cassettes – not only as subversive activists against the law or challengers to hegemonic Western music, but also as harbingers of a new age in Israel. Their cassettes were even compared with those used by Ayatollah Ruhollah Khomeini in Iran, since cassettes were the medium through which his revolutionary words were spread (other political Islamic movements, too, have relied on cassette tapes).

Post-Zionist music tended to be more Arabic in style and dotted with lyrics that conveyed some sort of challenge to basic Zionist truths. But in the domain of mainstream music, few of Israel's pop singers who imitated Western models were willing to risk their relationship with the wider public by being 'political'. One interesting exception was the pop star Aviv Geffen, at least until 2000, when he, like many others, winced under the ideological pressue. His lyrics included sharp, though simplistic, criticisms of Israeli militarism, and he himself refused to serve in the army. It was, however, his Michael Jacksonesque performance and histrionics, rather than his message, that made him popular. Nevertheless, his continuing appeal did signify an increased local tolerance for nonconformist lyrics that could perhaps have heralded a wider acceptance of less nationalistic ideas among the youth. Alas, it failed to do so.[5]

A New Written Word?

While music appealed to all walks of life, in the 1990s the more educated élite were exposed as never before to the possibility of narrating the idea of Israel through literature and poetry in ways that could be confrontational and, occasionally, even subversive.

It is somewhat difficult to ascertain whether there really was a post-Zionist literature. Reading was an important pastime in Israeli society, which was always endowed with excellent writers in the Hebrew language. When it came to post-Zionist ideas, there were clear differences between fiction and poetry in Israel. Very few prose writers crossed the consensual lines or were willing even to acknowledge that they worked within the constraints of an ideological orientation imposed by Zionism. Poets, on the other hand, found it easier to experiment with alternative viewpoints. The First Lebanon War of 1982 led some highly regarded poets to write pacifist or at least anti-war poetry, and the tendency to decry the evils of the Israeli occupation through the medium of poetry continued throughout the First Intifada. These poems were never collected in an accessible form; in any case, poetry was and is not widely read in Israel. One trend worth noting, however, was the growing body of Hebrew translations of Iraqi, Lebanese, Palestinian, and Syrian poetry, a trend that had been building since the 1970s. The literary monthly *Iton 77* began to publish such poems regularly in the 1980s, and even though one is free to doubt the broader impact of a journal read by a limited audience, the translations had the potential to disperse the one-dimensional and negative perception of 'Arab culture' and to some extent weaken the desire that Israel be a European cultural bastion. Unfortunately, the demise of the post-Zionist era killed these various possiblities at the budding stage.

On the other hand, in the realm of literature, mainstream publishing houses showed a growing interest in translations of famous writers from the Arab world, especially Palestinian and Egyptian novelists. Palestinian stories that carried a political message were generally not bought or distributed widely. On the other hand, the Hebrew translation of a novel by the Palestinian Israeli novelist Emile Habibi that reconstructed the evil days of the military regime imposed on the Palestinians in Israel until 1966 introduced the Jewish public to a period and to crimes by the state of which they would otherwise have known nothing. His early works were translated by fairly esoteric publishing houses, but he later became a household name, included on the lists of leading publishers, and in 1992 he was awarded the Israel Prize.

When mainstream interest in Habibi and in novelists throughout the Arab world petered out in the late 1990s, there was a noble but ultimately failed attempt to continue this important work. Usually the publishers that took on the task were one-man – or, in the case of the most prolific among them, Andalus, one-woman – enterprises. In the opening decade of the present century, Andalus specialised in translations from Arabic to Hebrew. The works were sensitively chosen by the owner, Yael Lerer, who was willing Israeli readers to a variety of Palestinian and Arab works, including works focused on how the West and Israel are perceived by the Arab world and the Palestinians. She thus enabled Israeli readers to become more deeply acquainted with the Egyptian Nobel laureate Naguib Mahfouz (who had earlier been translated by a mainstream publishing house) and to be introduced to more avant-garde writers such as the Sudanese Tayeb Salih. One important landmark in this respect was the Hebrew translation of the epic *Bab al-Shams* by Elias Khoury, the powerful saga of the Nakba and its consequences.

As for works originally written in Hebrew, so far only a handful have provided anything approaching a new view of Palestinian or Israeli society. Such writers were located on the margins and certainly were not part of the national canon. Shimon Ballas, for example, was quite well known in Iraq, where he had grown up as a communist, but was either neglected by mainstream critics in Israel or denigrated as having produced a primitive form of literature. Needless to say, publishing houses followed suit; Ballas's works, which criticised Zionist or Western Orientalism as well as the willingness of Arabs in general to internalise Orientalism, were rejected as unprofitable or as having inadequate cultural value. In his book *Zionism: The Limits of Moral Discourse in Israeli Fiction*, published in the 1990s, Yerach Gover commented that Ballas, by presenting himself as an Arab Jew, offered a counter-narrative, a self-declared identity as an Arab Jew who was bound to be perceived by genuine or cynical upholders of Zionism in Israel as someone who betrayed his nation.

Albert Swissa, who was born in Casablanca in the late 1950s, emigrated late to Israel – 1963.[6] His most famous novel, *Bound (Aqud* in Hebrew), tells the story of the trials and tribulations of Ayush, a Moroccan boy in 1970s Israel. The tale, and the many articles Swissa wrote, presented a softer Arab Jewish counter-narrative, which is probably why he won a prestigious literary prize in 1991. But he never published another book and left off writing to manage a cafe in Jerusalem.

The most influential writer within this trend was Sami Michael, who was widely read and was better known in Israel than Ballas or Swissa. His main contribution lay in his ability to reveal to Hebrew readers the Palestinian perception of Israeli reality. He, too, eventually left the counter-hegemonic route for a less contrary, and highly productive, existence.

A different kind of counter-narrative was provided by the poet Yitzhak Laor in *The People, Food Fit for a King*, a novel that uses every possible literary device, from the names of the heroes to the twists of the plot, to question basic truisms about Israeli society.[7] The story of an army unit about to enter the 1967 war, the novel has several endings and butchers more than one sacred Israeli cow. Laor ridicules the sanctity of the army and its heroism on the battlefied and rejects common Israeli notions about genuine friendships forged in war. Here is how the Nakba makes its appearance in another book of his, which tells the story of a tank column that finds itself mistakenly in Tel Aviv on the Day of Independence:

The procession reached the new commercial centre. The cries echoed all over the country: 'Who Are We? – Israel! Who Are We All? – Israel!' One incident, however, spoiled the overall joy, one that really knew no boundaries (the procession hit circles of dancers that blocked its way, and the dancers were asked to halt for a while so that the procession could continue). The incident involved 'crazy Zamira', who was the youngest granddaughter of the Iraqi communists in the neighbourhood; she was one of those kids whose parents were never summoned to school when she misbehaved and was punished. They did not trust them more than they trusted her. Suddenly Zamira yelled, 'You have not heard about Dir Yassin? You criminals! You murderers! You did not hear?' And she ripped off the military uniform she had donned for the festive day. Everybody laughed at Zamira and the history teacher said, 'This is not an excuse.'[8]

Finally, David Grossman's work on the Israeli occupation and the status of the Palestinians in Israel presented sights and sounds generally inaccessible to Jews in Israel. Unlike the novelists mentioned above, Grossman ranked high on the best-seller lists for some years. He may have been more mainstream and at times less critical, but his wide readership made him an important part of the challenge.[9] His cautious inputs did at least familiarise a wider audience with the Palestinian point of view, even if this greater familiarity did not lead to a recognition of its legitimacy or even validity.

A Post-Zionist Media?

The readiness of the Israeli media to open its doors to the new academic viewpoints, albeit for a very short while in the 1990s, can be understood as part of the ambiguous role played by the media in Israeli society. Traditionally, it acted in many ways like a state press in a non-democratic environment, imposing restrictions on itself to an extent unparalleled in democratic countries. Legally, the press operated according to the emergency laws enacted by the British Mandatory authorities in 1945, which were subsequently adopted by the young State of Israel. Although these regulations were used almost exclusively against the Palestinians in Israel, they were also used on rare occasions against the press, notably in the temporary closures of the Hebrew communist daily *Kol Ha'am* in 1953 and the daily *Hadashot* in 1984.[10] In addition, the press revised its own code of conduct, subordinating the 'right to know' to 'security considerations' in times of national emergency. There is no Israeli law guaranteeing the press freedom to operate; it is an assumed practice in a self-declared democracy but one which is not protected by law.

Until 1977, the press accepted the state's guidance in all matters concerning foreign policy and defence. Thus, 'sacred cow' topics such as Israel's 'retaliatory' policy against the Arab states in the 1950s, its atomic policy in the late 1960s, or its arms trades during the 1970s were avoided. This consensual approach to 'security' meant that there was no need for the state to impose sanctions on any of the main newspapers. The same situation applied to broadcast media. With the arrival of Internet media, which were far more pluralistic and beyond the reach of government, a new reality unfolded. Nevertheless, self-censorship still held sway.

Until 1965, Radio Israel was part of the prime minister's office. That year, it began to be operated (soon to be joined by television, which appeared in Israel in 1968) by a public company, the Israel Broadcasting Authority, whose advisory board comprised representatives from several political parties. One of the main reasons for the smooth cooperation between the government and the press during Israel's first decades was that most journalists were affiliated with the Labour movement, which held power from the creation of the state until 1977.

The ascension of the Likud to power created a schism between the more left-leaning press and the right-wing government. The press, for instance, did not accept Likud's aggressive settlement policy in the West Bank and the Gaza Strip, and was not enthusiastic about the Lebanon War of 1982. Vigorous criticism of government policy, however, did not lead to any change in the basic approach to the 'sacred cows' that make the idea of Israel what it is today.

The press was (and is) guided by a self-appointed committee of editors-in-chief who met regularly with the military censor, accepting his advice on matters concerning state security. The Editors Committee, established in 1948, reviewed every piece of information the press wanted to publish concerning the army or the security services. It should be noted that this self-censorship had wide public support throughout the 1980s: opinion polls showed that the majority of Jewish Israelis favoured limiting the media's freedom to report on 'national security' issues. Overall, then, the press did not deviate from the Zionist consensus, either in the tone of its reports or the orientation of its lead articles.

Nor did the press, in its by-and-large dismissive presentation of

Arabs, especially the Palestinians, deviate from the public imagery of Israeli Palestinians as a 'fifth column' of aliens from within. The term 'Israeli Arabs' or even *Bnei Miutim* (members of minority groups) were in common use, the latter term having been coined in the early years of the state. When dealing with Jewish and Palestinian fatalities, whether caused by accidents or acts of terrorism, the press employed different font sizes and placed the items in more or less prominent sections of the newspaper, giving extended and careful detail where Jews were concerned and only brief and general references where Palestinian casualties were reported.[11] Even tragedy or loss operated on different scales. Indeed, the very presence on newspaper staffs of 'our special reporter on Arab affairs' to cover Arab politics within Israel – even infrequently and in a limited fashion – underscored the segregation (there was no Arab correspondent who was an expert on Jewish affairs).

In the 1990s, changes began to occur in the Israeli press, as they did in academia, caused in part by new ideological insights but also facilitated by the partial privatisation of the print and electronic media at that time. The three leading dailies, *Haaretz, Maariv,* and *Yedioth Ahronoth*, were owned by three families, and Israel's second TV channel, which appeared in the 1990s (as well as channel 10, which arrived with the advent of cable TV), was run by private companies that shared time on the screen.[12] This turned the media into a kind of liberal watchdog, a function it had not previously fulfilled. Now granted a greater degree of free speech and opinion, the press took stands against human rights abuses in Israel, which concerned Palestinians. Privatisation also led to the first bold articles exposing corruption and financial embezzlement in the army and the security forces.

Another factor that contributed to the relative openness and pluralism of the media was the debate concerning the First Lebanon War and the First Intifada. Although the intifada was launched at the end of 1987, it was not until 1989 that Israeli journalists, especially print journalists, began to report what the national television and radio had avoided presenting: the daily brutalities inflicted on the population in the occupied territories. There were several reasons for this delay. As long as the national unity government was still in power (the Labour–Likud coalition was in office 1984–90), the press, with its pro-Labour orientation, hesitated to criticise the IDF's actions in the territories. The right-wing coalition under Yitzhak Shamir that took over in 1990 was an easier target.

Among the Israeli reporters who already stood out for coverage of this debate was Gideon Levy of *Haaretz*, who brought to the attention of Israeli readers the human tragedies arising from the continuing closures of the West Bank and the Gaza Strip and their moral implications. Also in *Haaretz*, columnist Amira Hass, who lived for three years in Gaza, made Israelis aware of life under occupation and later in the 1990s graphically conveyed the illusions and disappointments generated there by the Oslo Accords.

In those years, a few newspapers even stood up to the military censor. Since the early 1990s on a number of occasions, for example, *Haaretz* chose not to cooperate with the censor. The now-defunct daily *Hadashot* took the lead in this respect, and as early as 1984 was closed for several days for disobeying a direct instruction not to publish a photograph of two captive Palestinian guerrillas who had hijacked an Israeli bus. The Shin Bet objected to the photograph because it was the only evidence showing that the guerrillas, who were battered to death by senior commanders in the organisation immediately after the photograph was taken, had been captured alive.

In general, the print media were more advanced in their presentation of diverse views than were the electronic media, particularly television. The very division of print-media information into news sections, editorials and commentary by in-house and guest contributors, and cultural and weekend supplements offered more scope for unconventional thinking. It was in the cultural supplements that the debates of the 'new historians' and later of post-Zionist scholarship first appeared. Around the mid-1990s, echoes of the debate were reflected in the editorials, thereby enlarging the number of readers exposed to post-Zionist views. The debate also moved to cultural programmes on television, which, despite their relatively low ratings, still reached a wider and more diverse audience than academic journals or conferences. The very fact that debates on post-Zionism came to be included in the print media and on both television channels (on educational programmes) was indicative of a significant change. This inclusiveness would have been inconceivable ten or fifteen years earlier. The term 'Palestinians in Israel' appeared not only in the editorial columns and commentaries, but even in the news sections of the press. The term 'post-Zionist' was now in common use, in both a positive and a negative sense.

Nevertheless, one should not exaggerate the extent of the transformation in the press or its impact in those days. The media was still Zionist, even if it allowed post-Zionist voices now and then to be presented in its midst. The cases cited above were exceptions that did not disprove the general conduct, even of *Haaretz*. No matter how frequently articles criticising the government's policy towards its own Palestinian citizens and towards the Palestinians in the occupied territories appeared in the editorial pages, the representation of the Other in the news columns did not fundamentally change. The 'factual' news reports – radio, television, and print – continued to reflect an overall national agenda and employ a nationalistic discourse. TV and radio interviewers of Palestinians or Arab personalities continued to act as if they represented the government, or at least the consensual point of view.

The press's approach to conflicting interpretations of the current reality was well illustrated in its coverage of the September 1996 clashes in the occupied territories. That month, the Netanyahu government had decided to open a tunnel under the Haram al-Sharif, angering and infuriating the Arab and Muslim worlds and triggering a mini-uprising in the West Bank. The press was almost unanimously critical of this decision. Nonetheless, with respect to the clashes that followed the decision, most of the journalists took it for granted that the Palestinian Authority had ordered its police to fire on Israeli soldiers. The possibility, as reported in the international media, that the Palestinian police might have been moved to enter the fray by the spectacle of trigger-happy Israeli soldiers shooting at unarmed Palestinian protesters was not deemed credible in any of the major Israeli papers or TV programmes.

The operating style of the Israeli media involved a combination of self-imposed national censorship on the one hand and an attempt to act as a liberal marketplace of ideas on the other. This produced a reality wherein the press served two masters that were sometimes, indeed often, at odds with one another, and this reality fed the self-image of the Israeli press as being a liberal organ but not unpatriotic. It was an intentional ambivalence, probably based on the reasonable assumption that the news sections were read more widely and were more influential than the columns and commentaries. Still, there was some improvement. Several years earlier, the Palestinian or Arab version of events was not mentioned at all; now it was mentioned at times, though with an obvious preference for 'our' version.

It should be noted that there were attempts to found newspapers that would present the news in an integrated fashion – that is, seeking a 'post-Zionist' or 'non-Zionist' approach to the way the news itself was covered and commented on. Most of these attempts did not last long. Uri Avnery tried with *HaOlam HaZeh*, but even his use of succulent gossip and unclad females did not help the paper survive, and it finally closed in the early 1980s as a financial failure. *Hadashot* tried fashioning itself as a tabloid with an ideological, non-Zionist edge; as a daily paper, it presented a different discourse, more neutral and at times even radical, but it, too, was forced to close after nine years because of financial problems. The local Jerusalem weekly, *Kol Ha'ir*, was the only paper in Israel which continued the fair-minded – which in Israeli eyes meant radical – reporting of daily events in the country and the region.

Despite the various failures, attempts at creating an alternative press continued. A Hebrew version of the weekly report prepared by the Alternative Information Center appeared in the 1990s, aptly called *Mitsad Sheni* (The Other Front). It provided a window not only into the official Palestinian position but also introduced Hebrew readers to the pluralistic nature of Palestinian politics and culture, so often misrepresented in a one-dimensional and reductionist way by mainstream media. Behind such a publication stood the still unfulfilled goal of establishing a common front between all those who have been victimised by Zionism in modern times. In those days, the potential partners included Hamas, the leftist Palestinian anti-Oslo organisations, Palestinians in Israel, Mizrachi Jews in the development towns, and feminist organisations. But it appeared that *Mitsad Sheni* was read only within the world of activists and did not reach the wider public – it was simply a weekly circulated among interested people.

One should wait and see if, in future, similar enterprises will be able to open the eyes of the conventional Israeli reader. *Socialism Now* tried presenting an anti-Zionist agenda for a short period. *Mitan* (the Hebrew word for both a bomb and a burden) is still in print. The Democratic Front for Peace and Equality, Hadash, publishes a Hebrew weekly, *Zo Haderech* (This Is the Way) and 2005 saw the founding of an excellent monthly edited by Yitzhak Laor, *Mita'am* (not an easy term to translate, it means both on behalf of – either the authority or the counterforces – but is also associated with the Hebrew word for 'taste'), which ceased publication after seven years of providing one of the few genuinely critical spaces for public debate.

In recent years, the media struggle around knowledge and information has moved to cyberspace. Several very active websites and blogs are there for any Israeli reader who wishes to know the truth about the occupation and the oppression inside Israel, or to be introduced to more profound analytical pieces about Zionism, globalism, US imperialism, or anything else that places local realities in a regional and international context. It is still difficult to tell at this point how influential these efforts have been. While Facebook networking enabled a toothless and depoliticised Israeli protest movement to emerge in the summer of 2011, neither Facebook nor similar electronic arenas have had an impact on the continued allegiance of knowledge producers and consumers to the classically Zionist idea of Israel or even, of late, its new, neo-Zionist interpretation. The most vibrant among these websites is Ha-Oketz (The Sting), a rare open forum for challenging views in a society rigid with censorship.

The Diet-Zionist Media

Finally, what of the journalists themselves? Except for the notable cases of Gideon Levy and Amira Hass, and also perhaps Tom Segev, who has displayed similarly critical instincts, few other names from either the 1990s or the present day can be added to the list.

For the media, post-Zionism did not signify a legitimate position. It was not the left pole of the political field; it was located outside it. 'Left' in Israel meant, and still means, a willingness in principle to give up territory for peace and to recognise the Palestinian right to self-determination. It is a definition which had very little to do with a socialist point of view or economic issues.

Consequently, the journalists on the left have presented an agenda very different from that of the academics and artists of the 1990s. They limited their criticism to post-1967 Israeli policy and conduct towards the Arab world and specifically the Palestinians. In this way they legitimatised what the State of Israel, and before 1948 the Zionist movement, had done to, and in, Palestine up to 1967. They adopted what might be called an Israeli-centric or Judaeocentric concern about the effect of the continued occupation of the Palestinian territories on Israel's external image and on its internal and eternal 'soul'; the plight of the Palestinians was of secondary importance, if indeed it figured at all. Their desire for peace with the Palestinians derived more from a wish to enclave (if I may coin a verb) the Palestinians in a way that would absolve Israel from any future responsibility for them, and less from a desire to redress historical injustice or to end immoral behaviour. Their approach also excluded from any future solution two Palestinian groups: the refugees and the Palestinian minority within Israel. The refugees, according to this point of view, could return to whatever would be defined as the future Palestinian state; any other suggestion, such as the return of the refugees to Palestine as a whole, was and still is regarded as an existential threat to the Jewish state. As for the sizeable Palestinian minority within pre-1967 Israel – a problem that cannot be solved by the creation of a Palestinian state next to the State of Israel – any inclusion of them in peace talks is interpreted in a similarly hysterical way. Indeed, left-leaning journalists have avoided including the Palestinians in Israel in any discussion on the question of Palestine. To do so could open a debate on the very nature of the state, bringing to the fore its more racist and non-democratic features – issues no one on the Zionist left has been willing to address. This point of view would also garner substantial support among mainstream academics who viewed themselves as left but fought the post-Zionist and anti-Zionist scholars of the 1990s harder than anyone else.

These journalists and academics had a political home – the liberal Zionist party Meretz (although some remained loyal to the Labour Party) and a daily paper, *Haaretz*. The academics of the left Zionist parties are the ones who populated the op-ed sections of the more liberal publications and were brought in as guest commentators on news bulletins and talk shows. In our present century, many of the leading journalists in *Haaretz,* as well as those who had 'leftist' radio shows, joined either Meretz or Labour as politicians. One of them, Shelly Yachimovich, led the Labour Party in the 2012 elections.

A typical example of the liberal Zionist discourse is a book by Yaron Ezrahi, a political theorist who made frequent media appearances during the 1990s as the voice of reason and the left. His book *Rubber Bullets: Power and Conscience in Modern Israel* was one of a number of such books unleashed by liberal Zionist journalists in reaction to the outbreak of the First Intifada in 1987.[13] The book is a combination of personal soul-searching and academic analysis – one of the best in this genre. It is also the best example I have found to convey the esprit de corps of the liberal Zionist media, of which *Haaretz* is also a prime example and which lately has become well represented by additional forces and organisations, such as the J Street lobby in the United States and internationally renowned Israeli movies such as *Waltz with Bashir* and *The Gatekeepers*.[14] *Rubber Bullets* is a well-balanced book that moves smoothly between the personal and the general, as well as between the immediate reaction to particular events in the Intifada and the more distant assessment of the process overall. In this sense, readers interested in the psychological and, above all, ideological world of a peace activist on the Israeli

Zionist left could not wish for a more authentic presentation – one that reveals not only the strength but also, more important for the present discussion, the absurdity and ambiguity of this position.

This book is, in essence, a thorough examination of what might be called diet Zionism. That is, it revisits the acclaimed links between Zionism and liberalism, and all in all comes back worried and uncertain at the end of the journey. Juxtaposing liberal and modernist concepts of morality against the ideologies and practices of Zionism throughout its history, Ezrahi concluded that liberal humanism had a tough time penetrating or integrating into the political culture of Israel. However, he seemed to be ambiguous in his analysis of the causes for this poor state of affairs. Leaders of Zionism and Israel, when willing to admit the existence of such a problem, justified the dismal conditions of liberalism in Israel by pointing to the 'objective environment' that forced them to be economical on human and liberal rights. At times Ezrahi ridicules this excuse, but at times he wholeheartedly endorses it.

The reason for this ambiguity becomes clearer as one gets to the end of *Rubber Bullets*. It is a matter of periodisation. In pre-1967 Israel, according to the author, Zionist leaders were justified in their inability to make a clear choice between power and morality or between human rights and nationalism. Ezrahi, in fact, devotes only two pages in the book to a discussion – an indirect and elusive one at that – to the implication of the Palestinian Nakba on Israeli consciousness. Beyond those two pages, readers will not find in the book either the term 'Nakba' or other references to the 1948 Palestinian catastrophe. Ezrahi describes the immorality of the choice made after 1967 in an original manner, by highlighting the use of rubber bullets during the Intifada. Israelis considered this ammunition to be more humane than live ammunition. In the book, the phrase 'rubber bullets' becomes a concept, not just a kind of ammunition. The concept of rubber bullets appears here as yet another of many Israeli attempts to square the circle – it is immoral to use live ammunition against defenceless youths, but covering the bullets with rubber makes them kosher. However, Ezrahi applies this exercise in Israeli morality only to the post-1967 period, and particularly to the post-1977 period, during the rule of the Likud Party. This ambiguity is inherently imbued in the psyche and outlook of the Israeli Zionist left. This is why the words of praise attached by Shimon Peres to the book ring true: 'This excellent book will serve as a means for the non-Israeli to understand the contemporary reality of Israeli society well beyond the fog of myth and conventional wisdom'.[15]

Indeed, the book is a manifestation of the Zionist left interpretation of the present reality in Israel, but the fog of myth still lingers – the myth of the small and harmless pre-1967, and especially the 1948, Israel. As the opening words of the book convey so clearly, the images of the Intifada were indigestible to Ezrahi. This gut reaction, analysed in a lucid manner in the book, led to the development of a moral and logical position supporting the rights of the Palestinians for their own state and was an important factor in pushing a sizeable proportion of Israeli Jewish society behind the Oslo Accords. However, people like Ezrahi perceive peace as constituting only a termination of the Israeli occupation of the West Bank and the Gaza Strip, an end that will cleanse the Hebrew language from absurd terms and free the army from immoral actions such as the use of rubber bullets.[16]

But the Palestinians expect more than that. They want compensation or rectification of past evils dating back to 1948. Thus, what is missing in this approach is a gut reaction, similar to the one prompted by what Ezrahi witnessed during the Intifada, to the ghastly images from the criminal Israeli uprootings and massacres that took place during the 1948 war and afterwards. Palestinians are not likely to get such a reaction from Ezrahi, who does not want, as he clearly shows in the book, to confront his father with the past follies of Zionism, although he does want to educate his own son on the basis of the horrific pictures from the Intifada.

The book reveals an only partial foray into the darker side of the Israeli collective soul. It comes from within the Ashkenazi 'yuppie' groups of Israelis, who are willing to compromise with the Palestinians provided it will extract them from the Orient, the Middle East, the Arab world. They become less liberal and compromising when they encounter their 'own' Palestinian minority or those Arab Jews who succeeded in escaping the efficient machinery of de-Arabisation within the State of Israel.

Rubber Bullets is a genuine description of the paradoxes that currently tear Jewish society apart; it is also convincing proof that there is a metanarrative of Zionism, the implementation of which omits from a prospective solution of the Arab–Israeli conflict the Palestinians in the refugee camps, the diaspora, and those inside Israel itself. The book thus describes the transformation of the Zionist left within the boundaries of that metanarrative.

When, optimistically, I wrote in the 1990s about a post-Zionist media, I wrongly assumed that the liberalism of the left Zionist media would allow more confrontational views on Zionism to be aired freely and engaged with fully. But it was impossible for the Israeli press to display such tolerance for long. The film-makers had a far more interesting divide, between non-Zionist and liberal Zionist artists, and their post-Zionist legacy has lingered longer and might even have a more lasting effect on the idea of Israel in the future. The next chapter, which is this book's last to describe this unusual decade in the history of knowledge production in Israel, is devoted to it.

TEN

On the Post-Zionist Stage and Screen

We kiss your ass, General Boom,
If it were not for you we would have kissed *Kloom* ['nothing' in
Hebrew]
I remember how you lowered your shoulders when the soldiers
fell, General Boom,
I have lost my two sons, but if it were not for you I had *Kloom*
I remember how your red eyes were flooded with blood, General
Boom
I was also flooded a bit with blood, but if it were not for you I
would have nothing left but *Kloom*
This is why we love you, General Boom, your blushy cheeks in
the receptions
and your upright chin in the evening papers
Therefore we kiss your ass, General Boom
If it were not for you we would have been left with *Kloom*.

In this passage from *You, Me and the Next War*, the Israeli playwright Hanoch Levin ridiculed the most revered group of people
in Israel's ethos and history: the combat generals. Levin was born
in 1943 in Tel Aviv and staged this play at a small cabaret in the
summer of 1968, when the Israeli public was engulfed by messianic
euphoria after the June 1967 war.[1]

From then on, scores of his plays displayed this unwillingness to accept the militarised, nationalistic, Zionist nature of the local culture, politics and human attitudes. He also masterfully brought to the stage the ordinary life of ordinary people, with all their miseries, cruelties and dreams. His play *The Queen of the Bathtub*, staged in 1970, was a series of sketches that left very little of the Israeli ethos intact. The bruised political élite reacted by censoring the play; years would pass before it would be allowed to be shown again. Other, no less biting plays followed suit in the 1980s and 1990s, always accompanied by public outcry and an attempt by the public censor to silence this highly original and gifted playwright, who died in 1999.

Levin was not the only courageous Israeli playwright, though. Long before the 1990s, Yosef Mundi, Joshua Sobol and many others understood that the stage was a space where the worst could be said through the voices of others. When theatre became less popular, and hence less important in the eyes of the powers that be, these playwrights became even bolder and began to touch the rawest nerves of Zionism, as did the scholars and artists of the post-Zionist age.

But they were only a handful. Israeli theatre, apart from these exceptional cases and the relatively open period of the 1990s, was not only loyal to Zionism, it was a blunt reflection of the idea of Israel. In his comprehensive 1996 book *The Image of the Arab in Israeli Theatre*, Dan Urian showed that in most plays, Arabs were portrayed as shallow, one-dimensional figures, the objects of the playwrights' hatred, fear, and hostility.[2] Directors generally embellished the racist texts on stage with 'typical' Arab traits such as sloppy clothing and slurred speech. These stereotypes were present in plays as early as 1936 and were not limited to the work of right-wing cultural producers alone.

Self-criticism in the theatre, as in other artistic domains, was largely limited to post-1967 Israel and focused on the moral implications for Israeli Jewish society of the never-ending occupation of the West Bank and Gaza Strip. This self-imposed limitation, namely, not to pry beyond 1967, was particularly clear in the plays written by liberal and left-leaning Zionists, which appeared in the wake of the First Lebanon War. Since the focus was the effect on the Jews, not the experiences of the Arab victims, in even the more seemingly subversive plays the Palestinians appear as cardboard figures playing secondary roles, while the fully developed Jewish heroes engage in shooting, killing, and torture, but then regret their actions.

There was a non-Zionist approach in the theatre as well, but it was marginal in commercial terms and had no political impact on the society at large. This approach appeared both in translated Palestinian works and in original non-Zionist Israeli plays. One of the translated works was a Hebrew adaptation of Ghassan Kanafani's story 'Men in the Sun'.[3] The play, which appeared on the local stage in the 1980s, was a commercial disaster but hinted at the potential of such a glimpse into Palestine cultural production. It is the story of three Palestinian refugees who are trying to escape from Iraq and go to Kuwait, a journey that reflects the despair of being a refugee because of the Nakba. Original Hebrew works, however, were more popular. For example, some of Sami Michael's stories were adapted for the stage, becoming the first plays to humanise Palestinians by endowing the traditionally shadowy figures with names, histories, and ambitions.[4] In this context, one might mention fringe theatre, where one was able to see plays written by Palestinian Israelis depicting the occupation and the lives of Palestinians in Israel through personal and individual stories. An example of this was the 1994 national co-production in Jerusalem, by Palestinian and Israeli theatre groups, of a contemporary version of *Romeo and Juliet*.[5]

Yitzhak Laor, although primarily a poet, was one of the few Israelis who created clearly non-Zionist work for the stage, incorporating his general critique of Israeli militarism. Unlike the extroverted liberal Zionists, Laor was less interested in what happened to Israeli society as a consequence of the occupation than in the suffering of the Palestinians themselves. His play *Ephraim Hozer La-Tzava* (Ephraim Returns to the Army) included realistic descriptions of Shin Bet interrogation and torture; when staged in the mid-1980s, it was censored for a time because of the connection it made between Nazi behaviour and Israeli occupation policies.[6]

Joshua Sobol may have been less willing to tackle the essence of Zionism but he was very clear when it came to the evils of the occupation. In his 1985 play *The Palestinian Girl*, he provides a softer version of what Laor conveyed. A prolific playwright who was born in Palestine in 1939, he succeeded in covering in his sixty or so plays every aspect of life in Israel. More often than not, he did so critically, and occasionally even subversively. One of his recent plays, *Darfur at Home*, has one character shouting the following words, which capture very well the manipulation of Holocaust memory that was explored above:

> If you really believed there was a Holocaust, you would not have allowed the Israeli members of Knesset to pass a law that prohibits giving a glass of water to a refugee [referring to the African refugees who began to reach Israel in 2005]. You in your indifference, and the members of Knesset you have elected, who mete out a punishment of twenty years to anyone helping a refugee, you are the proof there was no Holocaust.[7]

But this was the exception, not the rule. Mostly it was the horrors of the occupation that made their way into the more open-minded and, in a way, post-Zionist theatre of the 1990s. Those who produced these plays are still at it today, but the medium's popularity has dimmed, and its share of 'political' plays has dropped dramatically.

Post-Zionist Celluloid

In the early 1970s, the Israeli film director Ram Levy decided to adapt to the screen S. Yizhar's (Yizhar Smilansky's) famous story on 1948, 'Hirbet Hiza'. The story was unusual in that the ethnic cleansing, in this case of a fictional and eponymous village, was described in detail, and raised some moral questions about the criminality of this policy through poignant dialogues between the soldiers.[8]

Levy went in search of a village, and in talking to Yizhar he discovered that the fictional village was based on a real one, in which similar events indeed did happen. But that village, like another five hundred or so, had been wiped out, and in its stead stood a Jewish colony. After touring the West Bank (in those days, Israelis could move quite easily in the occupied territory), he found a village that, according to Yizhar, resembled the one of 1948. Levy succeeded in persuading the mukhtar, the head of the village, to let him shoot the film there, but the mukhtar agreed on condition that the local villagers would not be used as extras. With the help of the area's military governor, Levy then found a more cooperative village willing to supply the people for the film; as the director recalled later, they were transported in with trucks as if it were a military operation.[9] The movie turned out to be a powerful fictional representation of the Israeli crime, which only one or two post-Zionist films of the 1990s succeeded in reproducing. The feature-film industry could have challenged the idea of Israel had its practitioners been willing to do so. We will return to it shortly.

The Israeli film industry travelled in a somewhat similar trajectory to that of the theatre. But when it took a critical stance, it went further than any other medium in presenting fundamental challenges to the Zionist historical narrative and discourse. Moreover, any change in approach to reality carried far more significance in cinema than in other forms of media. Film was one of the most popular pastimes in Israel, especially when one considers that the country already had an important and expanding cable system that broadcast commercial films on television about a year after they were shown in movie houses.

The pioneering works of this kind were produced in a highly unlikely place: the studios of Israeli national television. It is possible that this took place because directors who worked for the national television service in the 1970s, unlike their colleagues in the commercial or private film industry, tended to be given funding and not be constrained by ratings (there was only one channel) or commercial consideration. As a result, if they had a radical idea, they could at least make an attempt to translate it into a film – unless they were stopped by politicians, which did happen every now and then. Moreover, as long as there was only one state-owned television channel, considerable effort was invested in creating local drama, much of which was highly politicised.

Levy's *Hirbet Hiza* was screened in 1976 on the national television channel, Channel 1, and not in the movie houses. In those days, television programming was supervised by a council of politicians, and when the film was prescreened, they banned it. In an unprecedented reaction, technicians and journalists in support of freedom of speech managed to darken the TV screen at the time that had originally been scheduled for the screening of the now-banned film. A public and legal campaign enabled its brief reappearance.

Subsequently, still using the national television channel, Ram Levy became one of the more prolific contributors to a genre of docudrama that heralded a wave of post-Zionist productions in the 1990s. It began with *Ani Ahmad* (I Am Ahmad), produced in 1966 before television existed which criticised the state's treatment of Israeli Palestinians, and continued with *Bread* (1986), a powerful exposure of Mizrachi life in Israel's development towns.

Outside the television channels, the film industry followed the nationalist agenda until the early 1970s more closely than any other cultural form except for children's books. Arabs were depicted on the screen as stereotypical figures – evil, cruel, stupid, pathetic – who end up yielding to the superior Israeli hero. As mentioned above, a not uncommon plot involved Israeli schoolchildren single-handedly capturing armed Arab terrorists or invaders. In what I have been calling the post-Zionist cinema, that approach was radically transformed into a more complicated and humane representation of the Palestinians, in particular those who resisted Israeli aggression and occupation.

The First Lebanon War of 1982 catalysed local cinema's move in this new direction. Israeli film-makers began to give voice to underprivileged individuals and groups within Israel, though the transformation was of the 'diet-Zionist' variety. None of the films deviated from the Zionist metanarrative or from the major chapters in the mythical historiography taught in the schools; rather, they limited themselves to Israel's post-1967 Palestinian dilemma. Even so, and despite the fact that the film-makers preferred to tell the story of the conflict through romance, this was an impressive development if compared with the 1960s. On screen, the Palestinians became real human beings and, at times, even heroes.

Diet Zionism was replaced for a while during the 1990s with a bolder cinematic effort to engage directly with the essence of Zionism. In fact, film became the vanguard in the local Jewish attempt to reassess Zionism. The relative political openness of the early years after the signing of the Oslo Accords meant that critique and the representation of voices of the deprived could also sell well. Selling is the key factor for cinema, as it is for culture in general, and for a short while it transpired that a film with a radical message could be relatively profitable.

Compared with the academics, the film-makers appeared to be more open about their own ethnic, national, or gender agendas, which they discussed in interviews and seminars that followed film screenings as well as in dialogue written into the scripts. Films for the first time represented the world of Israel's Arab Jews, whose socio-economic status had only slightly improved since 1948. The films portrayed their growing frustration with the prospering Ashkenazi upper classes, their geographical and social marginality in the development towns and peripheral slums, their limited access to financial resources, and their distorted image in the national narrative. Some of the film-makers who portrayed Mizrachi life also dealt with the Palestinians. Ram Levy, for example, whose above-mentioned films *Hirbet Hiza* and *Ani Ahmad* addressed the Palestinians' situation, dealt with the development towns in *Lehem* (Bread), a tale of the helplessness and hopelessness of a North African Jewish family pushed to the geographical and social margins of Israeli Jewish society with very little chance of extracting themselves from the dismal reality.

Jad (Yehuda) Ne'eman, a film-maker and scholar who was a powerful voice in the 1990s, commented that those new films conveyed through their texts and subtexts a radical criticism of Zionism.[10] Thus far, both fictional and documentary exposure of the abuses of Zionism or the problematic involved in the idea of Israel had had only limited impact on the society. The main reason had to do with the socio-economic background of the film-makers. For all its

radicalism, there was still an Ashkenazi predominance in this new
wave cinema: most of the films that could be classified as having a
non- or even anti-Zionist stance depict the Arab–Jewish relationship
in Israel from the perspective of yuppies in Tel Aviv. In the 1980s,
Ashkenazi film-makers still dominated the film industry, and they
were more interested in the conflict with the Palestinians than in
the plight of the *Mizrachim*. A radical, leftist agenda was defined by
one's position on the Arab–Israeli conflict; not on social issues. Thus,
because their agenda was political rather than social, these films could
appeal to people living in relative comfort, who could afford to identify with the Other. They were, of course, accepted warmly by Israel's
Palesinians, and in that sense strengthened Arab–Jewish cooperation,
but mass audiences in the more deprived areas may have received
them differently.

Nonetheless, the fact that some of the films that depicted the
Israeli as occupier and coloniser and the Palestinian as victim were
shown for several weeks was an indication that they were intriguing
enough to create empathy, or at least interest. Indeed, it does seem
that the critique genre, whether hidden or fairly overt, was quite
popular for a while. This popularity was the result of the curious
fusion of an aggressively free-market political economy with the rise
of multiculturalism in Israeli society. The continued capitalisation of
the Israeli economy also explains the success of, and even the drive
for, a more critical response to the local cultural market, not just
as a fulfilment of an ideological agenda. As Pierre Bourdieu commented so aptly, both academic and cultural products represent not
only political and social transformations but also economic products
that need to be marketed.[11] This is clearer in the case of the cinema
than in that of academia.

In some instances, however, commercial considerations were secondary. What such film-makers wished to do was to connect, or
reconnect, to the world they came from – and this was particularly
true of Mizrachi and Palestinian film-makers. The Mizrachi film-
makers were producing their more critical work at a time when the
Mizrachi Jews' overall economic, judicial and political conditions
had improved. But improvement was not enough, at least in the eyes

of these artists. They, like other members of their community, were in fact frustrated at the persistent social and economic polarisation within Jewish society in Israel and in particular with the marginal position of their own community in the national myth and narrative.

Yet despite these impressive forays into other perspectives, the treatment of the Other in films and plays was inhibited by the projection of an Israeli image onto the Palestinian. It was as if the other side could be understood only if its heroes acted like Israelis or subscribed to an Israeli concept of reality. For instance, in the 1986 film *Avanti Popolo*, an Egyptian soldier, speaking in a Palestinian dialect (which Israeli Jewish viewers would not notice), conveys the message of human values common to both sides by quoting Shakespeare's Shylock. An Anglophile Egyptian common soldier must have been a very rare sight on the Sinai battlefield and yet he was invented to provoke sympathy from the Israeli audience.[12]

Some of the bravest attempts to show the world through the eyes of Zionism's victims, as suggested by the late Edward Said, were woven into fictional or real tales of impossible love.[13] Romance and sex sell, and romance was the main sweetener for the new views offered to Israeli filmgoers. Most of these films were modelled on a Romeo-and-Juliet sort of plot: a Jewish woman falls in love with a Palestinian man against the wishes of their respective families and societies. In reality, this was and is an extremely rare occurrence – and one which indicates how exclusionary the project of Zionism was. More than a century of settlement did not produce any significant romantic, let alone familial, ties between the settlers and the native population. No other settler society has been that 'pure', apart from the whites in South Africa.

The eroticisation of the conflict generates a sensual identification with the heroes. As with Hollywood films about African Americans, so in the 'enlightened' Israeli film industry the 'Arabs' were exceptionally handsome or beautiful. The focus on sex and beauty permits what psychologists call displacement: instead of identifying with the cause of the general suffering inflicted on the other side, the viewer identifies with the broken heart of an attractive hero. Also worth considering with regard to cooperation, friendship, and even romance across the divide is the interesting difference between the attitude of historians, especially in the new age of relativism and even postmodernism, and that of film-makers. While the historians may deduce an optimistic conclusion from such incidents in history, the cinema usually presents them through the lens of tragedy, as an indication of the unbridgeable abyss that separates the two sides and cannot be overcome. Thus, fiction is far more realistic in its depiction of relationships on the ground than the typical academic illusions about humanity and human beings.

Still, the films in which Jews apppeared as villains and Palestinians as heroes did seem to have an effect at the time. Switching conventional roles challenged the image of the Arab in the Zionist metanarrative. No academic work could reach such a broad audience or produce such a clear message. The best of this kind was the 1989 film *Esh Tzolevet* (Crossfire), which went beyond the subject of romance and presented, in a way never before seen in an Israeli feature film, a Palestinian perspective on the 1948 war. It warrants extensive mention here.[14]

Humanising the Nakba: *Esh Tzolevet* (Crossfire)

However progressive some of the films appearing in the post-Zionist decade were with respect to the occupation and the conflict, almost all of them lacked empathy towards Palestinian positions on the Nakba, in particular the sense of catastrophe and the right of return. What the more critical films did was to challenge the 1967 occupation, although it is true that the Arab, in a timeless sense, does become more humanised and appears, on several occasions, as the hero.

Most of these films lacked a historical dimension; they were located outside any well-charted chronological or geographical framework. The viewer never knew whether the locus was inside or outside the Green Line, or what time or year the events took place. Even so, they did present a Jewish occupier/colonialist and a native Arab/Other.

Crossfire is one of the few post-Zionist feature films that, like the classic Zionist films, dealt directly with the 1948 war. Very few people in Israel have seen the film, either when it first appeared or afterwards, and its maker, Gidon Ganani, does not belong to the ranks of Israel's hegemonic culture producers. Therefore it is not a good example of any salient trend or development. Yet it clearly shows the potential for an alternative representation of the idea of Israel.

The film is based on a true story: an impossible love affair between George Khouri, a Palestinian, and Miriam Seidman, a Jew. They meet accidently at a British checkpoint circa 1947. While searching Miriam's belongings, the soldiers toss her basket on the ground, spilling its contents. George helps her collect her things and thus they become acquainted with each other. Miriam works in her mother's restaurant in northern Tel Aviv, and George makes his way there on the pretext that he had to stop nearby because his car's engine got overheated and he needed water. On his second visit, he is thrown out by Miriam's brother, a member of the Hagana, and his mates. Miriam's apology gives rise to another meeting and then another, always due to Miriam's insistence and initiative. Although the meetings take place at intimate sites, such as the Andromeda Rock in Jaffa where they go for a night-time swim, they do not lead to a more intimate relationship between the two, because George does not take advantage of the many opportunities falling his way. As the overall situation deteriorates and tensions between the Palestinians and Jews increase, the meetings move to a British club. During one of those meetings, two Stern Gang terrorists enter and murder a British officer. Stern Gang members follow the couple on the suspicion that Miriam may be working with the enemy.

Miriam tells George she will never leave him, and it is her sheer determination that keeps the romance alive. Now the meetings are all in Arab Jaffa. But they are constantly interrupted by her brother, Shraga, known for his fanaticism and hot-headedness. He batters Miriam badly but leaves the couple alone. However, the Stern Gang hooligans finally find a pretext to move against Miriam and George: they both witnessed the killing of the British officer in the club and therefore have to be eliminated. The gang builds a case against them, which includes the allegation that Miriam assisted George to plan the attack on their headquarters in Tel Aviv. While Miriam awaits George for a final meeting in Palestine, after which they plan to leave the country for good, the Stern Gang executes her.

As mentioned, the template in post-Zionist movies about love affairs between Arabs and Jews ends in tragedy, specifically death. The futility of such a death and the predictability of such an ending are beautifully shown in a scene in which a Palestinian shepherd takes a picture of the two and gives it to Miriam's brother, who fails to develop them and then has to create a photomontage in order to show the two together. This is the essence of the romantic relationship: artificial, liminal, and in reality impossible. Even the only seemingly feasible solution for such an impossible love – running away abroad – cannot materialise.

But beyond the overtly tragic message of the film, there are hidden ones as well, which turn this film into the only one I know of in which the Palestinian narrative of 1948 is not merely respected but also accepted as accurate. By itself, the execution of a Jewish woman by Jews challenges the conventional image of the bloodthirsty and inhuman Arab. Moreover, and probably even unintentionally, the movie went further than most in its historiographical view: it presents Palestinian viewpoints on 1948 as rational and deserving of empathy. The most illuminating scene in this respect is one set in November 1947, in which the patrons in an Arab coffeehouse listen anxiously to the wireless as it broadcasts the UN voting process on the partition resolution. This is the first and only time in an Israeli movie that the scriptwriter demonstrates an awareness of the fears experienced by the other side, which are diametrically opposed to those of the Jewish side. A scene of Jews listening anxiously, anticipating the opposite result of the vote, has appeared often in documentary as well as feature films since 1948, and it is followed by ecstatic dancing in the streets.

Another striking aspect of the narrative is how it is positioned with respect to the explanation for the war's eruption. In the classic Zionist narrative, as mentioned earlier in the context of the film *Dan and Sa'adia*, the war breaks out for some unexplainable reason when the Arabs, out of the blue, decide to attack. Here it breaks out after the Arab governments lose the vote in the United Nations and David Ben-Gurion declares the Jewish state. By taking these events into account, the connection between the fury felt by the Palestinians and their frustration and consequent assault on Jewish convoys and settlements becomes clearer. This connection is explained in dialogue by one of George's friends in a scene that takes place in a pool hall in Jaffa. He speaks about UNSCOP (the UN Special Committee on Palestine, appointed in the spring of 1947 to propose a solution for the conflict in Palestine) and the fact that it permitted Jewish immigrants to flood Palestine while it discussed the country's future. It was clear that these new immigrants would be staying put, regardless of what the UN ended up proposing. 'And now the Arabs will stay defenceless, after the British leave, when they face these immigrants', says George's friend. This narration reflects not only the Palestinian narrative of the war, but also some of the claims made by the new Israeli historiography about it.

Yet another aspect of this film is that it brings out the human side of the Palestinians, who appear as victims of Jewish attacks on Jaffa. In one of these attacks, George's friend and relative Pierre is killed. George is seen stooping over his body and caressing his face. George is handsome and elegantly dressed; he drives a fancy car and is far more educated than Miriam. His English is flawless, and this we know because Miriam needs him to help her speak to the Brits. As it happens, all the major Palestinian characters in the film are Christians. This is first and foremost out of loyalty to the true story but tends inadvertently to suggest that the positive Arab image is limited to Christians. However, the Muslims who appear in the film in subsidiary roles are also depicted as normal, multidimensional human beings. Unlike in *Dan and Sa'adia*, here we know what they aspire to and what they fear, and more than anything else we learn what drives their actions. They win our empathy because their conduct is rational and because we are exposed to subtle and intelligent dialogue among themselves.

What contributes to the film's credibility is that not all the Palestinians are positive and admirable human beings. Thus, for instance, after Pierre is killed, George and his friends plan to exact revenge. But this is in fact the reverse of the way Zionist historiography characterises not only the 1948 war but every conflict with the Arabs: an Arab action and an Israeli retaliation. Here the Israeli action comes first. In addition, the Arab retaliation in this case fails, because one of the Palestinians is greedy enough to sell for good money their plan to the Stern Gang, and the same person is also providing the information on Miriam that the gang uses to incriminate her.

The Jewish characters, by contrast, are quite negative. The worst is Shraga, Miriam's brother. He appears in the movie with all the paraphernalia of a Hagana fighter and behaves like a mindless thug. To his underlings, when they fail to hit the targets during gun training sessions, he says, 'Imagine you are shooting an Arab, or a British soldier – it will help.' He contemplates expelling George from Palestine before deciding to kill him. And expulsion is the single historical fact that best connects the new Israeli historiography with the Palestinian narrative.

Even Shay, the military intelligence wing of the Hagana, appears to be acting on the basis of racism and fanaticism. They throw unfounded accusations at Miriam not because she constitutes an existential danger but because of her forbidden love for an Arab. Such a depiction could be found only in the boldest of the new historians' works – namely, the possibility that the young State of Israel followed certain policies or that its political élite took certain decisions towards the Palestinians, not on the basis of security considerations, but out of sheer racism.

Nonetheless, one-dimensional Arabs are not replaced by one-dimensional Jews. Israel, Shraga's best friend, is gentle and good-hearted, although he is torn to pieces because he is in love with Miriam and knows that this is why he collaborates with Shraga in the violent expulsion of George. Few members of Shay are appalled by the option of murder (but not battery and expulsion). Indeed, the Hagana's image in this film is fascinating. Its representatives do engage in direct killings, but they debate and hesitate, much more so than the Stern terrorists. So, in a typical Zionist way, they are absolved from the accusation of violence for the sake of violence. It thus seems easier to attribute the violence in the film to the Stern Gang and not the Hagana. George asks Miriam, 'Have you known any of the assassins of the British officer?' and adds, 'You are all brothers-in-arms.' He also associates the murder of another British officer with a potential death threat to Miriam, posing the rhetorical question 'You know what these murderers will do when they finish the British?' The terms 'murderers' or 'assassins' appear in the film many times when the Stern Gang is mentioned. In the final scene of the movie there is a photomontage of the couple, along with a text which reads: 'Miriam Seidman was executed and shot by the Stern Gang after being found guilty of treason. Her guilt was never proven, her name was never cleared, and those responsible for her death were never brought to justice.'

But this is not just a story of the Palestinian tragedy. It aspires to be a more universal tale about humanity in general. In general, when dealing with issues such as this, cinema has an advantage over historiography, as is made clear by the immediacy of this film, which could not easily be produced by a written narrative. It pointedly associates geography and politics. Thus, most of Miriam's encounters with George take place on the beach where the border between Jewish Tel Aviv and Palestinian Jaffa runs. Only there is it possible for the two to detach themselves temporarily from the hostile environment. The director juxtaposes these encounters on the shore with discussions at the Hagana's headquarters about Miriam's fate.

The stark contrast between the two protagonists and the murky, hostile, violent environment is also achieved through the way George and Miriam appear on the screen, as well as the physical surroundings where they meet. They are both handsome, young, and clothed in beautiful fabrics, very different from the dreary khaki uniforms worn by those around them. They are filmed against sunsets and maritime panoramas, while the rest of the scenes take place amid the ugly hustle and bustle of militarisation.

Again and again, Miriam and George try to disengage from the national plot into which they were tossed. George throws a bomb into the sea that he promised to detonate in a Jewish area; Miriam's face appears gloomy amid the sounds of cheering Jews, celebrating diplomatic victory in the UN. All this comes across in the film, despite the film-makers' more limited ability to identify with the other side compared with the capabilities of the historians. Cinema focuses on individuals, and its creators can therefore more easily display sympathy with the other side – and with respect to one's own national myth and narrative, calling up that sympathy poses a challenge. Generally, sympathy arises from emotive identification with a screen hero or from a more universal and critical view on life; rarely is it based, as is the case with historians, on new facts. New documentation for a film with a historical dimension is essential, but it is not the crucial component in the creation of a new historiographical picture of the past. Historical films of course have scriptwriters and directors who must support a historical plot with documentary material, but they can readily identify the more imaginative parts of the story. Even if a film tells a basically true story, such as Oliver Stone's *JFK* and *Frost/Nixon*, or Richard Attenborough's *Ghandi*, they are still an admixture of fiction and reality. Such licence is obviously a luxury that documentarians cannot permit themselves.

The Documentary Post-Zionist Challenge

Esh Tzolevet was not the only film in Israel that exposed dilemmas and taboos. A few films went so far as to take on the manipulation of Holocaust memory in Israeli politics and discourse. Ilan Moshenson's 1979 movie *Roveh Huliot* (The Wooden Gun), for example, conveyed Israeli uneasiness over the possible link between the Nazi wish to annihilate the Jews in Europe and the Zionist desire to see the expulsion of the Jews from Europe for the sake of the Jewish community in Palestine. Some of these themes were treated in television docudramas. Motti Lerner's 1994 three-part TV miniseries *The Kastner Trial*, for instance, was based on the true story of a Zionist activist who saved Hungarian Jews by bribing Nazis and who later tried to cleanse his name in a libel trial but failed. The film highlighted the uneasy connection between the Jewish leadership in Palestine and the Holocaust, and put forward the uncomfortable conclusion that the survival of the community in Palestine always came first. A 1995 docudrama by Benny Brunner, based on Tom Segev's book *The Seventh Million*, focused on Jewish leaders' decision not to become involved in operations to save Jews that did not bring survivors to Palestine and to concentrate on efforts to save Jews who were physically and mentally fit and likely to contribute to nation-building.

Beyond the makers of docudramas are the documentary film-makers, who intervene very little in the raw reality they film, believing strongly that it speaks for itself. One of the best among them is Eyal Sivan. An early film of his, *Yizkor: Slaves of Memory*, tested the limits of how far one can challenge from within one's own national ethos and mythology. In the film he follows the manipulation of Holocaust memories in the Israel high school system during the period between the Passover festivities through Holocaust Remembrance Day Yom Hashoah, and up to the celebrations of Independence Day, Yom Ha'atzmaut. The camera hardly leaves the classroom or schoolyard, and an extended version includes an extremely poignant interview with Yeshayahu Leibowitz, who was mentioned in Chapter 4 above. For me the unforgettable remark in this interview was that the Holocaust is not a Jewish problem: 'We did not do it. The Germans did, and it is therefore their problem.' By contrast, the occupation should concern the Israeli Jews, because this is an evil of their own doing. Calling on Israel to focus on its own crimes and less on its victimisation was a demand rarely heard of even at the peak of the post-Zionist era.

Yizkor leaves the viewer with a mixture of optimism and despair. The school manufactures a false and unconvincing Jewish narrative of self-righteousness and victimisation that lumps together the ancient stories of the Hebrews in Pharaonic Egypt with accounts of Nazi Europe and the 1948 War of Independence. The students do not always seem to fall prey to this metanarrative, but neither are they offered any alternatives, and thus are likely to become the slaves of this manipulated memory in future. What it also shows is the grotesque business of enslaving memory for ideological purposes: there is an efficient use of materials employed for the various memorial ceremonies, which have an almost postmodern character in which everything is the same whether it happened five thousand years ago or yesterday. An efficient teacher, then, will instruct the students not to waste the posters describing the exodus from Egypt so that they can be used again in a Broadway-style presentation on the various death camps of the Holocaust. On Yom Hashoah, each student is assigned a banner with the name of one of the camps on it, and the viewer almost senses a competition among the children to receive the banner that represents the worst site of the Nazi genocide.

An original angle on Holocaust memory manipulation and its relationship with the Mizrachi Jews has been taken by the prolific film director Asher Tlalim in *Don't Touch My Holocaust*.[15] In the film, Tlalim monitors a group of Arab and Jewish actors from Israel who participate in a play about the Holocaust, and poses the question of what later generations should know and understand about the horrific event. Tlalim would go on to explore the exilic and Holocaust background of Jewish experience through his 2000 film *Galoot* (Exile).

Tellingly, both Sivan and Tlalim left Israel and emigrated to Europe. In exile, Sivan would make ten films, two of which dealt with the history of Palestine. One of his latest is called *Jaffa, The Orange's Clockwork*, which follows the Zionist narrative through a multilayered deconstruction of the story of Jaffa oranges. It uses the Zionist takeover of the citrus industry in Palestine as a microcosmic struggle that represents the conflict in the Land as a whole. Sivan had already dealt with the history of Palestine. His second film was made in cooperation with Palestinian director Michel Khleifi; together they made *Route 181: Fragments of a Journey in Palestine–Israel*, a film that follows the fault lines of UN Resolution 181, the Partition Plan, and thus allows them to tell the story of the Nakba through the eyes of both victims and victimisers in a fascinating cinematic conversation.[16]

Sivan is one of the few Israeli film-makers who have engaged directly with the Nakba. In the early 1990s he was joined by David Benchetrit, whose documentary *Through the Veil of Exile* is both a tribute to and an uncensored stage for the victims of the 1948 catastrophe. Benchetrit's film is a profile of three Palestinian women from different walks of life, background and education. Each of them commences her story in 1948. Dalal Abu Kamar comes from the Al Shata refugee camp, Mary Hass is from Haifa and has lived in Gaza since 1967, and Umm Muhammad is from the Ayn Sultan refugee camp near Jericho. The year 1948 serves as a departure point for their personal stories. The story accepts, without any caveats, the chapter of refugeehood as it appears in the Palestinian narrative. The coerced lifting of people into trucks and their expulsion from their homes is accurately reconstructed and powerfully portrayed, as it would be in Palestinian films. By telling the story of Palestinians as real human beings and victims of Zionism – persons with names, pains and hopes, victims not just of 1967 Israel but also of the small and beautiful Israel that all liberal Zionists have nostalgically longed for – this film embodies everything that the cinema, historiography and literature of the classic Zionist era could not have portrayed.

The identification with the other side's narrative comes out clearly at the very beginning of the film. An Arabic psalm of longing is played while a picture appears of a lorry overloaded with people, passing through arid land, followed by a shot of a refugee camp. The link between the refugees and the world that was wiped out physically in the war is personified in the story of Dalal who is the first witness in the film. The wiping out of her house does not take place in a vacuum; there is a wiping hand as well, that of Israel. Dalal represents a very significant chapter in the national Palestinian narrative, one which had not yet been validated in Israeli fiction. She talks about the sense of temporality that accompanied the first years in the refugee camp; it is this sense that explains why the refugees refused to build stone houses in the camps, and why they believed that the UN Resolution 194 of December 1948, gave them the right to return. This resolution was the basis for their hopes of return and repatriation, regardless of what Israel had done to the Palestinians' homes or to the course of the Arab–Israeli conflict.

A different aspect of the story of dispossession emerges from Mary Hass's narrative, in which she describes how the State of Israel's Caterpillar D9 bulldozers demolished her home. Through its footage, the film confirms her account of Jewish families taking over Palestinian homes in the neighbourhood of Wadi Nisnas in downtown Haifa. Her description corroborates those found in the documents made available in the 1980s as well as the analyses of the new Israeli history. It is interesting that Mary Hass on one occasion reaffirms the Zionist narrative claim that Palestinians left because they heard on the radio that they should leave, which was proved unfounded by both Erskine Childers in 1961 and Benny Morris in 1992, both of whom saw no evidence for such announcements.[17]

Benchetrit, who is of Moroccan origin, went on to produce a trilogy on the Moroccan Jews. At the end of April 2004, while he was in the midst of making a film about refuseniks and the First Lebanon War of 1982, he went to the Israeli Ministry of Defense for a scheduled interview with the IDF spokesperson. Instead, he was handcuffed, pushed to the floor, and viciously battered by security personnel in the chamber, and spent a long time in hospital with a broken leg and a bruised body. The security team later explained that they thought he was an Arab.[18]

Not every film-maker went through such tribulations, but maybe this is why these critical, politically orientated documentaries remained the exception that did not represent the rule. Most documentary films were rather more inhibited. Made mainly for national television, they tended to be quite faithful to the official line. Although documentaries shown on television required scholarly consultation, most of the consultants hailed from the mainstream. The lack of empathy for the other side was evident when pictures of Palestinian refugees were shown: the running commentary did not disclose even a modicum of compassion, and the word 'refugee' was rarely mentioned.

Some documentary film-makers initially gravitated towards fundamental critique and then returned to the mainstream and tamed their earlier, more subversive instincts. Such was the case of Amos Gitai. At the beginning of his career, in the early 1980s, he already stood out. His first documentary film, *Bait* (home or house, in both Arabic and Hebrew), made in 1980, told the story of a house in Jerusalem undergoing refurbishment. The house had belonged to a Palestinian physician until 1948 when it was expropriated by the authorities and sold to an immigrant couple from Algiers. The film introduces all the tenants and all those involved in maintaining the house, including the Palestinian masons. A house is often a symbol of stability and certainty, but after 1948 this house, like the homeland, became a symbol of conflict. The film acknowledges the basic Palestinian demand for return, while not questioning the legitimacy of the Algerian couple's ownership. Similar themes can be discerned, but with much less conviction and clarity, in Gitai's later films.[19]

This careful navigation between a sober look at the idea of Israel, combined with an inability to be totally dissociated from it, comes to the fore most forcefully in *Tkuma* (Rebirth), an important Israeli documentary series of the post-Zionist era.[20]

Failed Navigation: *Tkuma*

The connection between scholarly and media representations of the past during the heyday of the post-Zionist critique is best demonstrated through a focused look at the television series *Tkuma*. It presented the history of the State of Israel and was broadcast on the country's official television channel in 1998, during the jubilee celebration of the founding of the state. It was meant to be the centrepiece of Israeli television's efforts to participate in the festivities. The name of the documentary is very much in line with Zionist mythology: *Tkuma* means the resurrection of the Jewish people in the redeemed land of Palestine. But this explicitly Zionist title was attached to a television programme that in part conveyed a post-Zionist message, or at least experimented with post-Zionist interpretations of major chapters in Israel's history. The title was the wrapping of the package, the framework within which the message was conveyed, and it blunted the sharper edges of post-Zionist criticism. Moreover, the post-Zionist views were presented within a traditional Zionist metanarrative that interpreted the reality of Palestine as exclusively Jewish. But while the history was still told as a Zionist story, there were indications that there was a counter-story as well. The fact that the other side's story received less coverage than the Zionist one created an imbalance that might have indicated to the viewer which story was the more truthful. Still, on several occasions the program provided Israeli participants' verification of Palestinian claims. At times, even the narrator himself presented the Palestinian view as just, and in so doing left viewers with an ambiguous and probably confused impression.

The tension between the wish to retell the Zionist story and, on the other hand, the desire to be even-handed by presenting the Palestinian view takes different forms. Each segment is prefaced by a bombastic and sentimental pro-Zionist monologue by Yehoram Gaon, one of Israel's most popular singers. A narrator then tells the story with great pathos, from a Zionist perspective, but at times the narrative is interrupted and challenged by eyewitnesses: Palestinians, Egyptians, Jordanians, and, for the segments dealing with Israel's conduct towards its Mizrachi citizens, North African and Iraqi Jews.

Given the demise of the post-Zionist approach, or at least its temporary disappearance in the early twenty-first century, one can assume the series did not have a significant impact. However, it is interesting to view it through its ambiguities, as these lie at the core of any future success or failure of critiques of Zionism from within. *Tkuma* demonstrates the tension between conformity and criticism, and exposed the abortive attempt to navigate safely between them.

Tkuma had twenty-two segments, but I will deal here only with those relating to the subjects at the heart of the post-Zionist critique: the essence of Zionism, the 1948 war, and the treatment of Israeli Arabs and Mizrachi Jews in the early 1950s. The series was quite openly critical of Israel after 1967, but as mentioned in previous chapters, this kind of criticism fell well within the parameters of legitimate Zionist discourse. Hence, these later segments, though quite poignant and intriguing, were of less interest as examples of post-Zionism. Although the historical picture of the pre-1967 events was still very much 'diet Zionist' in character – in that it cherished the period before 1967 as blissful and just while attributing all of Israel's wrongdoing to the 1967 occupation – the series did reveal significant cracks in this idyllic view. In general, it suggested that Israel was less moral in its conduct in 1948–49 than had commonly been depicted, that it was discriminatory and abusive in its treatment of its Arab and

North African Jewish citizens, and that it was aggressive towards its neighbours and inflexible when there was a chance of peace in the region. The post-1967 chapters showed how past conduct explained present behaviour, and how these early characteristics continued in various guises into the 1990s.

There were also more mundane reasons for the different approaches seen in the different chapters and periods. Though the series had a general editor, each segment was written, produced, and directed by a different team. And while a committee of five well-known mainstream historians acted as consultants for the entire series, the directors of the various segments tended to be far more critical and more post-Zionist in their views than were the general consultants.

As the program is devoted to fifty years of Israel's existence rather than to the history of Zionism per se, the origins and essence of Zionism were minimally addressed, and those references to the pre-1948 period that did exist were very much in line with the official Zionist version. Hence, by not dealing with the essence of Zionism – for instance, by not examining Zionism as a colonialist project – the series' overall message was a far cry from the message that emerged from the works produced by post-Zionist academics in the 1990s.

The two segments devoted to 1948 were important because they served as an overture to the entire series. One of the consultants for these two segments was Benny Morris. He was not a chief consultant (that is, a member of the consultative committee), but he was mentioned in the credits, and more important, one can feel his imprint. Some of the episodes described in the segments covering 1947 and 1948 read like passages from his book *The Birth of the Palestinian Refugee Problem, 1947–1949*. The most important effect of Morris's involvement was the relative centrality accorded to the refugee problem in the historical discussion of the 1948 war. Hitherto, the refugee problem had occupied only a marginal place in the overall picture drawn by official Israeli historians. Not only did the refugee issue assume greater importance in the story presented here, but also included was a discussion of why the Palestinians had left their homeland. The answer, however, was a diluted Zionist and 'Morrisian' one: half the population fled, and half were expelled. The segments made no mention of Israel's traditional explanation for the exodus: a general Arab order for the population to leave.

The programme introduced the evidence through eyewitnesses; there were no historians, just participants. A few Palestinian witnesses mentioned their belief at the time that they could leave because they would later be saved by the Arab world, but none mentioned a call or an order to leave. Most told a story of outright expulsion and uprooting. The segments also dealt at relative length with the question of massacres. There was an admission that Deir Yassin was not an isolated case. Other massacres were mentioned in general terms, though only Balad al-Shaykh was referred to by name (on the very last night of 1947, Jewish troops massacred the men of this whole village, on the eastern outskirts of Haifa, as retaliation for an assault on Jewish workers in the nearby refineries). This was a far cry from even Morris's own guarded accounts of many other massacres, let alone what is engraved in the collective Palestinian memory as described in seminal works such as Walid Khalidi's *All That Remains: The Palestinian Villages Occupied and Depopulated by Israel in 1948*, or even what was since proven as valid by other works with a less Zionist tint.[21] Still, an Israeli confession of atrocities committed in the past represented a breakthrough. In the course of the programme, a senior Israeli officer utters a sentence that has haunted me ever since I heard it. When asked about the 'purity of arms' – that Israeli oxymoron born in the 1948 war – he shrugs off the question with a bitter expression on his face. Of course, he says, the Israelis could not have adhered to the 'purity of arms' while fighting the civilian population. Each village became a target, he says, and they all 'burned like bonfires'. He even repeats the horrifying description: 'They burned like bonfires they did, like bonfires' (*Hem ba'aru kemo medurot, kemo medurot hem ba'aru*). And in those conflagrations, he admits, the innocent as well as the combatants perished.

As the programme also clearly conveyed, until May 1948 there was a paucity of fighters on the other side. In a segment that explored the case of Haifa, which was mostly based on eyewitness accounts, one could detect a more critical approach than could be gleaned from the account in Morris's book, which talks about flight, not expulsion.

But eyewitness accounts, together with rare documentary footage, showed an act of expulsion in Haifa. A tale about Golda Meir's visit to the city and her uncharacteristic shock at what had been done to the Palestinian population there reinforced the impression that it was not an isolated occurrence. Apparently it reminded her of pogroms and made her consider, for a brief moment, the Palestinian tragedy and particularly the Zionist role in bringing it about. But this soul-searching did not last long, nor did it transform the future prime minister's later anti-Palestinian stances.

Finally, on the 1948 war itself, the episodes showed how the houses of the Palestinian urban population were taken over, immediately after their eviction or flight, by Jewish immigrants. Unmentioned, however, was the story of rural Palestine, a major issue in the descriptions put forward by Israel's 'new historians' and documented in the works of Palestinian historians, as well as constituting a major theme in Palestinian novels and poems. Here in *Tkuma* there was no reference to the obliteration of villages and the takeover of their lands, either for existing Jewish settlements or for the construction of new settlements atop their ruins, settlements that quite often bear Hebraicised versions of the old Arab names.

Considerable footage was devoted to the peace efforts after the 1948 war, the very mention of which was a novelty of sorts. In the collective Israeli memory, nothing happened between the warring parties from the time of the armistice arrangements until Oslo in 1993. Having once been attacked as a 'deceiver' by one of Israel's leading historians for suggesting that Israel's first prime minister, David Ben-Gurion, did not seek peace with the Arab world after the 1948 war, I was therefore pleasantly surprised to hear the narrator assert that this was indeed Ben-Gurion's position, reflecting the description in my book *The Making of the Arab–Israeli Conflict, 1947–1951*, which had been published few years earlier. Nonetheless, the same narration ended not with the view (held by Morris, Avi Shlaim, and myself) that we missed out on peace because of Israel's intransigence, but rather with the view offered by the mainstream Zionist historian Itamar Rabinovich, Israel's ambassador to Washington and then the president of Tel Aviv University, who claimed that peace was 'elusive'.[22]

In sum, while these episodes relating to the 1948 war did indicate some of the findings of the 'new historians', and did show a desire to present the other side's point of view, it must be pointed out that these revelations and sensitivities were expressed within a mainstream Zionist general framework. They were not the main issue. The sequences dealt mainly with Israeli perceptions of the events of 1948. The viewer thus took in the Palestinian point of view and the Palestinian disaster in only small doses.

There was an overall tone of sadness in the 1948 chapters. Melancholy music accompanied them, and the Jewish eyewitnesses were carefully chosen to present a unified tragic voice. In fact, the 1948 war as presented in the programme was first and foremost a tragic event in the history of the Jewish people. True, this was a very different approach from that taken in previous documentary films, which tended to look at 1948 as a miraculous year of joy tinged with sadness. But the sadness conveyed by *Tkuma* was not about the cruelty or futility of war; it was about the need to sacrifice one's sons for the homeland. In the same vein as liberal Zionism's assertion that what happened to the Palestinian people was a small injustice inflicted to rectify a greater injustice (the Jewish Holocaust in Europe), the final impression left by the series was that the main tragedy of 1948 was what befell the Jewish community in Palestine. The Palestinian tragedy of 1948 was dwarfed by the personal stories of loss and bereavement on the Jewish side. Again, as with liberal Zionism's construction of the use of force – a response resorted to only reluctantly, in the face of Arab hostility – the films showed a Jewish tendency to ponder the consequences of a just war, in the mode of the soldiers who 'shoot and weep afterwards', if I may again repeat the phrase that emerged as a major theme in collections of conversations among Israeli soldiers following the 1967 war. One suspects that a different director might have chosen footage that would have shown triumphant smiles and warlike enthusiasm on the faces of Israeli soldiers after they had occupied and destroyed yet another Palestinian village. Instead, viewers of *Tkuma* saw the tormented face of a highly moral, civilised society that found itself, through no fault of its own, in the midst of war. I know of no other

national televised representation of such events that devotes so much
footage and energy to moral agonising over what, in truth, was a
quite common crime against humanity.

Moreover, there seems to be a clear method in the way the
Palestinian and Jewish eyewitnesses were chosen. The eyewitnesses
on both sides ostensibly represented the rank and file, ordinary
people. In reality, this was not so. On the Israeli side, the witnesses were highly articulate, usually senior officers, who described
with great eloquence and sensitivity what they went through. The
Palestinian witnesses, on the other hand, who were usually old men
and almost invariably Israeli Arabs (not one had actually lived all his
life in a refugee camp), presented clouded memories, often in broken
Hebrew, usually in slogans, and not always coherently. This, I feel,
was no coincidence. Even if unconscious, the selection represented
a means of depreciating the Palestinian point of view. Had someone
wished to create it, a very different impression of the Palestinian side
could have emerged.

The segments of *Tkuma* that dealt with the 1950s, particularly
the state's attitude towards the Jews from Arab countries as well as
towards the Palestinian citizens of Israel, likewise presented a partially
post-Zionist view. The Zionist role in encouraging the local Jewish
communities in the Arab world to leave for Israel was barely touched
upon, though the illusions spread by the Zionist messengers were
sufficiently conveyed. The main issue dealt with here was the absorption, or the lack thereof, of the immigrants after their arrival in Israel.
The way the newcomers were treated by the more veteran Israelis
clearly conveyed their negative attitude towards anything Arab – an
attitude soon translated into colonialist policies in education and
welfare. The process of geographic, social, and occupational marginalisation was strongly projected through the stories of individuals
who eventually succeeded in carving out better lives for themselves.
The message was: Israel was still the land of open opportunities.

With respect to this issue, there was one genuinely new piece of
evidence in the film. I think very few Israelis knew that the general
compensation Israel received from Germany was unevenly distributed among Jewish citizens of the state. The reparations, as they were

called, raised the average standard of living of the Ashkenazi Jews but did not help the *Mizrachim* at all, thus further widening the socio-economic gap between them. An Iraqi Jew in the program tells how he noticed the material improvements in the public life of Tel Aviv – people wearing new clothing, more food in the stores, automobiles, new amusement places – whereas in his own neighbourhood, all he could see was stagnation and continued deprivation.

For me, the most acute reference in this segment on immigrant absorption – the one that made the greatest impact, and which I think encapsulated the essence of the Mizrachi immigrant experience – was a statement by a Yemeni Jewish woman who arrived in Israel in the 1950s. When reunited in front of the TV cameras with the Ashkenazi woman who had been her teacher forty years earlier, she asked why her teacher had chosen to work with such a deprived and marginalised group. 'Was it because you were a Zionist, or because you felt it was your obligation as a human being?' she wanted to know. The response from her former teacher was confused and unclear, but it gave the impression that ideology had been a stronger motivation than humanity and, as such, had led to some tough treatment of the newcomers by the earlier Zionist settlers.

In other footage, it appears that other Mizrachi Jews felt that the Zionist discourse concealed acts of manipulation and dishonesty. The episode on the Palestinian citizens of Israel, titled 'The Pessoptimist', after Emile Habibi's book *The Secret Life of Saeed the Pessoptimist*, was by far the best segment of the entire series, the only one that did not play the game of 'balancing'.[23] Here, the director clearly did not feel compelled to show 'another side' to the story of discrimination against the Palestinians in Israel, but instead communicated the impression that there was no other side, that there were no extenuating circumstances for the abuse and maltreatment inflicted during the eighteen years of 'emergency rule' imposed on the Palestinian citizens (1949–66). The viewers watched the expulsion of villagers from their homes in the name of security considerations in the early 1950s. Military governors admitted that they were kings who harassed the local population with impunity on a daily basis. What was missing from the analysis in 'The Pessoptimist', unfortunately, was the connection with the situation of the Palestinians in Israel in the 1990s; this chapter conveyed a picture of an almost inevitable process of modernisation and Israelisation of the local Palestinian minority. In any case, this segment, together with another one on Israeli behaviour during the First Intifada, provoked a political upheaval and caused the prominent Israeli singer Yehoram Gaon to resign as the chief narrator of the segments lest he seem to be supporting Palestinian fighters.

Interestingly, though *Tkuma* largely ignored the Zionist right (it was the Zionist left that it held responsible for the expulsions, massacres, discrimination, and manipulations involving the Arabs), Likud spearheaded the protests against what it termed a 'post-Zionist' programme. Indeed, Likud appointed itself guardian of national virtues, assuming responsibility for what the nation did and does. Thus, according to the Likud minister of communications at the time, Limor Livnat, it was necessary that all these deeds be presented as just and moral. The director-general of the Israel Broadcasting Authority, Uri Porat, promised to screen an additional four segments that would balance the 'distorted' picture of the past. One of the reasons for the government's wrath was the fact that the programme enjoyed very high ratings and the post-screening video cassettes were selling well. Although the Ministry of Education forbade *Tkuma's* inclusion in the curriculum, there was a growing demand from high schools for copies to screen in the classroom, officially or unofficially.

In those days, the increased interest was not surprising. To adopt a wholly Zionist perspective on the past was seen as not only anachronistic but boring. Teachers and students alike wanted a refreshing angle, especially an angle that might provide an answer to the question of why Israelis found it so difficult to rejoice on their fiftieth anniversary. Indeed, it would seem that rather than celebrate their country's jubilee, Israelis preferred to deliberate on the connection between their history and the present. The deliberation was painful and left little room for rejoicing. It forced the Israelis to abandon the pious posture so dear to both secular and religious Jews. *Tkuma* threw into sharp relief the contrast between the programme's name – 'Rebirth' – and the reality of the nation after fifty years of existence, a reality that was unstable and insecure, since state and society had failed to reconcile with the people whom they expelled, whose land they took, and whose culture they destroyed. As became clear at the beginning of the next century, it would take more than a television programme with a mildly post-Zionist critique to make reconciliation possible.

ELEVEN

The Triumph of Neo-Zionism

The post-Zionists reject Zionism as a valid ideology and insist it does not fit the needs of our times ... [T]hey do not necessarily adopt the old anti-Zionist position. For them the social, political and cultural problems Israelis and Jews abroad face cannot be tackled within the Zionist discourse and cannot be solved through the current Zionist political and ideological agenda.

    – Adi Ofir, founder and first editor, *Theory and Criticism*[1]

If the Second Intifada did not totally obliterate post-Zionism, it definitely sent it underground. Even before, the members of this school found it hard to infiltrate academia, but now they shun the term.

    – Neri Livneh, journalist, *Haaretz*[2]

You couldn't mistake the atmosphere that enveloped Independence Day this year: It was an atmosphere of satisfaction ... [W]hat best explains this optimistic mood is the invalidation of post-Zionism. Since the start of the 1990s, Israel was under heavy attack by the post-Zionists. For some twenty years they enjoyed the halo of being fashionable, of being at one with the times. For all that they claimed we were ugly, they were beautiful. For all that they claimed we were evil, they were good. For all that they portrayed us as South Africa, they portrayed themselves as Nelson Mandela.

The post-Zionists' systematic attacks on the Jewish national home, on the Jewish national movement and against the Jewish people won them global acclaim. Their unconscious cooperation with anti-Semites, old and new, made them the darlings of international academia and the world media ...

Americans, Europeans, Arabs and Israelis are now being exposed – whether they know it or not – to the enormous gap between the (human) dimensions of Israeli injustice and the (inhuman) intensity of the brutality that surrounds it. This gap has opened people's eyes and explains some of the things we've had to do and the immense accomplishment we've achieved. It has made post-Zionism obsolete, explains the feeling of deep pride that we felt on Independence Day, and defines the challenge that we face in our 66th year.

– Ari Shavit, senior correspondent, *Haaretz*,
on Israel's Independence Day, 2013[3]

The Appearance of Neo-Zionism

In the mid-1990s a young American Jewish scholar by the name of Yoram Hazony founded a new institution, the Shalem Center, a think tank (and now a college) intended to confront what he saw as the dangers posed by post-Zionism. At one point, Hazony served as Benjamin Netanyahu's ghost writer and was part of his team of advisers. In 1996 Shalem published the first issue of its journal, *Azure: Ideas for the Jewish Nation*. Money came from the prime minister's office (and from conservative US funders), as did some of the centre's senior writers and fellows.

Hazony expressed his vision of the corrupting force of post-Zionism in *Azure* in the summer of 1996:

By now post-Zionist truths have become so self-evident as to constitute an Israeli 'political correctness' justifying – let no one be surprised – the censorship of opposing views …[N]owhere has the strange fruit of post-Zionist policy been more apparent than in the Foreign Ministry … The Jewish state is first and foremost a political idea. Armies may menace it physically, but it is on the level of ideas that the gravest threats are registered.

Azure provided the ideological infrastructure for a new era in the history of the State of Israel, in which the idea of Israel would be interpreted as an existential struggle against the Palestinians, particularly those who were Israeli citizens, as well as against the enemies from within, which is to say, whoever would be deemed a post-Zionist. The first struggle would be conducted in the Knesset and the second in academia. But the battlefield also extended to foreign policy – aggression towards the state's neighbours and the Palestinians under occupation – and towards the educational system and the media.

Ofir Haivry, the editor of the new journal, explained that his team hoped to set up in the near future a Zionist academia and media, since these realms had, from his point of view, been overtaken by post-Zionists. At the time, the centre and its members looked esoteric at best and pathetic at worst. Within a decade, however, their agenda had become the idea of Israel in the twenty-first century. Not only was it a far cry from post-Zionism; it was also a very different animal from the Liberal or Labour Zionism that had informed the idea in the previous century. The gist of it is quite familiar today: a highly nationalistic, racist and dogmatic version of Zionist values overrule all other values in the society, and any attempt to challenge that interpretation of the idea of Israel is considered unpatriotic and in fact treasonous.

The Impact of Post-Zionism

Let us examine first if indeed post-Zionism was as prevalent and hegemonic as the founders of the Shalem Center and their supporters asserted it was. As mentioned in the two previous chapters, the post-Zionist interpretation of Israel's past and present was widely filmed and broadcast. But merely the fact that it had been adopted by the knowledge producers was not an indication that their message was widely accepted in 1996 by the knowledge consumers. We now know, in 2014, that it was in fact basically rejected by the vast majority of them, though we did not know this at the time.

In general, it would be fair to say that the novels, plays and films that seriously transcended the Zionist narrative and its negative portrayal of Arabs did not become part of the Israeli canon, even in the heyday of post-Zionism. They did not represent a dominant cultural position, and their producers were not among the leaders of the Israeli cultural scene. Nonetheless, the 'new historians', poets, writers, film-makers, and playwrights did operate within the system that produced and shaped the country's cultural identiy, and they could conceivably have affected the society had they been able to persist with their critique beyond 2000.

The continuing scholarly debate, joined by other cultural producers, signalled not merely a scholarly rift but an identity crisis in a society that had been exposed to the possibility of peace in 1993. Peace had the potential to undermine the national consensus, which was based on the need to act jointly against common enemies. Relative economic success and security had already led deprived groups to demand a fairer share, just as it encouraged the Palestinians in Israel to lay bare the tension between the country's pretence of being a democracy and its insistence on remaining a Jewish state. Genuine peace demanded a radical change in the Israeli mentality and in the basic Jewish views about Arabs, specifically Palestinians. So a small number of people, with access to the public via the universities, schools, press, and movie screens, began to offer starting points for such a transformation. The point of departure was the acknowledgement that reality could be interpreted in a non-Zionist way, or at least that Israel's cultural identity must be more pluralistic.

The cultural identity of a society is shaped by historical and contemporary reality as well as by how this reality is interpreted by those who control sociopolitical power. By the time of this exceptional chapter in Israel's history, the nation's cultural identity could be characterised as a cultural product, shaped by the heritage and human geography of the land of Palestine and by the conscious national (that is to say, Zionist) attempt to change the identity of that land. From the very beginning, Zionism rejected the Palestinian identity of Palestine and successfuly used force and power to Judaise it. However, certain people and groups challenged the Zionist identity: Palestinians, some of the Jews who had been brought in from the Arab countries, and a small number of individuals, such as this writer, who were born in the country after the establishment of the state and who voiced their dissent in the 1990s.

The Zionist identity of the land and the society was continuously the challenged not because of 'new historians' or anti-Zionist novelists. The political demands of the deprived groups, the continuing occupation of the West Bank and Gaza Strip, and the frozen peace accord all contributed to a process capable of turning Zionism into either an anachronism or a concept that could be implemented only through an aggressive policy such as that adopted by the settlers. These processes of challenge began in 1977, when the hegemony of the Ashkenazi élite was questioned; they continued with the 1982 Lebanon War and the First Intifada; and they culminated with the assassination of Yitzhak Rabin and the May 1996 election, which brought a tougher kind of Zionism – the Likud version – back to power.

So yes, there was some truth in what the Shalem Center insisted on, but what they described was not the reality but rather a possible path that Israeli Jewish society could have chosen in the mid-1990s. But it did not do so. Not only was the path not taken, but those who pointed to it were gradually silenced and crushed. And in fact, it was not Hazony and his colleagues who began the counter-attack; instead, it was the Liberal Zionists who took the lead in closing the minds of those whose job and duty it was to produce knowledge for the benefit of the society as a whole.

Initial Reactions

From the perspective of mainstream Zionists, the post-Zionist interpretation of the past had gained a large following within Israeli universities and centres of cultural production by the 1990s. It was further believed that although every known historian in the Zionist camp had been recruited to refute the post-Zionist version of the past, it won legitimacy in the Western world. At the time, it was also wrongly assumed that because of its relative academic success, post-Zionism won over large segments of the Israeli public as well. For the briefest moment in the state's history, its parliament discussed post-Zionist legal initiatives that all, in one way or another, pointed towards a transformation of Israel from a Jewish state to a state of all its citizens. These suggestions had no chance of being endorsed by the parliament, but it was not forbidden by law to present them. As a result, at this peculiar juncture, these initiatives were put on the Knesset's agenda. But that chain of events was a rare exception. The rule was that the critical, and therefore far more pro-Palestinian, evaluation of past and present has not led to the wide acceptance of a non-Zionist, let alone an anti-Zionist, vision of the future.

When it became clear that a sizeable number of Israeli academics were not toeing the ideological line, mainstream academic institutions and persons began to react. As the dominant group, these mainstreamers could best be called, in hindsight, classical Zionists. Later they would be challenged not only by post-Zionist scholars but also by neo-Zionist academics, the kind associated with the Shalem Center, which helped to define their boundaries in a clearer way.

Classical Zionists were those who were neither non- or anti-Zionist Jews in Israel nor fundamentalist or ultra-Orthodox Jews. Ever since 1948, and even when classical Zionism's political fortunes had run down as they did in the 1970s, mid-1990s, and early twenty-first century, they continued to occupy a prominent, indeed a hegemonic, presence as a socio-ideological group within Israeli academia and media. Many, if not a majority, of those who controlled the academic and polemicist venues in Israel defined themselves as Zionists who were utterly opposed to 'both extremes' of the Israeli political spectrum.

For a long period there was no need for articulators of the classical Zionist view to clarify their positions on the past. It was the appearance of what was dubbed post-Zionist scholarship that forced the gatekeepers of classical Zionism to reassert their historiographical interpretations as well as their moral convictions. Collective memory and moral self-perception are closely linked, and it is no wonder that the post-Zionist critique on the past triggered a public debate from which much can be learned about classical Zionism's position on history. This position fed the policies of the first Netanyahu government, as well as the Barak, Sharon and Olmert governments, which takes us to the spring of 2009. Several members of the classical Zionist camp have remarked, albeit disparagingly, that the only merit they saw in post-Zionist scholarship was that it compelled them to redefine, clarify, and update their understanding of the Zionist and Israeli past.

The first scholars to attack the post-Zionist position did so in a very angry way. They denounced the new works as a purely ideological attempt to de-Zionise Israel or as a typical intellectual manoeuvre by self-hating Jews in the service of the enemy. Yoav Gelber, the head of the Herzl Institute for the Research and Study of Zionism at the University of Haifa, likened me and my colleagues to collaborators with the Nazis. Similar views were voiced by a leading liberal jurist, and for a while Israel's minister of education, Amnon Rubinstein, who already in 1995 wrote in *Haaretz* that post-Zionists were Holocaust deniers and haters of Israel who wished to eradicate Zionism.[4] Their work was 'an onslaught on the very essence and right of existence of the Jewish people and homeland ... it is not an academic work but a frontal ideological attack'. Another liberal professor of culture, Nissim Calderon, supported Rubinstein's view and described the latter's article and subsequent book on the topic, *From Herzl to Rabin: The Changing Image of Zionism*, as representing the enlightenment (Zionism) in its war against the darkness of post-Zionism.[5]

The attack intensified in the latter part of the 1990s. The post-Zionist scholars were not simply attacking Zionism; they were, in the words of two of Israel's most prominent scholars, determined to end academic discourse in Israel altogether. These two, Anita Shapira, the doyen of Israeli historiography, and Moshe Lissak, the state's leading sociologist, depicted post-Zionism as a corrupting method and theory.[6] They joined a group of Israeli historians and sociologists who in 2003 published a huge volume under the title *An Answer to a Post-Zionist Colleague*.[7] In it, post-Zionists were depicted as self-hating Jews and bad scholars, who were intentionally or unintentionally cooperating with anti-Semites. Elhanan Yakira, of the philosophy department at the Hebrew University, devoted an entire book to establishing the connection between Holocaust deniers, old and new anti-Semites, and post-Zionism; it bears the dramatic title *Post-Zionism, Post-Holocaust: Three Essays on Denial, Forgetting, and the Delegitimation of Israel*.[8]

It took some time, but Zionist academia did decide it needed to bring down the influence of post-Zionism. It was seen, in the words of a self-recruiter for the mission in the late 1990s – one of the shining new knights of Zionism, David Ohana – as a salvage operation. (The title of his book, too, is rather dramatic: *The Last Israelis*.)[9] The rescue operation was meant to salvage Zionism from both its neo-Zionist enemies on the right, and its post-Zionist foes on the left. This rescue operation was done in the name of liberalism and humanism as well as Zionism. In the eyes of these self-appointed rescuers, Zionism was a national movement, humanist, liberal, socialist, which brought modernisation and progress to primitive Palestine, caused the desert to bloom, rebuilt the ruined cities of the Land, and introduced modern agriculture and industry for the benefit of everyone, Arabs and Jews alike. In this version, Zionism was resisted due to a combination of Islamic fanaticism, pro-Arab British colonialism, and the local culture of political violence. Against all odds, and despite a most cruel local resistance, Zionism remained loyal to humanist precepts of individual and collective behaviour and stretched its hand, unrelentingly, to its Arab neighbours, who kept rejecting it. Against all odds, the Zionists also miraculously established a state in the face of a hostile Arab world – a state that, notwithstanding an objective shortage of space and means, absorbed one million Jews who had been expelled from the Arab world and offered them progress and integration in the only democracy in the Middle East. It was a defensive state, trying to contain ever-growing Arab hostility and world apathy; it was a state which took in Jews from more than a hundred diasporas, gathered them in, and made of them a single, new Jewish people. It was a moral and just movement of redemption, which unfortunately found other people on its homeland, but nonetheless offered them a share in a better future, which they foolishly rejected. This idyllic picture, so runs the reconstruction, was undermined and riven by the evil consequences of the 1967 war and the political earthquake of 1977 that brought the Zionist right to power. After and because of 1967, the state may have developed negative features, such as territorial expansionism and religious fanaticism on the right, and self-doubt and hatred on the extreme left. But it was a reversible development, which could be stopped by returning to old and traditional Zionist values of humanism, democracy and liberalism.

The U-Turn

Despite these volleys of angry prose, the post-Zionist point of view continued until roughly 1999 to be held by a relatively large number of academics, artists, film-makers and educators. Local academia's ability to tolerate, and even for a while to listen to, challenging voices depended very much on the country's general political mood. As long as the mood was sanguine and the Oslo Accords seemed to be leading somewhere, the mainstream was reasonably tolerant. Oslo's demise returned the society to a mood of intransigence and narrow-mindedness that left no room for critiques from the left, only from the right. Israel was back at war.

It was with the assassination of Prime Minister Yitzhak Rabin in 1995 that optimism began to wane. Pessimism set in, along with a growing distrust in the Palestinians, a move to the right, and a scaling back of Oslo's implementation and goals. At the same time, the popular appeal of the 'new historians' and their post-Zionist manifestations began to fade away until they were perceived as not only irrelevant but also as embodiments of national treason. What brought the 'post-Zionist decade' – and the historiographical debate on 1948 – to a definitive end was the outbreak of the Second Intifada in late September 2000. To be more precise, it was the Israeli narrative of the causes for the intifada and its overall description that contributed to the conclusion of this rare moment of grace in the history of the State of Israel.

Almost as soon as the first news about Palestinian mass demonstrations and disturbances began to circulate in the early days of October 2000, journalists, academics and politicians re-embraced the Zionist consensus. This newfound unity, arising from the abyss that the Rabin assassination prised open, was greatly facilitated by the fact that Israel's mainstream media uncritically accepted and widely disseminated the government's propagandist version of why violence had erupted. In that version, Yasser Arafat and the PLO were not only the initiators of the Second Intifada; they were also fully to blame for the failure of the 2000 Camp David summit, at which Arafat and Ehud Barak, with their host, President Bill Clinton, were supposed to tie up all the Oslo loose ends and present the world with a final settlement to the 'Palestine question'. From the viewpoint of Jewish society and its political élite, Israel had done all it could do to achieve peace but was met with extremism and intransigence, forcing the government to shift from peace to war. The Palestinians had proved themselves to be enemies, thereby justifying the brutality of the Israeli response to the Second Intifada and the closing of the public mind. Ariel Sharon's election by a wide margin in February 2001 confirmed the magnitude of public support for the new policies, while the events of 9/11 facilitated the government's depiction of Arafat as an arch-terrorist associated with Osama bin Laden and of Israel's response to the uprising as part of the 'global war on terror'. As in the past, the media and academia were the principal agencies providing professional and even scholarly scaffolding for these interpretations.

The uprising in the occupied territories and especially in Israel itself, where a large number of Palestinian citizens in Israel joined the intifada in demonstrations of an intensity and scope never seen since 1948, had a devastating effect on the movement to foster a post-Zionist critique. Within a few weeks after October 2000, public discourse in Israel had been reshaped along strictly consensual lines. The new discourse of unity engulfed everyone. 'New historians' such as Benny Morris and post-Zionist philosophers such as Ilan Gur-Ze'ev and others, appeared with *mea culpa* statements, reasserting their allegiance to Zionism, declaring their distrust of the Palestinians and their animosity towards the Palestinian minority in Israel. Here is how a right-wing newspaper, the weekly *Makor Rishon*, described Gur-Ze'ev's transformation: 'He was the assistant of the notorious post-Zionist philosopher, Adi Ofir ... who underwent a philosophical and ideological metamorphosis'. Gur-Ze'ev told the paper: 'I was part of an intolerant fashion with which I was supposed to collaborate, and even be one of its main heroes', and he declared, 'What we were preaching was a new anti-Semitism'.[10]

The public discourse revealed a sense of relief – a decade of disintegration and disunity was over, replaced by a unity which re-embraced even the settlers' movement in the occupied territories. This newly birthed consensus was reflected in the new political formations of the twenty-first century. In the century's opening decade, Israeli politics were dominated by a party named Kadima (Forward). Founded by Ariel Sharon; it comprised major sections of the Labour and Likud parties of the past and was the recipient of two significant electoral successes in 2006 and 2009. In ideological terms, Likud, Kadima, and the Labour Party (currently reduced to insignificance) shared a similar understanding of the idea of Israel, and their interpretation regained the space that had been occupied for a short while by the post-Zionist version of that idea.

From 2000 onwards, there remained no trace of the formerly impressive presence of the post-Zionist point of view. It was replaced by the new, consensual interpretation of Zionism, represented in the Knesset by the main parties. This consensual takeover competed with an even harsher and less compromising version of Zionism, which I shall call here neo-Zionist. In the 2012 elections, its representatives in the Knesset were grouped under a new party, the Jewish Home. The power base for this harsher Zionism were the settlers in the West Bank and in pockets within pre-1967 Israel where fundamentalist Judaism had grown exponentially in recent years. While classical and neo-Zionism seemed to collaborate well politically, they clashed culturally on the degree of religiosity that the society should require and on the optimal tactics for truly achieving the Zionist project, given the fact that there were still larger numbers of Palestinians than Jews inhabiting the Land of Israel. But since the debates were tactical, and the two streams were equally unwilling to make changes in the occupation or in the oppression of Palestinians inside Israel, the sense was that the Jewish state had nothing in particular to worry about. Hence Ari Shavit's sigh of relief expressed in *Haaretz* on the occasion of the state's sixty-fifth birthday, as quoted above.[11] The way he saw the situation, the only ideological rift in Israel was created by post-Zionism, but following its defeat, a more complete Jewish Israel was able to emerge.

The announcement of the untimely (some would say) and long overdue (most Israelis would say) death of post-Zionism was broadcast, as expected, by the liberal Zionist paper *Haaretz* as part of the paper's overall attempt to assess the impact on Israel of the Second Intifada, then entering its second year.[12] Tom Segev, who in 2001 had just published a book in Hebrew on post-Zionists, remarked that post-Zionism had been sent into exile abroad and could become quite popular there.[13] In retrospect, one would say he might have been right. But the point is that he, a veteran observer of cultural and intellectual life in Israel, concluded that its demise had already taken place in Israel itself.

Devout anti-Zionists did not lament the disappearance of a term that grouped them with those who were not categorically against Zionism. With the demise of post-Zionism, they now could return to their splendid isolation as eccentric academics and pundits, who were seen by their society as insane at best and traitors at worst. Amnon Raz-Karkozkin told *Haaretz* he detested the term 'post-Zionism' – but alas for him he was and still is regarded as a post-Zionist. In 2001 as in 1994, when we first used the term, we included him as someone who dared to question the very essence of Zionism and the idea of Israel. Given the small number of those bold enough to embark on this route, few writers had the tenacity or patience to divide them further into anti- and 'less anti-' Zionists. In the West, however, the left has always been more concerned with stressing its differences from the ally next door than with the enemy outside.

Like Segev, Shlomo Sand began to publish books on post-Zionism at an awkward moment – in 2001, when it fell out of favour. But he was given to keeping hope alive: 'The rumours of the death of post-Zionism are premature', he declared optimistically. Considering the popularity of his books, which severely attacked the basic historical assumptions underlying the idea of Israel – namely that the Zionist settlers were the genetic and authentic successors of the Jews who had lived in Roman Palestine – he may have had a point. In 2001 he urged me to be more patient, as the process would continue and succeed. For him it did, but alas the rest of academia seemed to go in the opposite direction.

Consider, too, a comment by the political philosopher Yossi Yonah of Ben-Gurion University, who noted that even at the peak of its success, 'for every post-Zionist member of academia there were ten if not a hundred Zionist academics'.[14] His university was singled out in 2001 as the last bastion of post-Zionism, centred around a journal called *Hagar*, edited by the post-Zionist geographer Oren Yiftachel. In 2012 the government tried to close the bastion within the larger bastion, the university's Department of Politics and Government, as it still included too many post-Zionists. So far this effort has not succeeded.[15]

One remaining point of interest in this situation is to see how mainstream academia – which has always wished to be seen outside Israel as liberal and democratic, a pretence long since dispensed with by Israel's politicians and diplomats – navigated between its declared noble values and its desire to remain part of the emerging consensus. As I will show later, in the epilogue, academia was recruited once more by the state, this time to a campaign called Brand Israel, meant to counteract what the recent Netanyahu governments saw as a growing delegitimisation of the Jewish state. This recruitment further complicated life for those who wanted to retain at least residual freedom of thought and expression, along with a modicum of self-criticism, within a society that increasingly regarded both (as demonstrated by one survey after another) as redundant values or objectives.

The next chapter will, I hope, illustrate how the idea of Israel has been interpreted in light of new research on the 1948 war, as one of many indications of the future orientation of the Jewish state. In the present chapter, however, I have the unpleasant task of recording the demise of post-Zionism. I shall do this by highlighting three landmarks, in the fields of politics, legislation and education, that heralded the coming of a neo-Zionist era in Israel. Post-Zionism may have been a bonbon tasted by Israel's chattering classes, most of whom shunned activism of any kind and disappeared from the ranks of advocates and supporters with the first potential risk to their own career, and perhaps also their own life. But while it occupied a place at the table, those chatterers did illuminate the possibility not only of a different Israel but also of a different Palestine. What we have without them explains the world's dilemma about Israel, with which I begin and end this book.

The Downfall – Dispensing with Political Plurality

Although post-Zionism had no political representation as such – possibly apart from the Communist Party and the two Palestinian national parties whose political agendas were similar – it produced a certain pluralism in the political discourse of 1990s Israel. That pluralism vanished, and with its disappearance, the gaps between the various political parties narrowed so much that it became difficult to tell the differences between them on the crucial elements of Israel's twenty-first-century agenda. Most of these parties, as mentioned, were swallowed by one central party, Kadima, notably at its inception, when Ariel Sharon was still active.

This was a long process in the making. It began in 1996, when Labour and Likud decided, following Rabin's assassination, to adopt a similar interpretation of past and present realities. This joint interpretation envisaged an Israel that extended over parts of the West Bank and the Greater Jerusalem area, and that existed next to a small Palestinian autonomous area or even a state. The newly enlarged state was also to include Syria's Golan Heights. This view was translated into practical terms through the way succeeding governments of Israel implemented the 1993 Oslo Accords. The reality they created in the mid-1990s was based on two assumptions. The first was that the pre-1967 Israel was non-negotiable. Hence, the future of the refugees or a discussion about Israel's role in the making of the problem – were off the negotiating table, not to mention the categorical refusal to include the Palestinians within Israel in any Israeli–Palestinian dialogue on the future. The second assumption was that parts of the West Bank, whose final demarcation would be defined later, would permanently be part of Israel; in 2013 these were more clearly marked and constituted nearly 40 per cent of the West Bank.

In the remainder of the space that had been Mandatory Palestine, Israelis would control the perimeters while the Palestinians would have a measure of autonomy. This formula had already been devised in the first days after the June 1967 war, as I have shown elsewhere, and was legitimised internationally as a peace plan that even won Nobel Peace Prizes for some Israeli politicians along the way. It also won over a Palestinian partner for a while and, in 1994, brought the world the Palestinian Authority, an entity that was expected to bless a scheme which would make Palestine a bantustan occupying less than 60 per cent of the West Bank plus 60 per cent of the Gaza Strip until 2005 and the whole of Gaza after that. There would be a mini-capital at Abu Dis (a neighbourhood on the eastern slopes of Jerusalem's mountains), but no solution for the refugee problem and no dismantling of Jewish settlements.

This vision also had an economic dimension, which cut across national boundaries. Part of it involved the introduction of a capitalist, free-market economy that would connect Israel and the future 'Palestine'. Under the Paris Protocol, which was the economic component of the Oslo Accords, signed in 1994, Israel and Palestine were to be a single economic unit. This can be seen in the connections between the customs bureaus and the imposition of a joint taxation policy. This unification was ensured by the decision to postpone any substantial negotiations over the introduction of a Palestinian currency. Furthermore, the protocol granted Israel the right of veto on any development scheme put forward by the Palestinian Authority. What all this meant was that the monetary and developmental policies of Israel and its currency exchanges were to play a dominant role in the Palestinian economy. Other aspects of the Palestinian economy, such as foreign trade and industry, would also be totally dominated by the Israelis.

The introduction of the Israeli version of a capitalist society into the Palestinian areas soon proved disastrous. With a very low GNP and the absence of a democratic structure, such an introduction and integration as offered by the Oslo/Paris agreements turned the areas under the control of the Palestinian Authority into the slums of Israel. An excellent example of such a development was evident already then in Erez, the buffer zone between Israel and the Gaza Strip. There the Israelis, with the blessing of the Americans and the European Union, opened an industrial park. Let the name not mislead the readers: it was a production line where all the workers were Palestinians and all the employers Israelis, who could enjoy the very low wages they paid their workers. Israel had similar visions for such parks on the border with Jordan and the West Bank – which was why industrialists in Israel saw themselves as belonging to the peace camp. Another aspect of the capitalisation of the peace process was the support given by a limited number of Palestinians who could benefit from such economic transactions.

Perceptive observers understood that the double burden of economic misery and the lack of genuine progress on the national front could lead to a Palestinian attempt to revolt against the post-Oslo reality; similarly, there was obviously nothing in that reality that could have served as an incentive for the Israelis to alter the post-Oslo situation. For the majority of the Jewish population in Israel, the peace was based on an unbeatable logic, a logic often reiterated by the late prime minister, Yitzhak Rabin. According to his vision, the Palestinians were locked in a dismal situation prior to Oslo; they were now offered an improvement – not a very impressive sort of improvement, but nevertheless better because it would mean that Gaza, Jericho, and Ramallah would fly the Palestinian flag and be guarded by Palestinian policemen. Most Palestinians saw it differently; what was on offer was a non-democratic authority that replaced Israeli occupation with Palestinian security services. But for most Israelis this was peace, provided there was no terror and no bombs; peace was equated with their daily security, and by around 2005, it was enhanced by the Oslo process.

The two main political parties, then, shared this vision of the future. They also saw eye to eye on the method needed to implement it: dictating the solution to the Palestinians. This line of action became evident soon after the Oslo Accords were concluded. The notion of dictation enjoyed wide support among the Jewish population and still does so today, and that support was clearly manifested in the 1996 election results, when a vast majority of Jewish voters elected parties which vowed to impose the Oslo reality on the Palestinians in even harsher conditions, the ones suggested by Likud. The same public mood informed the Barak government, which succeeded the first Netanyahu government in 1999. The latter's fall from power arose from his overall incompetence and a downturn in governability. The composition of the 1999 Barak government and its teams of principal negotiators (ex-generals such as Matan Wilnai, Dani Yatom, and Yossi Peled) produced a similar approach, even if the Likud chose not to join the new government.

So by the time the Second Intifada broke out, there was already a political consensus, and when Sharon came to power in 2001 he upheld that consensus, with one caveat – he was not interested in keeping settlers in the Gaza Strip and preferred to focus instead on turning the West Bank into the future Israel. As the Israeli journalist Amira Hass commented, at that point the vast majority of Jews in Israel lost interest in the Palestine question. The next election campaign proved the point – the issue of Palestine was absent from the agenda of the various parties. For all intents and purposes, it had been solved.

The Neo-Zionist Version of the Idea of Israel

Even the Mizrachi ultra-Orthodox party Shas and the Ashkenazi ultra-Orthodox party Agudat Yisrael were willing to go along with this geopolitical vision. But this vision of the future was not just a matter of defining borders or containing Palestinian national aspirations and rights. It was also a matter of the identity and essence of the society. And here we encounter the neo-Zionist vision, shared by the settler community and by supporters of the National Religious Party, the ultra-Orthodox parties, and a new secular right that was closely associated, both financially and ideologically, with the New Right in the United States. Among its adherents was a new right-wing party of Russian immigrants that would be a powerful actor in the next few years: Yisrael Beiteinu – Israel Our Home, led by Avigdor Lieberman.

Unlike the post-Zionists, following the 1999 elections the neo-Zionist alliance had representation in the Barak government – about six ministries, although compared with Netanyahu's government, they had of course lost power. They were able to join the Barak government because their interest had shifted from territorial and political borders to socio-cultural questions. They regarded the mini-state offered by Barak to the Palestinians to be irrelevant, but they decided not to insist on their ultimate vision: a completely de-Arabised West Bank, along with the construction of the Third Temple instead of the Muslim mosques in the heart of Jerusalem.

In elementary sociological terms, they thrived on the link between the decrease in external tension and the rise of internal tensions. Post-Oslo Israel was more than ever a multi-ethnic, multicultural society, deeply divided on issues of culture, law, morality and education. The Jewish population shared the same attitudes towards the Palestinians wherever they were, but basically differed on everything else. When there was no sense of external or existential threat, the various groups that constituted Israeli society tended to stress their separate identities at the expense of the state's identity, a tendency manifested in the way that questions of taxes, of conforming to general civil duties, or of a commitment to shared causes were handled. It was also apparent in the 1996 elections that the particular interests of Ethiopian, Russian, North African, secular Tel Avivian, and Palestinian Israelis could be best served in sectarian voting. The 1996 elections were carried out after a revision in the election law: Israelis would now vote separately for a prime minister and a party. Now they could divide their loyalties by voting realistically for one of the usually two possible candidates for prime minister, but voting more emotionally for the party which represented their narrower interests. This dangerous fragmentation ended with the abolition of this provision in the electoral laws in 2001.

During the 1999 elections, however, the trend towards fragmentation only strengthened. Neo-Zionism's greatest attraction for the Jewish majority in Israel was its simplicity. It conveyed confidence, not confusion, about the future. Its main tactic was to present itself as having the key to the unification of a disintegrated and polarised Israeli society, that key being a crystal-clear version of Judaism as a national movement, which the spokespeople and intellectuals of Labour Zionism never succeeded in promulgating. The neo-Zionists could present themselves as a unifying force, bridging the wide spectrum of conflicting interpretations of Judaism, both as a religion and as a national movement. While the post-Zionist scholars suggested that the fractured reality be understood as an indication for the need to turn Israel into a state for all its citizens and not try to identify the state with one group at the expense of others, the neo-Zionists proposed that only a Jewish religious and nationalist cement would secure Israeli society from further fragmentation and disintegration.

Four parallel processes forged this neo-Zionist option: the radicalisation of the national religious groups in Israel (whose strongholds were in the settlements and in a wide network of state-funded yeshivas); the Zionisation of the previously anti-Zionist ultra-Orthodox Jews; the ethnic insulation of segments of the Mizrachi Jewish community, caused by their being pushed to the geographical and social margins of society; and finally, the rapid integration of Israel into the stream of capitalist globalisation, which added to the alliance an intellectual neoconservative component, à la the American New Right (to which the Russian immigrants were mainly attracted).[16] These four groups shared the vision of an ethnic Jewish state stretching across most of what had been historical Palestine.

They were divided, however, on the issue of religion. The Russian immigrant community, almost one-sixth of the Jewish population by then, wanted the state to be a secular nationalist entity. The other groups envisaged a theocracy as the best means of facing Israel's external and domestic problems. The dominant group among them were religious leaders, be they rabbis, magicians, healers, politicians or educators. This new religious élite shared a highly derogatory view of secular Jews and non-Jews in Israel. According to one account, this alliance of fanatics saw secular Jews as the 'Messiah's donkey': having done their job in carrying Jews back to the Holy Land, they were now obsolete and could be treated as non-Jews. In other words, non-Jews are like beasts; Jews are allowed to utilise and exploit them, and may at times fear them, but always hold the moral high ground above them. As Sefi Rachlevsky's book *Messiah's Donkey* and similar publications show, medieval Jewish thinking, constructed to provide balance and solace in the face of a profoundly hostile Gentile environment, is reused here as a basis for a racist modern ideology that constructs a clear axis of exclusion/inclusion for the future. Its goal is an Israel without secular Jews and non-Jews.[17]

This concept was formulated and upheld by the national religious thinkers, primarily rabbis. It was presented as Zionism, not Judaism, and was connected to the Zionist precept of fulfilment, *Hagshama*, which, according to its old interpretation, meant only one thing: settling the Land. At first, neo-Zionists regarded settlement of the West Bank, Gaza Strip and Golan Heights as the ultimate act of patriotism and felt connected to all the previous colonisation projects of the Land that had been initiated since the late nineteenth century. But earlier settlement targets there had been almost met in full. Fulfilment now meant geographically reorientating settlement energy into the heart of mixed Palestinian–Jewish towns in Israel, such as Ramla, Lod, Jaffa and Acre – a move that had already sparked many violent clashes and heightened tensions in places where Palestinians and Jews had coexisted quite peacefully in the past. Such actions are upheld by rabbis who issue injunctions prohibiting the letting or selling of flats to Arabs, befriending Arabs, and most definitely marrying an Arab.

Neo-Zionist energy was also directed towards the attempt to impose stricter religious rule over public space, over the judiciary and on legislation. Its main target was the Supreme Court, because of its attempt to safeguard the public sphere from religious interference. So far, the secular Jews in certain areas, such as Tel Aviv and

Haifa, have quite successfully rejected these initiatives, whereas those in Jerusalem decided to leave and rebuild their lives in suburbia.

The neo-Zionist view on the past is even more nationalist and romantic than the consensual Zionist view of it. Israel of the Second Temple era was the glorious past which must be reconstructed. The resemblance between the neo-Zionists and India's Bharatiya Janata Party adherents is quite striking. Both here and there, these groups wished to demolish a past of several hundred years in the name of a more distant past of several thousand years. As a result, neo-Zionists took seriously the idea of rebuilding a Third Temple to replace Haram al-Sharif and preparing cadres of priests to serve there when the time would come – although they differ on how to achieve this goal, whether by exploding the two mosques on the Temple Mount, or waiting for divine intervention to pave the way for their scheme.[18]

The Next Generation: Education in Twenty-First-Century Israel

Apart from having a principal role in every Israeli government since 1996, the neo-Zionists' greatest success was having prolonged control over the educational system in Israel. In the late 1990s, they still shared the office with Meretz, a left Zionist party that was soon pushed out of mainstream politics. This impossible double control over the educational system, of a leftist minister of education and a neo-Zionist deputy, reflected the post-Zionist period of knowledge production in Israel. Throughout the 1990s, the balance of power in academia tilted towards the post-Zionist view, whereas the balance of power in the political field was still in the hands of classical Zionism; given the strong neo-Zionist opposition, the field of education had an unclear balance of power. But by the time the decade had come to an end, the academic as well as the educational system had shed all post-Zionist inclinations and resumed knowledge production in a classical Zionist way, with a growing tendency to paint history in neo-Zionist colours. For most of the first half of the twenty-first century the Ministry of Education was under the firm control of the

---

Likud and oversaw the ousting of all textbooks that were suspected of being even slightly influenced by post-Zionist scholarship. The Knesset's education committee assisted enthusiastically in this process, so all in all there was no need to have a neo-Zionist minister from the extreme right to execute the new strategy.

Under the Likud ministers of education, in cooperation with a cohort of academics, many of whom hailed from the national religious Bar-Ilan University and its satellite, Ariel University, in the occupied West Bank, the neo-Zionist interpretation of the idea of Israel constituted the ideological infrastructure for the official educational system. The neo-Zionists produced several educational kits (textbooks, curricula, and so on) which would have the power to impact the next generation of Jews in Israel. These kits could produce only one type of graduate: racist, insular, and extremely ethnocentric. The message that came through clearly, as found in research conducted by Daniel Bar-Tal of Tel Aviv University and, more recently, by Nurit Peled-Elhanan of the Hebrew University, is to fear the Other inside and around you – the Other being the Arab world around Israel, the Palestinian neighbourhoods, the Palestinian citizens inside Israel, and non-Jewish immigrants. A good example of that sort of thing is the school textbook titled *Those Were the Years – Israel's Jubilee*, which covers the state's chronicles since its foundation in 1948.[19] The Palestinians barely figure in the book – they are not mentioned with regard to the 1948 war, or as citizens of Israel under a military regime up to 1966, or as an occupied population in the West Bank and the Gaza Strip since 1967. The presence of Palestinian refugees is something the readers will not know about. They will only become aware of the existence of Palestinian terrorism, which emerged sometime in the 1960s for unknown reasons.

Another crucial element was the militarisation of the educational system. In 1998 the Ministry of Education announced a new master plan devoted to linking students more closely with the army. The basic idea was to follow children from kindergarten through high school graduation so as to ensure that they would be well prepared for 'military environment and values' and that they would 'be able to cope with situations of pressure and developing leadership skills on a battlefield'.[20] The level of physical fitness required by the army would be a precondition for matriculation and graduation, and an obligatory, integral part of the future educational system would be participation in army manoeuvres and military indoctrination. This was to be complemented by enriched lessons on Zionism and Eretz Israel studies. In the final three years of high school, the scheme aimed at 'increasing the motivation and preparedness for the IDF'. During the initial year there would be a focus on 'the individual's commitment to his or her homeland', and in the following two years, on 'actual participation in military life'.[21] In a way, this had always been done at schools, but always as a marginal part of school life; moreover, its features were formulated by more mainstream Zionists. Now the individual pupil would learn the history of the land according to the neo-Zionist interpretation – an education bound to shape his or her vision of the future. At the time, the universities seemed to offer some sort of counterbalance, but already, even before the demise of post-Zionist scholarship, it was doubtful how much a post-Zionist lecturer could do, even if he or she were lucky enough to have the opportunity to voice different opinions.

While the neo-Zionist education plans began to be implemented, the final products of the post-Zionist era didn't arrive at the Ministry of Education until the Ehud Barak government was in office (1999–2001). After all, it took several years for the books that had been commissioned back in 1993 to be produced. Consequently, the finished post-Zionist products were handed to a minister from the left Zionist party Meretz, who, as mentioned, had a neo-Zionist deputy in keeping with the impossible coalition that Barak tried to sustain. So, while the schools were slowly being introduced to the new version of neo-Zionism, they were also being given post-Zionist textbooks. This contradiction created a bit of mayhem that even reached the front page of the *New York Times*.[22] The fact was, these were only mildly post-Zionist textbooks that probably would not have attracted any special attention in the early 1990s, but that later, when they actually entered the classroom, represented sacrilegious and heretical views. In any case, they were soon cleansed from the system.

But they were worth looking at, again as an exercise to gauge where the post-Zionist challenge could have, but has not, taken Israel. How hopeful and naïve in a way were those who prepared the books one can gather from a statement by a member of a committee preparing such books, Avner Ben-Amos of Tel Aviv University, who explained to *Haaretz* in 1996 the raison d'être of the project:

> In the past the teaching of history [in Israel] was dominated by a version which claimed that we [the Israelis] had an unquestionable right to the land to which we returned after 2,000 years of exile, and we reached an empty land. Nowadays we cannot divorce the teaching of history from the debate inside academia and the professional literature. We have to insert the Palestinian version into the story of Israel's history, so that the pupils would know that there is another group that was affected by Zionism and the Independence [1948] war.[23]

From the vantage point of 2013, when this book is being written, the saddest and in many ways most disappointing aspect of my survey of the post-Zionist decade is its almost complete lack of influence on the educational system in Israel. Despite, or perhaps because of, the impossible wedding of post-Zionist and neo-Zionist control over the educational system during the days of the Barak government, only one side left a legacy that endured into the next century – the neo-Zionist's. When the new Netanyahu government came into office in 2009 (and again in 2012), both the mandatory and optional kits available for teachers in the State of Israel conveyed the neo-Zionist point of view.

But far worse was the absolute absence of any post-Zionist influence on legislation in Israel, especially legislation in the area of human and civil rights in 'the only democracy in the Middle East'.

Legalising Apartheid: The Neo-Zionist Version

An especially intensive and energetic wave of legislation against the Palestinians in Israel began in the twenty-first century. The Second Intifada was only a pretext for this; the true trigger was a demographic anxiety, prevalent in the very centre of the establishment, that natural birth and immigration could not tip the population balance in such a way as to ensure Jewish exclusivity and supremacy.

These phobias were articulated most clearly in the annual meeting devoted to the 'national agenda', which took place at the Interdisciplinary Center Herzliya (now a private university) on the northern outskirts of Tel Aviv. Ever since the late 1980s this venue had served as a kind of old people's home for famous Israeli academics, most of whom identified with the Labour Party. Every year they published a report on the state of the nation, based on speeches delivered to them by the country's top politicians, generals and strategists. Their report, commissioned by successive Israeli governments, set the national agenda for the next few years.[24] From the 1990s onwards the report included implicit recommendations for the transfer of Palestinians from Israel if and when they doubled their share of the population (from 20 per cent to 40 per cent) and for the reintroduction of nationalist indoctrination into the school system, a recommendation enthusiastically endorsed by all the governments, as we have seen.

It took a few years for the first recommendation to be implemented; apparently, implementation required the shock of the October 2000 events inside Israel to be activated. That month, the Palestinians in Israel joined in massive demonstrations in support of the Second Intifada, and the brutal police reaction left thirteen Palestinian citizens dead. The vast majority of media regarded these protests as acts of treason, and the politicians followed suit by blaming the Palestinians and their leaders for the bloody outcome of the protest movement.

And yet until 2009, no initiative for apartheid-like legislation succeeded in passing the final stages required for such initiatives to become law. This self-imposed inhibition disappeared with the

re-election of Netanyahu, however, although it must be acknowledged that the prior governments – those of the political midgets
who succeeded Sharon, such as Ehud Olmert and Tzipi Livni –
were already giving vent to policies from which Israel had refrained
during the 1990s, instigating two brutal and massive assaults, one on
Lebanon in 2006 and one on the Gaza Strip in late 2008.

Domestically, it was Netanyahu's government that channelled this
aggression towards the Palestinians inside Israel as well as dissenting
Jewish voices in the society. The Knesset became a venue for legalis-
ing neo-Zionist attitudes towards these two groups. The former were
far more important and in much greater danger of being affected
by such new legislation. Numbering a million and a half, they were
already living under a regime of oppression that unfortunately was
unknown and unnoticed outside Israel. It did not help that even the
consensual NGO in the state, the Association for Civil Rights in
Israel, reaffirmed the deterioration in the conditions and rights of
this minority since 2000. Its 2012 report summarised the reality for
this group of Israeli citizens as follows:

> Aside from the violation of Arab citizens' right to equality, their
> lack of access to services, and the discomfort inflicted on them,
> the exclusion of Arabic from the public space infringes on the
> dignity of a fifth of Israel's population and generates a feeling of
> discrimination and alienation, testifying to their inferior status
> and damaging their feeling of belonging in Israeli society. On the
> symbolic level, the absence of Arabic delegitimises the presence of
> Arabs in the public space.[25]

Below are listed just a few of the laws that make the Israel of 2014
what it is. This is the Israel that must be marketed inside and outside
as the fulfilment of Yosef Gorny's and Ari Shavit's claims of its being
the most successful modernisation and enlightenment project in
modern history.

The Nakba Law of 2009 is probably the most outrageous. It stipulated that whoever would commemorate Israel's day of independence
as a day of mourning would be arrested. Under international pressure

it was slightly revised: arrest was replaced by the denial of any public funding to any entity that would commemorate the Nakba. There is not one Palestinian school, cultural centre, NGO, or home in Israel that does not remember and commemorate the Nakba.

The 2011 amendment to the Citizenship Law of 1952, called the Law to Revoke Citizenship for Acts Defined as Espionage and Terrorism, along with similar laws from that year, allows the state to revoke the citizenship of anyone accused of terror and spying. Needless to say, support for the Palestinian struggle against the occupation is declared a terrorist act by Israeli law.

Another law from 2011, the Admissions Committees Law, legalised a known practice in Israel that can ban Palestinian citizens from living in areas that Jewish citizens wish to keep free of Arabs. The law allows existing and new Jewish-majority communities, wherever they are and however they live, to reject requests by Palestinian citizens of Israel to live among them, on the basis of their 'social suitability', in other words their ethnicity or nationalism.

And finally, more than once a bill has been introduced in the Knesset that would give preference to Jews (defined in the law as those who served in the Israeli army) in public service, jobs, salaries, and houses, which would compound the effect of a law to mandate every non-Jewish new citizen to swear allegiance to the 'Jewish and democratic' State of Israel.[26]

And that is just a short list of the worst. Ever since 2000, discriminatory practices and informal policies have been legalised by the Knesset, and this is still taking place. The construction of the legal infrastucture for an apartheid state is important for Israel, because its recent governments, including the one elected in 2012, believe in a unilateral annexation of Area C, 40 per cent of the West Bank, as a final act of geographical expansion, even though it adds Palestinians to the overall demographic balance. In that area, Israeli law would be imposed, hence the need to prepare a racist infrastructure for the future, expanded, and possibly final State of Israel.

Post-Zionists were also targeted. The most important law in this respect is the 2011 Law for Prevention of Damage to State of Israel Through Boycott, which defined as a criminal act, bearing the risk of lengthy imprisonment, any support for a boycott of Israel or for an action abroad considered to constitute delegitimisation. To this was added more recently a proposal for a law that would limit foreign funding for human and civil rights organisations in the state. As yet it has not passed.

Finally the legal reality in Israel reflects the ideological stance of the powers that be. Past ambiguities, remorse, and debates about the idea of Israel – all are gone, replaced by the joy felt on Independence Day by Shavit and most other senior journalists.

With the legal, political, and educational systems almost completely taken over by this new, energised version of the idea of Israel, one might have looked to the media and the universities to provide counterbalance and response. The media, however, became so united in its reactions after 2000 that it does not warrant further discussion. As for academia, I return at the end of this book to that domain and illustrate, for the sake of comparison, the earlier scholarly engagement with the history and historiography of Israel's foundational year of 1948 (after all, it was the work of a handful of serious historians concerning that particular year that triggered the unique 1990s in the Jewish state), on the one hand, and new research on the other, in which one can see how that hesitant journey into the past, fuelled by hopes of creating a different future, ended as if it had never existed at all.

TWELVE

The Neo-Zionist New Historians

Honest readers [of the work of the New Historians] cannot deny most of the facts presented by these historians about Zionism's policies in the past … and yet it seems that the conclusions that these historians were looking for are aimed at undermining the very legitimacy of the fathers of the nation, who are not alive anymore … We cannot underrate the perils of such an attack … No nation would be able to keep its vitality if its historical narrative were to be presented in public as morally defunct. [Moreover,] the novelty of what the New Historians did was in the perspective not the facts … these are not facts, but deep moral assessments.

– Daniel Pilser, *Techelet*, 2000[1]

The time that elapsed between the challenge posed by the 'new historians' addressing 1948 and their disappearance from the scene was short – less than two decades. The reason for this brevity is doubtless to be found in the fact that the 1948 war is not only a story closely linked to current politics but also a foundational myth. According to Louis Althusser, foundational myths are those most easily absorbed by society and according to which the social order is structured and maintained.[2] They provide the narrative that justifies the existence of the state, and as long as they remain relevant to the existing social order, they retain their force. In the case of Israel, of course, and despite the appeal and prominence enjoyed by the post-Zionist discourse for a time, the social order had not changed, which could explain why the society so quickly reverted to its long-held beliefs. And because the history of the 1948 war is also linked to matters of war and peace, to relations with the Palestinians, and therefore to the entire future orientation of the country, any scholarly or academic conclusions about it were and are extremely relevant to an understanding of the political scene. This was recognised by the scholars themselves, as well as by the politicians involved in the peace process.

In this final chapter I would like to show how the pendulum switch from a post-Zionist to a neo-Zionist version of the idea of Israel has impacted the Israeli scholarly community, most particularly its professional historiography. Deciphering what lies behind the decision to produce a certain narrative is still an enigma – we are much better at exposing a narrative than we are at exposing the motives for constructing or revising it. Therefore, I have limited my attempt to pointing to the ways in which changes in the political atmosphere are reflected in the narrative of the works produced by practising historians who focused on the 1948 war. According to the ethos of academia, the work of these historians should in principle not be affected by changes in public mood or general political orientation. However, the case of the current Israeli historiography of 1948 indicates that, in this conflict especially, the writing of history absorbs and represents ideological disputes and political developments to a degree comparable to any other cultural medium. The difference is that other media or discourses do not pretend to be objective or neutral.

As described in the previous chapter, almost immediately after the outbreak of the Second Intifada a reinvigorated Zionist consensus, which had somewhat eroded at the height of the Oslo days, reasserted itself with force. Public discourse in Israel was reshaped along strictly consensual lines. Thus, just as the atmosphere and politics of the early 1990s had been conducive for local historians to open a window onto the Palestinian narrative and even to contemplate acceptance of some of its major claims, so the changed conditions after 2000 provided fertile soil for a new generation of historians to entrench and barricade the narrative behind a wall of negation and fortify the collective identity in the face of renewed struggle.[3]

It is important to emphasise that while the new Zionist consensus was immediately restored and re-embraced, the new historiographical narrative, which had already begun to assert itself prior to 2000, did not exactly reproduce the classical Zionist narrative. It is not only history, but also historiography, that does not repeat itself. What emerged instead was a new/old narrative, updated to fit the shifting political realities on the one hand and to take into account and absorb the new information coming out of the Israeli archives on the other.

The new historiography was Zionist in its ideological orientation, its mode, and its colouration, but it avoided the omissions, distortions, and denials of fact that had characterised the classical Zionist version. The post-Zionists and 'new historians', whose work had been based on Israeli archival sources to the extent that these were accessible at the time, had brought to light new facts concerning expulsions, massacres, and other war crimes committed in 1948 that the neo-Zionist generation could not ignore. Most important for their emergence was the release in 1998 of major new documentation from the archives of the Israel Defense Forces (IDF) and the Hagana, enabling professional historians in Israel to see with their own eyes, in government documents, the magnitude of the 1948 ethnic cleansing. Even 'nationalist' and Orientalist historians, who had scorned Arab or Palestinian sources and relied exclusively on Israeli sources, could no longer deny the massive, intentional expulsions.[4]

Thus, from a purely factual standpoint, the neo-Zionist version of 1948 did not differ significantly from that of the post-Zionists or the new historians. The difference lay in the response or interpretation of the facts. What the new historians saw as human and civil rights abuses or even as atrocities and war crimes are treated in the new research as normal and sometimes even commendable actions by the Israeli military. What the post-Zionists interpreted as shameful chapters in Israeli history are, in the new research, justified.[5]

From the neo-Zionist perspective, acceptance of the factual claims of the new historians was accompanied by the categorical rejection (shared by the Israeli public at large) of the *contemporary* moral implications that these critical new historians drew from their findings concerning Israel's crimes in 1948, first and foremost being the dispossession of the Palestinians. The neo-Zionists did not merely reject the interpretation of the post-Zionists but also attacked them on moral grounds for dangerously undermining the legitimacy of the state. This approach is succinctly articulated in the quote that opens the present chapter.

That quote sums up the essence of the neo-Zionist response to the new historians: acceptance of the basic facts that they unearthed, combined with a castigation of them on moral grounds. This ambivalence produced something of a division of labour between the neo-Zionist scholarly attempt to reassert hegemony in Israel's production of knowledge, specifically in the presentation of the 'academic' narrative of 1948. One group undertook to challenge the moral underpinnings of the critical historiography, while the other group focused on a re-examination of the factual evidence, so that a new/old Zionist narrative of the 1948 war could be (re)constructed in a way that would reflect the post-2000 mood in the state and an updated interpretation of the idea of Israel.

The Critique of the New Historians and the Moral Debate

Paradoxically, even as the post-Zionist approach – and with it, the critical spirit within Israeli society – was totally silenced and marginalised with the outbreak of the Second Intifada, the attack on the new historians (except for Benny Morris) showed no signs of abating. Even in its greatly diminished condition, the critique of Zionism from within Jewish society continued to be depicted as a grave danger to the Jewish character of the state. From 2000 onward, questioning the national narrative in general and that of 1948 in particular was perceived as an ideological threat that needed to be countered by academia at home and abroad. It culminated quite recently with several new laws passed in the Israeli Knesset, as mentioned in the previous chapter, stipulating that, among other measures, public funding to any scholarly or educational entity that commemorates the Nakba be curbed, and academics who support the Palestinian academic boycott campaign be severely punished. It was followed by the exclusion of critical material from the educational system and the appearance of a new NGO, Im Tirtzu (If You Will It), whose main role is to monitor anti- or post-Zionist writing and teaching in academia. Im Tirtzu produced its own booklet on the Nakba, denying the new history of it in such a vulgar and insidious way that mainstream academia found it at best irrelevant and at worst embarrassing. This NGO is supported by another one, Israel Academia Monitor, whose board includes Israel's leading political scientists and historians and who employ their own team in every university to eradicate all residues of post-Zionism. It took a while before their intimidation began to bear fruit, as admitted by *Haaretz's* education correspondent Or Kashti:

The past four years mark a significant change from the past. During this period, the right has waged a systematic campaign that included delegitimisation, open and concealed threats and, at times, actual sanctions against whoever dared to undercut their complacent world view ... The seeds of delegitimisation spread through the air three years ago with the publication, by Im Tirtzu and the Institute for Zionist Strategies, of pseudo-scientific studies of the post-Zionist bias that supposedly prevails in Israeli academia. The seeds were then sown by these groups' supporters in the government, including Education Minister Gideon Sa'ar. And they were tended to by right-wing organisations like Yisrael Sheli.

Faced with the campaign being waged by the right to reshape reality, academia – as an institution based on values like skepticism, tolerance and pluralism – has barely raised its voice. At least, not in public. The number of academics who see public activism as part of their job description is declining. But even the larger organisations, like faculty groups, the various universities and the Israeli Academy of Humanities and Sciences, are trying to prevent any kind of statement being uttered about the increasingly ugly face of Israeli society. Self-censorship and conformity are more efficient than direct repression.

This was in 2013 but until then it seemed that the new historians' critique continued even as their influence disappeared, but now there were new grounds that reflected neo-Zionism's preoccupation with demonstrating the morality of the Zionist venture. Whereas in the early years of the post-Zionist challenge, the argument addressed the facts, it has now shifted to 'exposing' what lies behind the critical history and sociology that emerged in Israel as of the late 1980s. The earlier response was epitomised by Efraim Karsh, who accused the new historians of fabricating the facts – an allegation he summarised in his book *Fabricating Israeli History: The 'New Historians'* – but made no mention of morality.[6] In fact, the above-mentioned article in *Techelet* explicitly rebuked Karsh for failing to morally and ideologically confront the new historians while going to battle against 'undeniable facts'.[7] The editors of the journal concluded that Israeli academia could not permit the new historians to set the research agenda on 1948 – another critique absent from the earlier Zionist response.

The moral battle was waged energetically outside Israel, where the message of the post-Zionists had made more lasting inroads. Of the numerous books representing the neo-Zionist perspective on the 1948 war that appeared in the United States in the years following the eclipse of the new historians, the best example was a collection edited by Anita Shapira and Derek J. Penslar, titled *Israeli Historical Revisionism: From Left to Right*.[8] In their introduction, the editors declared that the new historians, whom they named the 'revisionists', excluding Morris, had been waging an attack on Zionism itself. But it was the political philosopher Michael Walzer who led the moral battle with the greatest passion. Presenting Zionism as a liberation movement of exceptional morality, Walzer characterised the debate over the 1948 war as an existential battle against the forces of evil.[9] He did not confront the facts but instead employed the discourse of 'complexity' to stifle debate. The dispossession of almost a million Palestinians, the discrimination against almost five million more, and the control through occupation were all characterised as complex issues. In a similar vein, Zionist historian Daniel Gutwein of the University of Haifa, after arguing that there was nothing new in the factual claims of the 'new history', depicted post-Zionism as a formidable enemy, a movement that, according to him, included postmodernists and nihilists bent on privatising the collective sacred national memory for their own selfish, if not perverse, interests.[10] Others, as we have seen, accused the new historians of outright treason.[11]

Before examining the works of the neo-Zionist historians, a few words should be said about Morris, one of the most important of the new historians, who, following what he described as his 'turning point' in 2000, could be said to embody both of neo-Zionism's hallmarks: its positivism and (in his political writings and interviews) its moral justification of the ethnic cleansing that took place during the 1948 war. Morris did not shy away from providing evidence damning to the Zionist narrative. His book *The Birth of the Palestinian Refugee Problem, 1947–1949*, provided the first systematic evidence, based on IDF sources, of major expulsions during the 1948 war. When the documents were first released in 1998, showing the expulsions to be far more premeditated, systematic, and extensive than had been shown in the more limited documentation available a decade earlier, Morris, ever the positivist, undertook what he referred to as the correction of a mistake, and so he revised and expanded his book to reflect the new evidence.[12] By the time the new edition was published in 2004, however, the Second Intifada was well underway, and the revelation of what would earlier have been seen as damning new information about 1948 now fused conveniently with the closing of the public mind with regard to the Palestinians in the wake of the uprising. In this new atmosphere, not only were Israel's brutal military operations against the Palestinians during the new intifada seen as justified, but so was their systematic expulsion in 1948. Morris, who had earlier been wrongly accused of being an 'Israel hater' and a post-Zionist, now set an example for the neo-Zionists, inasmuch as he was ideally situated to provide hindsight justification for the 1948–49 expulsions. In an interview with Ari Shavit published in *Haaretz* on 9 January 2004, he provided the ultimate justification for the ethnic cleansing in 1948: 'Without the uprooting of the Palestinians, a Jewish state would not have arisen here.'[13] Furthermore, he faulted Ben-Gurion for failing to 'cleanse' the 'whole Land of Israel, as far as the Jordan River', which 'would have stabilised the State of Israel for generations.'[14]

The Professional Writing of History Gets a New Face

Morris's description of the ethnic cleansing of 1948 as an act of self-defence, a choice 'between destroying or being destroyed', and his insistence that the 1948 war was one of those 'circumstances in history that justify ethnic cleansing'[15] were presented in an even cruder, more simplistic and quite fanatical way in his book *1948: A History of the First Arab–Israeli War,* first published in 2008. There the war of 1948 became a defence against a jihad, a kind of al-Qaida 1948 attack on the Jewish state that had to be fended off by every possible means. Indeed, in the dominant mood of post-2000, the Palestinian action and resistance of 1948 are recast in terms that reflect or echo modern-day terrorist organisations and their actions.[16]

This view, in various forms and shapes, aptly characterises the underlying spirit of neo-Zionist work on 1948 within the Israeli academy and in many recent collections on the war. In some of the new works, the moral defence of the war approaches messianic proportions. The introduction to one of the major collections on the war, the two-volume *Israel's War of Independence, 1948–1949,* by its editor Alon Kadish, is a good example. Kadish, a former head of the Hebrew University's history department, almost theologises the 1948 Jewish war effort, referring to the outcome as a victory of the 'just' over the 'unjust' in a battle that averted a second Holocaust,[17] and to the year 1948 as the last link in the chain that 'completed the redemption of the land and the return of the Jews to their homeland, as well as the renewal of their independence on the land'.[18] In general, Kadish's anthology, with its scores of articles focusing on military dimensions of the war, well exemplifies the mix of messianic Zionist discourse and the archival, positivist reconstruction that typifies the neo-Zionist approach. One might even suggest that it was thanks to the combined emphasis on messianic fulfilment and existential threat that the Judaisation and de-Arabisation of Palestine – and not just in the areas earmarked for the Jewish state in the 1947 UN partition resolution, but well beyond – is now fully recognised and morally justified as having been the principal goal of the Zionist leadership in 1948.

These elements (divine promise plus existential survival) had likewise constituted a crucial subtext of the 'old history' of 1948, written prior to the work of the new historians, though the old history, as already indicated, tended to be more discreet on such matters as expulsions and massacres. Another way in which the old mainstream Zionist historians differed from the neo-Zionist historians (and also from the new historians) was that they were generally not professional historians but rather journalists and pundits who were part of the political élite. Still, one of the main practitioners of the neo-Zionist narrative wrote an entire book to vindicate the early historiography of 1948 as valid and scholarly.[19]

Many of the neo-Zionist historians of 1948 are postgraduates or newly minted scholars, recently inducted into the community of professional historiographers. They not only have access to the documents released from the IDF archives in 1998 but have also been entrusted with selective and top-secret material that never would have been shown to scholars suspected of being critical of Zionism. Significantly, much of their work, which is in Hebrew, is published by the Israeli Ministry of Defense. The fruit of their efforts is voluminous and indicates both a new discourse and a fresh choice of subject matter, which generally moves away from the human dimensions of the war and towards its military aspects, with well-trodden military campaigns being reappraised from every possible angle. Modern themes such as Jewish civil society in wartime became favourites, redirecting the research away from the victimisation of the Palestinians to tales of the heroic steadfastness of the Jewish community in 1948.[20]

A number of works blamed the Palestinians for their fate, follow-ing established scholars who had steered clear of the 'new history', such as the various books written by the head of the Herzl Institute for the Research and Study of Zionism at the University of Haifa, Yoav Gelber.[21] But while the 'blaming the Palestinians' theme is often a subtext in these works, sometimes it is explicit, as in the case of Tamir Goren, who has focused specifically on the responsibility of the Palestinians for their exodus from Haifa.[22] Other topics include the recruitment of Jewish volunteers abroad and their fate; the role played by the settlements; logistical problems of infrastructure, poli-tics, and the military; and the costs of the war. Some of the new research reverts to subject matter more characteristic of the old Zionist narrative, such as the reinvention of 1948 as primarily a war of liberation against the British. Such work also reaffirms the Zionist claim of 'purity of arms', though this time vis-à-vis the British forces instead of the Palestinians. By contrast, post-Zionists focused on demolishing that myth.[23]

A number of the above-mentioned works appear in Kadish's two-volume set. Its title, *Israel's War of Independence, 1948–1949*, is typical of neo-Zionist historiography, which has abandoned the neutral term 'the 1948 war', which was used by the new historians, in favour of either the 'war of independence' or the 'war of liberation' – never asking, by the way, the question of independence from whom or lib-eration from what. When discussing this issue, I am always reminded of the Palestinians in my hometown of Haifa. Quite often we have met and strolled through a park in downtown Haifa called the Park of Liberation – which in fact would have to mean the liberation of Haifa from its indigenous population by the settler community that took their place.

Taken as a whole, the Alon Kadish collection exhibits many of the hallmarks of neo-Zionist historiography. Part of the new strategy, especially with regard to the expulsions, is to emphasise that these are common if not inevitable occurrences in war and then to treat them from an almost technical standpoint. This is effectively dem-onstrated in an article by University of Haifa geography professor Arnon Golan (published in 2003 in *Israel Affairs* and in an anthology

titled *The Israeli Palestinians: An Arab Minority in the Jewish State*),
which bears the wonderfully bland title 'Jewish Settlement of Former
Arab Towns and Their Incorporation into the Israeli Urban System
(1948–1950)'.[24] Golan, who had earlier taken a leading role in trying
to refute works by the new historians, here abandons his earlier denial
of the ethnic cleansing to write:

> The policy carried out with regard to the occupied Arab villages
> was their total destruction and the expulsion of the villagers who
> remained. The action was always implemented in keeping with
> the strictest interpretation of Plan Dalet ... There were also the
> phenomena of vandalism and revenge.[25]

The facts are there, recounted matter-of-factly, without any hint
of moral discomfort. Golan explains that both sides exercised the
same policy of expulsion, typical in times of war – a bewildering
statement that has no foundation whatsoever but sounds good. This
bizarre attempt to create a parity of victimhood had already been
attempted in his 1993 doctoral dissertation. This version of the 1948
war produced both Arab and Jewish refugees; thus, the issue was one
of 'equal victimhood'. It bears emphasis that, in contrast to most
writers claiming equal victimhood with reference to the Jewish refugees from Arab countries, Golan specifically refers to the few hundred
Jews whose settlements in what became the West Bank were dis-
mantled and to the residents of the Jewish quarter in the old city of
Jerusalem, all areas annexed to Jordan by prior Jewish consent. Golan
regrets the absence of a more effective and coordinating hand in the
division of the spoils of war resulting from the systematic Israeli pil-
laging of Palestinian property, houses, lands, and bank accounts, but
points out that the dispossession of the Palestinians was the only way
to make possible the absorption of so many Jewish immigrants after
the 1948 war.[26] His approving treatment of Israel's anti-repatriation
policy is another aspect of this approach.

Not surprisingly, many of the chapters of Kadish's *Israel's War of
Independence* reproduce the basic outline of events recounted earlier
by the new historians, yet now the results look very different. Dani

Hadari's chapter, for example, emphasises (as do the new historians) Plan Dalet's importance in precipitating the ethnic cleansing of Palestine.[27] Although Hadari does sanitise the terminology (he refers to the part of the plan detailing instructions to destroy Palestinian villages merely as 'an important military mission'), he makes no attempt to conceal actions that classical Zionist writers would have preferred to avoid discussing.[28] For example, not only does he write that the Jewish troops rarely honoured Plan Dalet's offer to let certain Palestinian villages surrender, he also commends the army for its harsh interpretation of the plan, ascribing it to the army's known propensity to 'take the initiative' – *litol yozma*.[29] He even highlights the case of Umm Zayant, a village that was promised immunity but was destroyed and its inhabitants expelled despite their overtures of peace. Hadari employs the same tone when discussing the army's policy of shooting villagers who tried to return to their villages after having been expelled. As with other such actions, he treats it as a purely military problem. Hadari has high praise for the IDF's de-Arabisation of the Galilee from May to October 1948. Interestingly, while the term 'ethnic cleansing' is almost never used by the neo-Zionists, the term 'de-Arabisation' has been adopted. Yet in pre-1948 classical Zionist discourse, Arabs were hardly mentioned at all, and such a term would have been unthinkable. The land, after all, was basically 'empty', and the task was therefore to colonise it. Only rarely was it acknowledged that colonisation required removal of the local population.

Among the numerous other examples of the neo-Zionist tendency to unapologetically recount events that earlier would have aroused uneasiness, at the very least, or simply been omitted from the account altogether, I will mention only a few. The writer Uri Milstein, for instance, describes in detail the massive looting of Palestinian houses but invokes it, not to criticise the acts themselves, but to expose the Hagana's disorganisation and failure to coordinate.[30] Two chapters in the Kadish anthology are also good examples of the neo-Zionist treatment of the systematically aggressive policy of the Zionist forces towards the Palestinian or mixed towns, where they premeditatedly drove out the Palestinian inhabitants. The chapter by Yoav Peled on the April 1948 operations in Jaffa corroborates the new historians' finding that the military confrontation in the town and the expulsion of its fifty thousand Palestinian inhabitants could have been avoided, but that Hagana commanders did not want the Palestinians to remain. A similar picture emerges from Moshe Arnewald's chapter depicting the expulsion of the Palestinian inhabitants of West Jerusalem during the same period. Both researchers find this policy acceptable, and neither shows any sign of the moral reservations typical of the new historians.[31] For example, the final pages of Peled's article describe how the Irgun carried out its operation to 'cleans[e] enemy outposts' by 'relentlessly bombard[ing] the Ajami quarter and other Arab neighbourhoods of the town centre with the objective of breaking the inhabitants' morale and creating chaos and havoc to cause mass flight'.[32] As recounted by Arnewald, the objective of the Jewish plan to take over West Jerusalem is identical: 'to cause a flight from the Arab neighbourhoods outside the Old City and the concentration of the Arab population in it'.[33] He comments that as a result of the attacks, 'the population density of the Old City by May 1948 was unbearable', its original population having doubled or even tripled.[34] Despite the 'gravity' of the living conditions and hygienic situation, and although 'on 8 May typhus broke out and riots began due to the scarcity of food and flour', he notes that the Old City's population did not leave because it felt secure.[35] In fact, the population, along with its refugees, did remain – because it was not expelled and was protected by the Transjordanian Arab Legion, which aborted all the Israeli attempts to occupy it. Elsewhere the situation was different; virtually the entire Arab population of West Jerusalem was driven out as a result of these actions.

Many, if not most, of Kadish's authors focus either on military operations and aspects that had a decisive impact on the direction of the war, or on prominent issues in the debate over 1948. By comparison, Aaron Klein's topic – the 1948 prisoners of war (POWs) – was little more than a sideshow.[36] Still, it is useful to spend some time on his chapter, as it is illustrative of many of the characteristics of the neo-Zionist historians we have been discussing. Klein had access to the IDF files released on the POWs, and his findings largely confirm those of Salman Abu-Sitta's study, which was based solely on oral histories and relevant reports from the International Red Cross (IRC) archives (both of which Klein cites among his sources).[37] In Abu-Sitta's account, the POWs were mostly citizens of the new state under international law who were not only imprisoned but also ethnically cleansed in that they were permanently uprooted from their villages, though permitted to remain within Israel's borders. About five thousand were systematically harassed and subjected to forced labour.[38]

Klein, who accepts Israeli policy towards the 1948 POWs as unavoidable, notes in passing that intelligence officers had permission to decide on the spot which Palestinians captured in military operations could be executed immediately – a reference that corroborates Palestinian oral recollections of summary executions in occupied villages and neighbourhoods throughout Palestine. Although Klein does report cases of barbarism and executions in the POW camps themselves, he states that these were not the norm and attributes excesses to the major logistical problems that become inevitable when thousands of men are taken prisoner. In his section titled 'Guards of the Camp' (Shomeri Hamahanot), he also notes that most of the camp guards were members of the Stern Gang and the Irgun, suggesting that if exceptional brutality occurred it came from the 'extreme right'.[39] According to Klein, anyone over the age of ten who appeared suspicious was a legitimate POW, and the troops were ordered to seize as many POWs as possible.[40] While not directly expressing misgivings about the tender age of the child POWs – whom he sometimes refers to as children and sometimes as soldiers – he does appear to want to fend off potential criticism. Thus, we are given the rather extraordinary explanation that small children were captured as POWs only after their mothers had been expelled. This is undoubtedly true, since the Zionist forces separated all male children and adolescents above the age of ten from their mothers before expulsion as a matter of course, but the implication here seems to be that the capture and imprisonment of very young children was a humanitarian act to save them from being left on their own.[41] With regard to the entire concept of forced labour, Klein commends the Israeli army for its efficient and purposeful use of the prisoners who fell into their hands. Most of the prisoners were Palestinian teenagers and young men in their early twenties, not soldiers, and were employed in hard labour.[42] The following passage about the construction of labour camps – based on an IDF document that would not have been made available to critical scholars – is a good illustration of neo-Zionist historiography's bland, matter-of-fact, technocratic approach, which contrasts so sharply with the moral indignation that such information would have occasioned in post-Zionist scholars even when not made explicit in their historical texts:

> The occupational potential present in thousands of Arab POWs was enormous. The Israeli market suffered from a serious deficit in working hands and the military system was in urgent need of new [military] bases and many camps. [Furthermore,] the realisation that employing the POWs would solve some of the problems and needs of the IDF led to the decision to build two special labour camps for captives – one in Sarafand and the other in Tel Litvinsky [Tel Hashomer Hospital today]. The building of the camps was completed in September 1948. Another special labour camp was opened for several months in Umm Khalid near Netanya ... The construction of labour camps was a significant quantum leap in the exploitation of manpower within the POWs, whose numbers kept growing.[43]

Finally, Klein commends the army for introducing order into the system and implies that the situation was beyond their control: 'Although the young military system of the IDF was not prepared for this affair ... it succeeded in organising itself in a reasonable manner and solving satisfactorily the problem of the prisoners'.[44] By the end of October or early November 1948, the employment of POWs had been systematised, backed by procedures, orders, forms, and reports. Nowhere in Klein's account is there any hint about the horrors described in the following first-hand account recorded in the immediate aftermath of the war by a Palestinian survivor:

We were loaded into waiting trucks ... Under guard we were driven to Umm Khalid ... and from there to forced labour. We had to cut and carry stones all day. Our daily food was only one potato in the morning and half a dried fish at night. They beat anyone who disobeyed orders. After fifteen days they moved 150 men to another camp. I was one of them. It was a shock for me to leave my two brothers behind. As we left the others, we were lined up and ordered to strip naked. To us this was most degrading. We refused. Shots were fired at us. When our names were read we had to respond 'Sir' or else. We were moved to a new camp in Al-Jalil village. There we were put immediately to forced labour, which consisted of moving stones from Arab demolished houses. We remained without food for two days, then they gave us a dry piece of bread.[45]

Klein says little about the camp conditions other than that the prisoners were well fed and paid for their work.[46] As reference for this latter claim, he quotes an IDF document summarising what the army told a delegation of the International Red Cross, making no mention that the IRC documents, which juxtapose the IDF report with the testimonies of the inmates, give exactly the opposite impression.[47] But at least he does not present the camp experience as something positive for those who lived through it. This is in contrast to the book's editor, who in his general introduction to the collection comments with regard to Klein's article that 'some of them [the Palestinian POWs] must have been happy since they sometimes worked in places where they had earlier been employed by the British'.[48]

The neo-Zionist historiographical paradigm has now also been introduced into Israel's educational system. In the late 1990s, two textbooks that hinted at the possibility of Palestinian expulsions in 1948 were under consideration for inclusion in the national curriculum, but after heated debate in the Knesset's education committee, they were rejected. What was taboo in 1999, however, has become legitimate since 2000, and the Ministry of Education's official curriculum now uses a book that teaches pupils that the Israeli army began to expel Palestinians and destroy their villages to prevent their return about a month and a half into the war. Given that the war is officially seen as having begun on 15 May, when the Arab armies entered Palestine (the implementation of Plan Dalet is not considered part of the war), a month and a half into the war would be early July.[49] Even leaving aside the rather extraordinary explanation that the expulsions were initiated because the population was no longer leaving voluntarily, there is no historical data to support this version; in fact, all of the evidence presently available in the IDF archives attests to systematic expulsions having depopulated more than three-quarters of the refugees by July. But what is even more noteworthy is that the expulsions are now unambiguously acknowledged in the school curriculum.

After thoroughly examining the history, geography, and civics textbooks addressing the 1948 war that are part of the curriculum, educator Daniel Bar-Tal concluded that the Zionist view of the conflict predominates and that the works convey an image of Jewish victimhood and a negative stereotyping of the Arabs.[50] Other authors corroborate the finding that Zionism pervades the pedagogy that deals with 1948.[51]

The transformation in the Zionist discourse is well illustrated by juxtaposing two quotes from Anita Shapira with regard to the expulsion of the Palestinians. In a 1999 review in the *New Republic*, she wrote:

> The Arab panic led to exodus, and to the collapse of the institutions of Palestinian society. The more the magnitude of the exodus became clear, the more admissible and attractive the idea seemed to Israeli leaders and military commanders – not because the Zionist movement had been planning such an evacuation all along, but because a remote option (even if there were some who harboured such hankerings) gained acceptance in the context of the behavior of both sides during the war.[52]

Five years later, the Palestinian exodus depicted by Shapira as a 'remote option', barely contemplated by the Israeli political and military leadership as late as spring 1948 (even though some may have 'harboured hankerings' for it) could suddenly be presented concretely and no longer qualified as contingent on the behaviour of the Arab side. In her 2004 biography of Yigal Allon, for example, Shapira wrote that he 'was the most consistent supporter of transferring the Palestinians and even committed massive expulsions in the war of independence' and 'had no hesitation in expelling the Arab population en masse'. She also approvingly quotes Allon's statement at a public lecture in 1950 that an 'eternal justification' (that is, the eternal right of the Jewish people to a homeland without 'aliens') validated the massive expulsion of the Palestinians. To this, she added that he 'did his best not only to occupy the land of Israel, but also to depopulate it'.[53]

The extent of the official or mainstream embrace of the reality of the expulsions as something positive, as the necessary prelude to the attainment of Jewish rights, is also well illustrated by the fact that the 'virtual campus' of Israel's Center for Educational Technology, an NGO that partners with, among other bodies, Israel's Ministry of Education, carries numerous references to the expulsion of the Palestinians in 1948.

In yet another example of facts formerly denied but now embraced, in the late 1990s the new historians had successfully demolished the characterisation of the 1948 war as a Jewish David against the Arab Goliath, a myth that was crucial for developing both contempt for Arabs and Palestinians and for cultivating a sense of invincibility of almost metaphysical proportions. At the beginning of the twenty-first century, the IDF released two documents revealing that the Israeli forces had a military advantage of two to one during the 1948 war, a fact now widely accepted but presented in a way that strengthens rather than weakens faith in this mythology. The following quote from Leah Segal of the neo-Zionist school of thought is a good illustration.

[These documents] teach us that 1948 was not a war of the few against the many. This is an undeniable fact today. But why do people claim that it debunks the myth of the few against the many? How did an army representing 65,000 people defeat armies that represented 35 million people? The answer is it was 'a war between quality and quantity'.[54]

Any other interpretation, she adds, is from the school of historians 'such as Ilan Pappe and Avi Shlaim', who willingly became the spokespeople of Palestinian propaganda.

It is evident, then, that the transition in Israel from a hopeful period of peace to the pessimism of war has been reflected in professional historiography and ideological debates within Israeli Jewish society. As noted in the previous chapter, this was part of a more general trajectory travelled by the idea of Israel, as a historical narrative, since the appearance of the 'new history'. The post-Zionist critique of Israel's past and present conduct, sometimes to the point of questioning the fundamental legitimacy and moral validity of the Zionist ideology, was replaced by a neo-Zionist stance which strongly adheres to the basic tenets of classical Zionist ideology.

This vacillation indicates ideology's powerful hold on scholarly Israeli historiography. The contribution of ideology was already evident in the early 1990s, when the scholarly debate in Israel regarding what happened in 1948 was conducted not only on the academic stage but even more so in the public arena, where a discourse of patriotism and humanism was often employed to justify both positions. That the professional Israeli historiography of 1948 is so clear an example of the biased nature of the historiographical enterprise arises from the central role of 1948 in the national narratives of both Palestinians and Israelis. The Zionist movement regards 1948 as a miraculous year, whereas the Palestinians regard it as a cataclysmic catastrophe, having produced both the State of Israel and the Palestinian refugee problem. Both issues will remain open as long as the conflict continues.

A review of the reversals of fortune of post-Zionism and the concomitant ascendance of neo-Zionism in the research on 1948 can serve other purposes besides demonstrating how ideology impacts academics in agitated societies such as Israel. First, it can provide a barometer of intellectual and cultural orientation of Jewish society in Israel, aspects which are often neglected at the expense of the near-exclusive focus on government policies and military strategies as the only determinants of a state's position on a given reality. Second, it confirms once again that the struggle over memory will remain a crucial factor in shaping the conflictual reality of Israel and Palestine and will impact the chances for any future reconciliation.

As a final footnote, I would add that the currently prevailing consensus in Israel, with its many justifications of whatever happened during the 1948 war, has far-reaching political implications. It reveals an Israel unwilling to reconcile with the past and with the Palestinians, an Israel overly confident that its policies of ethnic cleansing and dispossession can be morally justified and politically maintained as long as there are Western academics and politicians who are reluctant to apply the same set of values and judgements to the Jewish state that they have applied, quite brutally, to countries in the Arab and Muslim world.

Brand Israel 2013

The Domestic Front

In 2010 the Israeli minister of culture and sport, formerly the minister of education, Limor Livnat, initiated an award for Zionist-oriented art. The prize would be given to artists who have produced a work that reflect Zionism, Zionist values, the history of the Zionist movement, or the return of the Jewish people to their ancient homeland. It would be given 'in all fields of culture – performing arts, plastic arts, and cinema', said the minister, 'in a bid to make it clear that we are against boycotts and in favour of Zionist culture'.[1]

The choreographer Noa Wertheim won it for her piece *The Birth of the Phoenix*: 'In her work this artist has stressed the links between a man and his environment, in the same way as Zionism stressed this association.' The piece is 'an eco-dance, updated and in tune with nature – as is Zionism'.[2] Thus Zionism is not in fact the theme in this piece, but the artist had no problem in its being characterised as such, inasmuch as a 50,000 NIS prize is a hefty sum in Israel.[3]

The playwright Pnina Gery also received the prize for a play titled *An Eretz Israel Love Story*. The play was exported with a slight change to the name, *An Israeli Love Story*. It is a tale that erases any trace of self-criticism of the post-Zionist variety. The love story spans the period from the Holocaust through the 1948 Arab–Israeli War, the war that Israelis call the War of Independence. There are hardly any Arabs or Palestinians in its chronology of the first three years after the Holocaust in Palestine. As in Theodor Herzl's utopian Palestine, they appear once – as Bedouins who bless the arrival of the Jews. In Herzl's novel it was a grateful citizen of the Judaicised Haifa; in the play it is a sheikh in the northern valleys who calls the settlers 'my brothers'. The narrative and background resemble those of the early Zionist theatrical productions about the 1948 war. Here it appears as a war of liberation against inexplicable Arab barbarism, and is meant to be a depiction of heroism against all odds. The metanarrative is fed into the play through news bulletins that tell the 'true story' of what happened in Palestine between 1945 and 1948. A worthy play indeed for the annual Zionist art award, and again an indication of how the idea of Israel was domestically marketed.[4]

Then there is Zionist film. The singer David 'Dudu' Fisher, a cantor who became a pop star in Israel (and on Broadway), has ventured into Zionist documentaries, the most recent being *Six Million and One* (2011), which, through a personal story, concludes that only the State of Israel could have been the answer to the Holocaust. The film was nominated for the 2012 Ophir (the local Oscar) Award for Best Documentary. Noam Demsky of the Ma'aleh School of Television, Film & the Arts, Jerusalem, received 40,000 NIS in 2013 from Minister Livnat for a film called *The Strength to Tell*, which seeks to communicate 'a new sense of relevancy of the Holocaust and its lessons'.[5]

In 2012 the composer Doron Toister received a prize for his Zionist musical piece *We Are Your People*. One can assume that there was nothing Zionist about the music, the arrangement or the composition, so the award must have been given for the title. Appropriately Zionist poetry is now to be found in a new journal, *Meshiv Ruah* (Fresh Air), devoted to 'national religious poetry'. There is also a Zionist plastic art, it seems. Yoav Ben-Dov and Serjio Daniel Chertko won a prize for their piece *In the Spirit of Hope*. 'This work was particularly pleasing [for the ministry]', wrote the critic Alon

Idan, cynically, in *Haaretz,* since 'it constantly fused the Star of David and the national anthem, "Hatikva", in their work' while broadcasting the universal and national meanings of Zionism.[6]

An obvious winner a year later was the author A. B. Yehoshua, who up to 2000 was active in Israel's liberal left, together with Amos Oz and David Grossman. Minister Livnat declared that his work was a proof that 'Zionism can inspire qualitative and excellent works of literature'. She also added: 'All these works express, from different artistic angles, the Zionist narrative that unites the people in Israel. We are talking of very important works of art that enrich the Israeli culture'. The chair of the prize committee was the fiddler on the Zionist roof, Chaim Topol, who oversaw a budget of 53 million NIS for encouraging Zionist culture in Israel.[7]

To their credit, some artists expressed discomfort with governmental encouragement for Zionist art and culture. As they wrote to the minister of culture when the prize was issued in 2011, 'This is a prize that encourages recruited art for the sake of political goals. We demand its abolition and would like to channel its funding to the depleted budget that is supposed to support free art in Israel.'[8] The ministry rejected the protest, and its funding for 2013–14 increased.

Winning the prize was also the most effective way of absolving oneself from past allegations of post-Zionism. This is what happened to the pop band Habiluim. Named after one of the first Zionist settlers' movements of the late nineteenth century, they were regarded as part of the 'radical left' in the 1990s. Not bothering to hide their desire to win the prize (unless this is a very sophisticated and subversive form of protest), they adapted their lyrics to its requirements by writing about the wish of the left in the past to make territorial concessions:

> Maybe we should give the Arabs everything;
> Maybe this is Zionism to leave a rotten place
> and rebuild everything from the beginning[9]

Perhaps it is still a post-Zionist song nonetheless, thus explaining why they did not win the prize in 2013.

While official ministries were now openly encouraging Zionism as cultural production, it was left to less clearly identified bodies to spot the residues of post-Zionism in the local culture, academia and media. An organisation called NGO Monitor (their motto: Making NGOs Accountable) posts a highly detailed list – the NGO Index – of hundreds of groups that in some way address in a post-Zionist matters connected with Israel, in some cases including the precise amount of funds they have received from abroad. Ten groups are selected for special attention, but the index includes all the human and civil rights NGOs in Israel as well as the local branches of Amnesty International. These bodies have indeed been active, and I trust that history will judge them favourably for having kept alive a pacifist, humanist and socialist alternative to the way the idea of Israel has been implemented in the second decade of the twenty-first century. But for the time being, these critical NGOs number just a handful, and indeed, as some of the more acute observers of the scene have noted, the battle for the idea of Israel has moved abroad.[10]

Brand Israel: The International Version

In 2007 a poster of an almost naked Miss Israel, Gal Gadot, and a poster of four fit young men, equally barely dressed, were the faces of Israel in a campaign named Brand Israel, commissioned by the government and the Jewish Agency for Israel. The young woman (Miss Israel 2004 and a star in the 2009 Hollywood blockbuster *Fast and Furious*) was meant to attract the heterosexual young American to a rebranded Jewish State, while the young men became the faces advertising Tel Aviv as the gay capital of Israel. One wonders how Theodor Herzl or even David Ben-Gurion and Menachem Begin would have regarded this presentation of Zionism as a soft-porn wet dream. But policymakers had decided that anything and everything was appropriate in the struggle to fend off Israel's negative image. The local team explained that such posters 'allowed us to gear our message to the younger generation, especially males, and towards a demographic that did not see Israel as relevant or identify particularly with

Israel'.[11] But in fact the campaign targeted people in all walks of life with images and texts tailored to the inclinations and preferences of every group. If the idea of Israel became a prize at home, abroad it became a product.

The campaign began in the summer of 2005, when the Israeli Ministry of Foreign Affairs, the Prime Minister's Office, and the Israeli Ministry of Finance concluded three years of consultation with American marketing executives and launched Brand Israel: a campaign to recast and rebrand the country's image so as to appear relevant and modern instead of militaristic and religious. Huge sums of money (the sums would be revealed some years later) were allocated for marketing the idea of Israel abroad in order to combat what the political and academic élite in Israel regarded as a global campaign to delegitimatise the Jewish state. It was to be a gigantic effort, and the team appointed to see it through was accordingly called BIG (the Brand Israel Group).[12]

The first unit of the regime thrust into this campaign was the foreign ministry and its diplomatic service. But it needed an academic team, especially in the areas of political science, international relations and history. Using lessons developed in the study of anti-Semitism, they provided a narrative of the origins of this new challenge to the idea of Israel, a challenge that called for boycott, divestment, and sanctions. The initial attempt to define the origins was more descriptive than analytical, but it did succeed in locating the moment of birth: the UN's World Conference on Racism, which took place in Durban, South Africa, in early September 2001. According to the initial academic narrative, this meeting, with its obvious interest in Palestine, marked the launch of the delegitimisation campaign against Israel. The fact that it culminated on 8 September, three days before 9/11, did not escape the Brand Israel team, and thus the two events were directly linked as being two sides of the same assault against the free world.

This connection between 9/11 and the so-called delegitimisation campaign was made very openly by Benjamin Netanyahu on various occasions. In a speech given in the Knesset on 23 June 2011, for instance, he referred to an unholy alliance between radical Islam and the radical left in the West against the free democratic world, of which Israel was the ultimate symbol. He lumped together in addition to the UN meeting in Durban and 9/11, the International Court of Justice in The Hague ruling against Israel's apartheid wall in 2004 – and then, he added to that history for good measure, the famous case of the MV *Mavi Marmara*, an attempt by an international humanitarian-aid flotilla to reach besieged Gaza in the spring of 2010.

The main task of Brand Israel was to depict the country as a heaven on earth, a dream come true. Israel would now be identified with beauty, fun and technological achievement. This was the new version of the idea of Israel, and the messengers were newly created front organisations. One of them was the David Project in North America, which became very active in articulating the campaign among college students. One of its many actions was to try to counter the view of Israel as one of the most hated states in the world, together with such countries as Iran and North Korea, and stress that it was among the top twenty-five states whose citizens were glad to be part of it.[13] The project's purpose was to convince everyone that Israel was one of the happiest places on earth because of its high-tech achievements.

The Brand Israel team felt that Israel's history was another asset that would help sell the country in the twenty-first century:

> In terms of heritage benchmarks, Israel is home to fundamental religious and historical landmarks, including the Western Wall, Church of the Holy Sepulcher, Al-Aqsa Mosque, and the Baha'i Temple in Haifa. Israelis boast a high quality of life, and the country's democratic values focus on inclusion and political representation of all its citizens, including women and religious and racial minorities.[14]

The David Project came up with its own explanation for the discrepancy between what the country had to offer and its negative global image:

We know misperceptions of Israel are rampant in the media; ordinary citizens across the globe see Israel cast as yet another violent nation in a region steeped in unrest and war. Conversations taking place in print, on television, and in the blogosphere often regard the Arab–Israeli conflict as both all-consuming and myopic; the diversity and excitement of Israeli society is often subsumed by twenty-second sound bites focusing on only one aspect of the Israeli story.[15]

And it pinpointed the mission for the Brand Israel team:

How do we change perceptions? How do we introduce nuance into global conversations surrounding Israel? How do we discuss the highlights and achievements of Israeli society, while also recognising its weaknesses and shortcomings? What needs to happen to remove Israel from the bright spotlight of a violent conflict?[16]

The answer to these challenges appeared on the official website of the Israeli Ministry of Foreign Affairs. Rather than winning the argument with facts, information or moral viewpoints, the ministry proposed, it would be far more useful to brand Israel and market it like a product. Gideon Meir of Israel's foreign ministry told *Haaretz* in 2007 that he would 'rather have a Style section item on Israel than a front-page story'.[17]

What this meant in practice was that any PR campaign for Israel should avoid any association with the conflict or the Palestinian issue. This was the spirit of the guidelines given to yet another front organisation founded to help disseminate the new take on the young country. In 2001 a group in California, ISRAEL21C, began its work to 'redefin[e] the conversation about Israel' and 'show how Israeli efforts have contributed incalculably to the advancement of healthcare, the environment, technology, culture, and global democratic values worldwide'. As in the famous episode of the British sitcom *Fawlty Towers*, when the hotel owner is trying not to mention the Second World War to his German guests, so too this NGO was instructed not to mention the war or the Palestinians. The other side of the equation was elegantly articulated on America's East Coast by a PR expert on the team, who advised his colleagues to give up the attempt to win the argument against the Palestinians, because, as his words were paraphrased in *Jewish Week*, 'proving that Israel is right and the Palestinians are wrong may be emotionally satisfying for advocates, but not necessarily effective in changing people's way of thinking about Israel'.[18] This expert, the executive vice president of ISRAEL21C, also remarked that discussing Israel in terms of its conflict with the Palestinians was probably the wrong way to go about it: 'You have a narrow bandwidth, where Israel can only win some of the argument. We are trying to broaden the bandwidth to include Israel's accomplishments.'[19]

Soon after, the separate efforts of the various organisations and individuals were put under one management. This was an operational decision taken by the foreign ministry's first-ever Brand Israel Conference, convened in Tel Aviv in 2005, which officially kicked off the campaign. Foreign Minister Tzipi Livni appointed Ido Aharoni to head the brand-management office and gave him a $4 million budget, in addition to the $3 million established annual budget for *hasbara* (propaganda) as well as the usual $11 million for the Ministry of Tourism's promotional efforts in North America.[20] Funding was also earmarked for work in Europe. It is noteworthy that the politicians in Israel decided to focus on the United States, where they sensed that delegitimisation had become particularly ripe and successful. One might have thought that the Israelis saw the US as a safe, long-time bastion of pro-Israeli bias, but apparently not. As we shall see towards the end of this chapter, the academics would try to convince politicians that the plague was rampant in the United Kingdom, which they saw as the preferred main target for the Brand Israel campaign.

Aharoni recruited top people in the advertising world. It included the Saatchi brothers (reportedly they did the work for free) and PR experts such as David Saranga, the former consul for media and public affairs at the Israeli consulate in New York. Saranga told the industry's major publication, *PRWeek*, that the two groups Israel was targeting were 'liberals' and sixteen- to thirty-year-olds (hence the posters of the minimally clad Miss Israel and the fit gay men in bathing suits). In 2005 Aharoni's office hired TNS, a market research firm, to test new brand concepts for Israel in thirteen different countries, and also funded a billboard pilot program in Toronto.[21]

At the centre of the team were members of Brand Asset Valuator, or BAV, the world's largest brand database, working alongside the best publicists and marketing people. BAV specialised in exposing the target community's emotional attachments to brands. Fern Oppenheim, an advertising and marketing consultant and a member of the Brand Israel group, said that the BAV data would be part of a long-term strategy that would also include ongoing research and evaluation: 'We want to be a resource everyone can benefit from, the way a corporate management team would manage a brand'.[22]

Another expert, David Sable, who was connected to Young & Rubicam, told the diplomats that Israel had not ranked among the well-liked countries because, at least in the United States, people 'know a lot about Israel, just not the right things. They think of Israel as a grim, war-torn country, not one booming with high-tech and busy outdoor cafes'.[23] So, in 2005 the orientation was to sell Israel as, in effect, a branch of American society. This task was handed to Young & Rubicam. David Sable again: 'Americans don't see Israel as being like the US'.[24] Israel, as a brand, was already strong in America, but 'it is better known than liked, and constrained by lack of relevance'. He went on to say that Americans 'find Israel to be totally irrelevant to their lives, and they are tuning out, and that is particularly true for 18- to 34-year-old males, the most significant target'.[25]

Brand Israel intended to change this by selecting aspects of Israeli society to highlight, and then bringing Americans directly to them. They started off with a free trip for architectural writers, followed by one for food and wine writers. The goal of these efforts was to 'show Americans that there was another Israel behind the gloomy headlines' and convey an image of Israel as a 'productive, vibrant, and cutting-edge culture', as Gary Rosenblatt of *Jewish Week* put it. He summarised the blueprint for the next few years this way:

Think of Israel as a product undergoing an overhaul to make it more competitive in the marketplace. What's called for are fewer stories explaining the rationale for the security fence, and more attention to scientists doing stem-cell research on the cutting edge or the young computer experts who gave the world Instant Messaging.[26]

It was not only American PR and branding wizards who were recruited. The government also asked for deeper involvement from the public. In a show of total mistrust in its professional diplomats, it recruited commercial Israeli television to seek alternative messengers for the new idea of Israel through a reality show called *The Ambassador*. The winner of a thirteen-week elimination contest won a job with a Zionist advocacy group called Israel At Heart to boost the diplomats with the best of Israel's youth. One of Israel At Heart's initiatives was to send Ethiopian Jews to speak in black churches in the United States. (Consider the idea of bringing African Americans from inner-city US ghettos to tell people in Brixton about the 'American dream', and you may grasp the absurdity of such a move.) High school student cadres later took over the mission.[27]

Moreover, the Ministry of Foreign Affairs asked every Israeli artist, acting troupe, and dance company to include a Brand Israel component in their shows. A typical example of such a tour was the one undertaken in 2012 in the US and UK by the dance company Batsheva; the tour was openly described by the ministry as part of the Brand Israel campaign and the dancers as 'the best global ambassadors of Israel'.[28]

The Ministry of Tourism went a step further. It was not enough to present an image of the most relaxed, groovy, fun country in the world. In 2009 the state miraculously succeeded in getting rid of Palestine and the Palestinians, and received the Golan Heights as a gift from Syria. The ministry's updated maps of a greater, border-free Israel, which were shown worldwide in ads and posters, including in London's Underground, indicated no Golan Heights or Palestinian areas. Hundreds of protests caused the removal of the posters from the Underground.[29]

By 2010 the Israeli financial daily *Globes* reported that the foreign ministry had allocated a hundred million shekels (more than $26 million) to branding during the coming years. This money was mainly destined to help fight the delegitimisation that was becoming increasingly evident in social networks and cyberspace generally. The ministry was optimistic about the chances of such a campaign, since its research unit had determined that Web surfers relate well to content that interests them, regardless of the identity or political affiliation of the source.[30]

Another collaboration launched in 2010 was aimed at the gay community, emphasising Tel Aviv as a gay- and lesbian-friendly destination for European LGBTs. The collaborators included Israel's Ministry of Tourism, the Tel Aviv Tourism Board, and Israel's largest LGBT organisation, the Agudah, and their campaign was called Tel Aviv Gay Vibe. Critics called it a version of 'pinkwashing', comparing the use of women's rights in the nineteenth century to justify colonisation with the use of gay rights as a tool to legitimise the continued oppression of the Palestinians.[31]

Re-Branding the Rebrand – New Plans and Visions

Despite all the activity, the reports of success did not even convince those who published them. A new actor was asked to join the crew to find out why success was still elusive and what else could be done. The Jewish Agency works with several think tanks; one such was the Reut Institute. The institute claimed in 2010 that the threat to the State of Israel in the areas of diplomacy and international relations was on the rise. It described the 2009 report of the UN Fact Finding Mission on the Gaza Conflict, headed by Justice Richard Goldstone of South Africa, as epitomising the delegitimisation campaign, its origins, logic and possible consequences.[32]

What became known as the Goldstone Report gently accused Israel and Hamas of committing war crimes during the Israeli assault on Gaza that began at the end of 2008. Later, under Zionist pressure, Goldstone, who is Jewish, partly retracted the mission's findings. In

early 2010 the institute characterised the report as the centrepiece
of efforts to subject Israel to 'increasingly harsh criticism around
the world' and said that in certain places, 'criticism ha[d] stretched
beyond legitimate discourse regarding Israeli policy to a fundamental
challenge to the country's right to exist'. The institute's own report,
The Delegitimisation Challenge: Creating a Political Firewall, connects
the Goldstone Report to the international condemnation directed at
Israel after its second attack on Lebanon in 2006. That condemnation, according to Reut, is the product of a radical Islamist ideology
emanating from Iran, assisted by Hezbollah and Hamas.

The problem, the report suggested, was 'a conceptual inferiority'
of the ideological forces within the Jewish state. Israel had failed to
market itself as a peace-seeking Jewish and democratic state, hence
the great success of the vicious delegitimisation campaign. If this
campaign continued, warned the Reut Institute, Israel would become
a pariah state and there would be no solution for the Palestinian
question, bringing a one-state solution to the fore. When Zionist
bodies warn against the danger of a one-state solution, what they
mean is what Israeli prime minister Ehud Olmert warned against in
2007: that Israel would necessarily end up as an apartheid state under
such a scenario.[33] 'A tipping point in this context would be a paradigm shift from the Two-State Solution to the One-State Solution
as the consensual framework for resolving the Israeli–Palestinian
conflict', states Reut. Even a comprehensive permanent status agreement would not be capable of putting an end to the delegitimisation
campaign, because inherent in those efforts, contends Reut, is the
negation of Israel's right to exist.

So what is to be done? 'It takes a network to fight a network',
concludes the Reut report. Israel's diplomacy and foreign policy
doctrine requires urgent overhaul: 'Allocating appropriate resources
will be essential, but it must be recognised that there is a "clash of
brands"': 'Israel's re-branding is strategically important', but 'it is
equally important to brand the other side'. Since Israel's adversaries
have succeeded in branding it as 'a violent country that violates international law and human rights', Israel must isolate the delegitimisers,
work with NGOs, mobilise pro-Israel factions internationally, and

cultivate personal relationships with 'political, financial, cultural, media, and security-related elites'.

In other words, at least according to the Reut Institute/Jewish Agency, all the money and experts in the world could not help rebrand Israel as a peaceful, fun country. One might have thought a less violent policy would help, but no. Instead, Reut wanted the government to seek ways of pressuring the Western élites to broadcast a different image of Israel and to hope that Jewish communities could deliver the goods.

Another group connected with the Jewish Agency for Israel (in fact, created by it in 2002) is the Jewish People Policy Institute, commissioned to face threats to Israel's national security. Although a collection of demographers, historians, sociologists and propagandists, it is treated, in the context of the war against delegitimisation, as a military unit. Its master document on the topic, arising out of the 2010 Conference on the Future of the Jewish People, warned that the 'delegitimisation has to be understood not only as a threat to Israel but to Jewish existence everywhere'.[34] In a similar way, the 2010 'State of the Nation' conference at the Interdisciplinary Centre Herzeliya called Israel's marketing campaign a war, but not just a war – a matter of 'asymmetric warfare … conducted on the battlefield of ideas'. Since Israel had not been defeated militarily or economically, its enemies were trying to destroy it with ideas. There was an imbalance because the enemy was ubiquitous and powerful.[35]

Three years earlier, this Jewish Agency think tank associated its previous worry – about the assimilation of US Jews in the Gentile community – with the unequal war. It concluded that younger Jewish Americans were 'distancing themselves from Israel'. This was reaffirmed by a famous article by Peter Beinart in the *New York Review of Books* in 2010, but Beinart, like Norman Finkelstein, attributed this distancing to the wish not to be identified with the occupation and the criminal policies of the state.[36] The Jewish Agency would have none of that. For them, the reason was that Reform Judaism, which was very popular in the United States, was not sufficiently respected in Israel and was not allowed to convert non-Jews on Israeli soil. Thus, while the Reut Institute was asking for more aggressive lobbying, the Jewish People Policy Institute sought the façade of an Israel that would be more pluralist in Jewish matters.

Given that Brand Israel was not producing the desired results in 2010, local academics were also recruited. Until then, they had been busy struggling against the post-Zionists on the domestic front. First, it was Bar-Ilan University, the national religious institution, that led the way, but soon it was joined by Tel Aviv University. The academy's main role was to explain why, in 2010, Israel was still delegitimised. The first to venture an answer were ex-generals and previous heads of security services working in academia or in semi-academic institutes that served both the universities and the intelligence community. Among the latter was the Meir Amit Intelligence and Terrorism Information Center near Tel Aviv, which identified the same web of enemies that everyone before and after it had named: radical Islam working together with anti-Zionists and anti-Semites.

The Israeli deputy foreign minister affirmed this new Elders of Anti-Zion conspiracy in a speech he gave to the Jewish Agency in October 2010, in which he declared that Israel's enemies recruit agents who work under the pretence of human rights activism to delegitimise the nation. To deal with this problem, the politician echoed the Jewish Agency's position, which called for 'a counter web made of Jewish and non-Jewish NGOs and academic institutions that would join forces in the front against the delegitimisation and describe the reality in the world as it really is'.[37]

By 2011, the government had already invested millions in creating centres for Israel studies in various universities around the world and in sending high school graduates – the most handsome and articulate among them – to market a youthful, Western Israel. Teams of Twitter users, Facebook users, and bloggers began to work 24/7, responding to anything that sounded remotely anti-Israel, while lobbies, modelled on AIPAC in the United States, began to operate on the European continent. The campaign was conducted with military precision. Major General Eitan Dangot, the coordinator of Israeli policy in the occupied territories, spelled this out when he said, 'The war on legitimisation and public opinion is not easier than that fought in the battlefield … there is a culture of lies, distortion and fabrication'.[38]

He happened to be referring specifically to Hamas, but indicated that the phenomenon was global.

For example, in 2011 in the annual 'State of the Nation' conference organised by the aforementioned Interdisciplinary Centre Herzliya, delegitimisation was chosen as a major theme. One speaker after another regarded this assault as part of the ills of a 'left-wing postmodernism' that wishes to 'conquer the sources of cultural production to control the truth'. As they put it, an op-ed in the *Guardian* or *Le Monde* would not turn them into Zionists. They also complained that Israel would be blamed, no matter what it does and asserted finally that Israelis should not wash their dirty laundry in public and must instead present a united Israel.[39]

The academics working for the Jewish Agency blamed the United Nations, Western legal systems, and Western academia for the ongoing assault. Britain was singled out as being at the centre of the campaign to tarnish the idea of Israel, owing to the growing number of Muslims in the UK, although it was pointed out that there were still corporations, such as Tesco, that could be trusted to remain faithful to both the old and new versions of the idea:

> Britain is the capital of communication in the world. It is the centre of the world's principal NGOs but it is also a country with a fragile Jewish community. Amnesty and Oxfam are preoccupied with delegitimising Israel. The government is more sympathetic, so what should be done? Whoever is the delegitimiser, including Israeli professors [who support the Boycott, Divestment and Sanctions campaign, or BDS], should be fought as in a war. They should be targeted and fought, not engaged intellectually, and all the means not used before should be employed. This is the battlefield for the Israeli right to function, defend itself.[40]

So far, it is the Harold Hartog School of Government and Policy at Tel Aviv University that has commissioned the most comprehensive analysis of the issue at hand. In 2008, it produced a ninety-page policy paper on the topic, 'The Israel Brand: Nation Marketing Under Constant Conflict'. Yet that paper, as well as luminaries such as Alan

Dershowitz, a frequent visitor to the university, were somewhat at a loss as to what countermeasures should be offered that had not been tried before. The paper's author, Rommey Hassman, proposed an interdisciplinary tool that would integrate strategic management, marketing, and branding approaches with diplomatic and ideological doctrines; underlying the mix would be the Jewish notion of *tikkun olam*, which, as Neil Gandal, the head of the Hartog School, wrote in his opening note, 'posits the ethical and moral responsibility of the Jewish people to the world'. Gandal contended that the State of Israel could improve its image by emphasising its contributions in the field of humanitarian assistance and development, while also strengthening its work in the developing world.[41]

The abstract of Hassman's paper sets forth three main steps through which the government of Israel should market the nation:

1. *Establish a national communications council*: This council would be established in the framework of the Prime Minister's Office, and would be headed by the government's chief spokesperson. It would administer and oversee a network of government spokespersons, coordinating their stand on policy, security, and economic and social issues.

2. *Market the nation*: To do this, the Ministry of Foreign Affairs would function as the international marketing arm of the State of Israel. In this capacity, it would coordinate the marketing of Israel, supervising international press secretaries and spokespersons, contact with foreign journalists and media, and monitoring the international media. The Ministry would also be responsible for all of Israel's embassies, consulates, missions and representatives throughout the world.

3. *Establish a Communications Division within the Israel Defense Forces (IDF)*: This unit would coordinate an expanded IDF Spokesperson's Bureau, any units in the military dealing with research and consciousness design, the network of soldier-spokespersons, and Israel Army Radio (*Galei Zahal*). In working

with the foreign media, the IDF Spokesperson's Bureau would function as an implementing body, acting on the recommendations of the Ministry of Foreign Affairs and under the guidance of the national communications council.[42]

He then ends the abstract by cautioning:

Since it is not possible to simultaneously address all target markets, priorities will have to be set. This paper prioritises nation marketing by country, based on a measure of the strength of the relationship between each country and the State of Israel.[43]

I introduce this lengthy quote in full because it constitutes the kind of knowledge that neo-Zionist academia is producing on Israel as we move into and through the second decade of the twenty-first century. The past has been rewritten as a Zionist narrative, while the present is depicted as a battlefield for survival. The impressive and hopeful challenge from within has disappeared. Here and there, yes, it is still alive in the work of brave NGOs such as Zochrot, New Profile, Ta'ayush, and others which, when counted together, form just a tiny minority within the society. But in the academy, media and other cultural stages, there remain few individuals who, under heavy censorship and a campaign of intimidation, still dare to offer alternative interpretations of past and present reality. As before, much of what they do relates organically to the Palestinian, native and indigenous narratives of the past and the information campaigns of the present.

But the sheer power of the Jewish state, and its potential to destabilise the region, if not the world, fuels the continuing attempt to comprehend the idea of Israel in the twenty-first century. Such efforts take place mostly outside the entrenched state, although quite a few fugitives from it are important partners in this enterprise. In the new division of labour, at present, Palestinians seek to redefine who they are, following a century of dispossession, fragmentation and colonisation. Meanwhile, the rest of the world, since Israelis have ceased to do so, is trying to grasp the nature and future intentions of the State created in 1948, with the blessings of the international community but against the wishes of the indigenous population and the region on which that State was forced. For everyone concerned, one issue is painfully – or gratefully, as the case may be – clear. The idea of Israel became a living organism: a state of seven million people, an advanced economy, a powerful army, a thriving culture and a third generation of settlers who become native as time goes by.

In recent years, two progressive paradigms have emerged in the scholarly/activist attempt to depict the phenomena of Zionism and Israel as accurately and ethically as possible. They are the settler colonialist paradigm and the apartheid paradigm. Both challenge effectively the official Israeli, and mainstream scholarly, approach, which insists on seeing Zionism exclusively as a national liberation movement and Israel as a liberal democracy.

And yet, despite their usefulness, both paradigms are unsatisfactory. They apply historical case studies with a known closure to an ongoing reality. In the conventional study of colonialism, settler colonialist states are states whose colonialist history is behind them. But until we find something more appropriate, these paradigms are the best we have. In this respect, we face difficulties similar to those faced by the academics, experts and pundits who try to explain the nature and orientation of the revolutions in the Arab world, the so-called Arab Spring. Both are open-ended phenomena. Their closure is yet to occur.

Pressure from the outside world reached a peak in the summer of 2013 with the decision of the EU to impose partial sanctions on Israel. The cartographic image Israel has broadcast of itself since 1948 – an island of stability, civilisation and morality in a sea of barbarism, primitivism and fanaticism – has already been challenged. Even the half million Israelis who demonstrated in vain for a better standard of living in Tel Aviv in the summer of 2011 recognised that this map is becoming reversed, not only in the eyes of the world but also in their own perceptions. 'Tel Aviv is the new Tahrir Square', they chanted, and in 2013 threatened to create a new Tahrir Square because the government that had been elected in 2012 was not meeting any of their basic demands for better housing, employment and education.

The powers that be in the State of Israel are thus far tolerating the uglier face of the Arab Spring, in particular that of the Syrian government as it sends its air force to bomb freely whatever it deems a strategic threat to the state. The Israeli élite are hoping that the Spring will once more produce a monstrous Islamic sea that will restore Israel's image as an island of stability. But this is not going to happen.

Even in the most chaotic and violent moments of this new historical process, world opinion has not absolved Israel from its continued oppression of the Palestinians. Israel is seen more and more as a colonialist state that survived the twentieth century but is maintained because of its usefulness to the United States and its effective role in the global capitalist economy. There is no longer any moral dimension for the global support, and when the more functional side of this support starts to weaken, the scenarios shared, for better or for worse, by post- and neo-Zionists alike – of life in a pariah state that maintains an apartheid regime – may come true. This book was written with the hope that these grim scenarios would not transpire, but with the uncomfortable sense that they are already unfolding before our eyes.

Notes

Introduction: Debating the Idea of Israel

1 Yosef Gorny, 'Thoughts on Zionism as a Utopian Ideology', *Modern Judaism*, 18: 3, (October 1998), p. 241.

2 Yossef Barslevsky, '*Did You Know the Land?*': *The Galilee and the Northern Valleys, Volume A*, Ein Harod, Israel: Hakibbutz Hameuhad, 1940, p. xi (Hebrew).

3 See report in *Haaretz*, 13 July 1994.

4 Here is how the debate was described in one of the dailies: 'Ilan Pappe claimed that Zionism is colonialism. He claims that the equation between the two became commonplace in Israel, because those who subscribe to it have tenure in the Israeli universities.' As a result, the report goes on, a more theoretical debate developed. 'Sounds boring? More than 600 people filled the university hall and gave up the game in which Bulgaria kicked Germany out of the World Cup.' Zvi Gilat, *Yedioth Ahronoth*, 13 July 1994.

5 I have described this in Ilan Pappe, *Out of the Frame: The Struggle for Academic Freedom*, London: Pluto, 2010.

6 See Francis Fukuyama, *The End of History and the Last Man*, New York: Free Press, 1992.

7 Gorny, 'Thoughts on Zionism as a Utopian Ideology'.

8 This is part of a campaign led by the Israeli Ministry of Information called 'The Faces of Israel' launched in 2000.

9 See Omar Barghouti, *Boycott, Divestment, Sanction: The Global Struggle for Palestinian Rights*, New York: Haymarket Books, 2011.

10 Edward Said, *Orientalism*, New York: Vintage, 1979, pp. 5–28. See also the discussion in Tikva Honig-Parnass, *False Prophets of Peace: Liberal Zionism and the Struggle for Palestine*, New York: Haymarket Books, 2011.

1 The 'Objective' History of the Land and the People

1 Based on 'Der Wacht am Rhine' and quoted in Michael Berkowitz, *Zionist Culture and West European Jewry Before the First World War*, Cambridge: Cambridge University Press, 1993, p. 20.

2 Naftali Arbel, ed., *The Great Epochs in the History of Eretz Israel, Volume I: A Land Without People*, Tel Aviv: Revivim, 1983 (Hebrew).

3 Noam Chomsky covers it in *Hegemony or Survival: America's Quest for Global Dominance*, New York: Metropolitan Books, 2003.

4 On Ben-Zion Dinur, see Gabriel Piterberg, *The Returns of Zionism: Myths, Politics and Scholarship in Israel*, London and New York: Verso, 2010, pp. 132–4. See also Yaakov Katz, 'Explaining the Term the "Heralders of Zion,"' *Shivat Zion*, 1 (1950), p. 93 (Hebrew).

5 Shmuel Almog, 'Pluralism in the History of the *Yishuv* and Zionism', in Moshe Zimmermann et al., ed., *Studies in Historiography*, Jerusalem: Zalman Shazar Centre, 1978, p. 202 (Hebrew).

6 Israel Kolatt, 'On Research and the Researcher of the History of the *Yishuv* and Zionism', *Cathedra*, 1 (1976), pp. 3–35 (Hebrew).

7 Almog, 'Pluralism in the History of the *Yishuv* and Zionism'.

8 See Norman Finkelstein, 'Disinformation and the Palestine Question: The Not-So-Strange Case of Joan Peters' *From Time Immemorial*', in Edward Said and Christopher Hitchens, ed., *Blaming the Victims: Spurious Scholarship and the Palestinian Question*, London: Verso, 1988, pp. 33–70.

9 D. F. Merriam, 'Kansas Nineteenth-Century Geologic Maps', *Transactions of the Kansas Academy of Science*, 99 (1996), pp. 95–114.

10 J. B. Harely, 'Deconstructing the Map', *Cartographica*, 26:2 (Summer 1989), p. 1.

11 Martin Gilbert, *The Atlas of the Arab–Israeli Conflict*, New York: Oxford University Press, 1993.

12 Ibid.

13 See the Palestinian point of view in Ilan Pappe, *A History of Modern Palestine: One Land, Two Peoples*, Cambridge: Cambridge University Press, 2003, pp. 105–7.

14 The British Government in Palestine, *The Palestine Survey*, prepared in December 1945 and January 1946 for UNSCOP.

15 Salman Abu-Sitta, *Atlas of Palestine, 1948*, London: Palestine Land Society, 2004.

2 The Alien Who Became a Terrorist: The Palestinian in Zionist Thought

1 Edward Said and Jean Mohr, *After the Last Sky*, New York: Columbia University Press, 1998, p. 4.

2 Directed by Michael Parzan, Israel First Channel co-production with Doc en Stock, January 2012.

3 Barbara Smith, *Roots of Separatism in Palestine: The British Economic Policy, 1920–1948*, London and New York: I. B. Tauris, 1993.

4 David Ben-Gurion, from a speech celebrating the twenty-fifth anniversary of the Second Aliyah, *The Book of the Second Aliyah*, Tel Aviv: Am Oved, 1947.

5 Ibid., Mendel Zinger, 'From Barodi (a Shtetl in the Ukraine) to Eretz Israel', p. 128.

6 Ibid.

7 Ibid., Moshe Beilinson, 'Rebelling Against Reality', p. 48, and Ben-Gurion's anniversary speech, p. 17.

8 Ibid., Zinger, 'From Barodi (a Shtetl in the Ukraine) to Eretz Israel'.

9 Ibid., Natan Hofshi, 'The Pioneers of Zion', p. 139.

10 Ibid., Yona Hurewitz, 'From *Kibbush Ha 'avoda* to Settlement', p. 210.

11 Natan Hofshi, 'A Pact with the Land', *The Book of the Second Aliyah*, p. 239.

12 Ben-Gurion's anniversary speech, *The Book of the Second Aliyah*, p. 17.

13 Ibid., Alexander Zaid, 'The Genesis', p. 169.

14 Michal Sadan, 'The Hebrew Shepherd', PhD Thesis, Tel Aviv: Tel Aviv University, 2006.

15 See Zaid, 'The Genesis', pp. 169–70.

16 Ibid.

17 Natan Shifris, 'The Memoirs of a Factory Worker', *The Book of the Second Aliyah*, p. 191.

18 Ibid.

19 Israel Kadishman, 'Neither by Might, Nor by Force', *The Book of the Second Aliyah*, p. 293.

20 Yossef Rabinowitch, 'Entries from the Rehovot Diary', *The Book of the Second Aliyah*, p. 234.

21 Ibid., p. 235

22 For these and other typical references, see Yair Baumel, *Blue and White Shadow: The Israeli Establishment Policy and Action, The Formative Years, 1958–1968*, Haifa, Israel: Pardes, 2007 (Hebrew).

23 See Ilan Pappe, *The Forgotten Palestinians: A History of the Palestinians in Israel*, New Haven, CT: Yale University Press, 2011, pp. 126–7.

24 Anita Shapira, *The Dove's Sword: Zionism and Force*, Tel Aviv: Am Oved, 1992, (Hebrew).

25 Golda Meir at a London press conference in 1969, quoted in Marie Syrkin, *A Land of Our Own: An Oral Autobiography*, New York: Putnam, 1973, p. 242.

26 Ilan Pappe, *The Rise and Fall of a Palestinian Dynasty: The Husaynis, 1700–1948*, Berkeley, CA: California University Press, 2011, pp. 212–42.

27 Shai Lachman, 'Arab Rebellion and Terrorism in Palestine, 1929–1939: The Case of Izz al-Din al-Qassam and His Movement', in Elie Kedourie and Sylvia Haim, ed., *Zionism and Arabism in Palestine and Israel*, London and New York: Frank Cass, 1982, pp. 53–69.

28 A view formed already by one of the leading Arabists of the Zionist movement, Ezra Danin, and adopted by generations of Israeli historians thereafter; see Ezra Danin, *Documents and Photos from the Archives of the Arab Gangs, 1936–1939*, Jerusalem: Manges, 1981 (Hebrew).

29 Jenny Laval, *Haj Amin and Berlin*, Tel Aviv: Hakibbutz Hameuhad, 1996 (Hebrew).

30 Benny Morris, *1948: A History of the First Arab–Israel War*, New Haven, CT: Yale University Press, 2010.

31 Benny Morris, *Israel's Border Wars, 1949–1956: Arab Infiltration, Israeli Retaliation, and the Countdown to the Suez War*, New York: Oxford University Press, 1997.

32 Jillian Becker, *The PLO: The Rise and Fall of the Palestine Liberation Organization*, London: Weidenfeld and Nicolson, 1984.

33 Morris, *Israel's Border Wars*.

34 Avi Shlaim, *The Iron Wall: Israel and the Arab World*, New York: Norton, pp. 143–56.

35 Ze'ev Schiff and Ehud Ya'ari, *Intifada: The Palestinian Uprising – Israel's Third Front*, New York: Simon and Schuster, 1990.

36 Yehoshua Porath, *The Emergence of the Palestinian-Arab National Movement, 1918–1929*, London: Frank Cass, 1974, and *The Palestinian Arab National Movement, 1929–1939*, London: Frank Cass, 1977.

37 Yehoshafat Harkabi, *Arab Attitudes to Israel*, New York: Wiley and Sons, 1974, p. 1.

38 Matti Steinberg, *Unending Quest: The Development of Palestinian National Consciousness*, Tel Aviv: Dekel, 2000.

39 Moshe Shemesh, *The Palestinian Entity, 1959–1974: Arab Politics and the PLO*, London: Frank Cass, 1988; Avraham Sela, *The Decline of the Arab–Israeli Conflict: Middle East Politics and the Quest for Regional Order*, Albany, NY: State University of New York Press, 1997; and Shaul Mishal, *The PLO Under Arafat: Between Gun and Olive Branch*, New Haven, CT: Yale University Press, 1986.

40 Noam Chomsky, *Powers and Prospects: Reflections on Human Nature and the Social Order*, New York: South End Press, 1999.

41 Pappe, *Forgotten Palestinians*, pp. 50–63.

42 Sammy Smooha, 'Arab–Jewish Relations', Ephrain Yaari and Zeev Shavit, eds, Trends in Israeli Society, Tel Aviv: Open University, 2001, p. 238 (Hebrew).

43 Sammy Smooha, *Israel, Pluralism and Conflict*, Berkeley, CA: University of California Press, 1978, p. 31.

44 Sammy Smooha, *The Orientation and Politicisation of the Arab Minority in Israel*, Haifa, Israel: The Arab-Jewish Centre, 1984.

45 Uri Ram, *The Changing Agenda of Israeli Sociology: Theory, Ideology and Identity*, New York: State University of New York Press, 1994.

46 Calvin Goldscheider and Dov Friedlander, 'Reproductive Norms in Israel', in Usiel Oskar Schmelz and Gad Nathan, ed., *Studies in the Population of Israel, Volume 30*, Jerusalem: Magnes Press, 1986, pp. 15–35.

47 Elia Zureik, 'Prospects of the Palestinians in Israel: A Review Article', *Journal of Palestine Studies*, Part I, 22: 2 (Winter 1993), pp. 90–109 and Part II, 22: 4 (Summer 1993), pp. 73–93.

3 The War of 1948 in Word and Image

1 Netanel Lorch, *The Edge of the Sword: Israel's War of Independence, 1947–1949*, New York: Textbook Publishers, 2003, p. 1.

2 Ibid. See also Alon Kadish, ed., *Israel's War of Independence, 1948–1949*, volumes I–II, Tel Aviv: Ministry of Defence Publications, 2004 (Hebrew).

3 Porath, *The Emergence of the Palestinian-Arab National Movement*.

4 Shemesh, *The Palestinian Entity*.
5 Lorch, *The Edge of the Sword*; Jon and David Kimche, *Both Sides of the Hill: Britain and the Palestine War*, London: Secher and Warburg, 1960.
6 Gershon Rivlin and Elhanan Oren, ed., *The War Diary, 1948, Volume I*, Tel Aviv: Ministry of Defence Publication, 1982, p. 9 (Hebrew).
7 *The Hebrew Encyclopaedia, Volume Six*.
8 Ibid.
9 Anita Shapira, *Walking Along the Horizon*, Tel Aviv: Am Oved, 1989, p. 54 (Hebrew).
10 See Ben-Zion Dinur's introduction in the opening pages of Yehuda Slutzky, *The History of the Hagana*, volumes I–III, Tel Aviv: Ministry of Defence Publication, 1982.
11 *Cathedra*, 1 (1976) was devoted to this debate.
12 Amiztur Ilan, 'The Prophecy of a Jewish State and Its Realisation, 1941–1949', *Ha-Ziyonut*, 10, p. 279 (Hebrew).
13 Michael Cohen, *Palestine and the Great Powers, 1945–1948*, Princeton, NJ: Princeton University Press, 1982; Ilan Pappe, *Britain and the Arab–Israeli Conflict, 1948–1951*, London: Macmillan, 1988.
14 See David Ben-Gurion, *When Israel Went to War*, Tel Aviv: Am Oved, 1975 (Hebrew).
15 David Greenberg, *The Cinema*, Tel Aviv: Am Oved, 1967, p. 212 (Hebrew).
16 Nurith Gertz, *Hirbet Hiza'a and The Morning After*, Tel Aviv: Hakibbutz Hameuhad, 1983, p. 168 (Hebrew).
17 Nurith Gertz, *A Story from the Movies*, Tel Aviv: Open University Press, 1993, p. 21 (Hebrew).
18 Directed by Thorold Dickinson in 1955. See Ella Shohat's critique of the film in Ella Shohat, Israel: *Cinema: East/West and the Politics of Representation*, Austin, TX: University of Texas Press, 1989, pp. 58–64.
19 Gilbert, *Atlas of the Arab–Israeli Conflict*.
20 *They Were Only Ten*, directed by Baruch Dienar (1961).
21 See Shohat, Israeli Cinema, pp. 70–1.
22 I have analysed the background for the British decision in Pappe, *Britain and the Arab–Israeli Conflict*.
23 Directed by Yossi Milo in 1967.
24 See Shohat, Israeli Cinema, pp. 120–1.
25 Directed by Nathan Axelrod in 1963.
26 *Waltz with Bashir* was directed by Ari Folman and *The Gatekeepers* by Dror Moreh.
27 The director was Menahem Golan and the film is based on a children's story by Yemima Avidar-Chernowitz, a famous children's author. In the original story the villian was German; in the film he was both a Nazi and an Arab.
28 The director was Gil Sadan in 1988.
29 The director of that sequence was Nissim Dayan in 1989.

4 The Trailblazers

1 Daniel Florentine, *Conversations with Maxim Ghilan*, Tel Aviv: Yaron Golan Publication, 1998 (Hebrew).

2 Ibid.

3 I have gathered his biographical details from, among other sources, an excellent article by Eli Aminov, 'Judaism, Zionism and Israel Shahak', in *Haoketz* (Haoketz.org), (1 December 2011). See also, 'The Life of Death: An Exchange', by Israel Shahak with a reply by Timothy Garton Ash, *New York Review of Books*, 34:1, (29 January 1987), and Morton Nezvinsky, 'In Memoriam: Israel Shahak', *Washington Report on Middle East Affairs*, (August/September 2001).

4 Israel Shahak, *Jewish History, Jewish Religion*, London: Pluto, 2010.

5 Ibid., pp. 79, 89.

6 Ibid., p. 125.

7 In 2010, Boaz Evron wrote a book on his life and writing titled *Athens and the Land of Oz*, published by Nahar Publications in Tel Aviv. On the Canaanite movement, see Yaacov Shavit, *The New Hebrew Nation*, London and New York: Routledge, 1987.

8 Boaz Evron, 'How Can One Enjoy from All the Worlds (How Can One Have the Cake and Eat It)', *Yedioth Ahronoth*, 8 December 1978, republished in his new book *Athens and the Land of Oz*.

9 Avraham Shapira, *Conversations Between Soldiers*, Tel Aviv: The Kibbutz Movement, 1967. See the analysis of this publication in Piterberg, *The Returns of Zionism*, pp. 232–333.

10 Boaz Evron, *A National Reckoning*, Tel Aviv: Devir Publications, 1988.

11 He said this on the Sixth Session in the Russian Social-Democratic Party's Second Congress, 1903, published by Index Books, London, 1978.

12 Evron, *A National Reckoning*, pp. 328–32.

13 There are not many English sources on the life of this brilliant scholar. There is a good summary in Joel Greenberg, 'Yeshayahu Leibowitz, 91, Iconoclastic Israeli Thinker', *New York Times*, (19 August 1994). His most important book in English is *Judaism, Human Values and the Jewish State*, Cambridge, MA: Harvard University Press, 1995 (and a book on Maimonides that appeared a year later).

14 Yeshayahu Leibowitz, 'After Qibiya', *Beterm*, 1953/1954 (in Hebrew).

15 Ibid.

16 These views are reproduced in Dror Moreh's film, *The Gatekeepers* (2012).

17 Yitzhak Laor, 'Israel the Grandfather, and Also a Scientist and a Hero Who Abhorred Heroism', *Haaretz*, (28 September 2012).

18 Yeshayahu Leibowitz, *Faith, History and Values,* Jerusalem: Magnes, 1982, p. 225 (Hebrew).

19 Ibid.

20 Uri Avnery, *In the Fields of the Philistines*, Tel Aviv: Zemora-Bitan, 1990 (Hebrew).

21 Uri Avnery, *The Other Side of the Coin,* Tel Aviv: Shimoni Publications, 1950 (Hebrew).

22 Nitza Erel, *Uri Avnery: Without Bias and Without Fear,* Jerusalem: Magnes Publications, 1990 (Hebrew).

23 Akiva Orr, 'How Did I Arrive at Politics, the Communist Party and Matzpen', matzpen.org, (1 September 2008) (Hebrew).

24 Avigail Abarbanel, *Beyond Tribal Loyalties: Personal Stories of Jewish Peace Activists*, Newcastle, UK: Cambridge and Scholars Publishing, 2012.

25 Akiva Orr with Moshe Machover, *Peace, Peace and No Peace*, Tel Aviv:

Matzpen, 1950. There is also a limited English edition, which can be accessed through Orr's open-access books site akivaorrbooks.org/hebrew, with the title *The Un-Jewish State: The Politics of Israel.*

26 See Michael Warschawski, *On The Border*, Tel Aviv: Carmel, 1989 (Hebrew), which also came out in English, under the same title with South End Press in 2005.

27 Ilan Halevi wrote a semi-autobiographical novel, *Allers-retours*, Paris: Flammarion, 2005.

28 Uri Davis, *Crossing the Border: An Autobiography of an Anti-Zionist Palestinian Jew*, London: Books & Books Ltd, 1995.

29 Uri Davis, *Apartheid Israel: Possibilities for the Struggle Within*, London: Zed Books, 2004.

30 This has also happened to the anthropologist Samadar Lavie, who taught in several Israeli universities before being forced to leave.

31 Nitza Erel, *Matzpen: The Conscience and the Fantasy*, Tel Aviv: Resling, 2010 (Hebrew). The word *matzpen* (compass) and the word *matzpun* (conscience) have a similar etymology.

32 Ran Greenstein, 'Class, Nation, and Political Organization: The Anti-Zionist Left in Israel/Palestine', *International Labour and Working-Class History*, 75 (Spring 2009), pp. 85–108.

33 Yitzhak Rubin (director), *Udi Adiv, A Broken Israeli Myth*, 2010 (Teknews Media Ltd).

34 Uriel Tal, 'Reciprocity Between General and Jewish History, *Yahdaut Zemanenu* 3 (1986), pp. 3–12.

35 The most comprehensive analysis of the Black Panthers in Israel can be found in Sami Shalom Chetrit, *Intra-Jewish Conflict in Israel: White Jews, Black Jews*, London and New York: Routledge, 2009, pp. 81–140 (and his notes on Abargel on pages 100–7).

36 See also Ilan Pappe, *A History of Modern Palestine: One Land, Two Peoples*, 2nd edition, Cambridge: Cambridge University Press, 2006, pp. 211–13.

37 Shmuel Noah Eisenstadt, *Introduction to the Social Structure of the Mizrachi Communities*, Jerusalem: The Szold Institute, 1948; *The Social Structure of Israel*, Beit Berl Publications, 1958; *The Israeli Society: Background, Development and Problems*, Jerusalem: Magnes, 1967; and *The Transformations in Israeli Society*, Jerusalem: Magnes, 1989. Although scores of his books on modernisation elsewhere in the world and on the theory of modernisation appeared in English, only the last book on Israel appeared in English.

38 Sholmo Svirsky, 'Notes on the Historical Sociology of the *Yishuv* Period', in Uri Ram, ed., *Israeli Society: Critical Perspectives*, Tel Aviv: Breirot, 1993, p. 80 (published originally in the University of Haifa *Notes on Critique and Theory*) (Hebrew).

39 Ibid., and Sammy Smooha, 'Class, Ethnic and National Cleavages and Democracy in Israel', in Uri Ram, *Israeli Society*, pp. 172–202 (Hebrew).

40 Smooha, 'Class, Ethnic and National Cleavages and Democracy in Israel', p. 183.

41 Baruch Kimmerling, *Zionism and Territory: The Socio-Territorial Dimensions of Zionist Politics*, Berkeley, CA: University of California Press, 1983; Yonathan Shapira's most important book in this respect is *Elite Without Successors: Generations of Leaders in the Israeli Society*, Tel Aviv: Poalim, 1984.

42 Yonathan Shapira, 'The Historical Origins of Israeli Democracy', in Uri Ram, *Israeli Society*, p. 52 (Hebrew).

43 Baruch Kimmerling, 'State-Society Relations in Israel', in Uri Ram, *Israeli Society*, p. 336 (Hebrew).

44 Shapira, *Elite Without Successors*.

45 Baruch Kimmerling's last book was *Politicide: The Real Legacy of Ariel Sharon*, London: Verso, 2006.

46 Erel, *Matzpen*.

47 Maxime Rodinson, *Israel: A Colonial-Settler State?*, New York: Monad Press, 1973.

48 Anita Shapira, *Visions in Conflict*, Tel Aviv: Am Oved, 1988 (Hebrew).

49 Ran Aaronson, 'Settlement in Eretz Israel – A Colonialist Enterprise? "Critical" Scholarship and Historical Geography', *Israel Studies*, 1:2 (Fall 1996), pp. 214–29.

50 Gershon Shafir, *Land, Labour, and the Origins of the Israeli-Palestinian Conflict*, New York: Cambridge University Press, 1989.

51 Deborah S. Bernstein, *Constructing Boundaries: Jewish and Arab Workers in Mandatory Palestine*, Albany, NY: State University of New York Press, 2004; David De Vries, *Diamonds and War: State, Capital and Labour in British-Ruled Palestine*, London: Berghahn Books, 2010.

5   Recognising the Palestinian Catastrophe: The 1948 War Revisited

1 The information about this episode is gathered from an article by Shay Hazkani, titled 'The Research That Was Meant to Prove That the Arabs Had Fled in 1948', published in *Haaretz* weekend supplement, (17 May 2013).

2 Ibid.

3 Ibid.

4 Ibid.

5 Rony Gabbay, *A Political Study of the Arab–Jewish Conflict: The Arab Refugee Problem*, Geneva: Librarie Droz, 1959.

6 Quoted in Hazkani, 'The Research That Was Meant to Prove That the Arabs Had Fled in 1948'.

7 Quoted in ibid.

8 See Noam Chomsky and Ilan Pappe, *The War on Gaza*, Penguin: London, 2010, pp. 19–56.

9 Simha Flapan, *The Birth of Israel: Myths and Realities*, New York: Pantheon Books, 1988, pp. 3–6.

10 Ibid.

11 Ibid.

12 Ibid.

13 Ibid., p. 33.

14 Ibid., pp. 55–81.

15 Ibid., pp. 82–118.

16 Israel Baer, *Israel's Security: Yesterday, Today and Tomorrow*, Tel Aviv: Maarachot, 1966 (Hebrew).

17 Flapan, *The Birth of Israel*, p. 19.
18 Ibid.
19 Ibid., pp. 119–52.
20 Ibid., pp. 152–87.
21 Ibid., pp. 187–212.
22 Benny Morris, 'The New Historiography', *Tikkun*, 3, (November/December 1989), pp. 19–35, reprinted in Benny Morris, *1948 and After*, Oxford: Clarendon Press, 1990, pp. 1–34.
23 The English version of Shabtai Teveth's critique appeared in an article 'Charging Israel with Original Sin', *Commentary*, (September 1989). A good summary of that stage in the debate can be found in Avi Shlaim, 'The Debate About 1948' in Ilan Pappe, ed., *The Israel/Palestine Question: A Reader*, London and New York: Routledge, 1999 (2006), pp. 287–304.
24 See the lecture by Aharon Shay and David Tal on the new history given in a Van-Leer Conference, 'The New History in Israel', March 1996.
25 Avi Shlaim, *Collusion Across the Jordan: King Abdullah, The Zionist Movement and the Partition of Palestine*, Oxford: Clarendon Press, 1988, pp. iii–vi.
26 Ibid.
27 Pappe, *Britain and the Arab–Israeli Conflict, 1948–51*.
28 Ibid.
29 Pappe, *Britain and the Arab–Israeli Conflict*, pp. 26–7.
30 Ilan Pappe, *The Making of the Arab–Israeli Conflict, 1947–1951*, London and New York: I.B. Tauris, 1992.
31 Ibid.
32 Pappe, *The Making of the Arab–Israeli Conflict*, pp. 16–46.
33 And remade in 1988, see Walid Khalidi, 'Plan Dalet: Master Plan for the Conquest of Palestine', *Journal of Palestine Studies*, 18:69 (Autumn 1988), pp. 4–20.
34 Ilan Pappe, 'Were They Expelled?: The History, Historiography and Relevance of the Refugee Problem', in Ghada Karmi and Eugene Cortan, ed., *The Palestinian Exodus, 1948–1988*, London: Ithaca Press, 1999, pp. 37–62.
35 Pappe, *The Ethnic Cleansing of Palestine*, London: Oneworld, 2006, pp. 1–10.
36 Shlaim, *The Iron Wall*.
37 Tom Segev, *1949: The First Israelis*, New York: Owl Books, 1998.
38 Meron Benvenisti, *Sacred Landscape: The Buried History of the Holy Land Since 1948*, Berkeley, CA: University of California Press, 2002.
39 Meron Benvenisti, *Sons of Cypresses: Memories, Reflections and Regrets From a Political Life*, Berkeley, CA: University of California Press, 2007.
40 See Ilan Pappe, *Out of the Frame*.

6 The Emergence of Post-Zionist Academia, 1990–2000

1 A short reference to the conference can be found in Pinchas Ginosar and Avi Bareli, eds, *Zionism: A Contemporary Controversy*, Sdeh Boker, Israel: The Ben Gurion Heritage Centre, 1996, p. 8 (Hebrew).
2 Again it would be good to refer here to Honig-Parnass, *False Prophets*, and Ephraim Nimni, ed., *The Challenge of Post-Zionism: Alternatives to Fundamentalist Politics in Israel*, London: Zed Books, 2003.

3 Lawrence Stone, *The Past and Present Revisited*, London: Longman, 1989, p. 8.

4 Hanan Hever, 'The Post-Zionist Situation', in Gil Eyal, ed., *Four Lectures on Critical Theory*, Jerusalem: Van Leer, 2012, pp. 73–94 (Hebrew).

5 Edward Said, 'New History, Old Ideas', *Al-Ahram Weekly*, (21–7 May 1998).

6 Ibid.

7 Ibid.

8 Perry Anderson, 'Scurrying Towards Bethlehem', *New Left Review*, 10, (July/August 2001), p. 11.

9 Oren Yiftachel, 'Ethnocracy and Geography: Territory and Politics in Israel/Palestine', *Middle East Report*, geog.bgu.ac.il/members/yiftachel/paper3.html

10 Sarah Ozacky-Lazar, 'The Military Rule as a Mechanism of Control of the Arab Citizens', *Hamizrah Hahadash*, 42, (2002), pp. 57–69 (Hebrew).

11 Dan Rabinowitz, 'Natives with Jackets and Degrees: Othering, Objectification and the Role of the Palestinians in the Co-existence Field in Israel', *Social Anthropology*, 9: 1, (2000), p. 76.

12 Hillel Cohen, *The Present Absentees: The Palestinian Refugees in Israel Since 1948*, Jerusalem: Van Leer Institute, 2000 (Hebrew); Yoav Peled and Nadim Rouhana, 'Transitional Justice and the Right of Return of the Palestinian Refugees', *Theoretical Inquires in Law*, 5:2, (2004), pp. 317–32.

13 Sharon Groves, 'Interview with Marcia Freedman', *Feminist Studies*, (22 September 2002).

14 Yuval Yonay, 'A Queer Look at the Palestinian–Jewish Conflict', *Theory and Criticism*, 19, (Autumn 2001), pp. 269–75 (Hebrew).

15 Eyal Gross, 'Theo Meintz is Gone', from his blog Eyalgross.com/blog, (14 June 2013) (Hebrew).

16 Michael Shalev, *Labour and the Political Economy in Israel*, New York: Oxford University Press, 1992; and Jonathan Nitzan and Shimshon Bichler, *The Global Political Economy of Israel*, London: Pluto, 2002.

17 Baruch Kimmerling, 'State Building, State Autonomy and the Identity of the Society – the Case of Israel', *Journal of Historical Sociology*, 6:4, (December 1993), pp. 369–429.

18 Yael Zerubavel, *Recovered Roots: Collective Memory and the Making of Israeli National Tradition*, Chicago: Chicago University Press, 1995.

19 Nachman Ben-Yehuda, *The Masada Myth: Collective Memory and Mythmaking in Israel*, Madison, WI: Wisconsin University Press, 1995.

20 Shlomo Sand, *The Invention of the Jewish People*, New York: Verso, 2009; Piterberg, *The Returns of Zionism*.

21 Amnon Raz-Karkozkin, 'Exile Within Sovereignty: Towards a Critique of the "Negation of Exile" in Israeli Culture', parts 1–2, *Theory and Criticism*, 4/5, (1993/94), pp. 23–56 and pp. 113–32 respectively (Hebrew). See an extensive discussion on these articles by Gabriel Piterberg, *The Returns of Zionism*, pp. 127–30.

22 Gur Elroi, *Immigrants: Jewish Immigration to Eretz Israel*, Jerusalem: Yad Ben Zvi, 2004 (Hebrew).

23 Zeev Sternhell, *The Founding Myths of Israel: Nationalism, Socialism, and the Making of the Jewish State*, Princeton, NJ: Princeton University Press, 1998.

24 Lev Greenberg, 'The Arab–Jewish Drivers' Union Strike, 1931: A Contribution to the Critique on the National Conflict Sociology', in Ilan Pappe, ed., *Jewish–Arab Relations in Mandatory Palestine: A New Approach to the Historical Research*, Givat Haviva: The Institute of Peace Research, 1995 (Hebrew); David

De Vries, *Idealism and Bureaucracy: The Roots of Red Haifa*, Tel Aviv: Hakibbutz Hameuhad, 1999 (Hebrew); Deborah S. Bernstein, *Constructing Boundaries*.

25 Shulamit Carmi and Henry Rosenfeld, 'The Emergence of Militaristic Nationalism in Israel', *International Journal of Politics, Culture and Society*, 3: 1, (1989), pp. 5–49.

26 Uri Ben-Eliezer, *The Making of Israeli Militarism*, Bloomington, IN: Indiana University Press, 1998.

27 Yagil Levy, *Israel's Materialist Militarism*, New York: Lexington Books, 2007.

28 Hagit Gur-Ziv, *Statements on Silence: The Silence of Israeli Society in the Face of the Intifada*, Tel Aviv: The Centre for Peace, 1989 (Hebrew); Nurit Peled-Elhanan, *Palestine in Israeli School Books: Ideology and Propaganda in Education*, London and New York: I.B. Tauris, 2012; Diana Dolev, 'Academia and Spatial Control: The Case of the Hebrew University Campus on Mount Scopus, Jerusalem', in Haim Yacobi, *Constructing a Sense of Place: Architecture and the Zionist Discourse*, London: Ashgate, 2004, pp. 227–45. An important figure in this trend was Rela Mazali, and one of her recent contributions is 'A Call for Liveable Futures', *Huffington Post*, (25 June 2010).

29 Uri Ram, *Israeli Society*.

30 Ibid.

31 Shoshana Madmoni-Gerber, *Israeli Media and the Framing of Internal Conflict: The Yemenite Babies Affair*, New York: Palgrave Macmillan, 2010.

32 For Zvi Efrat's work in English, see the book he co-authored with Meron Benvenisti, Nadav Harel, Gideon Levy et al., *A Civilian Occupation: The Politics of Israeli Architecture*, London: Verso, 2003.

33 Alexander Kedar, 'The Legal Transformations of Ethnic Geography: Israeli Law and the Palestinian Landholder, 1948–1967', *Journal of International Law and Politics*, 33: 4, (2001), pp. 923–1,000.

34 Haim Bereshit, 'Givat Aliya as a Metaphor: Three Aspects', *Theory and Criticism*, 16, (2000), pp. 233–8 (Hebrew).

35 Ilan Gur-Ze'ev, 'The Thirty-First Floor: The University Tower and the Phallocentrism of Zionism', *Theory and Criticism*, 16, (2000), pp. 239–43 (Hebrew).

36 Jonathan and Daniel Boyarin, *Powers of Diaspora: Two Essays on the Relevance of Jewish Culture*, Minneapolis, MN: University of Minnesota Press, 2002; and for more on Hever, see Honig-Parnass, *False Prophets*, p. 197.

37 Sharon Rotbard, *White Cities, Black Cities*, Tel Aviv: Babel, 2005 (Hebrew).

38 John Arthur and Amy Shapiro, ed., *Campus Wars: Multiculturalism and the Politics of Difference*, Boulder, CO: Westview, 1994.

39 See Tamara Traubman, 'The Ratio of *Mizrachim* in the Academia', *Haaretz*, (18 October 2007). Ever lower quotas are discussed by Yifat Biton in an interview with the weekly *Makor Rishon*, (20 May 2011).

40 Mira Ariel and Rachel Giora, 'An Analysis of Impositive Speech Acts: Gender Biases in the New Israeli Cinema Discourse', in Nurith Gertz, Orly Lubin and Judd Ne'eman, eds, *Fictive Looks: On Israeli Cinema*, Tel Aviv: Open University Press, pp. 179–204 (Hebrew).

41 From a paper she gave at an AAUP Conference on the academic boycott, February 2006, and which can be accessed at aaup.org

42 Anat Matar, 'Israeli Academics Must Pay Price to End Occupation', *Haaretz*, (27 August 2009).

7 Touching the Raw Nerves of Society: Holocaust Memory in Israel

1 Quoted in Noam Chomsky, *Fateful Triangle: The United States, Israel, and the Palestinians*, Cambridge, MA: Southend, 1999, p. 99.

2 Avraham Burg, *The Holocaust Is Over: We Must Rise from Its Ashes*, New York: Palgrave Macmillan, 2009, p. 252.

3 Israel Shahak, letter to the editor, Kol Ha'ir, (19 May 1989).

4 Ibid.

5 Shahak, *Jewish History*, p. 71.

6 Israel Shahak and Norton Mezvinzky, *Jewish Fundamentalism in Israel*, London: Pluto, 2004, p. 105 and in *Jewish History*, p. x.

7 Shahak, *Jewish History*, p. 135, n. 25.

8 He repeated these ideas in English in Boaz Evron, 'The Holocaust: Learning the Wrong Lessons', *Journal of Palestine Studies*, 10: 3, (1981), pp. 16–26. The original quote is from Boaz Evron, 'The Holocaust – A Danger to the People', *Iton 77*, 21, (May/June 1980) (Hebrew).

9 Ibid.

10 Ibid.

11 Yehuda Elkana, 'In Favour of Amnesia', *Haaretz*, (2 March 1988).

12 Ibid.

13 Ibid.

14 Reproduced in English in Amos Elon, 'The Politics of Memory', *New York Review of Books*, (7 October 1993).

15 Peter Novick, *The Holocaust in American Life,* Boston: Mariner Books, 1999; Norman Finkelstein, *The Holocaust Industry: Reflections on the Exploitation of Jewish Suffering*, London: Verso, 2003; and Lenni Brenner, *Zionism in the Age of Dictators*, Westport: Lawrence Hill and Co, 1983.

16 Novick, *The Holocaust in American Life*, p. 10.

17 Finkelstein, *The Holocaust Industry*, p. 47.

18 Tom Segev, *The Seventh Million: The Israelis and the Holocaust*, New York: Picador, 2000, appeared first in Hebrew and was the only direct reference in Hebrew to these connections. An even more explicit condemnation can be found in Moshe Zimmermann, 'The Zionist Dilemma', *Haaretz*, (28 October 2004).

19 Ahimeir's references are quoted in Brenner, *Zionism in the Age of Dictators*, p. 125; Ben-Avi's appeared in sequence in *Doar Ha-Yom*, August and November 1932.

20 See Segev, *The Seventh Million*, p. 33.

21 Ibid.

22 Hava Eshkoli-Wagman, 'Yishuv Zionism: Its Attitude to Nazism and the Third Reich Reconsidered', *Modern Judaism*, 19: 1, (February 1999), pp. 25–6.

23 Ibid.

24 He published his books in Germany and then they were translated into Hebrew. The most recent in which these views are articulated clearly is *Germans Against Germans: The Fate of the Jews, 1938–1945*, Tel Aviv: Am Oved, 2013 (Hebrew).

25 One local newspaper, *Yerusahlaim* (part of *Yeidoh Ahronoth*) claimed Zimmermann compared the settler youth to the Hitler-Jugend movement (22

September 1995). Zimmermann sued the paper for misrepresentation, but lost the case on 3 February 2005.

26 Brenner, *Zionism in the Age of Dictators*.

27 Ibid, p. 93.

28 Joseph Massad, 'The Last of Semites', Al Jazeera English, (21 May 2013).

29 Brenner, *Zionism in the Age of Dictators,* p. 93 and Segev, *The Seventh Million*, p. 31.

30 Ibid.

31 David Ben-Gurion's Speech, Labour Party Archives, Beit Berl, Mapai Secretariat, (7 December 1938).

32 Segev, *The Seventh Million*, p. 83.

33 *The Seventh Million: The Israelis and the Holocaust*, directed by Benny Brunner, 1995.

34 Marek Edelman, *Resisting the Holocaust: Fighting Back in the Warsaw Ghetto*, London: Ocean, 2004; Idith Zertal, *Israel's Holocaust and the Politics of Nationhood*, Cambridge: Cambridge University Press, 2005.

35 Benedict Anderson, *Imagined Communities*, London: Verso, 1983; Eric Hobsbawm and Terence Ranger, *The Invention of Tradition*, Cambridge: Canto Books, 1983.

36 Edelman, *Resisting the Holocaust*.

37 Quoted in Zertal, *Israel's Holocaust and the Politics of Nationhood*, p. 35.

38 Ibid., pp. 54–6.

39 Ibid.

40 Anderson, *Imagined Communities*, p. 57.

41 Primo Levi, *The Drowned and the Saved*, New York: Abacus, 1988, pp. 78–85.

42 Quoted in Zertal, *Israel's Holocaust and the Politics of Nationhood*, p. 27.

43 Ibid., p. 28.

44 Hannah Arendt, *Eichmann in Jerusalem: A Report on the Banality of Evil*, New York: Viking, 1968.

45 See Yair Auron, *The Banality of Indifference: Zionism and the Armenian Genocide*, New York: Transactions Publishers, 2001.

46 Ilan Gur-Ze'ev, 'The Morality of Acknowledging/Not-acknowledging the Other's Holocaust/Genocide', *Journal of Moral Education*, 27:2, (1998), p. 161.

47 Adi Ofir, 'On "Hidush Ha-Shem": The Holocaust as an Anti-Theological Tract', *Politika*, 8, (1986), pp. 4–5 (Hebrew). *Hilul Ha-Shem* means sacrilegious. *Ha-Shem* is one of God's names, and *Hidush* means Renewal.

48 See Eyal Sivan, *Yizkor*.

49 Nurith Gertz, 'The Early Israeli Cinema as Silencer of Memory', *Shofar: An Interdisciplinary Journal of Jewish Studies*, 24:1, (Fall 2005).

50 Ibid.

51 This is the excellent summary of Milton Viorst, 'After the Fact: A Review of *The Seventh Million*', *Journal of Palestine Studies*, 24:2, (Winter 1995), p. 94; see also Segev, *The Seventh Million*, pp. 123–40.

52 Hanna Yablonka, 'The Development of Holocaust Consciousness in Israel: The Nuremberg, Kapos, Kastner, and Eichmann Trials', *Israel Studies*, 8:3, (Fall 2003).

53 Idith Zertal, *From Catastrophe to Power: The Holocaust Survivors and the Emergence of Israel*, Berkeley, CA: University of California Press, 1998.

54 Yosef Grodzinsky, *Good Human Material: Jews Against Zionists, 1945–1951*, Tel Aviv: Maariv, 1998 (Hebrew).

55 See the episode described in Pappe, *The Making of the Arab–Israeli Conflict, 1947–1951*, p. 31.

56 Grodzinsky, *Good Human Material*.

57 Aviva Halamish, *The Exodus Affair: Holocaust Survivors and the Struggle for Palestine*, Albany, NY: Syracuse University Press, 1998.

58 M. M. Silver, *Our Exodus: Leon Uris and the Americanisation of Israel's Founding Story*, Detroit, MI: Wayne State University Press, 2010.

59 See Pappe, *The Making of the Arab–Israeli Conflict, 1947–1951*, pp. 24–5.

60 Arendt, *Eichmann in Jerusalem*, p. 229.

61 Quoted and discussed in Nicholas Patruno, *Understanding Primo Levi*, Miami, FL: University of South California Press, 1995, p. 122.

62 See Yablonka, 'The Development of a Holocaust Consciousness in Israel' and Zertal, *Israel's Holocaust and the Politics of Nationhood*, pp. 69–71.

63 Ibid., pp. 196–8.

64 Quoted in an interview he gave to *Yeidoth Ahronoth* on 18 June 1982.

65 Amos Oz, 'Hitler Is Already Dead, Mr Prime Minister', *Yeidoth Ahronoth*, (21 June 1982).

66 Novick, *The Holocaust in American Life*, p. 158.

67 Gur-Ze'ev, 'The Morality of Acknowledging/Not-acknowledging the Other's Holocaust/Genocide'.

68 Moshe Zuckermann, *Shoah in the Sealed Room: The 'Holocaust' in the Israeli Press During the Gulf War*, Tel Aviv: self-publication 1993 (Hebrew).

69 Also this year this alternative ceremony took place in the school.

8 The Idea of Israel and the Arab Jews

1 Yehouda Shenhav, 'The Jews of Iraq, Zionist Ideology, and the Property of the Palestinian Refugees of 1948: An Anomaly of National Accounting', *International Journal of Middle East Studies*, 31:4 (November 1999), pp. 605–30.

2 Ibid.

3 Ibid.

4 Ibid., p. 605.

5 This text is now available in English, see Ella Shohat, 'Remembering Baghdad Elsewhere: An Emotional Cartography', *Jadaliyya*, jadaliyya.com, (1 April 2013).

6 Ariella Azoulay, 'Mother Tongue, Father Tongue', Yigal Nizri, ed., *Eastern Appearances: Mother Tongue*, Tel Aviv: Babel, 2004, p. 160 (Hebrew).

7 Quoted in Smooha, *Israel: Pluralism and Conflict*, p. 88. See also the apologetic article by Meyrav Wumser, 'Post-Zionism and the Sephardi Question', *Middle East Quarterly*, 12:2, Fall 2005, pp. 21–30.

8 Quoted in Sammy Smooha, *Israel: Pluralism and Conflict*, Berkeley, CA: University of California Press, 1978.

9 Quoted in Sami Shalom Chetrit, *The Mizrachi Struggle in Israel, Between Oppression and Liberation, Identity and Alternative, 1948–2003*, Tel Aviv: Am Oved, 2004, p. 65 (Hebrew).

10 Quoted in Smooha, *Israel: Pluralism and Conflict*, p. 88.

11 Aryeh Gelblum, *Haaretz*, (22 April 1949).

12 Ilan Pappe, 'Edward Said's Impact on Post-Zionist Critique in Israel', Adel Iskandar and Hakem Rustom, ed., *Edward Said: A Legacy of Emancipation and Representation*, Berkeley, CA: University of California Press, 2010, pp. 321–2.

13 Eli Avraham, *The Media in Israel: Centre and Periphery – The Coverage of the Development Towns*, Tel Aviv: Breirot, 1993, p. 32 (Hebrew).

14 Edward Said, 'Zionism from the Standpoint of Its Victims', *The Edward Said Reader*, Moustafa Bayoumi and Andrew Rubin, ed., New York: Vintage, 2000, pp. 68–114; Ella Shohat, 'Sephardim in Israel: Zionism from the Standpoint of Its Jewish Victims', *Social Text*, 19/20, (Autumn 1988), pp. 1–35.

15 These ideas were gathered in Moshe Behar and Zvi Ben-Dor Benite, ed., *Modern Middle Eastern Jewish Thought: Writings on Identity, Politics, and Culture, 1893–1958*, Boston: Brandeis University Press, 2012.

16 Moshe Behar, 'Is the Mizrachi Question Relevant to the Future of the Entire Middle East', Kedma.org, (January 1997) (Hebrew).

17 Sami Shalom Chetrit, *Intra-Jewish Conflict in Israel: White Jews, Black Jews*, London and New York: Routledge, 2013.

18 See Yehouda Shenhav, ed., *Colonialism and the Post-Colonialist Condition*, Jerusalem: Van Leer, 2004 (Hebrew).

19 Quote from Lorenzo Veracini, *Settler Colonialism: A Theoretical Overview*, New York: Palgrave Macmillan, 2010, p. 1; see also Patrick Wolfe, *Settler Colonialism and the Transformation of Anthropology*, London: Bloomsbury 1998; and Edward Cavanagh, *Settler Colonialism and Land Rights in South Africa: Possession and Dispossession on the Orange River*, New York: Palgrave Macmillan, 2013.

20 Ella Shohat, 'The Invention of the *Mizrachim*', *Journal of Palestine Studies*, 29:1, (Autumn 1999), pp. 5–20.

21 Chetrit, *Intra-Jewish Conflict in Israel*.

22 Yossi Yonah, Yonit Naaman and David Machlev, ed., *Rainbow of Opinions: A Mizrachi Agenda for Israel*, Jerusalem: November Books, 2007 (Hebrew).

23 From his poem 'I Am an Arab Refugee', 2004. The best line in the quotation is an oath Jews use with regard to Jerusalem.

24 Smadar Lavie, 'Arrival of the New Cultured Tenants', *Times Literary Supplement*, (14 June 1991).

25 Yoav Peled, 'Towards a Redefinition of Jewish Nationalism in Israel? The Engima of Shas', *Ethnic and Racial Studies*, 21:4, (1998), pp. 703–23.

26 Traubman, *Haaretz*.

27 Chetrit, *Intra-Jewish Conflict in Israel*.

9 The Post-Zionist Cultural Moment

1 Quoted in Yigal Nizri, 'Foreword: From a Noun to Us' in Nizri, *Eastern Appearance*, p. 27.

2 Ibid.

3 Dror Mishani, 'The Mizrahi as a Linguistic Abberation' in Nizri, *Eastern Appearance*, p. 86 (Hebrew).

4 Sami Shalom Chetrit, *Poems in Ashdodit*, Tel Aviv: Andalus, 2003 (Hebrew). Ashdod, the former depopulated Palestinian town Majdal, is where Chetrit grew up.

5 Ilan Pappe, 'Post-Zionism and Its Popular Culture' in Rebecca L. Stein and Ted Swedenburg, ed., *Palestine, Israel, and the Politics of Popular Culture*, Durham, NC: Duke University Press, 2006.

6 Albert Swissa, *Bound*, Tel Aviv: Hakkibutz Hameuhad, 1985 (Hebrew), and Yerach Gover, *Zionism: The Limits of Moral Discourse in Israeli Hebrew Fiction*, Minneapolis, MN: University of Minnesota Press, 1994.

7 Yitzhak Laor, *The People, Food Fit for a King*, Tel Aviv: Hakibbutz Hameuhad, 1994 (Hebrew).

8 Yitzhak Laor, *In the Spring: After the Reserve Service (Early Stories)*, Tel Aviv: Keter, 2000, p. 137 (Hebrew).

9 David Grossman, *The Yellow Wind*, New York: Picador, 2002, and *Sleeping on a Wire: Conversations with Palestinians in Israel*, New York: Picador, 2003.

10 See Dina Goren, 'The Media in Israel', *Skira Hodshit*, 8–9, (August/September 1984), pp. 57–67 (Hebrew).

11 Issam Abu Riya, 'The Arab Minority and the Israeli Media' in Issam Abu Riya et al., ed., *Exclusion and Negative Images*, The Israeli Civil Rights Report, 2002 (Hebrew).

12 Calev Ben-David and David Wainer, 'The Controversy Over Israel's Business Élite', *Bloomberg Businessweek*, (7 October 2010).

13 Yaron Ezrahi, *Rubber Bullets: Power and Consciousness in Modern Israel*, New York: Farrar, Straus and Giroux, 1997.

14 *Waltz with Bashir*, directed by Ari Folman, 2008; *The Gatekeepers*, directed by Dror Moreh, 2012.

15 Ezrahi, *Rubber Bullets*.

16 See a very incisive analysis of liberal Zionism in Honig-Parnass, *The False Prophets*.

10   On the Post-Zionist Stage and Screen

1 Hanoch Levin, *The Labour of Life: Selected Plays*, trans. Barborn Harshaw, Stanford, CA: Stanford University Press, 2003.

2 Dan Urian, *The Arab in Drama and Israeli Theatre*, London and New York: Routledge, 1997.

3 See Ilan Pappe, 'A Text in the Eyes of the Beholder: Four Theatrical Interpretations of Kanafani's Men in the Sun', *Contemporary Theatre Review*, 3, (1995), pp. 157–74.

4 For example, *A Trumpet in the Wadi*, adapted and directed by Shmuel Hasfari, 1998.

5 Fouad Awad and Eran Baneil directed a local version of *Romeo and Juliet* for the Kahn Theatre in Jerusalem (an Israeli Jerusalemite theatre) and al-Qasaba (a Palestinian Jerusalemite theatre).

6 The play was censored in 1988 and was staged privately in 1989.

7 Quoted in an interview in *Yedioth Ahronoth*, (December 2009).

8 Ram Levi's adaptation was screened in February 1978.

9 Ram Levi in conversation with Ilan Pappe in *Zochrot*, (19 November 2012).

10 Jad Ne'eman directed about twenty films. His most well known is probably *The Stretcher's Journey*, released in 1977. Such a journey is the initiation of soldiers into the IDF's élite units.

11 Mathieu Albert presents a good summary of Bourdieu's position in 'The Relevance of Pierre Bourdieu's Social Theory for the Study of Scientific Knowledge Production', *Canadian Journal of Sociology Online*, (October 2002).
12 Laor has analysed the method of appropriation in this film and others in Yitzhak Laor, *We Are Writing You, Homeland*, Tel Aviv: Hakibbutz Hameuhad, 1995 (Hebrew).
13 Said, 'Zionism from the Standpoint of Its Victims'.
14 *Esh Zolevet* was directed by Gideon Ganani with a screenplay by Benny Barabash.
15 *Do Not Touch My Holocaust*, directed by Asher Tlalim in, 1994.
16 The film was banned for a while by the French Ministry of Culture.
17 For David Hoffman's review of the film, see 'Through the Veil of Exile', *Washington Post*, (12 November 1992).
18 See report by Ronni Singer in *Haaretz*, 22 April 2004.
19 He is one of Israel's most prolific directors. Since 1998, he has directed more than twenty films, many of them full-length feature films about the Arab–Israeli conflict.
20 Ilan Pappe, 'Israeli Television's Fiftieth Anniversary Series: "Tekumma": A Post-Zionist View?', *Journal of Palestine Studies*, 27: 4, (Summer 1998), pp. 99–105.
21 Walid Khalidi, *All That Remains: The Palestinian Villages Occupied and Depopulated by Israel in 1948*, Washington: Institute for Palestine Studies, 2006.
22 Itamar Rabinovich, *The Road Not Taken: Early Arab–Israeli Negotiations*, New York: Oxford University Press, 1995; Shlaim, *Collusion Across the Jordan*; Pappe, *The Making of the Arab–Israeli Conflict, 1947–1951*.
23 Emile Habibi, *The Secret Life of Saeed the Pessoptimist*, New York: Interlink, 2001.

11   The Triumph of Neo-Zionism

1 Adi Ofir, *The Work of the Present: Essays on Contemporary Israeli Culture*, Tel Aviv: Hakibbutz Hameuhad, 2001, pp. 257–8 (Hebrew).
2 Neri Livneh, 'The Rise and Fall of Post-Zionism' in *Haaretz*, (19 September 2001). The English version appeared a day later as 'Post-Zionism Only Rings Once'.
3 Ari Shavit, 'Post-Post-Zionism', *Haaretz*, (18 April 2013).
4 Amnon Rubinstein, 'Who Is a Post-Zionist?', *Haaretz*, (1 September 1995); see also his book *From Herzl to Rabin: The Changing Image of Zionism*, New York: Holmes and Meyer Publishers, 2000.
5 Mentioned in Livneh, 'The Rise and Fall of Post-Zionism'.
6 Anita Shapira, 'The Past Is Not a Foreign Country: The Failure of Israel's New Historians to Explain War and Peace', *New Republic*, (29 November 1999).
7 Tuvia Friling, ed., *An Answer to a Post-Zionist Colleague*, Tel Aviv: Yedioth Ahronoth, 2003 (Hebrew).
8 Elhanan Yakira, *Post-Zionism, Post-Holocaust: Three Essays on Denial, Forgetting and the Delegitimisation of Israel*, Cambridge: Cambridge University Press, 2009.
9 David Ohana, *The Last Israelis*, Tel Aviv: Am Oved, 1997 (Hebrew).

10 'The New Anti-Semitism – A Threat to the Spirit of Freedom and Humanity', *Makor Rishon*, (23 July 2010).

11 Shavit, 'Post-Post-Zionism'.

12 Livneh, 'The Rise and Fall of Post-Zionism'.

13 Tom Segev, *Elvis in Jerusalem: Post-Zionism and the Americanisation of Israel*, New York: Picador, 2002.

14 Livneth, 'The Rise and Fall of Post-Zionism'.

15 'The Politics Behind the Closure of the Department of Politics', *Haaretz*, (5 October 2012).

16 Nurit Stadler, 'Is Profane Work an Obstacle to Salvation? The Case of Ultra-Orthodox (Haredi) Jews in Israel', *Sociology of Religion*, 63:4, (2002), pp. 455–74.

17 Sefi Rachlevsky, *Messiah's Donky*, Yiedoth Ahronoth: Tel Aviv, 1998.

18 See Pappe, *The Forgotten Palestinians*, p. 260.

19 Daniel Bar-Tal and Yona Teichman, *Stereotypes and Prejudice in Conflict: Representations of Arabs in Israeli Jewish Society*, Cambridge: Cambridge University Press, 2009; Peled-Elhanan, *Palestine in Israeli School Books*.

20 The Ministry of Education, *Israel Jubilee*, Jerusalem, 1998. The book was covered in Associated Press reports when it came out and a review can be found in the Hebron Institute for Political and Religious Studies.

21 Ibid.

22 Ethan Bronner, 'Israel's History Textbooks Replace Myths with Facts', *New York Times*, (14 August 1999).

23 *Haaretz*, (29 March 1998).

24 A summary of this report appeared in *Haaretz*, (27 March 2001).

25 The report can be found on the society's website: acri.org.il.

26 See an analysis of these laws in Pappe, *The Forgotten Palestinians*, pp. 4–5.

12   The Neo-Zionist New Historians

1 Daniel Pilser, 'Making History', *Techelet*, (9 March 2000), p. 1 (Hebrew).

2 Louis Althusser, *Essays on Ideology*, London and New York: Verso, 1984.

3 Ilan Gur-Ze'ev and Ilan Pappe, 'Beyond the Destruction of the Other's Collective Memory: Blueprints for a Palestinian/Israeli Dialogue', *Theory, Culture and Society*, 20: 1, (February 2003), pp. 93–108.

4 Yoav Gelber, *Independence Versus Nakba: The Arab–Israeli War of 1948*, Tel Aviv: Devir, 2004 (Hebrew).

5 Friling, *An Answer to a Post-Zionist Colleague*.

6 Efraim Karsh, *Fabricating Israeli History: The 'New Historians'*, London and New York: Routledge, 2000.

7 Pilser, 'Making History', p. 1.

8 Anita Shapira and Derek J. Penslar, ed., *Israeli Historical Revisionism: From Left to Right*, London and Portland: Frank Cass, 2003, pp. iv–vi.

9 Michael Walzer, 'History and National Liberation', in Shapira and Penslar, *Israeli Historical Revisionism*, pp. 1–8.

10 Daniel Gutwein, 'Left and Right Post-Zionism and the Privatisation of Israeli Collective Memory', in Shapira and Penslar, *Israeli Historical Revisionism*, pp. 9–42.

11 Martin S. Kramer, *Ivory Towers on Sand: The Failure of Middle Eastern Studies in America*, Washington: Washington Institute for Near East Policy, 2001; and Gelber, *Independence Versus Nakba*.

12 Benny Morris, *Correcting a Mistake: Jews and Arabs in Palestine/Israel, 1936–1956*, Tel Aviv: Am Oved, 2000 (Hebrew).

13 Benny Morris, 'The Survival of the Fittest', interview in *Haaretz*, reproduced by *The Journal of Palestine Studies*, 33: 3, (Spring 2004). p. 168.

14 Ibid., p. 169.

15 Ibid., p. 168.

16 Morris, *1948*.

17 Alon Kadish, ed., *Israel's War of Independence 1948–1949*, 2 vols., Tel Aviv: Ministry of Defence Publications, 2004, pp. 11–13 (Hebrew).

18 Ibid., p. 14.

19 Mordechai Bar-On, *A Memory in a Book: The Early Israeli Historiography of the War of Independence, 1948–1958*, Tel Aviv: Ministry of Defence Publications, 2001, p. 60 (Hebrew).

20 Mordechai Bar-On and Meir Hazan, eds, *People at War: A Collection of Studies on the Civilian Society During the War of Independence*, Jerusalem: Yad Ben Zvi, 2007 (Hebrew).

21 Gelber writes that the 1948 war began because of the Palestinian rejection of the partition resolution and the Arab world's wish to destroy the Jewish state. In his view, whatever the Jewish forces did was in total, morally justified self-defence; see Yoav Gelber, 'Why Did the Palestinians Run Away in 1948?', *History News Network*, (17 June 2002), hnn.us/article/782.

22 Tamir Goren, 'Separate or Mixed Municipalities? Attitudes of Jewish *Yishuv* Leadership to the Mixed Municipality During the British Mandate: The Case of Haifa', *Israel Studies*, 9: 1, (Spring 2004), pp. 101–24.

23 Yakob Markovizky, 'The Gahal–Recruitment Abroad in the War of Independence', in Kadish, ed., *Israel's War*, pp. 525–38; Alon Kadish, 'Settlements Prepare for War', in Kadish, ed., *Israel's War*, pp. 801–48; Jonathan Fine, 'Basic Problems in Government and Logistics', in Kadish, ed., *Israel's War*, pp. 679–710; Amir Bar-Or, 'The War of Independence: The Supervision of the Political Institutions over the Hagana Organisation', in Kadish, ed., *Israel's War*, pp. 711–58; and Haim Barkai, 'The Real Cost of the War of Independence', in Kadish, ed., *Israel's War*, pp. 759–92.

24 Arnon Golan, 'The Reshaping of the Ex-Arab Space and the Construction of an Israeli Space (1948–1950)', in Kadish, ed., *Israel's War*, p. 912.

25 Arnon Golan, 'The Transformation of the Settlements Map in the Areas Abandoned by the Arab Population as a Result of the War of Independence in the Territory on which the State of Israel was Founded, 1948–1950', University of Haifa, 1993 (Hebrew).

26 Benny Morris, 'The Survival of the Fittest'; Morris, *1948*.

27 Dani Hadari, 'The War of Independence in the North', in Kadish, ed., *Israel's War*, pp. 119–70.

28 Ibid., p, 131.

29 Ibid., p. 133.

30 Uri Milstein, 'The Looting by Harel', *NEWS1*, 28 February 2005.

31 Yoav Peled, 'The Campaign in Jaffa and the Surrounding Area', in Kadish, ed., *Israel's War*, pp. 389–422; and Moshe Arnewald, 'The Military Campaign

in Jerusalem in the War of Independence, November 1947–April 1948', in Kadish, ed., *Israel's War*, pp. 341–88.

32 Peled, 'The Campaign in Jaffa', p. 417.

33 Arnewald, 'The Military Campaign', p. 362.

34 Ibid., p. 359.

35 Ibid.

36 Aaron Klein, 'The Arab POWs in the War of Independence', in Kadish, ed., *Israel's War*, pp. 567–86.

37 Salman Abu-Sitta, report on Israeli website *Zochrot*, zochrot.org, (19 May 2002) (Hebrew).

38 See Abu-Sitta's research in Ilan Pappe, *The Ethnic Cleaning of Palestine*, pp. 200–4.

39 The insensitivity displayed in Klein's choice of subtitles, which would send shivers up the spine of any Holocaust survivor, could be the result of overuse, and manipulation of Holocaust memory in Israel, or simply ignorance. His use of the term *Mahanot Haavoda* (labour prison camps) shows a similar insensitivity; see Klein, 'The Arab POWs', p. 577.

40 Ibid., p. 568.

41 Ilan Pappe, 'The Tantura Case in Israel: the Katz Research and Trial', *Journal of Palestine Studies*, 30: 3, (Spring 2001), pp. 23–5.

42 Klein, 'The Arab POWs', pp. 568, 576.

43 Ibid., p. 576.

44 Ibid., p. 583.

45 Nimr al-Khatib, *Palestine's Nakba*, Damascus, 1950 (Arabic).

46 Klein, *the Arab PoWs,* p. 580.

47 Klein's lack of interest in the testimonies is perhaps not surprising, but this is the only study I have ever seen about the POWs that totally disregards the testimonies of the prisoners themselves. Imagine reconstructing life in a Japanese prison camp without oral and written testimonies of the inmates.

48 Kadish, *Israel's War*, p. 24.

49 This is the basis of the argument also made in Yoav Gelber's book, *Independence Versus Nakba*, which inspired the curriculum choice.

50 Daniel Bar-Tal, *Living With the Conflict: Socio-Psychological Analysis of the Jewish Society in Israel,* Jerusalem: Carmel, 2007, p. 443 (Hebrew).

51 See Sami Adwan and Ruth Firer, *The Narrative of the Palestinian Refugees During the War of 1948 in Israeli and Palestinian History and Civic Education Textbooks*, Paris: UNESCO Publications, 1997.

52 Anita Shapira, 'The Past Is Not a Foreign Country'.

53 Anita Shapira, *Yigal Allon: A Biography*, pp. 154, 375.

54 Leah Segal, 'Between Myth and Reality: Few Against Many?', *Hazofeh*, (24 February 2004) (Hebrew).

Epilogue: Brand Israel 2013

1 From the official website of the Israeli Ministry of Culture and Sport, speech made on 3 May 2012; see mcs.gov.il. For the debate in English, see 'Ministry of Culture Offers Prize for "Zionist-Orientated" Art', *Haaretz*, (6 October

2011). The full list of the 2012 winners appears only in the Hebrew version of the Ministry of Culture website, but not in the English one.

2 'Ministry of Culture Offers Prize for "Zionist-Orientated" Art', *Haaretz*.

3 Ibid.

4 Ibid.

5 Ibid.

6 Ibid.

7 *Haaretz*, (28 April 2013).

8 *Haaretz*, (6 December 2011).

9 *Haaretz*, (25 May 2013).

10 See reports on website, ngo-monitor.org.il.

11 Sarah Schulman, 'A Documentary Guide to "Brand Israel" and the Art of Pinkwashing', *Mondoweiss*, (30 November 2011), mondoweiss.net/2011/11/a-documentary-guide-to-brand-israel-and-the-art-of-pinkwashing.html.

12 Ibid.

13 The David Project, davidproject.org.

14 Ibid.

15 Ibid.

16 Ibid.

17 Schulman, 'A Documentary Guide'.

18 Ibid.

19 Ibid.

20 Ibid.

21 *Yedioth Ahronoth*, (27 July 2011).

22 Gary Rosenblatt, 'Marketing a New Image', *Jewish Week*, (20 January 2005).

23 Ibid.

24 Ibid.

25 Ibid.

26 Ibid.

27 See israelatheart.org.

28 'Calls to Boycott Batsheva in the Edinburgh Festival', *Haaretz*, (17 July 2012).

29 *Guardian*, (22 May 2009).

30 Schulman, 'A Documentary Guide'.

31 Schulman, 'A Documentary Guide'.

32 'The Delegitimisation Challenge: Creating a Political Firewall', the Reut Institute, (14 February 2010), reut-institute.org (Hebrew).

33 *Haaretz*, (28 November 2007).

34 Jewish People Policy Institute, Annual Assessment 2010, Executive Report 7, p. 182.

35 Vera Michlin, 'Winning the Battle of the Narrative', the Tenth Herzliya Annual Report, (31 January–3 February 2010), pp. 56–60.

36 Peter Beinart, 'The Failure of the American Jewish Establishment', *New York Review of Books*, (10 June 2010).

37 Israeli Ministry of Foreign Affairs press report, (21 October 2010); see mfa.gov.il (Hebrew).

38 Eitan Dangot, 'Strategies for Countering Delegitimisation and for Shaping Public Perceptions', panel discussion, Countering Assaults on Israel's Legitimacy, The S. Daniel Abraham Center for Strategic Dialogue, Netanya Academic College, (16 April 2012).

39 The Summary of the Eleventh Herzliya Conference; see herzliyaconference. org.

40 Ibid.

41 Rommey Hassman, 'The Israeli Brand: Nation Marketing Under Constant Conflict', policy paper presented at the Harold Hartog School of Government, University of Tel Aviv, (April 2008).

42 Ibid., p. 5.

43 Ibid., pp. 57–8.

Further Reading

Classical Zionism

Adelman, J. *The Rise of Israel: A History of a Revolutionary State*, London and New York: Routledge, 2008.

Bar-On, M. (ed.) *Never-Ending Conflict: Israeli Military History*, Westport, CT: Praeger, 2004.

Halpern, B. and Reinharz, J. *Zionism and the Creation of a New Society*, New York: Oxford University Press, 1998.

Kaplan, E. and Penslar, D. *The Origins of Israel, 1882–1948*, Madison, WI: University of Wisconsin Press, 2011.

Laqueur, W. *A History of Zionism: From the French Revolution to the Establishment of the State of Israel*, Jerusalem: Schocken, 2003.

Penslar, D. *Israel in History: The Jewish State in Comparative Perspective*, London and New York: Routledge, 2006.

Shapira, A. *Israel: A History*, Boston: Brandeis University Press, 2012.

Shimoni, G. *The Zionist Ideology*, Boston: Brandeis University Press, 1995.

Wistrich, R. and Ohana, D. *The Shaping of Israeli Identity: Myth, Memory and Trauma*, London and New York: Routledge, 1995.

Post-Zionism

Alam, M. S. *Israeli Exceptionalism: The Destabilising Logic of Zionism*, New York: Palgrave Macmillan, 2010.

Ben-Asher, H. *The Zionist Illusion*, New York: iUniverse.com, 2010.

Beinart, P. *The Crisis of Zionism*, New York: Times Books, 2012

Butler, J. *Parting Ways: Jewishness and the Critique of Zionism*, New York: Columbia University Press, 2012.

Ellis, M. H. *Judaism Does Not Equal Israel: The Rebirth of the Jewish Prophetic*, New York: New Press, 2009.

Feldt, J. *The Israeli Memory Struggle: History and Identity in the Age of Globalisation*, Copenhagen: University Press of Southern Denmark, 2007.

Ghazi-Boullion, A. *Understanding the Middle East Peace Process: Israeli Academia and the Struggle for Identity*, London and New York: Routledge, 2013.

Hilal, J. and Pappe, I. (ed.) *Across the Wall: Narratives of Israeli–Palestinian History*, London and New York: I. B. Tauris, 2010.

Hilliard, C. *Does Israel Have a Future? The Case for a Post-Zionist State*, Washington: Potomac Books, 2009.

Isacoff, J. B. *Writing the Arab–Israeli Conflict: Pragmatism and Historical Enquiry*, New York: Lexington Books, 2006.

Kovel, J. *Overcoming Zionism: Creating a Single Democratic State in Israel/Palestine*, London: Pluto, 2007.

Lentin, R. *Co-Memory and Melancholia: Israelis Memorialising the Palestinian Nakba*, Manchester: Manchester University Press, 2010.

Lowenstein, A. and Moor, A. *After Zionism: One State for Israel and Palestine*, London: Saqi Books, 2012.

Masalha, N. *The Bible and Zionism: Invented Traditions, Archaeology and Postcolonialism in Palestine–Israel*, London: Zed Books, 2007.

Pappe, I. (ed.) *The Israel/Palestine Question: A Reader*, London and New York: Routledge, 2007.

Podeh, E. *The Arab–Israeli Conflict in Israeli History Textbooks, 1948–2000*, New York: Information Age Publishing, 2005.

Prior, M. *Zionism and the State of Israel: A Moral Enquiry*, London and New York: Routledge, 1999.

Ram, U. *The Globalisation of Israel: McWorld in Tel Aviv, Jihad in Jerusalem*, London and New York: Routledge, 2007.

Roberts, J. *Contested Land, Contested Memory: Israel's Jews and Arabs and the Ghosts of Catastrophe*, New York: Dundurn, 2013.

Rogan, E. and Shlaim, A. (ed.) *The War for Palestine: Rewriting the History of 1948*, Cambridge: Cambridge University Press, 2007.

Rotberg, R. (ed.) *Israeli and Palestinian Narratives of Conflict: History's Double Helix*, Bloomington, IN: Indiana University Press, 2006.

Sand, S. *The Words and the Land: Israeli Intellectuals and the Nationalist Myth*, London: Semiotext(e), 2011.

Shafir, G. and Peled, Y. *Being Israeli: The Dynamics of Multiple Citizenship*, Cambridge: Cambridge University Press, 2002.

Shatz, A. *Prophets Outcast: A Century of Dissident Jewish Writing About Zionism and Israel*, New York; Nation Books, 2004.

Silberstein, L. J. *The Post-Zionism Debates: Knowledge and Power in Israeli Culture*, London and New York: Routledge, 1999.

Slyomovics, S. *The Object of Memory: Arab and Jew Narrate the Palestinian Village*, Philadelphia, PA: University of Pennsylvania Press, 1998.

Yiftachel, O. *Ethnocracy: Land and Identity Politics in Israel-Palestine*, Philadelphia, PA: University of Pennsylvania Press, 2006.

Zerubavel, Y. *Recovered Roots: Collective Memory and the Making of Israeli National Tradition*, Chicago: University of Chicago Press, 1995.

Feminism and Gender in Israel

Abdo, N. *Women in Israel: Race, Gender and Citizenship*, London: Zed Books, 2011.

Abdo, N. and Lentin, R. *Women and the Politics of Military Confrontation: Palestinian and Israeli Gendered Narratives of Dislocation*, London: Berghahn Press, 2002.

Azmon, Y. and Izraeli, D. N. *Women in Israel*, New York: Transaction Publishers, 1993.

Bernstein, D. S. *Pioneers and Homemakers: Jewish Women in Pre-State Israel*, Albany, NY: State University of New York, 1992.

Dworkin, A. *Scapegoat: The Jews, Israel and Women's Liberation*, New York: Free Press, 2000.

Haberman, B. D. *Israeli Feminism Liberating Judaism: Blood and Ink*, New York: Lexington Books, 2012.

Halperin-Kaddari, R. *Women in Israel: A State of Their Own*, Philadelphia, PA: University of Pennsylvania Press, 2003.

Kark, R. (ed.) *Jewish Women in Pre-State Israel: Life History, Politics and Culture*, Brandeis: University of Brandeis Press, 2008.

Katz, S. *Women and Gender in Early Jewish and Palestinian Nationalism*, Miami, FL: University of Florida Press, 2003.

Mayer, T. *Women and the Israeli Occupation: The Politics of Change*, London and New York: Routledge, 1994.

Misra, K. and Rich, M. *Jewish Feminism in Israel: Some Contemporary Perspectives*, Boston: Brandeis University Press, 2008.

Naveh, H. *Gender and Israeli Society: Women's Time*, New York: Vallentine Mitchell, 2003.

Rom, M. and Benjamin, O. *Feminism, Family and Identity in Israel: Women's Marital Names*, New York: Palgrave Macmillan, 2011.

Sharoni, S. *Gender and the Israeli–Palestinian Conflict: The Politics of Women's Resistance*, Syracuse, NY: Syracuse University Press, 1994.

Swirski, B. *Calling the Equality Bluff: Women in Israel*, New York: Teachers College Press, 1993.

Holocaust Memory

Achcar, G. *The Arabs and the Holocaust: The Arab–Israeli War of Narratives*, London: Saqi Books, 2011.

Cohen, B. *Israeli Holocaust Research: Birth and Evolution*, London and New York: Routledge, 2012.

Fox, T. *Inherited Memories: Israeli Children of Holocaust Survivors*, New York: Cassel Academics, 1999.

Hilberg, R. *The Politics of Memory: The Journey of a Holocaust Historian*, New York: Ivan R. Dee, 2002.

Safdie, M. *Yad Vashem: Moshe Safdie—The Architecture of Memory*, Berlin: Lars Müller Publications, 2006.

Stauber, R. *The Holocaust in Israeli Public Debate in the 1950s: Ideology and Memory*, New York: Vallentine Mitchell, 2007.

Arab Jews and *Mizrachim*

Alcalay, A. *After Jews and Arabs: Remaking Levantine Culture*, Minneapolis, MN: University of Minnesota Press, 1992.

Bashkin, O. *New Babylonians: A History of Jews in Modern Iraq*, Stanford, CA: Stanford University Press, 2012.

Shabi, R. *We Look Like The Enemy: The Hidden Story of Israel's Jews From Arab Lands*, New York: Walker and Company, 2008.

Somekh, S. *Baghdad Yesterday, The Making of an Arab Jew*, New York: Ibis, 2007.

Culture in Israel

Barak-Erez, D. *Outlawed Pigs: Law, Religion, and Culture in Israel,* Madison, WI: University of Wisconsin Press, 2007.

Fuhrer, R. *Israeli Painting: From Post-Impressionism to Post-Zionism,* New York: The Overlook Press, 1998.

Kahn, S. M. *Reproducing Jews: A Cultural Account of Assisted Conception in Israel,* Durham, NC: Duke University Press, 2000.

Katriel, T. *Performing the Past: A Study of Israeli Settlement Museums,* London and New York: Routledge, 1997.

Mautner, M. *Law and the Culture of Israel,* New York: Oxford University Press, 2011.

Regev, M. and Seroussi, E. *Popular Music and National Culture in Israel,* Berkeley, CA: University of California Press, 2004.

Stein, R. L. and Swedenberg, T. (ed) *Palestine, Israel, and the Politics of Popular Culture,* Durham, NC: Duke University Press, 2005.

Talmon, M. and Peleg, Y. *Israeli Cinema: Identities in Motion,* Austin, TX: University of Texas Press, 2011.

Neo-Zionism

Gelber, Y. *Nation and History: Israeli Historiography Between Zionism and Post-Zionism,* New York: Vallentine Mitchell, 2011.

Hazony, D., Hazony, Y., and Oren, M. B. (ed.) *New Essays on Zionism,* Jerusalem: Shalem Press, 2007.

Hazony, Y. *The Jewish State: The Struggle for Israel's Soul,* New York: Basic Books, 2001.

Morris, B. *Righteous Victims: A History of the Zionist–Arab Conflict, 1881–2001,* New York: Vintage, 2001.

Mazur, Y. *Zionism, Post-Zionism and the Arab Problem: A Compendium of Opinions About the Jewish State,* New York: West Bow Press, 2012.

Index

Abarbanel, Avigail, 83
Abargel, Reuven, 93
Abu Kamar, Dalal, 235
Abu-Sitta, Salman, 26, 288
Achoti, 150
Adiv, Udi, 88
Agudat Israel, 263
Aharoni, Ido, 302–3
Aharonowitz, Yossef, 33
Ahimeir, Aba, 160
Al-Fanar, 150
al-Husayni, Al-Hajj Amin, 35, 37, 110,
    175–6
al-Qassam, Izz al-Din, 36
al-Rashid, Harun, 189
al-Said, Nuri, 179
al-Tall, Abdullah, 111
Ali, Tariq, 83
Allon, Yigal, 27, 292
Almog, Shmuel, 20
Aloni, Shulamit, 137
Althusser, Louis, 276
Amar, Amran, 62
Anderson, Benedict, 21, 35, 167
Anderson, Perry, 131–2, 165
Arab League, 117
Arafat, Yasser, 82, 175, 256
Arendt, Hannah, 167, 173–4
Ariel, Mira, 148

Arnewald, Moshe, 287
Attenborough, Richard, 232
Auron, Yair, 168
Austen, Jane, 146
Avangard (Workers' Union), 88
Avnery, Uri, 82, 87, 210
Avraham, Eli, 187
Axelrod, Nathan, 59–60, 63

Baader-Meinhof Gang, 39
Baer, Israel, 111
Ballas, Shimon, 199, 203–4
Bar-Tal, Daniel, 268, 291
Barak, Ehud, 78, 141, 253, 256, 263–4,
    269–70
Barenboim, Daniel, 200
Barslevsky, Yosef, 1
Baum, Dalit, 138
Becker, Jilian, 38
Begin, Menachem, 37, 52, 92, 94, 175,
    184, 298
Behar, Moshe, 188
Beinart, Peter, 307
Beit Mihush, 29
Beiteinu, Yisrael, 264
Ben Barka, Mehdi, 71
Ben Canaan, Ari, 172
Ben-Amos, Avner, 270
Ben-Avi, Itamar, 160

Ben-Dov, Yoav, 296
Ben-Eliezer, Uri, 140
Ben-Gurion, David, 17–18, 32, 49, 51, 73, 106–10, 111, 118, 120, 123, 126, 160–1, 163, 175, 183, 229, 241, 282, 298
Ben-Yehuda, Nachman, 139
Benchetrit, David, 234–6
Benvenisti, Meron, 121
Bereshit, Haim, 143
Bernstein, Deborah, 103, 140
Bevin, Ernest, 55, 116
Bharatiya Janata Party, 267
Bichler, Shimshon, 138
Biletzky, Anat, 148–9
bin Laden, Osama, 256
Biton, Charlie, 93
Black Panthers (Israeli), 93
Bourdieu, Pierre, 224
Boyarin, Jonathan and Daniel, 144
Boycott, Divestment and Sanctions Campaign, 5
Brenner, Lenni, 158, 161
Brunner, Benny, 233
Buber, Martin, 95, 109, 155
Bullock, Alan, 55
Bund, 78, 165
Burg, Avraham, 154

Calderon, Nissim, 253
Carmi, Shulamit, 140
Carr, E. H., 22
Carter, Jimmy, 23
Castoriadis, Cornelius, 83
Cathedra (newspaper), 21, 54
Cavanagh, Edward, 191
Chertko, Serjio Daniel, 296
Chetrit, Sami Shalom, 177, 189, 192–3, 195
Childers, Erskine, 114
Chomsky, Noam, 43, 148
Churchill, Winston, 24
Clinton, Bill, 256
Cohen, Gavriel, 55
Cohen, Michael J., 55
Cohen, Hillel, 136
Communist Party (Israel), 70
Cromwell, Oliver, 74
Crossman, Richard, 171

Da'am Workers Party, 88
Dangot, Major General Eitan, 308
David Project, 300
Davis, Uri, 83, 85–6
Dayan, Asaf, 59
Dayan, Moshe, 92
De Vries, David, 103, 140
Demjanjuk, John, 156–7
Democratic Front for the Liberation of Palestine, 39, 70
Demsky, Noam, 296
Derech Ha-nizoz (Through a Spark), 88
Dershowitz, Alan, 310
Dinur, Ben-Zion, 17–18, 20, 53
Dolev, Diana, 141
Dulles, John Foster, 106
Edelman, Marek, 165–7
Effrat, Zvi, 143
Effrat, Benny, 197
Eichmann, Adolf, 162, 167, 174–5
Einsenhower, Dwight D., 106
Eisenstadt, Shmuel Noah, 44, 95
Elkana, Yehuda, 156–8
Elon, Amos, 157
Elroi, Gur, 139
Ettinger, Shmuel, 20
Evron, Boaz, 76–7, 79, 156
Ezrahi, Yavon, 213–15

Fanon, Frantz, 191
Fatah, 38, 140
Finkelstein, Norman, 158–9, 172, 307
Fisher, David 'Dudu', 296
Flapan, Simha, 109–12, 114–15, 117–18, 120, 122
Foucault, Michel, 142
Four Mothers, 151
Freedman, Marcia, 136–7
Fukuyama, Francis, 4
Gabbay, Rony, 107–8
Gadot, Gal, 298
Ganani, Gidon, 227
Gandal, Neil, 310
Gaon, Yehoram, 238, 245
Geffen, Aviv, 201
Gelber, Yoav, 253, 284
Gellner, Ernest, 103
Gertz, Nurith, 56, 169
Gery, Pnina, 295

Ghilan, Maxim, 69–72, 76
Gilbert, Sir Martin, 24–6, 58
Giora, Rachel, 148
Gitai, Amos, 236–7
Goering, Hermann, 176
Goitein, S. D., 20
Golan, Arnon, 284–5
Goldmann, Nahum, 154
Goldstone, Richard, 305
Goren, Tamir, 284
Gorny, Yosef, 1, 4, 272
Gould, Elliot, 147
Gover, Yerach, 203
Green, David, 32
Greenberg, David, 56
Greenberg, Lev, 140
Grodzinsky, Yosef, 170–1
Grossman, Avishai, 78
Grossman, David, 205, 297
Gur, Hagit, 141
Gur-Ze'ev, Ilan, 143, 154, 168, 176, 257
Gurewitz, Adolph, 76–7
Gush Emunim, 84–5
Gutwein, Daniel, 281

Habash, George, 39
Habibi, Emile, 202–3, 244
Habiluim (pop band), 297
Hadari, Dani, 286
Hadash, 211
Hagana, 52, 58, 65–6, 82–3, 115, 162, 171, 230–1, 277, 286–7
Haim, Ben, 197
Haivry, Ophir, 249
Halamish, Aviva, 172
Halevi, Ilan, 83, 85, 88
Halperin, Uriel, 77
Hamas, 27, 36, 82, 211, 305–6, 309
Harely, J. B., 24
Harkabi, Yehoshafat, 42
Hass, Amira, 208, 212, 263
Hass, Mary, 235–6
Hassman, Rommey, 310
Hatzionut (newspaper), 21, 54
Hazkani, Shay, 108
Hazony, Yoram, 248, 251
Herut Party, 52
Herzl, Theodor, 296, 298
Hever, Hannah, 130–1

Hever, Hanan, 144
Hezbollah, 306
Himmler, Heinrich, 176
Histadrut, 83, 100
Hitler, Adolf, 55, 153, 157, 160, 169, 175, 177
Hobsbawn, Eric, 165
Hofshi, Natan, 30
Hurewitz, Yona, 30
Hushi, Abba, 94
Hussein, Saddam, 177

Idan, Alon, 297
Irgun, 37, 52, 288
Isha L'Isha, 150
Israeli Defense Forces, 52, 66, 115, 143, 208, 236, 269, 277, 281, 283, 289–92, 310

J Street, 213
Jabotinsky, Ze'ev, 25, 77
Japanese Red Army, 39
Jerusalem School, 20
Jewish Home Party, 257
Johnson, Lyndon B., 108

Kadima Party, 257, 260
Kadish, Alon, 282, 284–7
Kanafani, Ghassan, 219
Kaplan, Yirmiyahu, 86
Karsh, Efraim, 23, 280
Kashri, Or, 279
Kedar, Alexander, 143
Kennedy, John F., 106
Khalaf, Karim, 156
Khalidi, Walid, 110, 119, 240
Khleifi, Michel, 234
Khmelnytsty, Bohdan, 74–5
Khomeini, Ayatollah Ruhollah, 201
Khouri, George, 227–31
Khoury, Elias, 203
Kimchie, John and David, 51
Kimmerling, Baruch, 98–101, 102, 104, 138
Kipling, Rudyard, 64
Klausner, Joseph, 20
Klein, Aaron, 287–8, 289–90
Koenig, Yisrael, 33
Kolatt, Israel, 20

Kollek, Teddy, 121
Kulthum, Umm, 201

Labour Party, 213, 257, 260, 265
Labour–Likud Coalition, 208
Laor, Yitzhak, 81, 204, 211, 219–20
Lavie, Smadar, 195
Le Roy Ladurie, Emmanuel, 129
Leibowitz, Yeshayahu, 79–81, 83, 169, 233
Lerer, Yael, 203
Lerner, Motti, 232
Levi, Galia Zlamansov, 143
Levi, Primo, 166–7, 173
Levin, Hanoch, 217–18
Levy, Yagil, 141
Levy, Gideon, 208, 212
Levy, Ram, 220–3
Lieberman, Avigdor, 264
Likud Party, 92, 98, 206, 215, 245, 251, 257, 260, 263
Lissak, Moshe, 2, 253
Livnat, Limor, 245, 295–7
Livneh, Neri, 247
Livni, Tzipi, 272, 302
Lorch, Betanel, 48, 51, 54
Loren, Sophia, 58
Lubrani, Uri, 108
Lusin, Yigal, 58

Ma'oz, Moshe, 108
Machover, Moshe, 84, 86–8
Mahfouz, Naguib, 203
Malcolm X, 192
Mandela, Nelson, 248
Mapai (Labour Party), 98, 99
Mapam, 109, 119
Marciano, Sadia, 93
Marshall, George, 118
Marx, Karl, 97, 142
Massad, Joseph, 162
Matar, Anat, 148
Matzpen, 86–9, 133
Mazali, Rela, 141
Meinz, Theo, 137
Meir, Golda, 34, 41, 92, 155, 241
Meir, Gideon, 301
Meretz, 213, 267, 269
Merriam, D. F., 24
Meshulam, Uri, 143

Michael, Sami, 204, 219
Milstein, Uri, 286
Mishal, Shaul, 42
Mishani, Dror, 199
Mizrachi Democratic Rainbow Coalition, 193
Morris, Benny, 37–8, 112, 114–15, 119, 121, 123–4, 132, 154, 236, 239–40, 241, 257, 278, 281–2
Moshenson, Ilan, 232
Mossad, 40, 71–2
Muhammad, Umm, 235
Mundi, Yosef, 218
Muslim Brotherhood, 37, 38
Mussolini, Benito, 175

Nahon, Yaakov, 195
Nasser, Gamal Abdul, 38, 55, 135, 175
Ne'eman, Jad, 223
Netanyahu, Benjamin, 141, 209, 248, 253, 259, 263–4, 270, 272, 299–300
New Profile, 152
Novick, Peter, 158, 172, 176

Ohana, David, 254
Olmert, Ehud, 253, 272, 306
Ofir, Adi, 168, 247, 257
Oppenheim, Fern, 303
Orr, Akiva, 83–4, 86–9
Oz, Amos, 78, 175, 297
Ozacky–Lazar, Sarah, 136

Pa'il, Meer, 66
Palestine Liberation Organization (PLO), 38–42, 50, 70, 82, 85, 133, 256
Palestinian Academic Society for the Study of International Affairs (PASSIA), 26
Palestinian Authority, 261
Palmach, 65–6
Pappe, Ilan, 131–2, 293
Peel Commission, 17, 161
Peled, Yoav, 136, 195
Peled-Elhanan, Nurit, 141, 268
Peleg, Yoav, 286–7
Penslar, Derek J., 280
Peres, Shimon, 92
Peters, Joan, 23
Pilavsky, Oded, 86
Pilser, Daniel, 276

Piterberg, Gabriel, 139
Popular Front for the Liberation of
    Palestine, 39
Porat, Uri, 245
Porath, Yehoshua, 41, 49
Preminger, Otto, 172
Prinz, Joachim, 155

Rabin, Yitzhak, 8, 33, 92, 155, 165, 251,
    255–6, 260, 262
Rabinovich, Itamar, 241
Rabinowitch, Yossef, 32
Rabinowitz, Dan, 136
Rachlevsky, Sefi, 266
Ram, Uri, 141–2
Ratosh, Yonathan, 77
Ratz, 137
Raz-Karkozkin, Amnon, 139, 258
Red Front, 88–9
Reinhart, Tanya, 148
Revisionist Movement, 165
Revolutionary Communist Alliance
    (RCA), 88
Revolutionary Communist League
    (Matzpen Marxist), 89
Rodinson, Maxime, 101
Rosenblatt, Gary, 303
Rosenfeld, Henry, 140
Rotbard, Sharon, 144
Rubinstein, Amnon, 253
Ruppin, Arthur, 161
Rush , Richard, 147

Sa'ar, Gideon, 279
Saatchi brothers, 302
Sable, David, 303
Said, Edward, 10, 42, 131–2, 146, 186–8,
    190–2, 200, 225
Salih, Tayeb, 203
Sand, Shlomo, 139, 259
Saranga, David, 302
Sartre, Jean-Paul, 101, 109
Saud, Ibn, 37
Schwarzenegger, Arnold, 64
Segal, Leah, 292
Segev, Tom, 120–1, 162–4, 169, 212, 233,
    258–9
Seidman, Miriam, 227–31
Sela, Avraham, 42

Shaath, Nabil, 85
Shach, Eliezer, 194
Shafir, Gershon, 102–4
Shahak, Israel, 72–6, 78, 154–6
Shak'a, Bassam, 156
Shakespeare, William, 225
Shalem Center, 248–9, 251–2
Shalev, Michael, 138
Shamir, Moshe, 59
Shamir, Yitzhak, 37, 208
Shapira, Anita, 2, 34, 53, 102, 104, 253,
    280, 291–2
Shapira, Yonathan, 98–100
Sharett, Moshe, 120
Sharon, Ariel, 141, 253, 256, 257, 260
    263, 272
Shas Party, 194, 263
Shavit, Ari, 248, 258, 272, 274, 281
Shay (Hagana), 230
Shazar, Zalman, 167
Shemesh, George, 197
Shemesh, Kochavi, 94
Shemesh, Moshe, 42, 50
Shenhav, Yehouda, 180–2, 189, 192
Shiloah, Reuven, 107
Shin Bet, 219
Shlaim, Avi, 38, 112, 115–16, 120–1,
    123–4, 241, 293
Shohat, Ella, 57, 59, 182–3, 187, 190–2
Sivan, Eyal, 169, 233–4
Smilonsky, Yizhar, 220–1
Smooha, Sammy, 43–4, 96–8
Sobol, Joshua, 218, 220
Stalin, Joseph, 119
Steinberg, Matti, 42
Stern Gang, 37, 52, 71, 76, 227–8, 230–1,
    288
Sternhell, Zeev, 104, 131, 140
Stone, Lawrence, 129
Stone, Oliver, 232
Svirsky, Shlomo, 2, 96–7, 177, 192
Swissa, Albert, 204

Tal, Uriel, 90–1, 98
Teveth, Shabtai, 112, 123
Tlalim, Asher, 234
Topol, Chaim, 297
Toraty, Benny, 198
Trank, Elsa, 174

Truman, Harry, 118
Twister, Doron, 296

Urian, Dan, 218
Uris, Leon, 58, 172

Veracini, Lorenzo, 191
Verne, Jules, 64
von Mildenstein, Leopold, 161

Walesa, Lech, 165
Walzer, Michael, 280
Warschawski, Michel ('Mikado'), 83,
    84–5
Wertheim, Noa, 295
Willis, Bruce, 64

Wolfe, Patrick, 191

Yablonka, Hanna, 170
Yachimovich, Shelly, 213
Yakira, Elhanan, 254
Yehoshua, A. B., 297
Yevin, Yehoshua Heschel, 160
Yiftachel, Oren, 135, 259
Yonah, Yossi, 259
Yosef, Ovadia, 194
Yunay, Yuval, 137

Zertal, Idith, 166, 170, 174–5
Zerubavel, Yael, 138–9
Zimmermann, Moshe, 161–2
Zukerman, Moshe, 177